THE

CHURCH AND THE REBELLION:

A CONSIDERATION OF

THE REBELLION

AGAINST

THE GOVERNMENT OF THE UNITED STATES;

AND THE

AGENCY OF THE CHURCH, NORTH AND SOUTH,

IN RELATION THERETO.

By R. L. STANTON, D. D.,

PROFESSOR IN THE THEOLOGICAL SEMINARY OF THE PRESBYTERIAN CHURCH

DANVILLE, KENTUCKY.

NEW YORK:

DERBY & MILLER, 5 SPRUCE STREET

1864.

C. A. ALVORD, STEREOTYPER AND PRINTER.

TO THE

YOUNG MEN OF THE UNITED STATES,

OF

EVERY CREED IN RELIGION AND EVERY PARTY IN POLITICS,

WHO PREFER

FREEDOM TO SLAVERY;

WHO ARE LOYAL TO THEIR COUNTRY,

AND WHO ARE

AIDING TO SUSTAIN ITS GOVERNMENT AGAINST REBELLION:

This Volume

IS MOST RESPECTFULLY DEDICATED

BY

THE AUTHOR.

PREFACE.

THIS volume does not claim to be a History, though some of its chapters are chiefly historical. The time for writing the History of the Rebellion has not come. It is, however, just as opportune now as it will be at any future period, to inquire into the causes of the revolt against the Government of the United States, and to examine the agencies which have been concerned in initiating and impelling it forward. These lie upon the surface of observation and are patent to all men. Time can throw no light upon them which will essentially change their character.

Believing that the Church of God in this land,—or, properly speaking, many of those in the different branches of the Church who have been leaders in its councils, and who are largely responsible for the formation and character of its public opinion,—may be justly held to have done much towards precipitating the Rebellion, as well as aiding it during the whole course of its progress, it is one aim of these pages to set forth the proofs and illustrations, in some small degree, of a record so deeply humiliating. No complaint need be entered in behalf of those whose conduct we unfold. Least of all will they themselves complain, for they glory in what they have done, and call on the world to applaud them.

There is another reason why it is essential to examine this record. Politicians, secular and religious journals, pamphleteers, men in all classes of society, freely lay the blame of this Rebellion, in a great measure, or wholly, at the door of the Church; charging the ministry, more especially, with having caused it. This is a very prevalent sentiment, if we may judge from what has been said and written. There is undoubtedly justice or injustice in the charge, according to the direction given to it. It is then essential that the matter be probed, so that if the Church or its ministers are improperly impugned, they may have justice done them; and that the really guilty may be held responsible.

We have examined many works which have issued from the press, calculated to elucidate certain phases of the Rebellion and the War, but we have observed no one designed to meet the demand which this volume is intended to supply, or which at all occupies the ground which several of its chapters cover.

We are indebted to many writers for the facts we present, and as far as possible have endeavored to give them credit in the body of the work, though omissions may have occurred.

With this statement of the object of this volume, we lay it before the public, in the confident hope that the Church and the Nation may soon come out of this strife, purified and invigorated, restored to those principles which were the glory of the earlier and better days of the Republic, and prepared for that great mission to which we have always fondly believed they were destined by the Ruler of the whole earth.

NEW YORK, *August*, 1864.

CONTENTS.

CHAPTER I.

CHAPTER II.

CHAPTER III.

CHAPTER IV.

CHAPTER V.

CHAPTER VI.

CHAPTER VII.

CHAPTER VIII.

CHAPTER IX.

CHAPTER X.

CHAPTER XI.

CHAPTER XII.

CHAPTER XIII.

CHAPTER XIV.

THE CHURCH AND THE REBELLION.

CHAPTER I.

CHARACTER OF THE REBELLION.

THE rebellion against the Government of the United States, now in the fourth year of its progress, is among the most extraordinary phenomena in the annals of mankind. It is so remarkable in its objects, so determined in its spirit, and has brought into action, upon one side and the other, material and moral forces of such gigantic magnitude, that the world stands appalled at the spectacle it presents.

In any proper consideration of the subject, the logical order brings us first to look at the character of the rebellion. It has certain palpable features which might profitably admit of an extended examination. Our plan will allow us to give them only a passing notice.

AGAINST POPULAR GOVERNMENT.

1. The primal characteristic it exhibits is that of a violent demonstration against *the life-principle of Popular Government.*

The ultimate sovereignty and true source of all political power, under God, are in *the people*, for whose benefit civil society has been ordained. In God's providence, mankind are distributed into nations, in which political power is to be exercised through the modes which the people of each may devise. To establish government, and to alter its form or character, so as to meet the varying wants of society, are among the inherent rights of every people. These are very generally conceded as fundamental principles in political science. They are denied by those who contend for the divine right of kings, and who hold that the many were created for the few; but the ablest writers acknowledge these rights as belonging primarily to the people, and of which they cannot be justly divested.

In regard to changing the government which exists over a people, either in its form or in matters of substance, the modes are various. In a monarchy, a people may wish to go no farther than to demand and receive concessions from the sovereign, leaving the form and structure of the government intact. Under a despotism, tyranny may become so oppressive as to be unendurable, with no hope of relief from the ruling power. Then, revolution may become a duty. This remedy is deemed justifiable in extreme cases, and a right which a people can never surrender. The propriety of resorting to it must, for the most part, be determined by the circumstances of each case.

In a popular government, however, republican or democratical, whose form and structure have sprung from the free consent of the whole people, and where the rulers, from the highest to the lowest, are chosen and frequently changed by their common suffrages, the right of violent revolution would seem to be well-nigh or quite excluded. All abuses of power are subject to that peaceful remedy which the people always have in their hands. Any branch of the government, executive, legislative, or judicial, which usurps authority, may be speedily reached and the corrective applied,—as, for example, in the United States,—by impeachment, or by the ballot. If the remedy belong directly to the people, the determination is with the majority, in the manner prescribed by law; and, when made, the decision must be final if the people are the ultimate source of power. A denial of these simple principles renders popular government impossible.*

Now, it is the invasion of that life-principle which underlies the whole structure of popular government, that constitutes the primal item in the catalogue of crimes which make up the terrible guilt of this rebellion. It is an appeal from the ballot-box to the sword; a determination to defeat by war the results of a popular election, fairly conducted in all respects according to the Constitution and laws, as those who have revolted admit; an election in which they, equally with the rest of the nation, freely embarked, and by the results of which they were therefore solemnly bound. This is the charge which stands recorded against them in the face of the whole world.

SOUTHERN DOMINATION IN THE GOVERNMENT.

2. Another item in the character of the rebellion is, that it is waged against a Government whose administration the rebels, through the party with which they had generally acted, *had almost uniformly controlled, from the origin of the Government to the time of their revolt, and every branch of which was still in their possession.*

This is one of those facts in our history, so well known and so public that it will scarcely be questioned. But an authority so valuable as that of Vice-President Stephens, of the "Confederate" Government, may here be given.

* Says M. De Tocqueville, in his *Democracy in America:* "All authority originates in the will of the majority." "In the United States, the majority governs in the name of the people, as is the case in all the countries in which the people is supreme." "The very essence of democratic government consists in the absolute sovereignty of the majority." "The moral power of the majority is founded upon yet another principle, which is, that the interests of the many are to be preferred to those of the few."

In a speech at Washington, Georgia, June 8, 1861, he says :—

It has been our pride that out of the seventy-two years of the existence of the Government under the Constitution, it has been for sixty under the control of Southern statesmen. This has secured whatever of prosperity and greatness, growth and development, has marked the country's career during its past history. The Northern masses generally agreed with Southern statesmen in their policy, and sustained them. These were the democracy of that section. Mr. Jefferson said they were *allies*. Washington's administration lasted eight years. It was Southern, and in the line of Southern policy. Then came the elder Adams. He was from Massachusetts. Opposite ideas shaped his policy. At the end of four years, the people indignantly turned him and his counsellors out of power. Then came Jefferson, Madison, and Monroe, each eight years—all Southern men. Here we had thirty-two years of Southern administration to four Northern. Then came the younger Adams from the North. He was the great embodiment of those ideas which now control Lincoln's administration. At the end of four years he was turned out of power, and Jackson, a Southern man, came in for eight years. Then came Van Buren, a Northern man, for four years. Then Harrison, Tyler, and Polk, which added eight years more of Southern control. Next, Taylor and Fillmore. Fillmore was a Northern man, it is true, but his administration was sustained by the South, and so was Pierce's. These may be called Southern administrations; and so was Buchanan's—thus making sixty out of the seventy-two years of the Government's existence under the Constitution. All the important measures which have marked the history of the Government, which have made it what it is, or was before the dismemberment, and made it the admiration of the world, were the fruits of the policy of Southern statesmen.

This statement of Mr. Stephens requires one modification. The policy of Mr. Van Buren's administration was as intensely Southern as that of any one he claims. It was not till several years after his retirement from public life that he gave expression to those views which rendered him odious to his quondam Southern friends. The balance may then be adjusted so as to give to the South, upon the principle Mr. Stephens lays down, *sixty-four years* of control of the Government, and to the North *eight years;* and that, too, while the North had a large majority of the population of the country.

Besides thus wielding the power and shaping the policy of the Government from its origin, the party of which Mr. Stephens here speaks had control of every branch of the Government when the revolt began, and even the Executive was not to be changed for a period of four months. From this state of facts, it seems in a high degree probable, that, had this powerful party remained intact, and had its Southern leaders exercised only a *modicum* of that sagacity which had characterized them in its better days, it could have secured for the South all that the South had a right to demand under the Constitution, and saved the land from a deluge of blood. But the instigators of this rebellion wantonly threw away the power which they possessed, to grasp a shadow which their ambition had pictured.

FALSE CHARGES BY THE SOUTH.

3. While this is a rebellion against the Government proper, it was instigated *against an incoming Administration on false grounds.*

It was charged at the outset throughout the South, that it was to be the policy of Mr. Lincoln's Administration to destroy slavery. This charge was known and proven to be false in every possible way which the case admitted. It was denied in the most formal manner in the platform of the party, adopted in the National Convention by which the present Executive was nominated. It was denied by many of the leading men of the party, in their numerous speeches during the canvass, and by the resolutions of many assemblages of the people; and if there were any contrary declarations they were wholly without authority, in the face of the formal announcement of the

National Convention. And finally, it was denied by the President in his Inaugural Address.* In short, it would seem to be impossible to meet such a charge in any way in which it was not met. And yet, the revolt began immediately upon the result of the Presidential election

* The following is an extract from the Inaugural Address of President Lincoln, in which is embodied the resolution above referred to from the platform of the National Convention: "I do not consider it necessary, at present, for me to discuss those matters of administration about which there is no special anxiety or excitement. Apprehension seems to exist among the people of the Southern States, that by the accession of a Republican Administration, their property and their peace and personal security are to be endangered. There never has been any reasonable cause for such apprehension. Indeed, the most ample evidence to the contrary has all the while existed, and been open to their inspection. It is found in nearly all the published speeches of him who now addresses you. I do but quote from one of those speeches, when I declare that 'I have no purpose, directly or indirectly, to interfere with the institution of slavery in the States where it exists.' I believe I have no lawful right to do so; and I have no inclination to do so. Those who nominated and elected me, did so with the full knowledge that I had made this, and made similar declarations, and had never recanted them. And more than this, they placed in the platform, for my acceptance, and as a law to themselves and to me, the clear and emphatic resolution which I now read: '*Resolved*, That the maintenance inviolate of the rights of the States, and especially the right of each State to order and control its own domestic institutions according to its own judgment exclusively, is essential to that balance of power on which the perfection and endurance of our political fabric depend; and we denounce the lawless invasion by armed force of the soil of any State or Territory, no matter under what pretext, as among the grossest of crimes.' I now reiterate these sentiments; and in doing so I only press upon the public attention the most conclusive evidence of which the case is susceptible, that the property, peace, and security of no section are to be in any wise endangered by the now incoming Administration. I add, too, that all the protection which, consistently with the Constitution and the laws, can be given, will be cheerfully given to all the States when lawfully demanded, for whatever cause, as cheerfully to one section as to another." The foregoing sentences completely disprove the charge under consideration. The President closed his Address as follows: "In your hands, my dissatisfied fellow-countrymen, and not in mine, is the momentous issue of civil war. The Government will not assail you. You can have no conflict without being yourselves the aggressors. You have no oath registered in heaven to destroy the Government; while I shall have the most solemn one to 'preserve, protect, and defend it.' I am loath to close. We are not enemies, but friends. We must not be enemies. Though passion may have strained, it must not break our bonds of affection. The mystic chords of memory, stretching from every battle-field and patriot grave to every living heart and hearthstone all over this broad land, will yet swell the chorus of the Union, when again touched, as surely they will be, by the better angels of our nature."

(Nov. 6, 1860) becoming known, and four months before the Administration was to assume power, in those acts of secret and open aggression upon the public authority and property throughout the Southern States, with which the world is so familiar.

The third item, therefore, which characterizes the rebellion, is, that it began with a most barefaced and palpable lie in its right hand, forged by the leaders against the sovereign people of the United States, in the face of the most public and indisputable facts to the contrary, and employed as a rallying cry to deceive the masses at the South and precipitate the States into secession.

It cannot be said, in answer to this, that the event has proved the charge true; that the present policy of the Administration towards slavery shows that it was from the first its design to destroy it. There is no shadow of evidence that the President, or the party that elected him, intended originally to interfere with it in the States, but overwhelming proof to the contrary. But when open war was made in the interest of slavery, to supplant the Government and dismember the Union, the whole case was changed; and as, on the one hand, the rebels did not enter upon the war to prove their prediction true, so, on the other, the Administration were not bound to abstain from touching slavery in order to prove the prediction false.

AGAINST ALL MEASURES FOR PEACE.

4. After the rebellion began, it was persistently adhered to and prosecuted, *in spite of the most urgent means to preserve peace*, made by the party which had triumphed in the Presidential election, and by many of the patriotic of all parties.

Among other important measures which were taken during the winter and prior to the fourth of March, 1861, while President Buchanan was still in power, were three which deserve special notice: The Acts of the Peace Convention, as it was called; the proposed Amendment to the Constitution from the Committee of Thirty-Three of the House of Representatives; and the organization of the Territories.

The Peace Convention met in Washington in January, 1861, and continued in session several weeks. It was convened on the recommendation of the Legislature of Virginia, and composed of delegates from thirteen free States, and seven slave States; to devise measures which should be recommended to Congress for its adoption, in order to harmonize the views of the two sections of the country and prevent bloodshed. It embraced many of the ablest men of the country, of the different shades of political opinion in each State represented. Although it was a body of no legal authority, yet from the weight of character of the men composing it, presided over by one who had filled the office of President of the United States, and from its humane and patriotic objects, its proceedings were watched with intense interest.

As the result of its deliberations, this Convention presented to Congress the recommendation of an article for an amendment to the Constitution, consisting of seven sections. As the questions which divided the country related mainly to slavery, the provisions of this proposed article were framed with special reference to that subject. Among them were the following, some of which were made apparently to the demands and others to the fears of the party in revolt, and nearly all of which were most marked concessions to the whole South. The article restored the Missouri Compromise line, with very serious modifications, on the parallel of latitude of 36° 30′. It admitted slavery into "all the territory" south of that line, guaranteeing that the status of slaves then within it should "not be changed," and prohibiting Congress and the Territorial Legislature from passing any law against taking slaves into such territory. It guaranteed the admission of States into the Union from "any Territory North or South of said line," either with or without slavery, as the Constitution of each State should provide. It prohibited such a construction of the Constitution as would give to Congress any power whatever over slavery in any of the States; or to abolish slavery in the District of Columbia without the consent of Maryland, and without the consent or compensation of the owners; or to prevent any one from taking his slaves to and from the District of Columbia at pleasure; or to interfere with or abolish slavery in any place, either in State or Territory, "under the exclusive jurisdiction of the United States;" or to interfere with the domestic slave-trade between the slave States. It also prohibited such a construction of the Constitution as would "prevent any of the States," so disposed, "from enforcing the delivery of fugitives from labor" to their owners; and made it obligatory upon Congress to "provide by law that the United States shall pay to the owner the full value of his fugitive from labor in all cases" where fugitive slaves should be prevented from arrest or rescued from the officers of the law "by violence or intimidation from mobs or riotous assemblages." And finally, it provided that the sections embodying these several guarantees and prohibitions (with two minor exceptions), together with the several parts of the Constitution which now relate to slavery, should "not be amended or abolished, WITHOUT THE CONSENT OF ALL THE STATES." A majority of "three-fourths" only of the States is now requisite for amending any part of the Constitution.

It is perceived at a glance that these propositions of the

Peace Convention made concessions to the whole South in several important particulars. The only question touching slavery which was brought into the Presidential canvass of 1860, was that concerning the Territories, over which Congress has full jurisdiction; and the result of the election was deemed a solemn judgment by the people that the Territories then free should remain free. This was simply in accordance with a principle which Congress had recognized several times in our history, by prohibiting slavery in portions of the territory of the United States, and these prohibitions had been sanctioned as constitutional by Southern Presidents and by the general acquiescence of all political parties.* But after the revolt commenced, and

* Including the action of the Continental Congress under the Articles of Confederation, and the several acts of Congress under the present Constitution, there has been direct legislation many times, prohibitory of or interfering with slavery in the Territorial domain under the immediate jurisdiction of the Government of the United States, between that earlier period and the administration of President Polk. The Continental Congress passed the famous "Ordinance for the Government of the Territory of the United States Northwest of the Ohio River," July 13, 1787. Eight States were represented, and voted on this Ordinance, three of which were free at the beginning of the rebellion, and five were slave, each State having one vote, viz.: Free States, Massachusetts, New York, and New Jersey; Slave States, Delaware, Virginia, North Carolina, South Carolina, and Georgia. *Every one of these States voted for this Ordinance prohibiting slavery*, and also every member but one, Mr. Yates, of New York. The Constitution of the United States was adopted in the same year, and in the Convention which framed it were several of the same men who in the Continental Congress passed this Ordinance. One of the earliest acts of the First Congress passed under the Constitution and during the administration of General Washington as President, embracing again several men who had been in the Convention that framed the Constitution, was an act to enforce the Ordinance of 1787, excluding slavery from the Northwest Territory; and in doing this, the fathers who had *made* the Constitution so recently did not of course suppose they were *violating* it. Whatever else, therefore, may be said about this Ordinance and the Act of Congress last referred to, and whatever else they may have included or covered, it is clear that they *prohibited slavery* in United States Territory; and they so far forth show that, in the judgment of the men who understood the real intent and meaning of the Constitution as well probably as any men who have since lived, it is perfectly within the power of Congress to prohibit slavery in any Territory of the United States whenever in its opinion public policy demands it. Nor has the exercise of such power been pronounced an infraction of the Constitution by the Supreme Court, or been so deemed by any class of public men (and

solely for the sake of preventing bloodshed, the Peace Convention, in which were some of the leading men of the triumphant party, presented to Congress *for adoption into the Constitution*, the foregoing provisions, which would secure greater immunities to slavery than it had ever before enjoyed.

How were these generous proposals received? The leaders of the rebellion scouted them with scorn. Some of them publicly declared,—as in the case of the Hon. Lawrence M. Keitt, member of the House of Representatives from South Carolina,—that if a blank parchment were given them on which to write the demands which the North should grant, they would reject it with contempt. Mr. Tyler, the President of the Peace Convention, went home to Virginia, and with other leading men of that State used all his influence against the favorable reception of these proposals by the Legislature. We witnessed, personally, the manner in which these propositions were received in the Senate of the United States. On being reported from the committee to whom they had been referred, we heard five speeches made upon them which consumed the chief portion of one day's session. Messrs. Mason and Hunter, of Virginia, spoke earnestly against

never by any political party), until within a very recent period. The last instance in the series of Congressional prohibitory acts now referred to, occurred as late as the administration of James K. Polk, a Southern President. With a Democratic majority in both Houses of Congress, slavery was prohibited in the bill for the organization of the Territory of Oregon. The Southern doctrine, therefore, that the Constitution carries slavery into the Territories by its own inherent force, and that Congress therefore cannot prohibit but is bound necessarily "to protect" it there by positive law, is a modern notion—*very* modern. And yet, this question of *slavery in the Territories* was made a chief element in the South (see next chapter) for urging the people into rebellion. Dr. Thornwell but announces the new doctrine on this point upon which rebel statesmen and the whole South acted,—and it goes beyond *the Territories* and into *the States*,—when he says: "The Constitution covers the whole territory of *the Union, and throughout that territory* has taken slavery under the *protection of law.*"—*Southern Presbyterian Review*, Jan., 1861.

them, as did also Mr. Pugh, of Ohio, these three men being of the party in the Senate having the majority; while their adoption was earnestly and most eloquently urged by Mr. Crittenden, of Kentucky, and by Mr. Baker, of California, the latter being of the Republican party, and showing a few months later, in the unfortunate battle at Ball's Bluff, that he was as ready to pour out his heart's blood for his country, when the clash of arms had actually come, as he was to speak eloquently for peace as long as peace was possible.

What good fruit could be expected from the labors of the Peace Convention, when their extreme and generous concessions to the South were spurned with disdain by all those who controlled Southern opinion?*

The second measure to which we have referred, was taken in the same spirit which actuated the Peace Convention. It was another proposition to amend the Constitution, emanating from the Committee of Thirty-Three of the House of Representatives, of which Mr. Corwin, of Ohio, a

* The late Secretary of the Treasury, Hon. Salmon P. Chase, was a member of this Peace Convention. On visiting his home in Ohio, in October last, addressing his fellow-citizens in Columbus and again in Cincinnati, he incidentally refers to the labors of this Convention, as follows: "When he left the State, it had been at the invitation and appointment of his friend and most honored successor (Governor Dennison), a Governor, he must here take the opportunity to say, who had worthily discharged the great trusts the people had confided to his hands. In the Peace Conference, to which he had thus been appointed, he and his Northern colleagues had been animated by the sincerest and most anxious desire to preserve the peace and harmony of the Republic. They had no wish save to give effect to the Constitution and laws as they stood. They had assured the delegates from the South that if they would be content with slavery where it was, there was no considerable body of men anywhere who sought to interfere with them. Join us, then,—they had proposed,—in assuring your people of this plain, indisputable fact, and allay this dangerous excitement. Then call for a National Convention and let the whole country decide on the new claims you prefer. But for that fair, simple proposition, *not one single vote from a single slaveholding State was recorded.* John Tyler was the Chairman of that Convention. Mr. Seddon, the present rebel Minister of War, and nearly every other member from the South, was now identified with the rebellion. They did not consent to the proposition, because they had made up their minds before they entered the Convention, to rule the nation or ruin it."—*Cincinnati Gazette*, Oct. 13, 1863.

leading member of the Republican party, was the Chairman. It was in these words: "No amendment shall be made to the Constitution which will authorize or give Congress power to abolish or interfere, in any State, with the domestic institutions thereof, including that of persons held to labor or servitude by the laws of said State."

This proposed amendment was intended to meet the specific charge, made all through the South during the Presidential canvass, that the Republican party designed to interfere with slavery in the States. It was indeed a work of supererogation, for no statesman of any party had ever pretended that Congress had any such power as it was proposed here to restrict. But it shows how earnest were the national authorities to promote concord between the North and the South. This measure passed both branches of Congress by the requisite majority of two-thirds, and indeed almost unanimously. It is highly probable that it would have been passed by the required number of the States, had not the violent measures of those in rebellion soon revealed that a prevention of actual hostilities was hopeless.*

The third measure showing a disposition to remove all causes of complaint as far as possible, is seen in the action of Congress upon the organization of Territories. As before stated, the only question touching slavery upon which the Presidential election turned, was concerning its status in the Territories. Congress, before its close on the 4th

* To this proposition to amend the Constitution, President Lincoln referred in his Inaugural Address, as follows: "I understand that a proposed amendment to the Constitution (which amendment, however, I have not seen) has passed Congress, to the effect that the Federal Government shall never interfere with the domestic institutions of the States, including that of persons held to service. To avoid misconstruction of what I have said, I depart from my purpose not to speak of particular amendments, so far as to say, that, holding such a provision to be now implied constitutional law, I have no objections to its being made express and irrevocable."

of March, 1861, organized several Territorial Governments for the remaining portion of the public domain. But instead of ingrafting upon these bills any prohibition of slavery in these Territories,—which they had the power of numbers to do after the withdrawal of the Southern members, as well as the authority of many precedents by Congress from the earliest period, and which would have been in accordance with the sentiments of the people expressed in the election,—the whole question was left open to the decision of the people in each Territory when they should form their respective State Constitutions; thus practically allowing to the South all that had been yielded by the decision of the Supreme Court in the Dred Scott case, that they might go to the Territories with their slaves, and abide the decision of the people whether they should be ultimately free or slave States.*

When such advances were made to the party then in revolt, and when they were met in the well-known manner indicated, no seer was needed to predict the result. In the words of the Hon. Edward Everett, the leaders of the rebellion "were resolved not to be satisfied." They looked with proud contempt upon the men who endeavored to conciliate them, and regarded their most generous concessions as prompted by pusillanimity and cowardice. They believed that a people who could so act would not fight when the trial of arms should come—a mistake of which they have since had ample proof.

This characteristic of the rebellion thus exhibits the most indubitable evidence,—and it is furnished in many other

* In an account of a public meeting held at Louisville, Kentucky, the *Louisville Journal* of the next day, April 21, 1861, says: "The Hon. John Brown Young followed in a speech unsurpassed in power and brilliancy. This gifted young orator rehearsed the history of the last Congress, the efforts for compromise, *the surrender by the Republicans of the fundamental idea of the Chicago Platform, in the positive non-extension of Slavery in the formation of the new Territories.*"

public facts,—that while the people of the North, represented by their leaders, were disposed to go to extreme lengths in preserving peace, the leaders of the rebellion were as persistently determined, in the face of these overtures, to brave all the hazards and horrors of civil war to carry out their foregone purposes.*

* One of the most thorough specimens of sympathy with the South which we have met with in Northern literature, from a respectable source, since the beginning of the rebellion, is a pamphlet of thirty-two pages from the pen of Rev. Samuel J. Baird, D.D., of New Jersey, entitled "Southern Rights and Northern Duties in the Present Crisis." It is in the form of a Letter, dated February 6, 1861, to the Hon. William Pennington, then Speaker of the House of Representatives of the United States. Dr. Baird says: "When a free, enlightened, and Christian people,—and such are our Southern brethren,—are induced to peril all, to rend the ties which have hitherto held them, or even to hesitate upon venturing the fearful experiment of revolution, the causes must be such as stand justified to conscience, and appeal to the highest principles of our nature. Either they are victims of a gigantic fraud, or they labor under grievances of the most serious nature. Upon either alternative, their position is entitled to profound respect, generous forbearance, and anxious study to discover and expose the fraud if they have been deceived, or to rectify the wrong if they are the subjects of real grievance; by any honorable means to allay their anxieties and restore the Union." It is very clear, from the whole pamphlet, that he deems the South the injured party, and most grievously wronged; and the chief responsibility is laid at the door of the "*Republican party*" which put Mr. Lincoln into office, whose 'attitude" he is led to "examine more particularly," "because the power is in their hands at this momentous crisis." Hence he criticizes their platform and condemns their principles and general course, and in these finds justification or palliatives for the South. Here is a specimen: "So long, in a word, as the representatives of a great party, professing to reflect the sentiments and act in the name of the North, form intrenchments around the Southern States, with the avowed purpose of arresting their further expansion, it is in vain to deny that the South has the most grave and momentous cause of apprehension. * * * It may be our duty to treat the institutions of the South as a crime, and themselves as enemies, to be surrounded and kept in subjection. Upon that question I now say nothing. But, manifestly, the alternative is, that all this is wrong, and an *aggression which the South ought not to suffer;* or that if right, in absolving us from the obligations to the South which have been heretofore recognized, *it releases the latter from allegiance to the Union.*" Further on, Dr. Baird says: "My single object has been, to bear a testimony to the claims of justice against us on her behalf—to expose the assumption that it is our peculiar prerogative, as guardians of the Territories, to protect them from the crime and curse of our Southern brethren. To this purpose, it has been shown that *the South has just cause of grievance of the most serious character, which demands prompt and cheerful redress at our hands;* and rights in the Territories, which neither in honor nor honesty may we disregard." Again: "Our first and imperative duty, in faithfulness to our covenants and to the claims of

PERPETRATED BY FRAUD AND VIOLENCE.

5. The rebellion was carried through the forms of secession, in many of the States, *by fraud and violence, against the wishes, and in some against the direct vote, of a majority of the people.*

The facts which illustrate this are voluminous, and generally well known. We are compelled to glance at them briefly, and can refer to a few palpable cases only.

The popular vote of Louisiana upon the ordinance of secession was never officially made public. It was charged by the New Orleans papers at the time as being largely against secession, and the officers of the Convention were challenged to proclaim the result. To this day that duty has never been performed by them, while there is the most unquestionable evidence that the State was forced into

honor and justice, is to accord to the South any necessary protection against the piratical policy of abolitionism, and a distinct recognition of *her rights in the Territories* of the United States." What, then, does Dr. Baird wish to have done, and by whom? He would probably have had Congress, when assembled in December, 1860 immediately get down on its knees and beg the South's pardon that the people had elected Mr. Lincoln, even when that Congress had a *Democratic majority in both Houses.* Hear him: "No one capable of forming an intelligent judgment on the subject, can look over the progress of events at the South, and the results thus far, and doubt that *had Congress, at the opening of the present session,* PROMPTLY shown a spirit of magnanimous patriotism, such as was so eminently becoming from the stronger to the weaker, and which the circumstances so clearly demanded, the tide of secession would have been stayed on the borders of South Carolina; and that State would soon have returned to her place in our midst." We have shown what measures for "peace" Congress did actually propose when that Democratic majority had been reduced to a minority by the withdrawal of the Southern members. Dr. Baird, nevertheless, mourns over "Congressional inactivity," and denounces "the treacherous passivity of the present session." It is but just to suppose, however, that he would not have belabored Congress in exactly that style, had the proceedings of the whole session been before him at the time he wrote; especially when, at the opening, *his friends* were in the majority. But after making allowance for this, the character of his pamphlet is such, throughout, that, although by no means as we suppose so intended, it was well calculated and unquestionably did give "aid and comfort" to the rebellion, both among those who were then and long before had been mustering and arming soldiers for the overthrow of the Government, and their hearty sympathizers all through the North.

secession against the direct vote of a majority of the people.

Governor Hamilton, of Texas, in an address to the people of that State in January last, not going into any proof of the fact, but incidentally referring to what those whom he was addressing well knew to be true, says: "When you were *forced, by a minority*, into rebellion, you were in the enjoyment of every blessing ever conferred by civil government upon men."

Virginia, Tennessee, and North Carolina, were carried into secession by violence and terror, as many of their own newspapers and public men at the time declared. Proof of this which we have in possession would fill many pages. In some States, the whole work was done by a Convention, or by the State Legislature, without the voice of the people taken upon the ordinance of secession; in others, the submission of the question to a popular vote was but a burlesque on the elective franchise. We mention facts which are too recent and too familiar to be doubted, and only refer to them to exhibit another of the striking characteristics of the rebellion.

A single testimony, chiefly concerning the manner in which Virginia was carried "out of the Union," will serve as an example of other cases. It is furnished by a distinguished Southern statesman who was familiar with the scenes he describes:

In these circumstances was the *peaceful* process of secession set on foot, and the deceived masses of the Southern States stimulated into that unnatural frenzy which wildly hurried them into a treason from which retreat soon became impossible. When this drama of secession came to the stage of its formal enactment in the passage of secession ordinances, it was characterized by frauds only more stupendous than those I have described, because they implicated a greater number of actors and spread over a wider surface. Whilst some of the States, perhaps a majority of them, were in earnest in their resolve to secede the most important States were not; and if the people in these had been left to the free expression of their wish they would have refused. The Convention of Virginia had been elected by a vote which was largely against secession, and the Legislature which authorized that Convention had taken care to provide that no ordinance of secession should have any effect unless ratified by a subsequent expression of the popular will in the regular election. When the Convention assembled at Richmond, there was a majority of its members opposed to the ordinance. The scenes that were enacted in the sequence of the proceedings, by which that majority was reduced to a minority, are only partially known to the country. Whilst the sessions were open to the public observation the majority held its ground, but amidst what perils and appliances, every inhabitant of Richmond at that time knows. The best men of the State, and there were many, who had dared to speak in the Convention in favor of the Union, were exposed to the grossest insults from the mob that filled the lobbies, and by whom they were pursued with hootings and threats to their own dwellings. Still, no vote could be got sufficient to carry the ordinance. The Convention then resolved to exclude the public and manage their work in secret session. From that day affairs took a new turn. The community of Richmond was filled with strife. The friends of the Union, both in the Convention and out of it,—a large number of persons,—were plunged into the deepest anxiety and alarm. They felt that the cause was lost and that the sentiment of the majority of the State would be overruled. Quarrels arose. Ardent and reckless men were distempered with passion. It was no longer safe to discuss the subject of the day in the streets. The hotels were filled with strangers, loud, peremptory, and fierce. A friend of the Union could not mingle in these crowds without certainty of insult, nor even sometimes without danger of personal violence. The recusant members of the Convention were plied with every expedient to enforce their submission. The weak were derided, the timid bullied, the wavering cajoled with false promises and false representations of the state of opinion in the country. Those who could not be reached by these arguments, but who were found pliable to more genial impulses, were assailed by flattery, by the influences of friendship, by the blandishments of the dinner-table, and finally carried away by the wild enthusiasm of midnight revelry. If the Convention had sat in Staunton or Fredericksburg,—anywhere but in Richmond,—no ordinance of secession could have been passed. As it was, it was a work of long and sinister industry to bring it about. It became necessary to fire the people with new and startling sensations—to craze the public mind with excitement. To this end, messages were sent to Charleston to urge the bombardment of Sumter. * * * The whole South became ablaze. Men lost all self-control, and were ready to obey any order. The vote of the Convention had been canvassed from time to time during this process of ripening the mind for the act of secession, and it was now found that it might be successfully put. It was taken three days after the surrender of Fort Sumter, and the public were told that it was carried by a large majority. Subsequent disclosures show that upwards of fifty of its members stood firm and preserved their equanimity in this great tempest of passion. The scene at the taking of the vote is described by one of the members as resembling the riot of a hospital of lunatics. The ratification of this act was yet to be gone through, as prescribed by the law, in a vote of the people to be taken in May. That proceeding was substantially ignored in all that followed. An appointment of members to the rebel Congress was immediately made, to represent the State in the Provisional Government then established at Montgomery. The President of the new Confederacy was forthwith invited to send an army into the State; and accordingly, when the month of May arrived, troops were stationed in all those counties where it was supposed any considerable amount of loyalty to the Union existed amongst the people. The day of election appointed for the ratification found this force stationed at the polls, and the refractory people mastered and quelled into silence. Union men were threatened in their lives if they should dare to vote against the ordinance; and an influential leader in the movement, but recently a Senator of the United States, wrote and published a letter, hinting to those who might be rash enough to vote against secession, that they must expect to be driven out of the State.* Of course, the ratification

* Reference is here made to James M. Mason, now the Rebel Commissioner to London. His letter is dated "Winchester, Va., May 16, 1861," and was published in the *Winchester Virginian*. In this letter he says: "The ordinance of secession withdrew the State of Virginia from the Union, with all the consequences resulting from the separation. It annulled the Constitution and the laws of the United States within the limits of this State, and absolved the citizens of Virginia from all obligations and obedience to them." This is a little remarkable, when the Convention provided that the ordinance should be submitted to a vote of the people of the State. But we see from another paragraph of the same letter, what sort of an election this was to be: "If it be asked, what are those to do who in their consciences cannot vote to separate Virginia from the United States, the answer is simple and plain: honor and duty alike require that they should not vote on the question; if they retain such opinions, they must leave the State." All very "simple" and very "plain;" and the plan was very faithfully executed.

2*

found no opposition in any doubtful county. * * * My object is to show that the whole secession movement was planned and conducted in the spirit of headlong revolution and premeditated war. In Tennessee the proceeding was even less orderly than in Virginia. In Missouri it was no better. The attempt was made to carry Kentucky and Maryland by the same arts and the same frauds, but utterly failed. Maryland has repudiated secession and its abettors with a persistent and invincible loyalty. Kentucky, under severe trial and in the actual contest of civil war, has bravely and honorably preserved her faith and repelled every assault.

We have given this long extract, not because any proof is wanting of the fraud and violence by which the rebellion was inaugurated, but to show in these graphic details what loyal men all through the South suffered at the outset for opposing the insane movement. This authority is unquestionable. The extract is taken from the *National Intelligencer*, of Washington, D. C., of Feb. 23, 1864. The editor indorses the writer as "evincing ability, sagacity, and fine analysis, in laying bare the secret springs of the great insurrection," and says he is a "Southern gentleman who for many years occupied with distinction a seat in the National Legislature, and who subsequently held a responsible post in the administration of an important Executive Department of the Government."*

* At a Union meeting in Huntsville, Alabama, on the 5th of March, 1864, the Hon. Jeremiah Clemens, formerly a United States Senator from that State, addressed the meeting, and said "he would tell the Alabamians how their State was got out of the Union." He proceeded to say: "In 1861, shortly after the Confederate Government was put in operation, I was in the city of Montgomery. One day I stepped into the office of the Secretary of War, General Walker, and found there, engaged in a very excited discussion, Mr. Jefferson Davis, Mr. Memminger, Mr. Benjamin, Mr. Gilchrist, a member of our Legislature from Lowndes county, and a number of other prominent gentlemen. They were discussing the propriety of immediately opening fire on Fort Sumter, to which General Walker, the Secretary of War, appeared to be opposed. Mr. Gilchrist said to him: 'Sir, unless you sprinkle blood in the face of the people of Alabama they will be back in the old Union in less than ten days!' The next day General Beauregard opened the batteries on Sumter, and Alabama was saved to the Confederacy." Another distinguished statesman says upon the same gen-

PROSECUTED BY CRUELTY AND TERROR.

6. This rebellion was not only initiated by fraud and violence, through the means by which its ordinances of secession were enacted, but during every stage of its progress, from its birth to the present hour, *it has been prosecuted with the most atrocious cruelty towards those in the revolted States who have dared to oppose the designs of its leaders.*

From its inception till now, the world has been told by public men and by the organs of public opinion in the South, that the people were a unit in support of the rebellion, while the world has all the time had the most certain knowledge that this was only a stupendous falsehood, concocted and persisted in for political purposes. The evidence of this is overwhelming, and is sustained by facts which meet us at every stage of the movement.

The people have heard so much during the present year, since the opening of the rebel Congress in December last, of the sweeping conscription measures by which all from sixteen to fifty-five capable of bearing arms have been driven into the army, and of the total repudiation of plighted faith in forcing those to enter it who had secured legal exemption by furnishing substitutes, and other oppressive acts of a like character, that they forget that impressments into their armies by the most violent means have been a marked feature of their recruiting service from the beginning of the war. Looking back over

eral subject: "Future history will record, that, perhaps with two exceptions, the ordinance of secession would not have been carried in any of the seceding States, if the people could have been permitted a fair, uncontrolled election, by ballot upon it. But they were overwhelmed by fraud and force; and then they were told, according to the improved theory of State rights, that whenever a majority of a State had resolved to commit treason, the minority were bound not only to submit, but to share the sin and shame. Those whom argument failed to convince, the military despotism had silenced, for the time being."

the events of the spring and summer of 1861,—a period when rebel fervor was at its height, and when the expectation of speedy success to their arms was upon the lips of all their leaders,—we find that rigorous impressments pervaded all parts of the South. The proof is furnished in the Southern papers of that period, but we cannot occupy space with the details.

But these are among the least offensive measures which were taken to crush out loyalty to the United States. The tens of thousands of individuals and families who have been forced to flee for life, leaving home and property, penniless and friendless, and the many who have remained only to suffer imprisonment, indignity, and death, are facts well attested, and have occurred from the beginning of the revolt down to a late period.

As early as August 14th, 1861, after multitudes had fled from rebel tyranny, Jefferson Davis issued the following edict of banishment:

> I do hereby warn and require every male citizen of the United States, of the age of fourteen years and upwards, now within the Confederate States, and adhering to the Government of the United States, and acknowledging the authority of the same, and not being a citizen of the Confederate States, to leave within forty days after the date of this proclamation. And I do warn all persons above described who shall remain within the Confederate States, after the expiration of the said period of forty days, that they will be held as alien enemies.

All know what followed the issuing of this decree. The North was soon filled with Southern refugees. A well-informed witness declared at the time that "two hundred thousand men, women, and children, in the single State of Tennessee, had thus received 'notice to quit,' the most of them thus driven from the land that gave them birth."

The persons who have thus suffered persecution at home, and banishment, are from every rank in life, from the mechanic and day-laborer, to those in all the professions: clergymen, lawyers, physicians, members of Congress, United States Senators, and judges of the highest courts of the State and of the Nation. In the spring and summer of 1861, Senator Johnson and Messrs. Etheridge, Bridges, Maynard, Nelson, all then or previously members of Congress, were compelled to flee from the single State of Tennessee, or, being out of the State, found it unsafe to return. Judges Catron and Trigg, of the same State, with others of the bench, the former of the United States Supreme Court, were treated in like manner. Judge Catron did not dare, nor was he permitted, to visit his home in Nashville until Middle Tennessee was repossessed by the United States forces. Judge Wayne, also of the Supreme Court of the United States, whose residence was in Georgia, being in attendance upon his official duties at Washington when the rebellion began, and determined to remain loyal to his oath and his country, has never since ventured to visit his State, and will not be able to do so except under the protection of the arms of the Union. The only crime for which these men were exiled from the land of their birth, and for which others have suffered imprisonment at home, was their determination to adhere to the Government which had always given them protection, their regard for their solemn oaths of office, and their unwillingness to yield to the demands of a godless rebellion.

If persons of such distinction can be so treated, and were so treated at the beginning of the revolt, no large amount of credulity is demanded to believe that thousands of less note have been subjected to the most cruel doom. We have undoubted proof of this, relating to every period since the beginning of the war, and we fairly infer that there are multitudes of like cases of which the public never hear.

Among numerous testimonies at hand, we give an illustration of this point from the address of Governor Hamilton, of Texas, to the people of that State, issued in January last. We too well know that Texas does not stand solitary and alone in the work here graphically described. The same tale is true of every rebel State. Governor Hamilton begins by barely referring to his own treatment:

CITIZENS OF TEXAS: Through the instrumentality of ambitious and designing men, you have been for more than two and a half years engaged in rebellion against the Government of the United States. Hunted as a felon, and expelled from the State because I would not join the conspiracy to overthrow free government, I now, after an exile of eighteen months, return to it, charged with the duty of organizing such Provisional State Government as may be best calculated to aid in restoring you to the blessings of civil liberty. When you were forced, by a minority, into rebellion, you were in the enjoyment of every blessing ever conferred by civil government upon men. Not a single wrong had you ever suffered from the Government. * * * Martial law has been visited upon you, and in every town, and village, and neighborhood, some petty despot appointed, to whose edicts you were required to bow in meek submission. You have been denied the right to travel through the community near your homes, on the most necessary business, without the written permission of one of these tools of tyranny. You dare not convey to market the product of your farms and your labor without permission. Your wagons and teams have been seized by Government agents at home and on the road to market, in order to compel you to sell them your crops for a nominal price in worthless paper. No interest has been secure, and no right sacred. Law and order no longer exist among you. * * * The vicious and depraved, the murderers and ruffians of the country, are banded together in secret societies, known as "Sons of the South," and are from day to day sitting in judgment on the lives of the best citizens of the State. *Three thousand of your citizens have perished because they loved good government, and peace, and order in society—perished as felons. They have been hung, shot, and literally butchered; they have been tortured, in many instances, beyond any thing known in savage warfare.* Uncertainty, and gloom, and despair, are resting upon you to-day like the frown of God. Are you in love with this, and do you desire it to continue?

He then draws a picture of the condition of things just before the rebellion began, from which we take a single paragraph:

In our own State, during the summer and fall of 1860, *according to the published account of the murderers themselves*, two hundred and fifty of our free citizens were hung as felons, and thousands driven from their homes and compelled to leave the State, *because they were* SUSPECTED *of infidelity to slavery*. And, finally, gathering temerity from its successful war upon the rights and lives of the citizens, it lifted its unholy hand to destroy the Government to whose protection it owed its power.

We close these illustrations of rebel cruelty by one more quotation. It is from the distinguished Southern statesman referred to under the foregoing head, and commended so highly by the *National Intelligencer*, a journal that will not be suspected of favoring what is called "radicalism." He is speaking chiefly of the violence practised towards loyal citizens of Virginia, and says:

What argument can Virginia, for example, make in favor of a revolt against the authority of the Union, that may not be used with tenfold force by her own western counties to justify a revolt against her? Virginia herself had really no definable grievance against the Union. * * She has never yet indicated a single item of grievance resulting from the acts of the Federal Government. In fact, that Government has always been, in great part, in her own hands, or under the control of her influence. If she has not been happy and prosperous it is simply her own fault. I mean to say, she has no cause whatever to excuse her rebellion against the Union. Yet she revolted; we may say, gave to the revolution a countenance and support, without which it would have speedily sunk into a futile enterprise. Having come to it, she assumed the right to compel her unwilling citizens to cast their lives and fortunes into the same issue. A large portion of her people, comprising the inhabitants of many counties in the mountain region of the Alleghanies, have always been distinguished,—as, indeed, seems to be the characteristic of all our mountain country,—for their strong attachment to the Union. These people have an aversion to slaves, and have been steadily intent upon establishing and expanding a system of free labor. They have, therefore, very little in common, either of sentiment or interest, with the governing power of the State. When, therefore, the question of secession was submitted to them, they voted against it. From that moment they were marked, and when the State, under the control of its lowland interest, raised the banner of revolt, its first movement was to invite the Southern army to occupy the mountain districts, to overawe and drive the people there, not only into submission to the dominant power of the State, but into active hostility against the Union. To this end these loyal people were pursued with a bitter persecution, harried by a ruffian soldiery, hunted from their homes into the mountain fastnesses; their dwellings burned; their crops destroyed; their fields laid waste, and every other cruelty inflicted upon them to which the savage spirit of revolution usually resorts to compel the assent of those who resist its command. The inhabitants of these beautiful mountain valleys are a simple, brave, and sturdy people; and all these terrors were found insufficient to force them into an act of treason. They refused, and in their turn revolted against this execrable tyranny and drew their swords in favor of the Union. What more natural or righteous than such a resistance? And yet, Virginia affects to consider this the deepest of crimes, and is continually threatening vengeance against what she calls these rebels—Virginia, the rebel, denouncing rebellion! Her own plea is that she has only *seceded*, but Western Virginia *rebels*—there is a great difference.

When it is considered that unnumbered multitudes all through the South have been subjected to similar cruelties for the crime of loyalty to the Government, and for refusing to be driven into treason and rebellion against it,—and when this is contrasted with the "leniency" of our Government, which, as Governor Hamilton says, is without a parallel in the history of nations dealing with treason and traitors,—it places the unblushing cruelty of the Southern leaders and their minions out of the pale of all comparison with that of any tyrannical power, claiming to be civilized and Christianized, which the world has ever known.*

* In his address to the people of Texas, Governor Hamilton truly says: "In the history of the world, there cannot be found one example of a government dealing with a rebellion against its rightful authority with the mercy and leniency which have characterized the United States in this war. Out of the multiplied thousands who have been taken in arms against the Government, *not one* has been made to suffer for his

ITS DESOLATION OF THE COUNTRY.

7. We pass over some of the other characteristics of the rebellion, with a bare mention of them: *the wide-spread desolation which it has brought upon the whole disloyal region, to every interest, material, moral, social, and religious;* bringing to premature and dishonored graves the flower of a whole generation of their young men, with multitudes of aged fathers and stripling boys, pressed into their armies by the merciless conscription; leaving their land filled with widows and orphans, to mourn and weep out the remainder of an embittered life; the threatening of wide-spread starvation within their borders; the laying waste of nearly the whole producing regions of agriculture, from the desolation which more or less always follows the track of armies in civil war; the disbanding of their institutions of learning of the higher grades, to furnish material for their armies;* the injury which, from

treason. How has it been in Texas and throughout the South? Hecatombs of victims have been offered upon the altar of rebellion! The men who are responsible to society and to God for the blood of a thousand good citizens, are those who are prating about the tyranny of the President and the Government of the United States."

* We may perhaps take this as a specimen of what has befallen institutions of learning at the South. If this is true of North Carolina, where there has always been great disaffection with the rebel leaders, we may readily infer the condition of colleges in other States: "The effect of the rebellion on Southern Colleges is well illustrated by the case of the University of North Carolina at Chapel Hill. In 1860, it had four hundred and thirty students; in 1863, but sixty-three, nearly all of whom were too young or physically incapacitated for service. In 1860, eighty-four young men graduated, of whom one-seventh are known to have fallen in battle. Of the eight who ranked highest in the class, four are in their graves, a fifth is a wounded prisoner, and the others are in the army. Of the Freshman Class of that year, eighty in number, only one remained to graduate, and even he had been in the army, and was discharged for bad health. Though none of the fourteen members of the Faculty were liable to conscription, five enlisted, one of whom was killed; another has been taken prisoner; the third was severely wounded, and the fourth has a ruined constitution. Every son capable of service of the remaining nine, eight in number, entered the service, and two of them have been mortally wounded. Fifteen young men of the village, being more than half of the whole, have perished in battle."—*New York paper.*

the nature of the case, must have befallen the churches, and every interest of religion; and the inevitable condition of the South, in all these respects, for many years to come, which no pen can portray;—together with the blighting influence upon both sections of the country which must ever attend such a war, in the burdens of taxation, which must be felt for generations to come; in the social demoralization of the people at large, the corruption of public men, the familiarizing of the mind of the nation, and especially of the young, with scenes of bloodshed and carnage, and the desire for other wars, all which are the common fruits of all such conflicts; the like destruction, in the North as in the South, of the thousands of the noble and the brave who have fallen in battle, with the agony which has been brought upon the households of the whole territory of the Union; and the social alienation and bitterness which the strife has engendered, not only between the two sections of the country embroiled, but in many instances between those of the same household, both North and South.

This is but the bare mention,—and by no means all,—of that heritage of woes, now pressing, and long to be continued, every one of which is justly chargeable to this rebellion.

IT AIMED TO USURP THE GOVERNMENT.

8. Another characteristic of the rebellion is seen in *what it aimed at first to accomplish.*

Much declamation has been expended by public men and public journals, in both sections of the country, because the people in rebellion are not allowed to have their independence and separate nationality. But it was not for a separate Confederacy that the rebel leaders first inaugurated secession. They aimed to prevent the installation of the present Administration, to seize the Government and the public offices and archives at Washington, and by a *coup de main* to establish themselves in power as the legitimate succession to the present Government, and to impress upon it that character which they have given to their own Constitution; while their independence, as a separate nation, was resolved upon only in the event and as the result of the failure of their original plan.

That this was the programme laid down by the rebel leaders is the very general conviction of the intelligent and loyal people of the country, and many facts fully warrant this conclusion. It was the opinion freely expressed by members of Congress and other public men in their private circles, during the last two months of Mr. Buchanan's administration; and it is believed that to General Winfield Scott, more than to any other man, is the country indebted for the frustration of the scheme. The scattering of the small forces then composing the army of the United States to distant military posts, and the sending of the vessels of the navy to distant seas, by the respective Secretaries of the War and Navy Departments; the speedy gathering of a few hundred regulars, with several batteries of artillery, at Washington, by order of General Scott, when he apprehended danger, especially at the time the electoral votes were to be opened and counted; the wrathful speeches of Senator Mason, of Virginia, and other Southern statesmen, when they saw their plans foiled, because "the two Houses of Congress were surrounded by armed soldiers, as though they were sitting in an Austrian capital;" the subsequent well-matured plot to assassinate the President elect, as he should pass through Baltimore;*

* In a speech in the United States House of Representatives, April 8, 1864, Mr. Long, of Cincinnati, said: "A little over three years ago, the present occupant of the Presidential Mansion, at the other end of the Avenue, came into this city under cover

the vigilant preparations deemed essential at the time of Mr. Lincoln's inauguration, when the troops were stationed at different points in the city, and Generals Scott and Wool and other officers stood ready to mount at a moment's warning; these are all well-remembered facts, and the measures then taken by the illustrious head of the army reveal his sagacity and patriotism, and illustrate, in their warding off the threatened evil, the debt of gratitude due him from his countrymen.

The scheme of seizing the Government was not abandoned on the successful inauguration of Mr. Lincoln. On the evening of the 12th of April, 1861, when the citizens of Montgomery, then the rebel capital, were rejoicing in the prospect of Fort Sumter's speedy fall, the bombardment being then in progress, General Walker, the rebel Secretary of War, made the following declarations in a public speech: "That before many hours the flag of the

of night, disguised in plaid cloak and Scotch cap, lest, as was feared by his friends, he might have received a warmer greeting than would have been agreeable, on his way through Baltimore, at the hands of the constituents of the gentleman from Maryland." Mr. Long is one of the opponents of the present Administration. The *Albany Evening Journal* speaks of the contemplated assassination, and of the measures taken to prevent it, on the part of the President's friends, as follows: "They employed a detective of great experience, who was engaged at Baltimore in the business some three weeks prior to Mr. Lincoln's arrival there, employing both men and women to assist him. Shortly after coming to Baltimore, the detective discovered a combination of men banded together under a solemn oath to assassinate the President elect. * * * It was arranged, in case Mr. Lincoln should pass safely over the railroad to Baltimore, that the conspirators should mingle with the crowd which might surround his carriage, and by pretending to be his friends, be enabled to approach his person, when, upon a signal from their leader, some of them would shoot at Mr. Lincoln with their pistols, and others would throw into his carriage hand-grenades filled with detonating powder, similar to those used in the attempted assassination of the Emperor Louis Napoleon. It was intended that in the confusion which should result from this attack, the assailants should escape to a vessel waiting in the harbor to receive them, and be carried to Mobile, in the seceding State of Alabama." Then, speaking of Mr. Lincoln, the *Journal* says: "The party then took berths in the sleeping-car [at Philadelphia], and, without change of cars, passed directly through to Washington, where they arrived at the usual hour. Mr. Lincoln wore no disguise whatever, but journeyed in an ordinary travelling dress."

Confederacy would float over the fortress; and no man could tell where the war this day commenced would end, but he would prophesy that the flag which now flaunts the breeze here, *would float over the dome of the old capitol at Washington before the first of May.*" This speech of General Walker struck the key-note which was immediately echoed by the newspapers throughout the seceded States. Though Virginia had not yet seceded, the papers of that State sounded it. *The Richmond Enquirer* of April 13th, the day of the fall of Fort Sumter, had the following: "Nothing is more probable than that President Davis will soon march an army through North Carolina and Virginia to Washington. Those of our volunteers who desire to join the Southern army as it shall pass through our borders, had better organize at once for the purpose." This was published nearly a week before the Virginia Convention passed the ordinance of secession, and forty days before the people were to vote on the ordinance. This was also two days before President Lincoln issued his Proclamation (dated April 15th), calling for troops, and before it was known, either North or South, how the intelligence of the taking of Fort Sumter would affect either the Government or the people. Mr. Stephens, the rebel Vice-President, soon afterwards uttered the same sentiment respecting the taking of Washington, in a public speech at Richmond, on his arrival there before the secession of Virginia, and before the ordinance had passed the Convention, when on a mission to conclude a "military league" between that State and the Southern Confederacy.

There is nothing clearer in the early history of the rebellion, than that the primary plan of its leaders was to overthrow the Administration at Washington, to usurp its power and authority, and to install the rebel Government as its legitimate successor. This from the first was the battle-cry of their rulers, their armies, and their people. It is only because they were foiled in their original purpose that they have been content to seek to establish their separate independence.

POPULAR GOVERNMENT UNIVERSALLY ENDANGERED.

9. Another thing settled in the character of this rebellion, is, that its success would have *destroyed the hope for popular government throughout the world.*

A successful rebellion resulting in the overthrow of any other government on earth would be of little consequence in the great scale of human interests when poised against such a result to the Government of the United States. This is illustrated in the deep anxiety with which the contest has been watched on both sides of the Atlantic and by the people of every nation. The aristocracies of the Old World have aided the rebellion as far as they have deemed it safe, and have earnestly desired our dismemberment and downfall. They have felt that in such an issue their own power would be more secure. From the great heart of "the peoples" *alone* has there been for us a single genuine throb of sympathy. The only notable exception to this among the rulers in the monarchies of Europe is that of the Russian Empire. Even many of the middle classes of the nations of Western Europe, and among them many of the merchant princes of her marts of commerce, have given their good wishes and their active aid and their stores of gold to the rebellion, making a gain out of our national peril.

But the millions of the real people have desired our success and deserve our grateful remembrance. They feel that their own interests are bound up in our triumph. When, therefore, the nation shall come out of this strife successful, they will feel as do we, that what the nations of the earth have ever regarded as but "the American experiment," will be settled in favor of popular government for all time to come. One universal shout of rejoicing will then go up from the down-trodden millions of the world, and at its reverberations among the habitations of men, tyrants will everywhere tremble as they have never done before.

Among the characteristics, therefore, which stamp this rebellion with peculiar odium, is the fact not only that it is made against popular government, but in its success the last hope of liberty would have perished from among men. No people could have dared reasonably to hope for success in an experiment of free institutions after ours should have failed, commenced as it was under such favorable auspices, and having had such prosperity in all that can make a people great and glorious for nearly three generations.

It is too well known for doubt that a part of the original scheme of the rebel leaders was to establish an aristocracy, and perhaps a monarchy, and if we may judge from very recent utterances the plan is not abandoned. To this end, as well as to secure their independence, they have sought an alliance with several monarchical powers, and have been willing to place themselves under their protection without much scruple about conditions provided their independence could be gained.

Should the rebellion therefore succeed, and the plan of the Southern oligarchy be consummated, popular government throughout the world would thereby receive a double blow, in the dismemberment of that system of government, where it has now its fairest illustration, and in the establishment of aristocratic institutions in its stead over a large portion of the territory of the

United States, and over several millions of the people now embraced within its legitimate rule.*

TO PERPETUATE NEGRO SLAVERY.

10. And finally, this is a rebellion whose chief prompting impulse, at its inception and through its whole progress, has been *the security, the expansion of the area, and the perpetuation, of human bondage.*

That the slavery of the negro race, as the stimulating power, is the foundation on which the whole superstructure of this rebellion rests, is a fact patent to the eyes of all men. But as we reserve this point for a separate chapter, to be canvassed when we come to speak of the causes of the rebellion, we shall not dwell upon it here. We barely mention it now as completing the summation and forming the climax in the catalogue of those elements, —all of which we have not attempted to enumerate,—which give a special character to the rebellion, and stamp it as monstrous and diabolical without a parallel in the history of mankind.

When we speak of negro slavery as being at the bottom of the rebellion, we are aware that this is denied. The proof of our position, however, to be given hereafter, will be found in Southern testimony which cannot be confuted. We are also aware that other causes are assigned, the chief of which are: that the rebellion is the scheme of dis-

* No man better understands the character and aims of the rebellion and its leaders than Andrew Johnson, of Tennessee, a candidate for the Vice-Presidency. In a speech at Nashville, June 10, 1864, he said: "One of the chief elements of this rebellion, is the opposition of the slave aristocracy to being ruled by men who have risen from the ranks of the people. This aristocracy hated Mr. Lincoln because he was of humble origin, a rail-splitter in early life. One of them, the private secretary of Howell Cobb, said to me one day, after a long conversation, 'We people of the South will not submit to be governed by a man who has come up from the ranks of the common people, as Abe Lincoln has.' He uttered the essential feeling and spirit of this Southern rebellion."

appointed and ambitious politicians; a desire for an independent nationality; a wish to found an aristocracy, or a monarchy, or both; a strike for free trade, and to be rid of Northern competition; a vindication of the doctrine of State rights; a jealousy and chagrin at Northern growth and prosperity, in comparison with Southern; or, these and other similar causes all combined; and that slavery, and the Presidential election of 1860, were "a mere pretext." We grant the substantial truth of what are here given as *auxiliary* causes of the rebellion; and yet, it is further true, as we shall see, that it is NEGRO SLAVERY, in its emoluments in the Rebel States, in its fears of encroachment and apprehended dangers, and especially in its modern garb as "divine," and a political and social "good in itself" to all concerned, that underlies all other causes, and gives the *vital and essential force* to carry these desires and aspirations into execution in the form of open rebellion.

CHAPTER II.

CAUSE OF THE REBELLION.

It is among the marvels which our civil war has exhibited, that there should be a difference of opinion concerning the reasons which have prompted the rebellion now in progress against the Government of the United States. But if we may judge from the speeches of public men in Congress, in State Legislatures, upon the stump, from the messages of Governors of States, from the resolutions of political bodies, and from the current literature of public journals,—all confined, however, to the loyal States, but found in every stage of the contest from the beginning till now,—we see that there is as wide a variance upon this simple point as can be found upon any other question of fact or policy touching the rebellion, or any other matter concerning human interests upon which men are commonly divided. Upon discovering this, one might be led to the conclusion that there are inherent difficulties in the solution of the case. But it is one of the plainest of all things connected with the whole movement, and it is quite remarkable that there should be disagreement upon it, at least among truly loyal men.

SLAVERY THE CAUSE.

As perfectly decisive of the difficulty, if there be any whatever, it is well known that in the Rebel States and among those engaged in the rebellion, there has been but one prime reason assigned for it from first to last, as put forth by their public men and echoed by all their organs of public opinion. This is so plainly true, and the reason itself is so plain and so plainly stated, that it would seem a little wonderful, did we not know too well the political corruption which abounds, that all men in the loyal States, including those who sympathize with the rebellion, should not be content to permit the rebel leaders to make their own statement of the case on this point, and to allow that statement to be true. With all the frenzied fury and disregard of truth which they have shown, and the want of sagacity and ordinary good sense which have characterized ten thousand things which they have said and done in the progress of their horrid work, we must certainly allow a sufficient method to their madness to suppose that they at least knew and could tell *for what they rebelled.* They probably did know; they certainly have told; and they all agree.

In a word, they declare that it was FOR NEGRO SLAVERY that they rebelled: for its security against apprehended peril; for its expansion into free territory, wherever their inclinations and interests might prompt them to carry it; and for its perpetuation. This is what *they* universally present as the reason for their course, warranting, with certain discriminations, the concise remark we often hear, that "slavery is the cause of the rebellion," and that "slavery is the cause of the war."

Here then we might rest and dismiss the case. But as this is a controverted point, we shall present the opposite view as held by rebel sympathizers and certain Union men, and then give the conclusive evidence which sustains the position we take, that it was in the interest of slavery alone that the rebellion was undertaken; that "the duty" which devolved upon the South was "plain, of conserving and transmitting the system of slavery, with the freest scope for its natural development and extension."

AN OPPOSITE VIEW.

Among other distinguished witnesses to the position, that to secure greater immunities to slavery was *not* the cause of the rebellion, is found the Hon. George Robertson, a former Chief-Justice of Kentucky, and a friend of the Union. In a series of elaborate papers on national affairs, published a few months since in the *Louisville Journal*, he declared that it was not slavery,—" not security for an institution that needed none better than the Constitution,"—for which " the leading conspirators" rebelled; but it was because the " *South sought independence*." He presents seven reasons, formally laid down, for this opinion, concluding thus: " 7th and lastly. Some of the leaders, without contradiction or dissent, said in Convention (we presume the Judge refers to that of South Carolina), that they had been hatching independence for more than thirty years, and ridiculed the idea that antislaveryism, in any of its phases, was the cause of their secession." He elsewhere says: " Thus the treacherous and proscriptive concoctors of rebellion initiated this unholy war; and hence some of them truly said in Convention, that the warfare waged by abolitionists against the institution of slavery and the security of slave property, was a ' God-send' to the advocates of Southern independence."*

* We deem it but just to Judge Robertson to give his seven propositions together and in full: "That the leading conspirators South sought independence,—and not security for an institution that needed none better than the Constitution they so long conspired to destroy,—should not be doubted for these among other reasons: 1st. They knew that, from time to time, they had obtained every supplemental security which they had asked or desired excepting only the humbug of 'protection' in Northern Territories, where slavery could never long or usefully exist, and where majorities of the inhabitants would not want it. 2d. They knew that no person claimed for Congress power to abolish or disturb slavery in the States, and that Congressional non-intervention in Territories,—which they had secured as far as useful to the South by the Missouri Compromise of 1820, and everywhere by the 'finality' of 1850,—was all they wanted or had any right to expect. 3d. They wantonly threw away these

Our space will not allow us to quote more at large from the Judge; but as we have said he is a Union man, we give a sentence or two among many to show this, and to show his view of slavery as an institution, and that he would not allow it to come into competition with the preservation of the Union: "I am not, nor ever was, pro-slavery in feeling or in principle. I would delight to see all men free. But I know that this is impossible until the different races approximate more nearly to moral equality." Speaking of the "less ambitious masses" in the South, who "rushed inconsiderately into the maelstrom of this shocking rebellion," he says: "They ought to have known better, and set up for themselves. But, had they not been deluded,

securities for the normal expansion of slavery by their suicidal abrogation in 1854 of these pledges of national faith, thereby indicating that *their* agitations of moot questions of slavery were intended, not for that institution or its incidents, but only for independence and power. 4th. They knew, that, before President Lincoln's inauguration, Congress had organized all the new Territories without any interdiction of slavery, and proposed also an amendment to the Constitution expressly and irrevocably providing against any Congressional interference with slavery in any State; and they knew that the incoming President and party were committed, by their Chicago platform, against all such intervention; and, moreover, knowing that a majority of Congress and of the Supreme Court were on their side, enough of the Southern members of Congress abdicated to give the Republican party a majority, thus showing that they were plotting pretexts for revolt; not for security to slavery, but for independence and a different form of government. 5th. They knew or ought to have known that their peculiar institution would be safer and more peaceful under our National Constitution binding on *all the people*, North, as well as South, than under a 'compact' of Confederation by 'sovereign States,' without a semblance of legal obligation on any people or States not parties to it. 6th. They wantonly destroyed the unity and nationality of their Democratic party in 1860, and thereby promoted Mr. Lincoln's election, which they preferred to that of Douglas or Bell, and then made that election a prominent pretext for secession. 7th and lastly. Some of the leaders, without contradiction or dissent, said in Convention that they had been hatching independence for more than thirty years, and ridiculed the idea that antislaveryism, in any of its phases, was the cause of *their* secession."—*Louisville Journal*, Oct. 19, 1863. Many persons at the North, and some papers, both secular and religious, embracing those who are loyal and disloyal, have most strenuously maintained that slavery was not the cause of the rebellion; that it was not to render it more secure against supposed aggressions that the States seceded; that this was "a mere pretext." We shall see the fallacy of this position from testimony which cannot be overthrown.

and the issue had really been between the Union and slavery, even then they ought, for their own welfare, to have stood by the Union, which would surely be better without slavery than could be slavery without such a Union."

Judge Robertson's position as to the ground of the rebellion is very much like that of some others among loyal men. We are not, at this point, concerned with the reasons which he gives for it, but rather with the question of its correctness. But before adducing the proof for a contrary position, we will state some of the obvious discriminations which should be borne in mind.

IN WHAT SENSE SLAVERY IS THE CAUSE.

When slavery is charged with having caused the rebellion and the war, no more can justly be meant than that it is the occasion of both. Nor is this all. It is scarcely just to hold the institution, as such, to this responsibility. It has been *made* the occasion. Nor does this exhaust the proper distinctions of the case. It has been made the occasion only in the hands of wicked and designing men. Many slaveholders are as true and loyal to the Government, and have shown this during the whole progress of the rebellion, as any men in the country. Nor is this seen in the Border States only. If these designing men, whether open or secret rebels, are found among the slaveholders of every Border State, so also loyal slaveholders, who have been such from first to last, may probably be found in every seceded State. As our arms have advanced, this has been found true; not merely where men have avowed their loyalty in the hope of retaining their slaves, or of receiving compensation for them from the Government, but where some of the largest slaveholders have always retained their loyalty notwithstanding the terrors of rebel rule. We personally know such cases in the Southwestern States, those of men who have been obliged to keep silent, but who nevertheless have maintained their allegiance to the Government. It is also no doubt true, that many in those States who gave in their adhesion to the rebel leaders did so under duress, to save property and life, and who may therefore be regarded, without any straining of that charity and patriotism which both moral and political justice should extend to them, as truly loyal men. It would be among the strangest of all phenomena if these things were not so. It would be tantamount to saying that all men in the South conceded the superior wisdom and approved the measures of the rebel leaders, and sustained them on these grounds; whereas, it is known that from the first, many men in the seceded States, far more sagacious and less blinded by ambition than those who assumed the control of affairs, warned the people against rebellion, pointed out the failure of their schemes, declared the falsity of their prophecies, foretold the ruin which would come upon their section of the country, and the result has already vindicated their sagacity and sealed their patriotism. It is therefore not just to hold the institution of slavery, as such,—embracing, of consequence, all slaveholders,—responsible, either for the rebellion or the war.

What is true is this: that ambitious men, fearing without just cause that the Administration now in power, and the party that had put it in power, designed to destroy slavery in the whole country,—or, if not believing this, pretending at least to believe it, and taking this ground before the people, and convincing large numbers that this was their design,—induced the States to rebel, that they might give to the institution greater expansion, security, and power, and, with God's permission, perpetuate it forever. This was substantially the position taken by leading men, the controllers of public opinion, in both Church and State.

MODERN VIEWS AND POWER OF SLAVERY.

It is among the clearest facts known, that within the period of some thirty years or more, a total revolution had taken place in the Southern mind, extending to almost the entire people, regarding the *status* of slavery as an institution, embracing its political, social, and moral character and relations. The causes of this change were, in part, the enormous pecuniary profits of the institution, which led political economists and statesmen to defend and commend it, and thus to repudiate the views of the fathers of the Republic; and, in part, the teachings of the ministers of religion, who had discovered new light in interpreting the word of God, which led them to defend and commend it as a Divine Ordinance, and thus to repudiate the views of the fathers of the American Church. And it is a fact of marked significance, that, in this change of opinion, the clergy, in many distinguished instances, led the way, and they are no doubt justly held to a higher responsibility for it than any other class of men. They will not of course deem this any disparagement, although they might decline the distinction here given them, for they claim to have done a good work. Of the reality of this change, and who are mainly responsible for it, we shall give the evidence in due time.

This revolution in Southern opinion, made slavery, in many important respects, a totally different affair in Southern society from what it had ever hitherto been regarded. It was so interwoven with its whole structure, was so completely the basis of labor, in a section of country almost wholly agricultural, and brought to the coffers of the master such untold wealth, that it had become the most vital element in Southern civilization.* It gave social position and political power. It prescribed customs to the household and gave laws to the State. It influenced all their systems of education and made a tenet in their religion. The mechanic and the day-laborer, the gentleman of leisure and the man of business, the lawyer and the physician, the judge and the clergyman, all professions and all institutions, came under its sway and called it master. It was respectable, honorable, a necessity, divine. It had no traceable origin; it had always existed. It was sanctioned by the law of nature, by the consent of all times and all peoples, and by the law of God. It had come from the Patriarchs, was embedded in the decalogue, regulated by the institutions of Moses, sustained by the Prophets, vindicated by Christ and the Apostles. All this had become the staple of Southern thought, the touchstone of Southern fidelity. It was promulgated in books and newspapers, harangued from the stump and in legislative halls, taught in the schools, pronounced in the courts, and preached from the pulpit. Southern society had become permeated with these views. It lived and breathed in this intellectual and moral atmosphere. The sentiments and feelings which such a system begat, sustained men through the activities of the day, gave them repose at night, and administered consolation in the hour of death.

When matters had come to this pass, under the teachings of recent times and the golden reign of the Fibrous King, how was it possible for the leaders in such opinions to be content that slavery should remain in the strait-jacket put upon it by the fathers of the Republic? How

* "Must I pause to show how it (slavery) has fashioned our modes of life, and determined all our habits of thought and feeling, and moulded the very type of our civilization?"—*Dr. Palmer*, *Thanksgiving Discourse*, *New Orleans*, Nov. 29, 1860.

could they any longer revere the political maxims of Washington and Jefferson, Madison and Henry, any more than they could regard with favor their sentiments upon slavery? The institution had become so important in their eyes that verily they thought the whole country was theirs; that they could take their slaves to every State and plant them in every Territory; that Congress was theirs, that the Presidency was theirs, that the Supreme Court was theirs; that, indeed, the whole people were theirs, with the wealth, greatness, prosperity, and glory of the nation —in a word, that they had made them all.*

* "The unexampled prosperity and growth of the United States, have been in exact accordance with the development of the slave population, the slave territory, and the slave products, cotton, rice, tobacco, sugar, and naval stores, of the South."—*Dr. Smyth, of Charleston, S. C., in the Southern Presbyterian Review*, April, 1863. Dr. Palmer, contrasting the North and the South, speaks of "the exemplary patience with which she (the South) has endured a system of *revenue* legislation, flagrantly and systematically discriminating against her, and in favor of the North. But the abundant fertility of her soil has enabled her to grow rich, even whilst contributing *two-thirds* to the revenue of the Government."—*Ibidem*, April, 1861. To show the absurdity of Dr. Palmer's statement, we only need to present the official figures. The "revenue" raised from imports will be a proper criterion; and, with the exception of the public lands, duties on foreign importations were almost the only source of "revenue" to the General Government. We do not find in the *latest* census returns (for 1860) the amount so stated as readily to show what proportion was collected in the Free States and what in the Slave States; nor do we find, in any one year, returns from all the ports given in the tables. But in De Bow's "Compendium of the Seventh Census," the revenue for 1853, collected from the following ports, is stated. This is probably a proper standard for any year:

PORTS IN FREE STATES.		PORTS IN SLAVE STATES.	
New York	$38,289,341.58	New Orleans	$2,628,421.32
Boston	7,203,048.52	Baltimore	836,437.99
Philadelphia	4,537,046.16	Charleston	432,299.19
San Francisco	1,794,140.68	St. Louis	294,790.78
Portland	350,349.22	Savannah	125,755.86
Cincinnati	251,649.90	Mobile	102,981.47
Oswego	128,667.27	Richmond	73,992.98
New Haven	125,173.40	Louisville	48,307.67
		Norfolk	31,255.51
Total, eight Free ports	$52,679,416.73	Total, nine Slave ports	$4,574,242.77

When they at length found that the people of the whole land had become aroused by their aggressions, and in their sovereign majesty at the ballot-box, in November, 1860, pronounced against these extravagant claims, they resolved on rebellion, in the mistaken interest of slavery, and believed that they had only to do this to bring the whole civilized world to their feet. Every one who has been a close observer of passing events in Church and State for twenty years past, well knows that this is but a true picture of the change which has taken place in the mind of the extreme Southern portion of the country.

PROOF THAT SLAVERY IS THE CAUSE—OFFICIAL TESTIMONY.

It seems almost a work of supererogation to set forth the evidence of a fact so well known, that slavery, in the sense we have explained, caused the rebellion. Men might as well deny the testimony of their senses,—which do

By the same "Compendium," the total of revenue collected, was, from "all other districts, $1,678,206.04," to be divided between Free and Slave ports. It thus appears, that, so far from the Slave States "contributing *two-thirds* to the revenue of the Government," they did not contribute *one-thirteenth*, according to the above returns; and as *De Bow* was a ring-leader among the disunionists, at the very time he published this "Compendium," it is probable that *his* figures "don't lie." We are of course aware of the logic by which Dr. Palmer's statement is supported by some writers (though he gives simply the naked affirmation, as quoted), but it involves a greater absurdity than the statement itself. The revenue from foreign importations, comes, ultimately, from the consumer; and it is said that the *South* consume the vast amount of foreign goods, and therefore pay the mass of the revenue. It is not so easy to determine this by exact data from figures, as it involves so many minute details. But when that large class of the "poor whites" in the Slave States who never see, much less wear or use a dollar's worth of foreign goods, is deducted from those who consume them, and then the latter are compared with the millions of the vastly preponderating population of the Free States who use foreign articles of every description, it is the most preposterous of all conclusions,—a simple unsustained assertion,—to maintain that the consumption of imported goods in the Slave States comes within the longest cannon-range of the amount consumed in the Free States. Dr. Palmer is good at the "long-bow," and his unsustained statement has been so often made that many, both North and South, believe—or pretend to believe it.

sometimes deceive them,—and it is only because this is denied that we spend a moment in collating the proof.

The seventh reason which Judge Robertson assigns for his position, that "some of the leaders" in the South Carolina Convention "ridiculed the idea" that slavery or anti-slavery "was the cause of their secession," is plausible, and would seem to be conclusive, had we not testimony which completely overwhelms it. We place over against the sayings of these men, whatever they may have uttered in loose and heated harangues, the solemn, deliberate, *official act* of the Convention itself, which was passed *unanimously*. It sets forth, to use their own words, "the immediate causes which have led to this act"—the secession of the State. After a long historical statement from their peculiar stand-point, and an argument to show that secession is authorized by the Constitution of the United States, they state the grievances which have impelled them to secede. *There is not a solitary allusion in the ordinance of secession to grievances on any subject but slavery.* But the relation of the General and State Governments to that institution, and their apprehensions for the future, they argue at length. A sentence or two will show their position.

Those States (the non-slaveholding) have assumed the right of deciding upon the propriety of our *domestic institutions*; and have denied the rights of property established in fifteen of the States and recognized by the Constitution; they have denounced as sinful the *institution of slavery*; they have permitted the open establishment among them of societies, whose avowed object is to disturb the peace and eloin the property of the citizens of other States. They have encouraged and assisted thousands of our slaves to leave their homes; and those who remain, have been incited by emissaries, books, and pictures, to servile insurrection. For twenty-five years this agitation has been steadily increasing, until it has now secured to its aid the power of the common Government. * * * On the 4th of March next this party will take possession of the Government. It has announced that the South shall be excluded from the common territory, that the judicial tribunal shall be made sectional, and that *a war must be waged against slavery* until it shall cease throughout the United States. The guarantees of the Constitution will then no longer exist; the equal rights of the States will be lost. The slaveholding States will no longer have the power of self-government, or self-protection, and the Federal Government will have become their enemy.*

Whatever may be true about the justice of these charges, the proof is conclusive, from this official act, that *slavery*, in its extravagant claims and unfounded fears, was at the bottom of the secession of South Carolina. This conclusion cannot be avoided, unless we take the ground, either that the men of that Convention *did not know* and were unanimously mistaken as to what their own complaints were, or that they were utterly hypocritical in stating them and are not to be believed at all, and that too in a document intended to vindicate their course before the world.

The acts of secession, along with the other proceedings of the Conventions of the other rebel States, respectively,

* This ordinance of the South Carolina Convention was passed "by a unanimous vote of one hundred and sixty-nine," Dec. 20, 1860. The unscrupulous falsehoods solemnly declared in this official act, are palpable. The proof of several of them we have already given. We choose to speak plainly, and therefore say: It is notoriously FALSE (1.) To charge the "non-slaveholding *States*" as a *body* with *any* of these things; (2.) To charge *any one* of them upon the Federal Government; (3.) To charge that the "party" then to come into power "on the 4th of March," had ever declared its intention or assumed the right to wage war "against slavery until it should cease throughout the United States;" but this "party" had officially declared *just the contrary*, and this the South Carolina Convention PERFECTLY KNEW. That official declaration is given in a note to Chapter I. Mr. Lincoln's letter accepting the nomination of this "party" for the Presidency, dated "May 23, 1860," contains an explicit indorsement of that declaration, as follows: "The declaration of principles and sentiments, which accompanies your letter, meets my approval; and it shall be my care not to violate, or disregard it in any part." This letter of the Presidential candidate of this "party," the members of the South Carolina Convention HAD SEEN. They had, therefore, within their own positive knowledge, the complete disproof of their official charge; and thus their falsehood stands before all men.

show precisely the same cause for the revolt as that assigned by the Convention of South Carolina,—the assumed hostility of the General Government to slavery, and the corresponding sentiments of the people of the North,—and there is *no other reason given in any ordinance of secession.*

A more recent and conclusive official testimony is found in the action of the Rebel Congress, at Richmond, in an "Address to the People of the Confederate States," issued in February, 1864, in which they speak of the cause of their secession, as follows:

> Compelled by a long series of oppressive and tyrannical acts, culminating at last in the selection of a President and Vice-President by a party confessedly sectional, and *hostile to the South and her institutions,* these States withdrew from the former Union and formed a new Confederate alliance, as an independent Government, *based on the proper relations of labor and capital.* * * * The Republican party was formed to *destroy slavery* and the equality of the States, and Lincoln was selected as the instrument to accomplish this object.

INDIVIDUAL WITNESSES THAT SLAVERY IS THE CAUSE.

Besides this official testimony, many witnesses to the same effect might be cited from among leading statesmen and divines. We give a sample of this testimony.

Alexander H. Stephens, Vice-President of the Southern Confederacy, is a representative man among Southern statesmen, and one of the ablest of them all. In his speech at Savannah, Georgia, March 21, 1861, showing the superiority of their Constitution, he said:

> The new Constitution has put at rest forever all the agitating questions relating to our peculiar institutions,—African slavery as it exists among us,—the proper *status* of the negro in our form of civilization. *This was the immediate cause of the late rupture and present revolution.* Jefferson, in his forecast, had anticipated this, as the "rock upon which the old Union would split." He was right. What was conjecture with him is now a realized fact. But whether he comprehended the great truth upon which that rock stood and stands, may be doubted. The

prevailing ideas entertained by him and most of the leading statesmen at the time of the formation of the old Constitution were, that the enslavement of the African was in violation of the laws of nature; that it was wrong in principle, socially, morally, and politically. It was an evil they knew not how to deal with; but the general opinion of the men of that day was, that, somehow or other, in the order of Providence, the institution would be evanescent and pass away. This idea, though not incorporated in the Constitution, was the prevailing idea at the time. The Constitution, it is true, secured every essential guarantee to the institution while it should last, and hence no argument can be justly used against the constitutional guarantees thus secured, because of the common sentiment of the day. Those ideas, however, were fundamentally wrong. They rested upon the assumption of the equality of races. This was an error. It was a sandy foundation, and the idea of a Government built upon it—when the "storm came and the wind blew it fell." Our new Government is founded upon exactly the opposite ideas; *its foundations are laid, its corner-stone rests,* upon the great truth that the negro is not equal to the white man; *that slavery, subordination to the superior race, is his natural and normal condition.* This, our new Government, is the first, in the history of the world, based upon this great physical, philosophical truth.

The late Rev. Dr. Thornwell, of Columbia, S. C., was one of the representative men of the Southern Church. In a Fast-Day Sermon preached in Columbia, S. C., Nov. 21, 1860, upon "National Sins," occasioned by the then incipient troubles of the country, he says:

Let us inquire, in the next place, whether we have rendered unto our servants that which is just and equal. Is our legislation in all respects in harmony with the idea of slavery? Are our laws such that we can heartily approve them in the presence of God? Have we sufficiently protected the person of the slave? Are our provisions adequate for giving him a fair and impartial trial when prosecuted for offences? Do we guard as we should his family relations? And, above all, have we furnished him with proper means of religious instruction? These and such questions we should endeavor to answer with the utmost solemnity and truth. We have come before the Lord as penitents. *The people whom we hold in bondage are the occasion of all our troubles.* We have been provoked by bitter and furious assailants to deal harshly with them, and it becomes us this day to review our history, and the history of our legislation, in the light of God's truth, and to abandon, with ingenuous sincerity, whatever our consciences cannot sanction.

Immediately after the secession of South Carolina, December 20, 1860, Dr. Thornwell published an elaborate paper in its defence, in the *Southern Presbyterian Review*. In reference to the justifying cause of secession, we take from the article the following sentences:

The real cause of the intense excitement of the South *is not* vain dreams of national glory *in a separate confederacy;* * * * *it is* the profound conviction that the Constitution, *in its relations to slavery*, has been virtually repealed; that the Government has assumed a new and dangerous attitude upon this subject; that we have, in short, new terms of union submitted to our acceptance or rejection. *Here lies the evil.* The election of Lincoln, when properly interpreted, is nothing more nor less than a proposition to the South to consent to a government *fundamentally different upon the question of slavery* from that which our fathers established. * * * The Constitution covers the whole territory of the Union, and throughout that territory has taken *slavery under the protection of law.* * * * Let the Government permit the South to carry her persons held to service, without their consent, into the Territories, and let the right to their labor be PROTECTED, and there would be no quarrel about *slavery.* * * * We are sure that we do not misrepresent the general tone of Northern sentiment. It is one of *hostility to slavery*,—it is one which, while it might not be willing to break faith, under the present Administration, with respect to the express injunctions of the Constitution, is utterly and absolutely opposed to any further EXTENSION OF THE SYSTEM. * * * THE EXTENSION OF SLAVERY, in obedience to Northern prejudice, is to be forever arrested. Congress is to treat it as an evil, an element of political weakness, and to restrain its influence within the limits which now circumscribe it.

Another representative man among the Southern clergy is the Rev. Dr. Palmer, also a South Carolinian by birth. On the breaking out of the rebellion he was pastor of the First Presbyterian Church in New Orleans, a post which he maintained until a little before the recovery of that city by the Union forces. On Thanksgiving Day, November 29, 1860, he preached a sermon, entitled, "The South: Her Peril and Her Duty," in which he presents the grounds which justify secession. His fundamental proposition is, that it is the great "providential trust" of the South, "*to conserve and to perpetuate the institution of slavery as now existing;*" and that it is

Our present trust to preserve and transmit our existing system of domestic servitude, with the right, unchanged by man, to go and root itself wherever Providence and nature may carry it. * * * No man has thoughtfully watched the progress of this controversy without being convinced that the crisis must at length come. * * * The embarrassment has been, while dodging amidst constitutional forms, to make an issue that should be clear, simple, and tangible. *Such an issue is at length presented in the result of the recent Presidential election.* * * * It is nowhere denied that the first article in the creed of the new dominant party is the RESTRICTION OF SLAVERY WITHIN ITS PRESENT LIMITS. * * * The decree has gone forth that the institution of Southern slavery shall be constrained within assigned limits. Though nature and Providence should send forth its branches like the banyan tree, to take root in congenial soil, here is a power superior to both, that says it shall wither and die within its own charmed circle. * * * IT IS THIS WHICH MAKES THE CRISIS. Whether we will or not, this is the historic moment when *the fate of this institution* hangs suspended in the balance.

TESTIMONY OF RELIGIOUS BODIES TO THE SAME EFFECT.

All the religious public bodies of the South, which speak on the subject at all, present slavery as the cause of the disruption. Among other numerous instances, the "Address of the General Assembly of the Presbyterian Church in the Confederate States of America, to all the Churches throughout the Earth," adopted "unanimously," at Augusta, Georgia, December, 1861, states the matter as follows:

In addition to this, there is *one* difference which so radically and fundamentally distinguishes the North and the South, that it is becoming every day more and more apparent, that the religious as well as the secular interests of both, will be more effectually promoted by a complete and lasting separation. *The antagonism of Northern and Southern sentiment on the subject of Slavery* LIES AT THE ROOT *of all the difficulties which have resulted in the dismemberment of the Federal Union*, and involved us in the horrors of an unnatural war.

The Southern Baptist Convention, a body representing, as they say, "a constituency of six or seven hundred thousand Christians," sitting in Savannah, Georgia, May 13, 1861, "unanimously" adopted a paper in which they thus refer to slavery as the cause of disunion:

The Union constituted by our forefathers was one of coequal sovereign States. The fanatical spirit of the North has long been seeking to deprive us of rights and franchises guaranteed by the Constitution; and after years of persistent aggression, they have at last accomplished their purpose.

And similar testimony is borne by all the leading denominations of Christians at the South, which might be given did time and space permit; the purport of all being,—that slavery, its claims and apprehensions, as urged by the Southern leaders, caused the rebellion.*

* Besides the proof given from official sources, both secular and religious, and from distinguished civilians and divines, that slavery, in the sense explained, caused the rebellion, we add the statements of a few well-known public men of the South to the same effect, out of a thousand of a similar kind. Governor Andrew Johnson, of Tennessee, in a speech made at Nashville, in March, 1862, is reported as saying of the rebel leaders: "Look at the hypocrite Yancey, telling Great Britain *now*, that slavery was *not* the cause of the war. *They made the slavery question the sole pretext for their rebellious acts.*" In an address at Nashville, June 10, 1864, Governor Johnson says: "I told you long ago what the result would be, if you endeavored *to go out of the Union to save slavery*, and that the result would be bloodshed, rapine, devastated fields, plundered villages and cities; and therefore I urged you to remain in the Union. In trying to save slavery, you killed it, and lost your own freedom." Governor Hamilton, of Texas, in his Address to the people of that State, before referred to, says of slavery: "Gathering temerity from its successful war upon the rights and lives of the citizens, it lifted its unholy hand to destroy the Government to whose protection it owed its power. In its efforts to accomplish this, you have only been considered as so much material to be used." Hon. E. W. Gantt, of Arkansas, who had been a General in the rebel army, in his speeches in New York, Little Rock,

It is thus as clear as any proposition can well be made, from *testimony*,—and the testimony of those who *ought* to know,—that the great underlying cause of all which prompted the Southern rebellion, was the endeavor to give to the institution of negro slavery greater security, expansion, and lasting perpetuity; and the incitement to this step for these ends was the hue and cry falsely raised through the South, that the incoming Administration of the General Government was pledged to the people who had put it in power, to interfere with the constitutional rights of the institution, or wholly to destroy it.

Ark., and other places, says: "What is the cause of this war? *We know that there is but one disturbing element in the country.* In the South, where the struggle commenced, there were but two ideas, and they revolved around the negro. One was, we should stay in the Union to protect the negro; the other was, to go out, still to protect the negro. Had there been no negro slavery, there would have been no war. I say so, because I never saw any bitter contest in the country that negro slavery was not the foundation-stone to. Let us, fellow-citizens, endeavor to be calm. Let us look these new ideas and our novel position squarely in the face. *We fought for negro slavery.* We have lost. We may have to do without it." Governor Bramlette, in his message to the Legislature of Kentucky, says: "Ambitious men of the South, who first sought to create a sectional division upon the tariff, in order to build up a Government based upon the *aristocracy of the slave-owner*, having been foiled by the incorruptible patriotism and indomitable will of Andrew Jackson, next gave and accepted a sectional quarrel *about the slave.*" "The blinded ambition and obduracy of the Southern secessionists, *persistently thrust forward the slave as the object of strife*, although the Administration and the ruling powers for more than one year waived it aside, and refused to accept the issue." Hon. J. B. Henderson of Missouri, in a speech in the United States Senate, on the 7th of April last, "in favor of amending the Constitution so as to abolish slavery," thus speaks of the cause of the rebellion: "Shall it be answered that the South made the war before the institution was attacked, and that their *only* wrong consists in this? *The South declares that the rebellion was inaugurated to protect slavery against Northern aggression.* Then the Northern Democracy must admit, at the least, that such is the *character and influence of the institution* that it drove the Southern people into *unnecessary war before it was jeopardized by the action of the Government.*" "The Union is severed in the name of slavery. The civilized world regards slavery as the remote or proximate cause of the war." "In the interest of slavery, they claimed the right to sever the Union. They have done so, to the extent of their power." "If the South be wrong, the wrong springs, as they say, from slavery. *They themselves* GIVE NO OTHER CAUSE *for their withdrawal.*" To this testimony might be added that of the entire press of the South, both secular and religious, that slavery is the grand underlying cause of the rebellion.

INCIDENTAL CONFIRMATORY EVIDENCE.

A great many other public facts known to the whole country confirm this testimony. Secession has been attempted by the public authorities, more or less acting together, in every Border slave State. In Kentucky, in the year 1861, a patriotic and determined Legislature prevented the disloyal designs of Governor Magoffin and other officials. In Maryland, Governor Hicks, sustained by certain Union Senators, refused for a long period to call a meeting of the Legislature, when it was well known that their design, if assembled, was to pass an act of secession; and when at length the body did meet, they were prevented from consummating such a purpose only by the prompt action of the General Government. Governor Burton and other officials did all in their power, consistent with their personal safety, to carry out Delaware. Western Virginia was only saved to the Union by a division of the State. Governor Jackson, of Missouri, and the disloyal element in the Legislature, claimed to have carried that State into secession legally; at least by a process which commended itself to their political consideration. And thus, while *every one* of the Slave States has either formally enacted or attempted to enact secession, *not one* of the Free States has made such attempt.

Nor is this all. Some of the Border States which made the attempt to secede,—as in the case of Kentucky and Missouri,—pretended to organize regular State Governments, in connection with the rebel Southern Confederacy, and have since continued such organizations, "dwelling in tents" and itinerating like menageries, but still claiming authority over the territory of their respective States. For the past two years or more, every Slave State except Maryland and Delaware has been represented in the rebel

Congress. And finally, in full accordance with these significant facts, the State papers and military orders issued from Richmond, together with the whole Southern press, have always regarded every slave State as making a part of the Southern Confederacy.

ALL SLAVE STATES OFFICIALLY CLAIMED BY THE REBEL PRESIDENT.

Mr. Davis, the rebel President, gives, among other official proofs, incidental evidence of the position here taken, in his specification of Kentucky, when addressing Vice-President Stephens, in July, 1863, relating to his projected visit to Washington on the "Confederate steamer Torpedo." Mr. Davis says:

> The putting to death of unarmed prisoners has been a just ground of complaint in more than one instance; and the recent executions of *our officers in Kentucky*, for the sole cause that they were engaged in recruiting service in a State which is claimed as still one of the United States, but is also *claimed by us as one of the Confederate States*, must be repressed by retaliation if not unconditionally abandoned, because it would justify the like execution *in every other* State of the Confederacy.

This refers to the spies executed by order of General Burnside in Kentucky; although that State, in every popular election, in some half dozen instances since the rebellion began, has given overwhelming majorities for the Union as against secession.

Now, do these uniform, consistent, public, official acts (though of course without just authority), admit of any other explanation than that secession was undertaken, and that the rebellion has been prosecuted through every step in its progress, in entire subserviency to slavery? Their pretended rule was only claimed to extend over the *slave* States, but yet *over all of them*. All their acts were marked by a geographical line, and that line *bounding freedom* *and slavery.* Their independence, from first to last, they have insisted, must be acknowledged by granting to them *every slave State*, and their President, members of Congress, and public journals, have constantly declared that they will *never consent to peace on any other terms.**

It would seem that no proposition was ever more fully sustained by testimony of every species, both positive and negative, than that this rebellion has its life-spring in slavery. To preserve, perpetuate, and extend it, has animated its civic councils, furnished the theme for the eloquence of its pulpits, given prowess to its military leaders, sustained the heroic endurance of its soldiery, and nerved to the sacrifices and stimulated the prayers of its people. We know not what more could be possibly added to make out a plainer case.

In regard to the first six reasons presented by Judge Robertson to show that protection to slavery could not have stimulated "the leading conspirators," and in which he says "they knew" this and "they knew" that, we need only reply that *sane* men might have seen and known all he states, of the then past, present, and future. But the difficulty with those "leading conspirators" was that they were *not* sane. They were demented. The profits, the glory, and the divinity of slavery had intoxicated them to frenzy. They could see nothing as it was. Our belief is that God had smitten them with judicial blindness; and that, through their infatuation, He intended to accomplish for this nation great purposes of His own—of which we shall speak hereafter. But be this as it may, no truth in the world is better sustained than this, that slavery, as

* Among the "terms" of peace, on which alone the *Richmond Enquirer* says the rebels are willing to negotiate, this is stated: "2. Withdrawal of the Yankee forces from every foot of Confederate ground, including Kentucky and Missouri." "The North must yield all; we nothing." These "terms," in which they claim all the Slave States, are given in full, in a note to Chapter iv.

explained, is the cause of the rebellion against the Government of the United States.

UNLIMITED EXTENSION OF SLAVERY.

But it was not only to preserve slavery where it was established that the rebellion was undertaken. Nor was it, in addition, merely to carry it into the unoccupied domain of the United States. Their scheme was much more grand than this. They aimed to build up a great Slave Empire around the Gulf of Mexico. Mexico and the States of Central America, now free, were to be peopled with negro slaves; and the isles of the sea, now consecrated to freedom, were to be re-enslaved; and with Cuba, these fertile lands of the tropics, united to the Southern States, were to constitute the territory of a nation whose "corner-stone" was to be human bondage.

The proof that this was the magnificent plan contemplated, is overwhelming. General Gantt refers to this in his speeches, from which we have quoted. It was for this he himself fought in the rebel army. He says: "I was a very good *type of a pro-slavery man.* I said, if the Constitution of our fathers would not protect slavery, no guarantees would do it. I wanted to *give that power an expansion,* westward to the ocean, and in another direction to take in Cuba and a part of Mexico, *and all we could get beyond.*"

Any one who doubts that it was the scheme of the leaders of the rebellion to extend slavery south and west over countries now free, "to go and root itself," in the language of Dr. Palmer, "wherever Providence and nature might carry it," and "with the freest scope for its natural development and extension," has not had his eyes open to current and notorious events.

But this is by no means all. To make this "extension"

of slavery over so vast a region either practicable or profitable, another thing was absolutely essential. Where were the slaves to come from to occupy these immense domains of the tropics? or even profitably to develop our own unoccupied Territories, could slaves have been brought into them, or could the South have obtained the portion claimed by her on "an equitable division" of the Union? The answer to this is easy; but it is not found where certain "conservatives," so called, at the North find it.

It is one of the curious things which the discussions of the times have developed, that certain Northern men charge those who would hinder the "extension" of slavery into our own free territory, with throwing obstacles in the way of emancipation; declaring that the way to *perpetuate* slavery is to confine it where it is, whereas, to allow it to expand, according to the wishes of its friends, is the certain way to promote emancipation and eventually to *destroy* it.

THE RESTRICTIVE POLICY.

Among those who have taken this view is Rev. Dr. Samuel J. Baird, of New Jersey. In his letter before referred to, entitled "Southern Rights and Northern Duties in the present Crisis," he says upon the point in hand: "The distraction now realized by our country, has attained its portentous character in consequence of two assumptions which are both demonstrably false." Our present concern is with only one of these "assumptions," which he states thus: "It is assumed that the effect of the erection of new Slave States, is to increase the amount of slavery in the country." He then proceeds "to state the grounds upon which" he has "long held the opinion, that the restrictive, or free soil policy, so far from tending to the advantage of the negro, and the extirpation of slavery, has directly the opposite effect,—that its influence is to retard his elevation, and render early emancipation impossible."

Dr. Baird here takes precisely the opposite view of the "restrictive" policy from that taken by both Drs. Palmer and Thornwell. The former, in his Thanksgiving Discourse, before quoted, says: "The decree has gone forth that the institution of Southern slavery shall be constrained within assigned limits. Though nature and Providence should send forth its branches like the banyan-tree, to take root in congenial soil, here is a power superior to both, that says it shall *wither and die within its own charmed circle.*" Dr. Thornwell, in his article before referred to, says: "The extension of slavery, in obedience to Northern prejudice, is to be forever arrested. Congress is to treat it as an evil, an element of political weakness, and to restrain its influence within the limits which now circumscribe it." "You may destroy the oak as effectually by girdling it as by cutting it down. The North are well assured that if they can circumscribe the area of slavery, if they can surround it with a circle of non-slaveholding States, and prevent it from expanding, *nothing more is required to secure its ultimate abolition.* 'Like the scorpion girt by fire,' *it will plunge its fangs into its own body and perish.*"

There seems to be, then, a slight difference of opinion between the New Jersey Doctor and the High Priests of the Slavery Propaganda, as to the effect of the "restrictive" policy. He thinks, and has "long held the opinion," that the restriction of slavery "would render early emancipation impossible;" they, that "nothing more is required to secure its ultimate abolition." We judge that the Southern Doctors had the more ample knowledge and sounder view of the case. Dr. Baird reasons theoretically, while the other gentlemen reason practically.

THE EXPANSIVE POLICY.

But our main object in referring to Dr. Baird is to notice the other side of the problem; to compare his opinion of the "expansive" policy with the designs of Southern men. We do not aim, for want of space, to give his argument, but merely his positions. He says:

> It is true, as an ordinary rule, that dispersion tends to stimulate the increase of population; * * * but it is evident that this principle does not apply, in any appreciable degree, to the slave population. The responsibility of providing for the support of the family rests not on the parents but on the master. * * * In one word, the immediate effect of the wider dispersion of a given number of slaves is, to elevate and fit them for freedom, and to secure for them that boon, in the surest and safest manner. * * * As a question of State policy, it may be wise for the Northern States to prohibit the introduction of slaves from the South. But as a question of national policy, a question of humanity to the negro and emancipation to the slave—as a question of national strength, political and military, no proposition is more demonstrable than that the utmost possible dispersion of the slaves is the policy dictated by sound reason, and approved by enlightened humanity. It may be objected that the "curse of slavery" ought not to be inflicted on the Territories. Waiving all cavil as to the phrase, it would seem that true patriotism must have at least as great concern for the welfare of the people of the South as for the trackless wilds of the West.

The point here made is, that the wider the "dispersion" of the slaves, permitting the "extension" of the system into all the Territories as the South demanded, would tend to "emancipation," and be the proper "policy" for all who desired that end to advocate; just as the "restrictive" policy would tend to perpetuate the system. Does Dr. Baird then suppose that this was the motive the South had in view when demanding admission into the Territories?—that this was, with them, a measure of "emancipation?"—and that being refused, they sought to get out of the Union?

Or, if this was not their direct *motive*, does he suppose that they were not quite as well able to determine the "effect" of opening the Territories to slavery, as himself?—that they could not see whether such a course would promote "emancipation" or not? Is it not at least highly probable, that, as he is proved by Southern testimony,—from those who "live, and move, and have their being," in the atmosphere of slavery,—to be in error about the "restrictive," so also he may be about the "dispersive" policy? We would not call in question the correctness of his reasoning, in its general application, upon the "increase of population," under the aspects of the respective policies of a scattered or crowded condition; but it does not cover the present case. We shall see this when we understand the ultimate designs of the South concerning this question of "dispersion" through the Territories.

REOPENING OF THE AFRICAN SLAVE-TRADE.

There is too much known for doubt, that it was the ultimate plan of the rebel leaders to fill up the Territories, could they have free access to them, with slaves from the Old States, and to supply their places with *fresh importations from Africa*, or introduce those newly imported into both, as occasion might require.

They were to clamor for a repeal of the law prohibiting the African slave-trade as "piracy," and in case of failure were to evade it, or to pursue the traffic openly in spite of it, as was done in the case of the slaver *Wanderer* and others, that brought cargoes into Southern ports and sold and dispersed them through the Southwest a few years ago. Prosecutions against them would fail, as they did fail in some of these cases, because Southern Courts were corrupted by the prevailing opinion.

Thus, the "effect" pointed out by Dr. Baird of opening

the Territories to slavery, would not be to elevate the negro and ultimately to emancipate him through the policy of "dispersion;" but an expansion and perpetuation of the system on new ground, by new recruits from Africa, was the grand design of the rebel leaders. In case the war against this course should become too hot, or they should not gain access to the Territories, the plan was to go out of the Union, build up a Slave Empire around the Gulf of Mexico, and people the fair regions of Central America with their newly-caught victims.

REOPENING OF THE TRADE DENIED.

When this project of reopening the African slave-trade is charged, it is by some denied, even despite of the fact that it *was actually in progress* against all the power of American courts of law, and American and English fleets on the African coast. The fact which is often appealed to as perfectly conclusive, is, that the rebel Constitution, adopted at Montgomery, specially prohibited the opening of that traffic. But the power that made that instrument could change it, and undoubtedly would do so at the proper time. That prohibition was inserted manifestly for two reasons: to conciliate the Border States which had slaves to sell, and to conciliate European Powers whose favor they wished to gain. It certainly was not inserted because of any opposition to the traffic in itself considered, either on the ground of principle or policy. Such a supposition would belie the well-known sentiments of the leading spirits among its framers.

Even the good and great Dr. Thornwell, while denying that the desire for reopening the trade was a cause of the disruption, does not condemn, but rather palliates, if he does not actually approve, the traffic in itself considered, and when properly conducted. He is rather facetious, and seems to think that those at the South who have advocated it, have done it simply for the purpose of "teasing their enemies" and "providing hard nuts for abolitionists to crack." We shall soon see whether this is true. In the mean time, hear Dr. Thornwell, in the same article before referred to:

> It has also been asserted, as a ground of dissatisfaction with the present Government, and of a desire to organize a separate Government of their own, that the cotton-growing States are intent upon reopening, as a means of fulfilling their magnificent visions of wealth, the African slave-trade. The agitation of this subject at the South has been grievously misunderstood. * * * They wished to show that they could give a Rowland for an Oliver. Had abolitionists never denounced the domestic trade as plunder and robbery, not a whisper would ever have been breathed about disturbing the peace of Africa. The men who were loudest in their denunciations of the Government, had, with very few exceptions, no more desire to have the trade reopened than the rest of their countrymen: but they delighted in *teasing their enemies.* They took special satisfaction in providing hard nuts for abolitionists to crack.

Dr. Thornwell thus resolves the whole thing into a *joke;* regards the utterances of the leading spirits in Southern Commercial Conventions, and the deliberate resolves of those bodies for many years, with the advocacy of leading Southern papers and periodicals,—coming from the Yanceys, the Rhetts, the De Bows, and their colaborers, the very men who at length wielded power to carry the whole eleven States into that very rebellion which he defends with his powerful pen,—as evincing nothing more serious than the employment of their pastime in a little innocent "teasing." If he himself is serious, we pity his incredulity. The proof is too full to admit of a doubt among common men. But why should he present this *caveat* at all?—especially in the face of abundant testimony? He seems to have no objection to the reopening, on the ground of any *wrong* in the traffic; nor, according to him, does any one else in the South. The only thing is to see that it is well conducted. Hear him:

> There were others, not at all in favor of the trade, who looked upon the law as unconstitutional which declared it to be piracy. But the great mass of the Southern people were content with the law as it stood. They were and are opposed to the trade,—not because the traffic in slaves is *immoral*,—that, *not a man* of us believes,—but because the traffic with Africa is *not* a traffic in slaves. It is a system of kidnapping and man-stealing, which is as abhorrent to the South as it is to the North.

If then it could be divested of some of its odious features, it would all be right! But even if "the great mass of the Southern people" *were* against the African slave-trade, we only need to bear in mind that so also they were against disunion until led astray by demagogues in Church and State; and as "the men who were loudest in their denunciations of the Government," and finally led the people into rebellion, were the very men who were for opening the slave-trade, so, we may reasonably suppose, they would eventually have been equally successful, under the new Government, in carrying "the great mass" with them in favor of the latter scheme.

PROOF OF THE DESIGNED OPENING OF THE TRADE.

Let us now see what evidence there is that it was a part of the plan of disunion to reopen the African slave-trade.

De Bow's Review, an able commercial periodical published at New Orleans before the rebellion, was an acknowledged organ of the rebel leaders, and an oracle on all subjects connected with their movements. For several years it had openly advocated the reopening of the trade, and some of its articles made this a *sine qua non* with the

South for remaining in the Union. Its editor, Mr. J. D. B. De Bow, Superintendent of the Census Bureau under President Pierce, and many of his correspondents, wrote in favor of the project. Almost every number had something upon it. We can only give a specimen of this literature. The first citation is found in the number for November, 1857, in an article advocating a "Central Southern University," to educate young men in the political views peculiar to the South; and as a reason for showing its necessity, the writer thus speaks of American and European views of slavery and the slave-trade:

> These fifteen hireling States, together with all the rest of North America, except the slaveholding States mentioned, and more than one-half of South America, reinforced and sustained by England, France, and most of the other nations of Europe, have openly declared themselves against American slavery, and may be said to be engaged in a crusade against our domestic institutions. *The African slave-trade* has been denounced as piracy, not only by several European powers, but by the United States. From the beginning of the present century up to this time, the influence of the Government has been against the South;* and for fifteen years this Government has kept a fleet on the African coast for the express purpose, acting in conjunction with England and France, of suppressing the traffic in slaves, and for preventing their importation into America. And at least three-fourths of the expense of maintaining this fleet have been paid by the South. * * * *The difficulty between the South and the North can never arrive at a peaceable settlement.* The supreme and ultimate arbitor in the dispute now pending between them *must be the sword.* To that complexion it must come at last.

The foregoing is mild compared with what follows from the number for December of the same year. The article is upon the "Wealth of the North and the South: the

* And yet, from the *facts*, and the testimony of the rebel Vice-President, it appears that the Government was controlled by "the South" and its Northern "allies," *sixty-four* out of seventy-two years from its origin. This is shown in Chapter I.

Slave-Trade and the Union." Speaking of the North, the writer says:

Her industrious and enterprising population, her commercial, manufacturing, and mechanical skill, her fine harbors, her fisheries, and *her Union with and vicinity to the South*, are the true sources of her prosperity. *A revival of the African slave-trade at the South*, would furnish her with cheaper raw materials, cheaper provisions, and extend and improve the market for her commerce, merchandise, and manufactures. *This is probably the only measure that can save the Union.* It will meet with some opposition *from a* FEW *inconsiderate* Southern slaveholders, because it will lessen the price of slaves and of slave products. But it will greatly increase the price of Southern lands, *half of which are now lying waste and useless for want of labor*,* whilst Christendom is almost starving from the deficiency of Southern products. Such a step would give *political security to the South*, because it would identify still more closely the interest of ALL SECTIONS *in upholding and increasing Slavery.* Texas would speedily be settled, and Kentucky, Virginia, Tennessee, Missouri, and Maryland, with slaves at two hundred dollars around, would bring all their now vacant lands into successful cultivation. *It is most probable that New York, Pennsylvania, and the whole Northwest,* WOULD ALSO BECOME SLAVEHOLDING *with slaves at two hundred dollars.* EVENTS ARE TENDING THIS WAY. * * * It is our true interest to secure and preserve the monopoly of cotton production, and we can effect this only by the renewal of the slave-trade. It is highly creditable to the much abused "extremists of the South," that they, *with a few exceptions*, and their press, are the most prominent advocates of the revival of the slave-trade, which in a pecuniary way most of them think injurious to themselves. *But they are patriots, and ready to make great sacrifices to preserve peace and Union.* * * * Is it possible to conceive that THE NORTH will not, when it surveys the whole ground in controversy, ADVOCATE THE RENEWAL OF THE OLD SLAVE-TRADE as a measure of humanity, as well to the idle, savage, pagan negroes, as to the starving, laboring whites of Europe and the North? * * * All sections have confidence in the present Administration, but let it go out

* What, then, we would ask Dr. Baird and others who agree with him, could the South do with the Territories, except to introduce slaves from Africa, if "half" of the "Southern lands" in 1857 were "lying waste and useless for want of labor?" Nothing, clearly, unless on his principle they wished to promote "emancipation" by "dispersion."

of power—and "then the deluge." Mr. Buchanan will be the "last of the Presidents," unless abolition is arrested in its course, and some measure, some line of policy adopted, which shall plainly and obviously make *the extension of Slavery the interest of the North.* * * * An exasperated South will blow the Union to shivers, if hordes of Northern immigrants continue to seize upon and monopolize the whole of that territory, which she, the South, chiefly acquired, despite of much Northern opposition. *The revival of the African slave-trade,* the reduction in the price of negroes, and the increase of their numbers, will enable us successfully to CONTEND IN THE SETTLEMENT OF NEW TERRITORIES with the vast emigration from the North. NOTHING ELSE CAN. IT IS THE ONLY MEASURE THAT CAN PRESERVE THE UNION. * * * Let her (the North) examine the subject calmly, historically, religiously, morally, statistically, and philosophically, and she will find the proposed procedure quite as humane as profitable. If this does not satisfy her, calculate the costs and consequences of disunion, *for it has come to this*—EITHER A RENEWAL OF THE SLAVE-TRADE, OR DISUNION. There can be no drawn battle between abolition, and slavery and the slave-trade. Truth will prevail. One or the other must conquer. God defend the right.

We give but one more specimen, taken from the same periodical, *De Bow's Review* for May, 1859:

How often have we been told from our legislative halls, that Congress has no power or jurisdiction over slavery, as it exists in the United States—that each one of the States is sovereign, and competent to manage its own internal affairs. How comes it then, we ask, that Congress has, for so many years, legislated, and entered on her rolls, *laws expressly prohibiting the slave-trade, and entering into compact with foreign nations with force of arms to suppress it?* * * * Where is the propriety or fitness or evenness in action, to send a United States Marshal to aid in the recapture of a runaway slave in any of the miscalled free States, and at the same time having a fleet on the African coast to intercept and suppress it altogether? If any one can solve this riddle, why then we confess he is more shrewd than we are, and most cheerfully resign to him the palm of victory in discrimination. * * * Was not the seizure and capture and confiscation of the brig *Echo*, a direct preventive of the people of a certain latitude from the use of that kind of laborers only, and property suitable to their climate, soil, and production? * * * *Ever since the time that Congress first took action to suppress the slave-trade,* AT THAT CRISIS AND MOMENT WERE SOWN THE SEEDS OF DISUNION

THE CAUSE FULLY DEVELOPED.

We now see the ultimate purposes sought to be accomplished by the rebel leaders. We are now ready to draw the grand conclusion as to *the cause of the rebellion.* We are able, somewhat, to approach to an adequate conception of the enormity of that wickedness, to perpetrate which, through treason, fraud, war, and carnage, ministers of the Gospel and Christian Churches, with others,—as we shall see further on in these pages,—gave their personal and official influence at an early stage in this drama of blood, and in some instances took the lead in counsel and action, and have been its most ardent supporters to the present hour. We see the *special end* to be reached by an overthrow of the Government of the United States, and the building up of another nation in its stead, upon such a "corner-stone" as no other nation, according to Mr. Stephens, ever rested upon "in the history of the world."

The project was grand. The means were appropriate. The conception was worthy of the greatest intellects and the largest hearts. We seriously doubt whether any other people but "our Southren brethren" could have compassed it. It was not merely to perpetuate a system of human bondage which was the scorn of the whole Christian world outside of the immediate region in which it was upheld; not merely to preserve for themselves and transmit to their children the status of slavery as it existed among them; but it was to inaugurate and consummate a great system of Slavery Propagandism, and that not merely upon the virgin soil of the Territories; these modern

Apostles were to carry their missionary enterprise into the Free States; "New York, Pennsylvania, and the whole Northwest," were among the first benighted regions that were to be visited; and "with slaves at two hundred dollars" a head, every farmer could become a gentleman of leisure, with an abundance of laborers to till his grounds. To realize these glowing visions of wealth and the *otium cum dignitate*, the slave-marts of Africa were to be again thrown wide open, and "all sections" were to go in for "the revival of the slave-trade." Dr. Thornwell and other leading clergymen would approve of the traffic, and defend it in the Religious Reviews, as De Bow had long done in his Commercial Review, if it could only be divested of some of its repugnant adjuncts; and for the sake of enlisting their vigorous pens this could easily be done, or at least easily promised.

And why should not all hands at once join in this, and all become rich together?—and why should we not, too, "as a measure of *humanity*," when appealed to "calmly, historically, religiously, morally, statistically, and philosophically?" And, above all, we are appealed to *patriotically*. If we do not join in this grand religious and political regeneration of our country and the rest of mankind, "an exasperated South will blow the Union to shivers" and set up for themselves; "for it has come to this—either a renewal of the slave-trade, or disunion." But they do not wish to do so bad a thing—oh, no! "*They are patriots*, and ready to make great sacrifices to preserve peace and Union!"

As, then, the "renewal of the old slave-trade" is the "only measure that can preserve the Union," the responsibility of its preservation is upon the North. Why will she not step forward and sign the bond? Who can hesitate when such interests are in the trembling balance?—

wealth, ease, religion, humanity, patriotism, Union, and universal slavery; all made sure forever, with "the price of negroes at two hundred dollars" a head!

Another idea looms up under all this which certain moralists should ponder, and correct their logic. They have said all along that it was the "Abolitionists" who had bred all the trouble, and finally brought disunion. But let them take a lesson here from their Southern teachers. It was not the Abolitionists at all; not even the more moderate opponents of slavery; but it was opposition to the *slave-trade* which at the very first threatened to destroy the Union, just as a refusal to reopen it has led to its actual disruption. The Southern oracle says: "Ever since the time that Congress first took action to suppress the slave-trade, at that crisis and moment were sown the seeds of disunion." A truce then to this war upon the Abolitionists. The "seeds of disunion" were sown before they were out of their teens.

But to look at the matter "calmly," as we are exhorted to do: the AMERICAN PEOPLE may here behold the sumptuous repast to which they were sincerely and soberly invited by the leading spirits of the South, the men who controlled public opinion there, and were successful in precipitating the rebellion. Nothing short of consenting to these demands could have satisfied them. If the North had been ready for this humiliation, the Union and the Government could have been saved and peace maintained. But in no possible way could war have been avoided without this, except upon a complete abandonment of their ground by the South. That ground they would not abandon,—and hence the rebellion.

CHAPTER III.

RESPONSIBILITY FOR THE REBELLION.

As in regard to the cause of the rebellion, so also as to the responsibility for it, there has been a wide diversity of opinion. While the former is too plain to admit of doubt, there appears to be more plausible ground for difference about the latter; and yet, laying aside prejudice, the facts seem to place this also within the pale of complete moral certainty.

It has been very freely charged, and is still, by many in the loyal States, that the abolitionists have brought all the troubles upon the country, have provoked the South to rebel, and are therefore responsible for the war and all its consequences. Another class divide the responsibility about equally between the abolitionists and secessionists. Still another class charge the whole responsibility upon the rebels, insisting that whatever grievances they may have had, real or imaginary, they were not justified in seeking to redress them by revolution.

Few questions, either political or moral, connected with the contest, can be more important than this; important as affecting the interests of the country at large; important in the eyes of the nations of the world, and in the judgment which posterity will form; as well as important, officially and personally, to the rulers, and the leaders of parties, both North and South, and to every individual who has given aid on either side, in however small a degree; and not only important for the life that now is, but in reference to that account which all must render to God when He shall make inquisition concerning the responsibility for having plunged thirty millions of people, in a Christian land, into a war which has in its bearings and magnitude no parallel in history. No question, therefore, deserves to be approached with more candor and examined more dispassionately.

ABOLITIONISTS CHARGED WITH THE RESPONSIBILITY.

On this point we refer again to the papers of Judge Robertson; chiefly because he represents an extensive class. He condemns the secessionists unsparingly, but he holds the abolitionists largely responsible for the woes which have befallen the land. He says: "For that pernicious ferment, abolitionists are primarily and pre-eminently accountable, and are, therefore, justly chargeable with a large share of the responsibility for all the consequences; for, had there been no abolitionism, there would have been no secession yet, if ever, and had there been no secession there would have been no war." He plainly does not mean by "abolitionists" those who are simply *emancipationists*, or opposed to slavery, as nearly the whole North and many in the Border slave States are; for, he says, even of himself: "I am not, nor ever was, proslavery in feeling or in principle; I would delight to see all men free." By "abolitionists" he means those of the Garrison and Phillips school; for in the same article he describes them thus: "Abolitionists, it is true, have complained of the Constitution as 'a league with hell,' only because it tolerates and protects slavery in the slaveholding States; and this pestilent band of fanatics and demagogues have, for thirty years, been plotting a dissolution of the Union as the only or most speedy and sure means of abolishing slavery."

By this description the Judge means by "abolitionists" those whom the country commonly accept under this designation, headed by Garrison, Phillips, and their coadjutors, some of whom have heretofore joined with their opposition to slavery, opposition to the Sabbath, the ministry, the Church, and the Bible. He quotes one of their pet phrases which shows that he means them. We enter no defence of this class, as abolitionists. We have always been opposed to their schemes and to the spirit by which they seem to have been actuated. We make these quotations, however, and we remark upon them, for the purpose of endeavoring to determine where the real responsibility we are seeking lies. We believe in giving "the devil his due," and even William Lloyd Garrison and his associates are entitled to at least that measure of consideration. As we totally disagree with the eminent jurist in locating this responsibility, we cannot refrain from a vindication of these men, so far as the charge is concerned, that they are "primarily and pre-eminently accountable" for the rebellion and the horrors of the war. We not only deny the allegation, and shall give ample evidence to sustain the denial, and show where the responsibility lies, but we are amazed at the reasoning by which the Judge would sustain the charge, though we have frequently met with the like before.

FALLACIOUS REASONING TO SUSTAIN THE CHARGE.

In the first place, we do not see why, in the chain of sequences which the Judge employs, he should either begin or end just where he does. His point is, that the abolitionists are responsible for the war; "for, had there been no abolitionism, there would have been no secession yet, if ever, and had there been no secession there would have been no war."

Why may we not, with equal cogency, so far as the logic of the case is concerned, begin with at least one prior step?—thus: "Had there been no slavery, there would have been no abolitionism," &c. The case admits of this, beyond question. The proposition is logically true, and true in fact. Abolitionism, whether right or wrong, is aimed only at slavery, and could not exist without it. They have lived side by side, and they will die together. Nor is there any logical necessity for beginning with this one prior step. With perfect truth, we may reason thus: "Had there been no sin there would have been no slavery." And the chain might be extended further. But the position of slavery in this longer chain is not only logically correct, but it is so in morals; and this, too, whether slavery is a sin *per se* or not. It is, at the very least, the *fruit* of sin, as all classes admit, and one of the palpable signs of a fallen race. The ablest defenders of slavery as a divine institution, declare it to have originated in a "curse" inflicted for sin, and to be one of its most striking badges; and all this, while arguing that in these latter days it has been transmuted into a "blessing" to all concerned, political, social, and moral, by a sort of metaphysical alchemy in which its defenders are peculiarly skilled.

THEY WOULD DISCUSS THE SUBJECT.

But in the next place, passing by the logic of this passage, there is a moral aspect which the case suggests beyond that which we have incidentally stated. Remarkably few, taking the general judgment of Christendom, agree with the men of the extreme South in their modern views of slavery. With a unanimity that has few parallels, it is regarded as an evil, political and social; and by great numbers, as a sin. Whether they are right or wrong in their judgment is not now material; they claim the right to discuss the question. It is idle to tell men in our country that they shall not discuss any question of morals, politics, or religion. It cannot be prevented. There is neither authority nor power to prevent it; and we trust it will never be attempted, unless the liberty of speech or of the press shall be abused to the injury of individuals or of society.

Now it is notorious that the head and front of the offence committed by the class of whom Judge Robertson speaks, is that they would discuss the question of slavery; or, if the term suits any better, that they would "agitate" the subject. They had, as all the world knows, a peculiar way of their own; but if they transgressed no law, that peculiarity was a part of their right. They called hard names, and unnecessarily stirred up bitter feelings. In this they committed an offence against good taste and Christian propriety, and we have always disapproved of their course. But that they, in common with all men, had a perfect right to discuss the subject to their hearts' content, all must admit. If discussion disturbed slavery, as it is universally conceded it did,—and must necessarily do so, however conducted,—it was one of the misfortunes of the institution which from its nature could not be avoided, and for which it was alone responsible. And it will be seen in the sequel, that here is where the great "grievance" lies, when the case is sifted to the bottom. Mankind would discuss the merits of slavery. Hence the germ of Southern dissatisfaction.

ABDUCTION OF SLAVES.

But the abolitionists are charged with doing far worse than discussing the subject. It is said, they stole Southern property; when fugitive slaves were pursued, they made open resistance to the laws; and finally, their schemes culminated in the John Brown raid. We shall not defend any of these things. We have always condemned them. We have advocated in the pulpit, in a Northern State, obedience to the laws, active or passive, the Fugitive Slave Law included, specifying it by name, and have condemned mob violence, and our views have heretofore been published. We should take the same course with regard to any properly enacted law, without regard to its character. We know of no other course which a Christian can justly take.

But suppose it be admitted that the abolitionists did all that is here charged, what does it amount to as justifying or even extenuating this gigantic rebellion? South Carolina formally presents in her "Declaration of Causes which induced the Secession" of the State, and as "justifying" it, this spoliation of her slave property; and yet, South Carolina, as the men of her Convention must have known from the statistics extant, suffered very little in this regard, and even less than any other State. All the seceded States suffered comparatively little, and those most noisy about secession least of all, from their geographical position; while the Border States, from which the largest number escaped, were content to remain in the Union, and condemned in not very measured terms the course of the States farther South. This complaint of the rebel States, of the loss of their property, when presented to justify either secession or rebellion, is too well known to be the most shallow and hypocritical of all false pretences.

THE WHOLE NORTH CHARGED WITH IT.

The attempt has been made to implicate the mass of the Northern people in these breaches of the law and good faith towards the South. Certain newspapers, North and South, have rung with such charges, and certain Northern and many Southern orators in Congress have made them. But their falsity is obvious. No evidence has ever been found to sustain them, even after the most diligent search. It was charged, for example, that the whole North aided and abetted John Brown; or, at least, as was again said, the whole Republican party; or, with still another abatement, certainly the leaders of that party, though in the face of their positive denials. Senator Mason, of Virginia, was so sure of his game that he called for a Committee of the United States Senate, "with full power to send for persons and papers," to investigate the subject. He was promptly accommodated, and was made chairman. After a long research without let or hindrance, and with all the power of a willing Administration to aid him, he made a report and asked for the Committee's discharge. He found nothing—and reported it.

ABOLITIONISTS NOT REPUBLICANS.

In regard to the abolitionists, who are held "primarily and pre-eminently accountable" for the horrors of this rebellion, it is well known that they have ever formed a remarkably small fraction of the community, and that their influence with the mass of the people has been insignificant. They have never, in any Presidential election, as a party, acted with the Republican party, but have opposed it with violence and bitterness, always having their own candidate. Since the rebellion has been in progress, the leaders of that faction have sometimes been found supporting the Government and sometimes abusing it; according to our observation, most commonly the latter. Wendell Phillips, the most renowned orator among them, has frequently, and of late, denounced the President by name, and the Administration, for the policy pursued in conducting the war, and he has publicly identified himself with a party opposed to Mr. Lincoln's re-election.

But granting all that may with truth be said of these men, their numbers and influence have always been so small in the country, that it is perfectly preposterous to hold them "primarily and pre-eminently accountable" for the war and its consequences. Or, granting that the utmost that has been charged upon this class is true to the letter,—yea, and that vastly more than is charged specifically, is true of them,—yet, it cannot before God, nor will it before candid men, be deemed sufficient to justify, or in the least possible degree to extenuate, an open and bloody revolution against the General Government. And although it may be urged against the Garrison and Phillips school that they for many years strived to divide the Union,—and they freely admit the charge, at least their leaders,—their weapons were the tongue and the pen. They never, as a party, put themselves in battle array to overthrow the Government, seizing the ships, mints, custom-houses, and forts of the Government, and using them in a bloody contest for its destruction. These memorable deeds were left for the Southern chivalry,—"our Southern brethren,"—and for the sake of *slavery*.

ABOLITIONISTS COMPLIMENTED—THE PEOPLE DISPARAGED.

But do serious people see the bearing of such a charge? In holding the Abolitionists responsible, do they perceive what power over twenty millions of people in the Free States they ascribe to the merest fraction of the population?

Here is a small body of persons, led by some half a dozen orators, male and female, who have, within a few years, by meetings, speeches, and publications,—all peaceful and legitimate means under a free Government,—put forth their sentiments on a given subject, and have produced one of the most astounding revolutions in human history in the sentiments of an enlightened, educated, and religious people; leading this people, to such an expression of opinion at the ballot-box, as is deemed a solemn political judgment on one of the mightiest questions of State which ever affected any people resulting in so disaffecting another portion of the same nation, in population relatively not more than one-third of the whole number, as to induce them to take up arms to "recover their rights," and to induce the majority also to take up arms to maintain that political judgment; and thus exhibiting to the world one of the greatest and most bloody wars ever known among men. All this is charged upon this "contemptible faction," as it is called; but by no means contemptible, if the charge is true.

While this "faction" was engaged in this work, they were opposed, in both sections of the nation thus affected by them, by the much larger portion of the "fourth estate," the press, secular and religious, daily, weekly, and periodical; they were covered with reproach, and the most opprobrious epithets of the English language were heaped upon them, by orators in Congress and among the people, by the press, and by all the usual appliances for affecting public opinion. During all the earlier period of their career, they were frequently assailed with other weapons; showered with rotten eggs, their meetings broken up by mobs, their public halls burned, ordinary places for popular assemblages denied them, their printing-presses broken and their offices sacked and burned; and if one of them chanced to be found South of a certain line of latitude, or a person who was no more than "suspected" of being one of them, a coat of tar and feathers was the least compliment paid him; and if his visit was welcomed with whipping or hanging, it was deemed no more than was deserved for such sentiments and conduct as he was "reasonably suspected" of entertaining.

Beyond this, the mass of the religious portion of the nation was against them, and had no manner of sympathy with or for them. The pulpits belonging to the larger part of the various denominations were opposed to them, whether any thing was preached in that line or not. The pulpits they controlled, or even had access to, were remarkably small in number. In the religious bodies of every Church,—Conventions, Associations, Conferences, and General Assemblies,—resolutions were passed against them, again and again. To be known as an "Abolitionist," or to be branded as such, whether justly or otherwise, was enough to shut a man out of the social circle, and out of the sympathy of religious men and religious bodies, in many places where the cue was given to the habits and usages of the higher grades of society; while "distinguished consideration," with more than a diplomatic significance, was often shown at the North to men who were identified with Southern institutions, and simply because they were so identified.

All this is well known to the world. And yet, this "vile faction," in the face of such opposition, and with the simplest means, has revolutionized a mighty nation; has led even the mass of the people who have been their revilers to sustain the Government in now at length vindicating those sentiments, and sustaining by a powerful array of armies that cause, for the whole origin of which they are held responsible. This is the aspect which the charge puts on, from the lips of those who make it, when it is confronted with the facts. What power wielded by a "contemptible faction," thus to take twenty millions of enlightened people by the nose and mould them as though they were but a nose of wax! Did the world ever see the like before, except under Jesus of Nazareth and the twelve fishermen of Galilee? Either, then, it must be admitted that it was *the ideas* which this "faction" propagated which have done the work,—horrible as those ideas were held to be,—or we must look elsewhere for the responsibility for the revolution through which we are passing.*

RESPONSIBILITY OF ABOLITIONISTS DISCLAIMED AT THE SOUTH.

It is well to note, that the more considerate among the advocates and apologists of the rebellion, even at the South, in Church or State, do not hold the Abolitionists responsible, as furnishing in their conduct the justifiable ground for secession. Take one example, from the *South-*

* Here is a recent charge of the responsibility upon the abolitionists, from one of the most influential secular prints of the country, illustrating and sustaining what is said above. It is one of a thousand similar cases. The *New York Herald*, of July 16, 1864, closes an article upon "The Truth of History," thus:

"The abolition agitators did cause the rebellion at the South; for they gave the rebel leaders the only pretext they needed to fire the Southern people and drag them into civil war. The fire-eaters tried to raise a rebellion on the tariff question; but the people would not revolt. Then Greeley, Garrison, and the other abolitionists deliberately set to work to drive the South out of the Union. This has been confessed by Greeley, by Garrison, and by Wendell Phillips, all of whom were original disunionists. Greeley wrote the first article in favor of secession that appeared in a Northern paper; Wendell Phillips delivered the first speech in favor of the rebel confederacy from a Northern rostrum. Garrison declared that he trampled upon the infamous Constitution. *The rebel leaders simply took advantage of the utterances of these abolitionists to coax and frighten the people of the South into treason.* They used the weapons with which Northern fanatics supplied them. They employed the arguments which Greeley and his colleagues furnished them. They worked in concert with the abolitionists, and for the same traitorous end. When South Carolina seceded, Greeley and Wendell Phillips raised howls of joy, which were only silenced by fears of the consequences when Northern patriots began to arm themselves against the rebels. This, we assert, is the exact truth of history. If Greeley's history asserts any thing different it is a false and lying book, and if General McClellan is abused for stating these facts he is abused for speaking the truth, and Greeley knows it."

ern Presbyterian Review, April, 1861, where the grounds of secession are argued at length, and justified. This is a fair specimen of the view taken by the more calm and reflecting portion of the rebel leaders:

Let us proceed to the second question: Why do the cotton-growing States desire to secede? What reasons have induced them to brave all the real difficulties, and all the possible dangers of secession? Among the reasons assigned by the Princeton writer, only one is true, and that one is stated as it never entered the mind of any Southern man, living or dead, and could not, therefore, be subjectively a motive for their conduct. *The fierce ravings of the Abolitionists have not caused the secession of the Southern States.* This has, for many years, been a great annoyance; but it could hardly be called a *grievance.* The wild outcries of the Abolitionists have excited very various emotions in the breasts of different Southern men. Some have been aroused to anger and scorn; others have been amused; while those who agree with the Princeton Review, that their language and spirit are execrably wicked, have heard them more in sorrow than in anger. They have felt that the danger to be feared was for those in whose hearts these fierce fires were burning, and by whose lips such words of blasphemy were uttered. The high-spirited and fiery Southerners, as they are called, have borne for thirty years all that the fanatics could say, and they might very well have endured it a little longer. The proceedings of the incendiaries sent to the South to entice the slaves to abscond, or to stir them up to revolt and massacre, *have not caused the secession of the Southern States.* This is undoubtedly a very great *grievance*, but by no means so formidable as the people of the North generally suppose.

As this disclaimer comes from a high source in the Presbyterian Church at the South, and undoubtedly represents the sentiment of leading Southern men,—except among noisy politicians, who had sinister ends to gain by giving the abolitionists a prominence,—we ask for it the particular attention of a large class at the North (of whom Rev. Drs. Nathan L. Rice, of New York, and Samuel J. Baird, of New Jersey, are a good type among clergymen, and embracing also the editorial corps of the major portion of the religious press, weekly and quarterly), who have wasted much time in trying to convince the passing generation of mortals, that, among Northern men, the abolitionists, and others whom they have stigmatized and misnamed such, have been the great fomenters of discord between the North and the South; predicting that their course would at length bring the country into open conflict; and, therefore, holding *them* now chiefly responsible for a fratricidal war. The world well knows how persistently such declamation has been uttered for many years past. But the most serious-minded men of the South openly deny this. They "hardly" regard *such* opposition to slavery as a "grievance," in the manner in which they have most commonly waged it. The *real* cause of their secession is quite another thing; in a word, *the unwillingness of the whole people of the North and the National Government* to yield to their exorbitant demands.

And here is just where Judge Robertson and others make a serious mistake in interpreting the sayings of certain men in the South Carolina Convention. They deny that the "ravings of the abolitionists" had disturbed them seriously, just as the writer in the *Review* we have quoted does. But, at the same time, they present the fact that the *Northern people and Government* AS A WHOLE were against them; that is, could not agree in admitting "their rights" upon the slavery question to the full extent to which they demanded them; and *hence* they were determined to remain in the Union with them no longer.

Instead of the *abolitionists* being held to the responsibility for what has occurred, so far as the revolt has any extenuation in the conduct of Northern men, it may yet be found that the chief responsibility rests upon quite another class; upon many of those who have been the loudest in their denunciations of them, and who are ranked as leading men in the Church and in the State.

DISCUSSION THE GERM OF THE TROUBLING ELEMENT.

The real difficulty, so far as irritating the South is concerned, was far more wide-spread than any thing which could be charged upon the abolitionists. It was not so much that they would "agitate" and act in their peculiar way, as it was that *any action whatever* should be taken upon slavery. That man has been a poor observer of events who does not know that *the offensive manner* of dealing with the question was not the thing which gave the South uneasiness. It certainly was not, so far as the religious portion of the community was concerned. It was, rather, *the discussion of the subject at all*, in any manner, in any place, and by any persons. It had come to be fashionable to regard any entertainment of the subject as "agitation," and the term "abolitionist" was freely applied in order to frown down the most respectful inquiry. It had not been possible for many years to introduce the subject into any of the large religious bodies in which men of the extreme South were members, without giving mortal offence, and leading to threats of ecclesiastical secession. The pleas against it were specious and plentiful, and somewhat contradictory. The matter had been "acted upon and settled" by the Church, and therefore should be "let alone." It was a "political question, with which the Church has nothing to do," and therefore should not be introduced. It was a "troublesome subject, and would rend the Church asunder." These and many more reasons were given; while Southern extremists, who would keep the subject out of the Church lest the Church should be defiled by its examination, were ever contending that it was an institution sanctioned and regulated by the word of God. Any form of its consideration, by the most serious minded men, except in the favoring interest of slavery, was stigmatized as "wicked agitation." Nothing but utter silence upon the question, unless in its favor, was pleasing to the class of slavery propagandists. We speak from personal knowledge and extended observation, and declare only what is notorious.

At the very same time, the South was teeming with publications, the newspaper, the sermon, the pamphlet, the quarterly and the octavo volume, put forth by her ablest writers, her Thornwells and Palmers, her Hammonds and Cobbs, her Elliotts and Bledsoes, her Armstrongs and Smylies, statesmen, lawyers, divines, vying with each other to sanctify and glorify the system of Southern bondage as a "blessing," socially, politically, religiously; while, in perfect accord with all this, in the North were found apologists and defenders of the system from the same classes and professions, and through the same means; and yet, many of these Northern men were ready to raise the hue and cry of "agitation" and "abolitionism" if any thing were said against the system, unless it were emasculated of all the pungency and pith which would give it force. In a word, although discussion was feared as a fiend, it could be tolerated, and even applauded, provided it were on the right side.*

* To give an illustration of what some great men thought about discussion on this subject, and how it could be disposed of, we refer to the proposition of a distinguished statesman. In the early part of 1861, soon after the secession of South Carolina, when many men in the Border States were striving to produce a "reconciliation between the North and the South," the Hon. John P. Kennedy, of Baltimore, published a pamphlet, entitled, "The Border States: Their Power and Duty," &c. He gives a series of propositions which the Border States should submit to the two sections, and among them this about discussing the subject of slavery: "Finally, a pledge to be given by the free States to exert their influence, as far as possible, to discourage discussions of slavery in a tone offensive to the interests of the slaveholding States." The alternative, on the failure of the proposed negotiations, is thus

It is a notorious fact, as regards the great body of the people of the United States who were in principle opposed to slavery, that the utmost they did to manifest their opposition was to discuss and determine its merits; and this they felt bound to do, especially in consequence of its more recent and extravagant claims. The measure of *their* responsibility for the rebellion and the war is thus easily gauged. It is equally notorious, that this discussion, and the conclusions formed concerning the system, were the chief things which gave the concocters of the rebellion mortal offence. *Their* responsibility is thus just as easily determined. Who, then, are responsible for this heritage of woes? Must the South bear it all? Is the North to bear no share of it?

presented: "But in the adverse event of these stipulations, or satisfactory equivalents for them, being refused, the Border States and their allies of the South who may be disposed to act with them, will be forced to consider the Union impracticable, and to organize a separate Confederacy of the Border States, with the association of such of the Southern and free States as may be willing to accede to the proposed conditions." On a subsequent page he says, the italics being his own: "But let the free States everywhere, and the sober, reflective, and honest men in them, understand, that *the old Union is an impossibility unless the agitation of slavery is brought to an end.*" These extracts are suggestive: (1.) Mr. Kennedy, like some other men in the Border slave States, takes the position that slavery was not the cause of the rebellion, and yet *all* his proposals for "reconciliation" are made with reference to slavery in some of its bearings; giving thus, unwittingly, the proof that slavery was in reality the cause. (2.) The real difficulty was not that the subject was discussed "in a tone offensive," but that it was discussed at all. Discussion in any form or spirit was "offensive," unless it was in favor of the system. (3.) But the most remarkable thing here is, that so distinguished a gentleman, once a cabinet minister, should at any time have seriously proposed (and he is by no means the only statesman in this category) any State action, in a popular government, "to discourage discussion" on any subject; and especially with the alternative of dissolving the Union, unless his proposed concessions, demanded by the subject upon which discussion was to be precluded, were granted. But the country can well afford, at this later day, to pass over some things of this kind which then took strong hold of many minds; and of Mr. Kennedy this can be said on two grounds. He, like a large portion of his countrymen, has obtained some new ideas since then; and during the present year he has given his powers, with other leading men of Maryland, to the work of entirely removing slavery from that State. Some Border State men make no advance on the subject—unless it be backward.

WHAT CLASS OF NORTHERN MEN RESPONSIBLE.

Here is where the case pinches, and yet the solution of the question is most easy. We freely concede that a certain part of the people of the North have a portion of this responsibility to bear, but it is not that small and uninfluential class whom Judge Robertson, and other writers who agree with him, would hold up to the public gaze; nor yet that larger number who manifested their dissent by discussion. It is rather that class of men in Church and State,—politicians, editors, divines, and others, who are always influential in forming, controlling, or echoing public opinion,—who have ever been crying out about an infringement of Southern rights, making apologies for the South, courting the smiles of the Southern people, and yielding, step by step, to their extreme demands. So far as provocative action may be charged with responsibility, in yielding to the clamors of Southern passion, and exciting Southern men to demand more and more in concession to slavery, this class may be justly held to a large measure of it.

RESPONSIBILITY AMONG POLITICIANS NORTH.

The "claims of the South" were always in the market. They were put up to the highest bidder in the political contests of the country. They formed the central plank in political platforms. We state nothing more than is known and read of all men, when we say that that party which for many years before the rebellion began had commonly the control of the General Government, was always the successful competitor; and having once and long ago established with the South its subserviency and fidelity, it held its position undisputed. No slave was ever more obedient to his master. This was seen in its conventions, in its platforms, in its primary meetings, upon the stump, at elections, in Congress, in the Supreme Court. Certain concessions emboldened Southern politicians to demand what had never been dreamed of by the founders of the Government; but the demand was no sooner made than it was granted, and generally, in latter days, in the name of the supreme organic law; so that, at length, the doctrine of Southern Statesmen, and of nearly the whole Southern people, was precisely that stated by Dr. Thornwell, in his elaborate vindication of the secession of South Carolina: "The Constitution covers the whole territory of the Union, and throughout that territory has taken slavery under the protection of law;" a doctrine, as understood at the South, which would have startled the framers of the Constitution, and which is nevertheless but the echo of the celebrated declaration of President Buchanan about Kansas while it was yet a Territory, that slavery existed there in fact and by the Constitution of the United States, as truly as it existed in Georgia and South Carolina.

RESPONSIBILITY AMONG CHURCHMEN NORTH.

The subserviency of Northern politicians had its counterpart within the Northern Churches, and in those ecclesiastical bodies which extended into all parts of the Union. We do not mean that corruption, bargaining, and sale, for place and profit, occurred in like manner; but the disposition to apologize, extenuate, stifle discussion, and yield to Southern wishes, lest slavery should receive some damage, or somebody or something connected with it, somewhere or somehow, should be in some manner or in some degree hurt, in purse, feeling, or character; all this has been too frequently illustrated in the higher courts of the Church, and defended by religious journals, and makes too prominent and frequent a figure in our recent religious history, scarcely to need in these pages any recurrence to the facts except in a general statement. And yet it may be well to confirm this view by a bare reference to the influence this course had upon the South, as seen in Southern testimony.

SOUTHSIDE VIEW OF NORTHERN CLERGYMEN.

A man's standing and influence are generally pretty well determined by the estimation in which he is held by his judicious friends. Taking this as a fair criterion of judgment, we have only to turn the eye South to perceive how certain Northern men in the Church were regarded upon those questions which politically and religiously divided the country, and at length terminated in rebellion and war, and thus to see on which side their influence for many years, when these difficulties were culminating, was thrown.

If in taking this Southern observation we are led to give names, it is because we find them presented in the South, and because they are prominent persons and representative men of a large class at the North. If special distinction is given to individuals, it only shows how highly their services were valued; and if they are now found at last upon the side of the country and its real interests, it only serves to make the lamentation at the loss of their services the more bitter, and to give the sarcasm in which it is expressed a keener point.

The Southern Presbyterian, a religious weekly published at Columbia, South Carolina, is a good authority upon the point in hand. In its issue of February 23, 1861, it refers, as "a sign of the times," to a discussion then going on between Rev. William Matthews, of Georgia, and Rev. Dr. N. L. Rice, then editor of the *Presbyterian Expositor*, at Chicago. The Southern editor, Rev. A. A. Porter, says:

> We do not intend to report the particulars of this correspondence, which would be profitless. We allude to it for a different purpose. We have called it a sign of the times! We regard it as such for several reasons: Because Dr. Rice, who has heretofore been DISTINGUISHED *as a defender of slavery and the South,* and as an antagonist of the antislavery party, now has wheeled about with Dr. Hodge, and, like him, appears on the other side, against the South and Slavery. We have heard much of late about a reaction in the North in favor of the South, and have been assured that our cause was gaining ground there. Does this look like it?

To appreciate fully the point here made, it is only necessary to bear in mind that this comes from one who well knows the course of opinion and discussion in the Church and the country, and that it comes from the capital of *South Carolina.* If the course of Dr. Rice for twenty years past has such an estimation in such a quarter,—where, to be "a defender of slavery and the South," and to be "distinguished" as such, has a meaning whose significance cannot be mistaken,—it is better testimony than any *we* could give to show how great has been his influence, and on which side it has been exerted, during the gestation period of that gigantic iniquity which at length gathered sufficient strength from such nutriment to come forth armed and equipped to make war upon good government and popular liberty. This same article pronounces Dr. Rice "probably the adroitest debater now living,"—another indication of the high esteem in which his defences of "Slavery and the South" were held,—and thousands at the North well know, that had not the class of which he is so prominent a representative taken the course they did, there would have been formed such a public sentiment in the Church at least as would have checked the growing proslaveryism and spirit of domination in the South, and which would have gone far towards preventing secession, treason, rebellion, and war.

The name of Dr. Hodge occurs in the foregoing paragraph, associated with that of Dr. Rice. It appears, however, and we should in justice state, that he is not claimed as having given his influence to the South in the same manner. Southern men differ upon the point, it is true. Dr. Armstrong, in his "Christian Doctrine of Slavery," frequently quotes Dr. Hodge as sustaining his own views; and Dr. Armstrong, it is well known, as seen in that book and in his discussions with Dr. Van Rensselaer, though mild in his terms and eminently Christian in his spirit, maintained and vindicated the extreme view, substantially, of the system taken at the South. It is well known, too, that Dr. Hodge's writings on slavery have been extensively circulated and approved at the South, and have undoubtedly exerted a large influence to make the Southern people quite contented with the status of the institution, and quite willing it should be perpetuated. It is possible, also, that in the above paragraph the editor designs to put Drs. Rice and Hodge in the same category, and yet it is not probable; for in a subsequent paper he speaks very differently of the latter.

In reply to a correspondent, who refers to "the course of Dr. Hodge, Dr. Rice, Dr. Lord, Dr. Breckinridge, and Dr. Engles," in regard to the state of the country, as "unexpected," and who, notwithstanding that "course," says of them, "*They are every one with us, and against abolitionists, on the slavery question*,"—deeming the fact so important as to array the sentence in italics,—the editor, the Rev. A. A. Porter, in *The Southern Presbyterian* of March 30, 1861, thus excepts by name two of the persons concerned:

We cannot agree with our correspondent that the views of the eminent men whom he names, on the slavery question, are acceptable to Southern Presbyterians. Our readers, who noticed the communication of "Georgia," in our last number, must be convinced that there is a wide and radical difference between us and Dr. Hodge on that subject. Dr. Breckinridge, it is well known, is, and always has been, an emancipationist—that is, in favor of the gradual abolition of slavery. So is Dr. Hodge. So, we doubt not, are almost the entire body of Northern Presbyterians.

It thus appears, that while Dr. Hodge is quoted favorably by Dr. Armstrong at Norfolk, Virginia, he is not deemed sound in South Carolina and Georgia. Latitude sometimes affects men's views of moral questions. He is by no means put in the category with Dr. Rice, at the South; for, although Dr. Rice has said some hard things of slavery, and has been regarded as an "emancipationist" also, at least at the North, he has, nevertheless, always taken such a course, and illustrated so highly the peculiar skill of "the adroitest debater now living," that the South,—even "the extremists" among them, as we see,—claimed him as THEIR MAN *par excellence*, to do their work at the North, and thus give them substantial "aid and comfort." Hence they have always spoken of him kindly, and valued his services at a very high figure. This is shown as truly in their incidental references as it would be in a more elaborate commendation, and at the same time the thing is done with a better grace. Here is another specimen, in *The Southern Presbyterian* of April 27, 1861, where the South Carolina editor again laments that he can count no longer on the services of his quondam friend:

No less authority than Dr. N. L. Rice, *who has been regarded in the South as* OUR BEST FRIEND *at the North*, and who, if we mistake not, drew up the act of 1845, which was supposed by the South to be a *decision in our favor*, tells us that we must not interpret that as reversing former acts.

Et TU, *Brute!* The "decision" here referred to, is that made by the General Assembly of the Presbyterian Church upon slavery, and this is one of the incidental evidences to show how that famous paper, of which Dr. Rice is the author, was regarded by the South Carolina type of proslaveryism.

RESPONSIBILITY OF NORTHERN MEN THUS DETERMINED.

We need not go further in our citations. The fact is undeniable, that a large and influential class among clergymen and editors in the Church of all branches at the North, exerted such an influence for a long course of years, whether so intended or not, as to foster that spirit, and countenance those claims put forth by the South, which led Southern demagogues to believe that they could rule the country according to their own peculiar notions, and could count upon their Northern friends to sustain them; or, failing to rule it, could divide the country, and still look with confidence to their support. Hence their pitiful cries when, in the hour of need, they found they were forsaken.

In regard to certain religious men at the North,—and perhaps the same may be said of politicians, who, Mr. Jefferson said, were "allies" of the South,—we accord to them a sincere, though, we think, a mistaken course of speech and action. Some of them have since frankly acknowledged that their course was wrong. *It tended to deceive the Southern Church.* Since the rebellion began, Southern divines have denounced this class of men most unsparingly, and so have Southern journals, both of the weekly and periodical press. They have even pronounced them hypocrites. All this is very natural, even though we admit it to be unjust. But of those who have always opposed their extravagant claims, they have spoken with more respect, though, for them, they have manifested no warmer love.

It is likewise well known, that those Northern politicians who were Southern "allies," have been treated in no mild manner at the South, while the Republican party, and even the Abolitionists, have been spoken of with that higher consideration, comparatively regarded, which one esteemed an open foe always inspires. It is, for example, quite probable, that the reason why they so bitterly denounce General Butler, is as much owing to the fact that he was always so prominent and able in their political councils, and instead of taking a stand with them when the breach occurred, as they had hoped he would, was found in command of a Union army, as it was owing to the stringent rule he exercised in New Orleans. We do not hold this class of public men entirely responsible for the rebellion, though it is unquestionable, from the speeches of some of them, during the winter and spring of 1860–61, before the attack upon Fort Sumter, made in Congress and out of it, that the Southern leaders still counted upon them as "allies," believed they would stand by them in an open clash of arms, that the North would thus be divided, and that the rebellion would have an easy triumph. The fact cannot be denied, that there was good reason for believing that this reliance had a better foundation than many things that are taken for granted. It is undoubtedly true that the Southern leaders were so far forth deceived, and were thus emboldened to do what otherwise they might have been restrained from doing, and to this extent these Northern politicians were responsible; while, on the other hand, some of these "allies" were themselves deceived, believing that Southern men would not dare to strike the blow.*

* We do not put General Butler in this category. He did not, at this period, take

We have good reason to believe, also, that the leaders of the Southern Church, as we have already intimated, were stimulated to become active promoters of the rebellion, by virtue of the hold which they believed they still had upon their special friends at the North; supposing, at first, that their secession might be effected peaceably, or, if it came at last to an open clash of arms, that their faithful "allies" would still stand by them.

The responsibility for the rebellion, so far as the North is concerned, is thus not difficult of adjustment. It rests not upon the abolitionists; the South themselves repudiate this idea. It rests rather upon those, in Church and State, who have countenanced Southern extremists, and who were claimed by them as favoring their views; the "adroitest debaters" in Congressional halls and Church courts, and who upon the stump and through the press were "distinguished as defenders of slavery and the South;" in this manner nourishing and sustaining Southern men up to such

any course to deceive the rebels, nor was he himself deceived as to their designs. On the contrary, in December, 1860, soon after the secession of South Carolina, "General Butler went to Senator Wilson of Massachusetts, an old acquaintance, though long a political opponent, and told him that the Southern leaders *meant war*, and urged him to join in advising the Governor of their State to prepare the militia of Massachusetts for taking the field." "One thing he considered absolutely certain: there was going to be a war between Loyalty and Treason; between the Slave Power and the Power which had so long protected and fostered it. He found the North anxious, but still incredulous. He went to Governor Andrew, and gave him a full relation of what he had seen and heard at Washington, and advised him to get the militia of the State in readiness to move at a day's notice. He suggested that all the men should be quietly withdrawn from the militia force who were either unable or unwilling to leave the State for the defence of the Capital, and their places supplied with men who could and would. The Governor, though he could scarcely yet believe that war was impending, adopted the suggestion. About one-half the men resigned their places in the militia; the vacancies were quickly filled; and many of the companies, during the winter months, drilled every evening in the week, except Sundays."—*Parton's Butler in New Orleans*, ch. ii. It was unquestionably owing to General Butler's suggestions, as above related, that so large a number of Massachusetts troops were able to obey the call of the President so promptly, in April, 1861, occasioned by the attack upon Fort Sumter.

a point of preposterous demand for their claims, that at length the masses of the people rose in their sovereign majesty to throw off the incubus, and restore the Government to its true and original status.

NORTHERN RESPONSIBILITY IN ANOTHER LIGHT.

It has often been said that the people of the North had no business to trouble themselves about the question of slavery in any aspect of the case, as the South were alone responsible for the institution. This has been the short argument, many a time, employed against Northern men: "It is none of your business; if it is a sin, the Southern people only are guilty of it; if it is a social evil, or a political matter, it is wholly their concern; therefore, let it alone."

These are radical errors; and yet, so shrewd a man as Dr. Thornwell sustains them. He says:

> The *responsibility* of slavery is *not upon the non-slaveholding States.* It is not created by their laws, but by the laws of the slaveholding States; and all they do in the case of the fugitive from his master, is to remand him to the jurisdiction of the laws from which he has escaped. They have nothing to do with the justice or injustice of the laws themselves. —*Fast-Day Sermon,* Nov. 21, 1860.

> We have no complaint to make of the opinions of the North considered *simply as their opinions.* They have a right, so far as human authority is concerned, to think as they please. The South has never asked them to approve of slavery, or to change their own institutions and to introduce it among themselves. The South has been willing to accord to them the most perfect and unrestricted right of *private judgment.* But what we *do* complain of, and what we have a right to complain of, is, *that they should not be content with thinking their own thoughts themselves,* but should undertake to make the Government think them likewise.—*So. Pres. Rev.,* Jan., 1861.

These are erroneous opinions, in any true consideration of the case· and most flagrantly so in view of the changes which have occurred, within a recent period in our history, in Southern sentiment, upon the social, moral, and political status of slavery.

SLAVERY MAY BE EXAMINED AT THE NORTH.

These are errors, *politically* considered. Dr. Thornwell's argument, in both the articles above quoted, is to show that slavery is *national*. He says, as before given: "The Constitution covers the whole territory of the Union, and throughout that territory has taken slavery under the protection of law." Admitting for the sake of the argument that this is so, it follows that slavery is a matter for the consideration of the whole people, and their responsibility is involved in every national aspect of the institution; to see that its relations to the Constitution are understood aright and are properly maintained. His premises being admitted, the conclusion is inevitable. But without admitting the extreme views which Southern politicians have often advanced in more recent times, which are not sustained by the founders of the Government, and which we presume Dr. Thornwell intends to cover by the sentence just quoted, all statesmen agree that in any *true* relation of the Constitution to slavery, the institution, in some of its most important bearings, is one of national concern and national responsibility. More especially is this true in the light of Southern claims which are believed to be totally at variance with the Constitution. It was incumbent on every Northern statesman, and upon every Northern citizen, to note whither such sentiments were tending, and to act accordingly. It is perfectly immaterial, however, to the present point, which construction of the Constitution is right, the Northern or the Southern. In either case, slavery is a matter for national consideration. In a purely political light, therefore, Dr.

Thornwell makes a most ill-founded complaint of the people of the non-slaveholding States, in "that they should not be content with thinking their own thoughts themselves."

His position is equally false in *morals*. The relation which the people of the North sustain to slavery politically, makes its moral status of necessity one of just concern to them. If it is an evil in any sense, if a sin in itself, or if all its evils are merely incidental to the relation, still the inevitable connection of the whole people with it, through the structure of the common Government, fixes upon them the responsibility in no small degree of its moral status and relations, whatever they may be. It is utterly erroneous to say that the people of the non-slaveholding States "have nothing to do with the justice or injustice" of the institution, or even "of the laws themselves" by which it is regulated. If they are concerned with it at all, if they are obliged to return fugitives that escape from slavery to the jurisdiction of the laws from which they have fled, or if they have any other duty to discharge under that instrument which gives the institution any national status whatever, then they have a right to inquire into any thing and every thing which gives it character; and especially into its moral status, for they and the slaves themselves are moral beings. The whole people of the non-slaveholding States may consider every moral element and bearing of the institution, and may approve or condemn, in whole or in part, according to their best judgment, and act as righteousness demands. Nor can any past settlement of principles concerning it, or any opinion entertained of it, by the fathers, or by anybody else, preclude their right thus to do; for they must act on their own responsibility before God.

But most especially,—if, indeed, there can be any difference,—is it their privilege not only, but their right and solemn duty, to compass the whole subject, when the South, well nigh or quite universally, abandoning the opinions concerning it held substantially by the whole country in the early days of the Republic,—by statesmen and divines,—have latterly taught that slavery is right and a "blessing," is an "Ordinance of God" and a "school of virtue,"* and is vindicated throughout the whole Scriptures. What the people of the North have claimed, is, to examine these pretensions, to see whether the Fathers both of the Church and of the State in this country were right or wrong, and having formed a judgment to act accordingly; and this is the whole they have claimed.

A SUBJECT FOR ALL MANKIND.

Nor is this all. The moment the claim is made that Southern slavery is sanctioned and sanctified by the Word of God, and is on a par with the conjugal and parental relations, the whole subject is thrown open to the discussion of all people in this country not only, but to the entire Christian world to whom the Scriptures are given. Under the modern claims for Southern negro slavery, it is the idlest of all possible objections to say of Christians of even any foreign nation, that "they have nothing to do with the justice or injustice" of the institution. If it is a perfectly Scriptural system, as is claimed, they may inquire into it, as they may into any social system claiming such a sanction; as into polygamy in Utah, or into any of the

* "Strange as it may sound to those who are not familiar with the system, *Slavery is a school of virtue*, and no class of men have furnished sublimer instances of heroic devotion than slaves in their loyalty and love to their masters. We have seen them rejoice at the cradle of the infant, and weep at the bier of the dead; and there are few amongst us, perhaps, who have not drawn their nourishment from their generous breasts."—(*Fast-Day Sermon.*) Some naturalists tell us that there are certain "irrational animals" who give the same illustrations of "virtue."

systems of heathenism; and the same if it is not sustained by Scripture; and to determine whether it is or not thus sanctioned, they must examine it, for there is no other way of arriving at the truth.

And beyond this, we may say that the principle of self-defence and self-preservation,—"the first law of life,"—impels to this course. We have seen that it was a part of the scheme of the rebel leaders to make the whole North slaveholding, and to people its lands with slaves fresh from Africa. The same men think that Europe would be better off with slavery. If, then, such a change has taken place in this country as to lead men to applaud it where it was once only tolerated, and to declare it in every sense a "blessing," where once it was pronounced a "curse" to all concerned, who can tell but like transformations may occur elsewhere, and among other nations?

FREE SOCIETY PITIED AND LAMENTED.

Is it not well known that eminent Southern writers, not content to enjoy the blessings of slavery alone, have expressed their pity for the social condition of the North; have lamented "the failure of free society;" have become eloquent upon "the organization of labor;" have predicted that the North would be obliged to resort to their system to prevent anarchy and ruin; and upon these convictions have recommended themselves to imitation by all the nations of the earth? Dr. Thornwell says:

> We confidently anticipate the time when the nations that now revile us would gladly change places with us. In its last analysis, slavery is nothing but an organization of labor. * * * Society is divided between princes and beggars. *If labor is left free*, how is this condition of things to be obviated? The Government must either make provision to support people in idleness, or it must arrest the law of population and keep them from being born, or *it must organize labor*. * * * On what principle shall labor be organized so as to make it certain that the

laborer shall never be without employment, and employment adequate for his support? The *only way* in which it can be done, as a permanent arrangement, is by *converting the laborer into capital;* that is, by giving the employer a right of property in the labor employed; in other words, BY SLAVERY. * * * *That non-slaveholding States will eventually have to organize labor*, and to introduce something so like slavery that it will be impossible to discriminate between them, or to suffer from the most violent and disastrous insurrections against the system which creates and perpetuates their misery, seems to be as certain as the tendencies in the laws of capital and population to produce the extremes of poverty and wealth. *We do not envy them their social condition.* * * * We desire to see no such state of things among ourselves, and we accept as a good and merciful constitution the organization of labor which Providence has given us in slavery.—*Fast-Day Sermon.*

SLAVERY THE PROPER CONDITION FOR ALL LABORERS.

The plain English of the foregoing is, that Dr. Thornwell would have *all the laborers in every nation reduced to slavery.* He would not merely go to Africa for laborers, but would reduce every *white* man who is compelled to labor, from freedom to slavery. Dr. Palmer joins his lamentation over freedom to the laborer, and over the perils of free society, as follows:

The so-called Free States are working out the social problem under conditions peculiar to themselves. *These conditions are sufficiently hard*, and their success is too uncertain to excite in us the least jealousy of their lot. With a teeming population, which the soil cannot support—with their wealth depending upon arts, created by artificial wants—with an eternal friction between the grades of their society—with their labor and their capital grinding each other like the upper and nether millstones—with labor cheapened and displaced by new mechanical inventions, bursting more asunder the bonds of brotherhood; amid these intricate perils *we have ever given them our sympathy and our prayers*, and have never sought to weaken the foundations of their social order. God grant them complete success in the solution of all their perplexities!—*Thanksgiving Discourse.*

We sincerely thank the kind man for his "sympathy and

prayers" concerning a state of things of which he knows so little; but we do not think the greatest sufferers in "the so-called Free States" are quite willing to say they are ready to be reduced to that "system of organized labor" which is here marked out for them.

The mild and amiable Dr. Armstrong, of Norfolk, Virginia, does not leave it to inevitable inference, but states it in terms, that *the white laborers of Europe* are the proper subjects of whom to make slaves. This is his view of the matter:

> It may be that such a slavery, regulating the relations of capital and labor, though implying some deprivation of personal liberty, will prove a better defence of the poor against the oppression of the rich, than the too great freedom in which capital is placed in many of the Free States of Europe at the present day. Something of this kind is what the masses of free laborers in France are clamoring for under the name of the "right to labor." * * * It may be that *Christian slavery* [the author's italics] is God's solution of the problem about which the wisest statesmen of Europe confess themselves "at fault."—*Christian Doctrine of Slavery.*

These Christian Doctors of Divinity, so eloquent and earnest upon "Christian Slavery;" so tearful and prayerful over the condition of society at the North; so anxious to have all laborers, white and black, blonde and brunette, in America and Europe, reduced to slavery, the only distinction being that the "rich" shall be the masters and the "poor" their slaves,—and who would, upon this principle alone, illustrate "the organization of labor" in every nation upon earth, allowing masters only to carry a pocket dictionary from a Southern press (if the South ever printed one) to define "poor" and "rich,"—are of course supported in all this by the politicians and economists of the South. In *De Bow's Review* for November, 1857, one of them discourseth as follows, on "Southern Thought:"

We must teach that *slavery is necessary in all societies*, as well to protect, as to govern the weak, poor, and ignorant. This is the opposite doctrine to that of the political economists. We should show that slave society, which is a series of subordinations, is consistent with Christian morality—for fathers, masters, husbands, wives, children, and slaves, not being equals, rivals, competitors, and antagonists, best promote each other's selfish interests when they do most for those above or beneath them. Within the precincts of the family, including slaves, the golden rule is a practical and wise guide of conduct. But in free society, where selfishness, rivalry, and competition, are necessary to success, and almost to existence, this rule cannot be adopted in practice. It would reverse the whole action of such society, and make men martyrs to their virtues. * * * We, of the South, can build up an ethical code founded on the morality of the Bible, because human interests with us do not generally clash, but coincide. Without the family circle, it is true, competition and clashing interests exist, but slavery leaves few without the family, and the little competition that is left is among the rich and skilful. and serves to keep society progressive. It is enough that slavery will relieve common laborers of the evils of competition, and the exactions of skill and capital. * * * Southern thought will teach that protection and slavery must go hand in hand, for we cannot efficiently protect those whose conduct we cannot control. * * * It is the duty of society to protect all its members, and it can only do so by subjecting each to that degree of government constraint, or slavery, which will best advance the good of each and of the whole. Thus ambition, or the love of power, properly directed, becomes the noblest of virtues, because power alone can enable us to be safely benevolent to the weak, poor, or criminal. *To protect the weak,* WE MUST FIRST ENSLAVE THEM, and this slavery must be either political and legal, or social. * * * Slavery is necessary as an *educational institution, and is worth ten times all the common schools of the North.* Such common schools teach only uncommonly bad morals, and prepare their inmates to gradu- te in the penitentiary, as the statistics of crime at the North abundantly prove. * * * We, of the South, assume that man has all along instinctively understood and practised that social and political government best suited to his nature, and that domestic slavery is, in the general, a natural and *necessary part of that government, and that its absence is owing to a decaying diseased state of society,* or to something exceptional in local circumstances, as in desert, or mountainous, or new countries, where competition is no evil, because capital has no mastery over labor.

WHO, NOW, IS RESPONSIBLE?

The reader is no doubt willing to rest here; these lessons in political economy are sufficient for his present reflection. The divines and the economists whose views are now given, are among the foremost leaders of the rebellion; were those who, at the earliest moment, urged it on, and those whose teachings for twenty years past had helped to prepare the Southern people for the work in which they are to-day engaged, on a hundred fields of carnage and blood, where lie the bleaching bones of the flower of a generation of young men; and they are those who have, during every step in the progress of the war, by prayers and counsels, and active aid in the armies of treason, given all their might to bring forth these legitimate fruits of the seed they have sown. This is their work; for it they are responsible.

The laborers and mechanics of the North,—all the "poor," indeed, of every class,—may see the feast which was elaborately prepared for them, and the destiny which inevitably awaited them, could the South have had their way in the unlimited and unchecked control of the Government; and they may learn, in this, the real character of that rebellion, to put down which the Government has called the people to arms.

All may see, in the light of these sentiments, the real nature of that system, and the real character of its supporters, that have found apologists and extenuators in the North for these many years past, in the "adroitest debaters" and most "distinguished defenders of slavery and the South," in Church and State. While these men were sowing broadcast these seeds through every means in their power, it was deemed a labor of love to prepare for them the soil. While they could teach their doctrines at will, and pity that condition of "free society," and mourn over that hardness of heart which would not receive them, it was deemed "agitation," "agitation," "agitation," nothing but wicked interference with matters which concerned them not, for pulpit, or press, or Church court, to raise even a gentle note of remonstrance. While some who had the sagacity to see what was inevitably coming upon the Church and upon the country from such teachings, and who had the boldness and the faithfulness to God's truth to declare it, —and whose far-sightedness the result has remarkably verified,—have been, for that very faithfulness, exiled by the Church from posts of usefulness to which their qualifications and labors eminently entitled them, others, chiefly instrumental in this ostracism, have been honored by Southern votes with high stations, and have illustrated *their* faithfulness by eminent subserviency to those who so long controlled them. But for all deeds there is a day of reckoning; and we are quite sure the Church itself is beginning to understand those who have been true to her interests and those who have dishonored and betrayed her.

When the day shall eventually come to write the history of this rebellion, it will not be difficult, so far as men of the North are concerned, to determine the true measure of their responsibility. And when the full character and aims of the rebel leaders shall be understood, it will be the judgment of the historian, as it is now the conviction of the loyal masses of the people, that such a disease as had thus fastened itself upon the body politic, could not be purged from it except through the agency of gunpowder —the means which the rebels themselves invoked.

CHAPTER IV.

RESPONSIBILITY FOR BEGINNING AND CONTINUING THE WAR.

THE South admit that they took the initiative for *secession*, but charge the North with having begun the *war*. This charge has been made from the beginning, and is deemed so clear that it admits of no dispute. It is found in their public journals, secular and religious, in the speeches of their public men, and is formally set forth and reiterated in the State papers of the rebel President and the members of his Cabinet, and by the rebel Congress.* From the moment of the actual outbreak of hostilities to the present

* "A sense of oppression and wrong, on the part of the North, in *instituting and sustaining* this war upon the South, is deep seated and abiding in their minds, and they will shrink from no sacrifices and turn away from no dangers in *resisting it*." —*Presbytery of Western District, Tennessee*, July, 1861. Rev. Dr. Thomas Smyth, of Charleston, S. C., when speaking of "the *defensive* character of the war of the South," says: "That war, as we have already proved, was *provoked, threatened*, perfidiously *commenced*, and openly proclaimed by the North."—*Southern Presbyterian Review*, April, 1863. In an "Address of (the Rebel) Congress to the People of the Confederate States," issued in February, 1864, it is said: "That a people, professing to be animated by Christian sentiment, and who had regarded our peculiar institution as a blot and blur upon the fair escutcheon of their common Christianity, should *make war upon the South* for doing what they had a perfect right to do, * * * was deemed almost beyond belief by many of our wisest minds. * * * These reasonable anticipations were doomed to disappointment. The red glare of battle kindled at Sumter, dissipated all hopes of peace, and the two Governments were arrayed in hostility against each other. *We charge the responsibility of this war upon the United States.* They are accountable for the blood and havoc and ruin it has caused. * * * The war in which we are engaged was wickedly, and against all our protests and most earnest efforts to the contrary, *forced upon us*." The rebel President, Jefferson Davis, in one of his messages to Congress, referred to in the above-mentioned Address, says: "Our efforts to avoid the war, *forced on us as it was* by the lust of conquest and the insane passions of our foes, are known to mankind."

hour, they have persistently declared that the General Government, sustained by the body of the Northern people, are alone responsible for having *begun*, and for having *continued*, the war.

They insist that secession was a peaceful remedy for their wrongs, against which war could not justly be made; and they declare, that, ever since war began, they have been ready to make peace, but that the General Government would not have peace.

These are grave issues, lying at the root of the controversy in which the two sections of the country are involved. We cannot here canvass the alleged right of secession, which is claimed to be a Constitutional remedy for the grievances complained of. Our object, at present, is different. Whether secession, under the Constitution, be a justifiable remedy for any invasion of right or not, it is only necessary, in reference to the immediate object now in hand, to show, that the kind of secession which the South undertook, was early begun, and was vigorously prosecuted, by acts which can have no other terms of description than those which belong to the vocabulary of war. To assume that such acts are authorized under the Constitution, that they are what it contemplated as proper to be done in carrying out secession, that these are acts of peace, and that therefore secession is a peaceful remedy for supposed wrongs, are propositions so monstrous, that no one can be deceived by them the moment the acts in question come to be examined in their nature and the time of their occurrence.

JOHN M. BOTTS ON SECESSION.

As introductory to a brief narration of early events, well remembered by the whole world, we refer to a letter of the Hon. John Minor Botts, of Virginia, dated Richmond,

January 24, 1861, written in answer to a request made to him to become a candidate for the Convention, which passed the Ordinance of Secession for Virginia. It is well known, that so eager were the Southern rebels for a disruption of the Union, that they rejoiced over the election of Mr. Lincoln to the Presidency, with exceeding great joy, as furnishing the justifiable ground for the step. Referring to this, Mr. Botts says:

> I am not willing to sacrifice the best interests of my State and my country, and the hopes of oppressed mankind throughout the world, in upholding South Carolina in a bad cause; in a wholly unjustifiable and petulant whim, which she avows she has indulged for thirty years. I am not willing to rush upon destruction, for a misplaced sympathy for a State that exulted over the election of a Republican President, burned their tar barrels and illuminated their cities, because it afforded them the pretext for rebellion, and that has violently seized upon the forts, arsenals, arms, and ammunition, and money of the United States, and has fired upon, and driven from her waters, an unarmed vessel bearing that flag of the Union which has borne us triumphantly through every war and every trouble.

NARRATIVE OF EVENTS.

These words of Mr. Botts, suggest the events of the fall and winter of 1860–61, which fix indelibly upon the South the responsibility of having *begun the war*, in repeated and long continued *acts* of war. The work of revolt began immediately after the election, and in the midst of the rejoicing at the result of it. State after State, by formal acts, openly repudiated the authority of the United States, and "seceded." The people of these States, in various localities, sustained by the public authorities, forcibly seized, as Mr. Botts declares, the public property of the nation. The forts, ships, mints, custom-houses, public money, arms, arsenals, ammunition, and other public property, were taken. All these, confessedly, belonged, not to the respective States, but to the United States. They were built, manufactured, or purchased, as the property and by the money and authority of the United States. The title was not questioned by any one. Many of these things were taken by force. The guards of mints and custom houses were eluded or overborne; and the forts and ships, in some of the former of which were garrisons, and in the latter armed officers, were seized by bodies of armed men in superior numbers, and the United States forces were compelled to surrender. These were not the acts of mere mob violence. They will take in history, as they have in the eye of public law, a different character. *These were* ACTS OF WAR; *the early measures of an open revolution.* They were directly authorized by organized States, which claimed to have thrown off the national authority. They were taken that they might resist by force any attempt on the part of the United States to repossess them, and to re-establish the authority which had been subverted. These acts were, therefore, severally, *acts of war*, so far as such acts can be, before war has been formally declared by competent authority, or in a revolution before there has been any forcible step taken to resist it. It is possible, that *technically* these acts may not be acts of war, for there was, as yet, no legal power to declare it; but *practically* such was, to all intents and purposes, their character.*

* Soon after the secession of South Carolina and the seizure of the Forts in the harbor of Charleston, and the like seizure of the Forts within the limits of Georgia and Alabama by those States, the sluggishness of Florida was thus chided by the *Charleston Mercury:* "To our friends in Florida we would respectfully pass a word. There are two powerful strongholds and most important points of military offence and defence in Florida—Pensacola and Key West. The States both of Georgia and Alabama have wisely taken time by the forelock, and put themselves in possession of such fortresses as lie within their borders." "In this view, it is important for the people of Florida to reflect that there are perhaps no fortresses along our whole Southern coast more important than those of Florida. These Forts can command the whole Gulf trade. And should Mr. Buchanan carry out what appears to be his present plan, he certainly must desire to hold possession of these Forts."

REBEL GOVERNMENT FORMED—THE SOUTH ARMING.

In the mean time, and before all these acts had been consummated, the several States which had "seceded," formed what they termed a Provisional Government, called the "Confederate States of America," in opposition to the Government of the United States, and soon afterwards adopted a Constitution, elected officers, and invested this Government with a permanent character and authority. This Government called out, as some of the seceded States had previously done, thousands of troops, armed and equipped them with the munitions taken from the United States arsenals, placing some of them in the forts and ships they had seized, the garrisons and crews of the national Government having already surrendered to them.

OUR GOVERNMENT INACTIVE.

During this time, and while all these things were publicly occurring, and the public journals of the country were publishing the details, the General Government *took*

"But let Florida hold these Forts, and the entire aspect of affairs is changed." "*The commerce of the North in the Gulf will fall an easy prey to our bold privateers; and California gold will pay all such little expenses on our part.*" In enumerating these and other seizures, in a Report made to the House of Representatives soon after, the Hon. John A. Dix, Secretary of the Treasury, says: "*Third.*—The seizure by Louisiana of all United States moneys, as well as those of private depositors in the mint and sub-treasury at New Orleans and other places. *Fourth.*—The seizure of revenue cutters, by arrangement between their commanders and the collectors of Mobile, New Orleans, and Charleston. *Fifth.*—The expulsion of the sick and invalid patients at the United States hospital at New Orleans, in order to provide accommodation for Louisiana troops." On the general subject, in this same Report, Mr. Dix says: "Throughout the whole course of encroachment and aggression, the Federal Government has borne itself with a spirit of paternal forbearance, of which there is no example in the history of public society; waiting in patient hope that the empire of reason would resume its sway over those whom the excitement of passion has thus far blinded, and trusting that the friends of good order, wearied with submission to proceedings which they disapproved, would, at no distant day, rally under the banner of the Union, and exert themselves with vigor and success against the prevailing recklessness and violence."

no measures to prevent them. If names are things, and if things have names descriptive of their character, these acts of aggression were *acts of war;* and to whatever we may now attribute the non-interference by the General Government, under the administration of President Buchanan,—whether to fear, timidity, imbecility, hope of restoring authority and preserving peace by doing nothing; or, to direct complicity with treason,—still, the facts will go down to history, that while the rebels were spending months in these acts of war, and in open preparation for war, the Government against which they had rebelled did nothing of a warlike character to oppose them.

SIEGE OF FORT SUMTER.

During the progress of these events, the rebels, not being able easily to seize some of the forts of the United States,—as Forts Pickens, Sumter, Moultrie, and others,—commenced against them a regular siege. Fort Sumter, in the harbor of Charleston, had a garrison of some seventy men, under the heroic Major Robert Anderson. Being instructed by the Government not to surrender the fort, *and also instructed not to fire upon the besiegers unless fired upon by them,** they were quietly permitted to en-

* President Buchanan, in his Annual Message to Congress, December 3d, 1860, speaking of the "property of the United States in South Carolina," says: "It is not believed that any attempt will be made to expel the United States from this property by force; but if in this I should prove to be mistaken, the officer in command of the forts has received orders *to act strictly on the defensive.* In such a contingency, the responsibility for consequences would rightfully rest upon the heads of the assailants." An order given to Major Anderson from the War Department, delivered at Fort Moultrie, December 11, 1860, says: "You are carefully to avoid every act which would needlessly *tend to provoke aggression,* and for that reason you are not, without necessity, to take up any position which could be construed into the assumption of a hostile attitude; but you are to hold possession of the Forts in the harbor, and *if attacked,* you are to *defend* yourself to the last extremity. The smallness of your force will not permit you, perhaps, to occupy more than one of the three Forts, but an attack on or an attempt to take possession of either of them, will be regarded as an act of hostility, and you may then put your com-

circle the fort with powerful siege-works, mounted by the heaviest guns belonging to the United States, until the reduction of the fort was made morally certain, whenever the rebels should choose to open fire. The force which was under arms to man and support the batteries erected around Fort Sumter, numbered, according to their own estimates, from seven to ten thousand men. They were armed mostly from the Government arsenals. Major Anderson could at any time have demolished the works in course of construction around him, or prevented their construction at all; but he was ordered by the Government to *stand strictly on the defensive.* Whether anybody had "blundered," most surely "all the world wondered." However humiliating to its loyal citizens such a course was, and reproachful to the national honor and power in the eyes of other nations, it is yet true that the Government made not one solitary effort of a warlike nature to recover its property or reassert its jurisdiction. Not a soldier was called out by the Government, while the rebels were mustering and drilling their forces.

CONGRESS NOT AGGRESSIVE.—STAR OF THE WEST.

Congress was in session during four months after these measures of revolt were initiated, and for several weeks after the warlike deeds referred to had well nigh reached their climax. Yet, Congress passed no act and took no step of a warlike character to meet these aggressions, but was, at this very time, maturing measures for peacefully settling, if possible, the difficulties of the country. In one instance, while Congress was in session, the Administration then in power (Mr. Buchanan's), as was clearly its

mand into either of them which you may deem most proper to increase its power of resistance. You are also authorized to take similar steps whenever you have tangible evidence of a design to proceed to a hostile act."

right and duty, sent the Star of the West, an unarmed vessel, with provisions for the garrison in Fort Sumter. The men were nearly in a starving condition, cut off from their usual supplies from the Charleston markets. The Star of the West was *fired upon*, and compelled to abandon the enterprise. This was another *open act of war*, committed by the assumed authority of the rebel Government. Yet, the Government of the United States did not retaliate. *Not a single shot was fired in return.* The brave garrison looked on in silence; no provisions were landed; their stores were nearly exhausted; they saw the flag of their country dishonored and fired upon by traitors; but all was borne, as the Government had so ordered.* Nor did Congress take any action, such was the disposition towards conciliation. It was during this very period that the several successive measures looking to peace,—by

* At this time, Major Anderson addressed a note to the Governor of South Carolina, in which he says: "Two of your batteries fired this morning upon an unarmed vessel bearing the flag of my Government." "I cannot but think this a hostile act, committed without your sanction or authority. Under that hope, I refrain from opening a fire on your batteries." "I respectfully ask whether the above-mentioned act was committed in obedience to your instructions, and notify you, if it is not disclaimed, that I regard it as *an act of war.*" This vessel was the *Star of the West.* The Governor replies to Major Anderson: "She was fired into. This act is perfectly justified by me." Governor Pickens further says: "Your position in the harbor has been *tolerated by the authorities of the State;*" and "the act of which you complain is in perfect consistency with the rights and duties of the State." Major Anderson rejoins: "I have deemed it proper to refer the whole matter to my Government." These notes bear date, January 9, 1861. The *Charleston Courier* of January 10, shows the amount of the firing at the vessel: "The Star of the West rounded the point, took the ship channel inside the bar, and proceeded straight forward until opposite Morris Island, about three-quarters of a mile from the battery. A ball was then fired athwart the bows of the steamer. The Star of the West displayed the stars and stripes. As soon as the flag was unfurled, the fortification fired a succession of shots. The vessel continued on her course with increased speed; but two shots taking effect upon her, she concluded to retire. Fort Moultrie fired a few shots at her, but she was out of range. The damage done to the Star of the West is trifling, as only two out of *seventeen shots* took effect upon her. Fort Sumter made no demonstration, except at the port-holes, where the guns were run out bearing on Morris Island."

the Peace Convention, and the proposed Amendments to the Constitution,—were under consideration. This forbearance, in the face of those repeated insults to the national authority and honor which culminated in firing upon the national flag without resentment, was mistaken by the rebels for timidity and cowardice. It only served to stimulate their determination toward resistance to that power which they could so easily defy, and whose measures had only inspired their contempt.

NEW ADMINISTRATION.—ATTACK ON FORT SUMTER.

Weeks passed on. The session of Congress had expired by its Constitutional limitation, and the new Administration, with Mr. Lincoln as President, came into power on the 4th of March, 1861. On the sixth of that month, only two days after Mr. Lincoln's inauguration, the "Confederate" Congress passed an Act authorizing a military force to be raised of *one hundred thousand men.*

At length the works for reducing Fort Sumter were nearly completed. At this time the garrison had but some two or three days' supply of provisions. This was well known to the rebel authorities. The Government, as in duty bound, determined on a second attempt to send a supply; and, at the same time, as a still further evidence of its forbearance and of its disposition to conciliation and peace, the Government gave the voluntary assurance to the besiegers that no reinforcement of men or munitions would be attempted, but that it would only supply the destitute garrison with provisions, and that no warlike demonstration would be made unless this should be interfered with. *This peaceful determination of the Government was made the occasion of an attack upon the fort, even before the provisioning vessels had arrived.* Here was another, and the climax in a series, of *open acts of war,* under express orders from the rebel Government at Montgomery; while the General Government, against which they were made, *had not called out a soldier, nor fired a gun, nor done one warlike act in opposition to them.* As an inevitable event, after a gallant resistance of an attack of some two days, by a circle of batteries constructed without opposition and completely investing the fort, the starved garrison of seventy men surrendered to the army of seven thousand.* It was then, *and not till then*, that the Government laid aside its forbearance, *that the President* MADE THE FIRST CALL FOR TROOPS, to defend the nation's honor and rights, to recover its property, and to restore its authority.

THE UNAVOIDABLE ISSUE.

The Government of the United States thus forbore as long as forbearance was possible, and perhaps much longer than was wise; until, indeed, this inevitable issue was presented,—that it must succumb, without resistance, to an open, well-organized, armed, and bloody rebellion, against its authority, property, honor, and power, and become a scoffing and a byword among all the nations of the earth, and a prey to their insults and rapacity; or that it must make at least an attempt to recover and maintain its rights by the sword, which God had put into the hand of its Chief Magistrate for the punishment of evil-doers and for the praise of them that do well. This simple alternative was forced upon the Government, as the whole world plainly saw.

The foregoing facts are so recent as to be within the mem-

* The *Charleston Mercury*, of May 3, 1861, gives the amount of "shot and shell expended during the bombardment of Fort Sumter," from fourteen batteries which had been specially erected for its reduction,—not including Fort Moultrie,—as "two thousand three hundred and sixty-one shot, and nine hundred and eighty shell."

ory of those who have paid attention to the current events of the early period of the war. And yet, it is with such facts before them, that the rebels and their sympathizers persist in asserting that "the Government of the United States is the aggressor," that "the North began the war," and that "the South is fighting in self-defence;" and it is upon the issue, thus falsely made, that much eloquence is expended in the endeavor to get up sympathy for "our oppressed Southern brethren," and to cast odium upon the National Government and upon those who are sustaining it in its effort to regain rightful authority over the whole domain of the Union.

The earliest possible date when the United States Government began, on its part, the war which it is now prosecuting to resist secession, and put down treason and rebellion, was April 15, 1861, when President Lincoln, by proclamation, called for seventy-five thousand troops. *Up to that moment, no warlike step for these ends had been taken.* And even then, by that proclamation, the rebels were allowed "twenty days to disperse and retire peacefully to their respective abodes." Had they availed themselves of this, no *act* of war upon their persons or property would have been committed; but they laughed this to scorn, and went on more vigorously in their warlike measures, which they had been steadily prosecuting *five full months.*

GENERAL M'CLELLAN'S OPINION.

General McClellan, in his address at the dedication of the Battle Monument at West Point, on the 15th of June, 1864, mentions the cause of the war, the unjustifiableness of the rebellion, and the necessity of maintaining our nationality, in the following terms:

Stripped of all sophistry and side issues, the direct cause of the war, as it presented itself to the honest and patriotic citizens of the North, was simply this: Certain States, or rather, a portion of the inhabitants of certain States, feared, or professed to fear, that injury would result to their rights and property from the elevation of a particular party to power.] Although the Constitution and the actual condition of the Government provided them with a peaceable and sure protection against the apprehended evil, they preferred to seek security in the destruction of the Government, which could protect them, and in the use of force against the national troops holding a national fortress. To efface the insult offered our flag; to save ourselves from the fate of the divided Republics of Italy and South America; to preserve our Government from destruction; to enforce its just power and laws; to maintain our very existence as a nation—these were the causes that compelled us to draw the sword. Rebellion against a Government like ours, which contains the means of self-adjustment, and a pacific remedy for evils, should never be confounded with a revolution against despotic power, which refuses a redress of wrongs. Such a rebellion cannot be justified upon ethical grounds, and the only alternative for our choice is its suppression, or the destruction of our nationality. At such a time as this, and in such a struggle, political partisanship should be merged in a true and brave patriotism, which thinks only of the good of the whole country.

Quot.

SOUTHERN ASSUMPTIONS VS. "NORTHERN AGGRESSIONS."

Taking the ground that the North began the war, the leaders of the rebellion have aimed to stimulate their own people, and to make out a case before the world, that they are fighting in self-defence.

Says Dr. Smyth, in the article before referred to, in the *Southern Presbyterian Review*, April, 1863: "By every instinct of self-preservation and defence, by the divinely authorized as well as inherent natural right of all her citizens in the Government ordained by them, as 'free,' and 'using their liberty' (1 Pet. ii.), the South was imperatively required to defend life, liberty, and the pursuit of happiness, even unto blood, against the arrogant and rapacious usurpation of the North." Dr. Smyth refers to "the conclusiveness of the facts adduced, in proof of the *aggres-*

sion of the North in originating this war," as set forth in an article of this *Review*, in 1861, on the "Battle of Fort Sumter," which we have not seen. From some incidental allusions, however, it is clear that he relies for "proof" upon certain "negotiations" attempted by the Southern leaders with the Government, in which they were unsuccessful, and which are known to the country. He takes the view of Southern writers generally.

The argument based upon this feature of the case they push with zeal; but their premises are false, their reasonings illusive, and their conclusions natural. Not being able to set aside the warlike character of the acts which we have detailed, they set forth that they were trying, at the same time, to negotiate with the Government a settlement between the North and South, but that the Government would not come to any terms, and thus forced upon the South the necessity of a war of self-defence in behalf of secession.

DIPLOMATISTS FROM SOUTH CAROLINA.

We need not go into any long statement of the measures on which the rebels rely to show that they were seeking a peaceful solution of their troubles by *negotiation*, while, as we have seen, they were making war *in fact*.

Soon after the secession of South Carolina, she sent three Commissioners to Washington, Messrs. Barnwell, Adams, and Orr, to treat with the General Government. They address a communication "To the President of the United States." They exhibit their credentials, and declare the object of their mission. They do not come to negotiate with the Executive about the "secession" of their State. That is, with them, a fact accomplished. Deeming the Constitution but a "compact," and not establishing a "Government" proper, but merely forming a "league" between several " nations," any one of them can withdraw at pleasure. The separation, or " secession," is a fact of the past. *One* party has dissolved the "compact;" and that is the end of the matter. These diplomatists have nothing to say on that subject; the deed is done; the case is closed. They are the accredited representatives of a Foreign Power; they are from the "nation" of South Carolina. They state to President Buchanan:

> We are authorized and empowered to treat with the Government of the United States for the delivery of the forts, magazines, light-houses, and other real estate, with their appurtenances in the limits of South Carolina; and also for an apportionment of the public debt, and for a division of all other property held by the Government of the United States, as agent of the Confederated States, *of which South Carolina was recently a member*, and generally to negotiate as to all other measures and arrangements proper to be made and adopted in the existing relations of the parties, and for the continuance of peace and amity between this Commonwealth and the Government at Washington.

They also furnish the President " with an official copy of the Ordinance of Secession," and intimate that they "*were* ready to negotiate" with him " upon all such questions as are necessarily raised by the adoption of this ordinance;" and they *had* hoped all things would go on well.

But the scene suddenly changes. " The events of the last twenty-four hours," say they, " render such an assurance impossible." What is the matter? Why, they hear that Major Anderson has " changed his base," and " retired" from Fort Moultrie to Fort Sumter. They complain bitterly; tell the President: " We came here the representatives of an authority which could, at any time within the past sixty days, have taken possession of the Forts in Charleston harbor;" but the game has flown. " Until these circumstances are explained," they say to the President, " we are forced to suspend all discussion as to any arrangement by which our mutual interests may be amicably adjusted."

And then, "in conclusion,"—for all documents must have an end,—they "urge upon" the President "the immediate withdrawal of the troops from the harbor of Charleston. Under present circumstances, they are a standing menace which renders negotiation impossible, and, as our recent experience shows, threatens speedily to bring to a bloody issue questions which ought to be settled with temperance and judgment."

The President makes a long reply; the Commissioners of the Palmetto "nation" put in a long rejoinder; and upon the latter the following indorsement is made: "This paper, just presented to the President, is of such a character that he declines to receive it." The inference is, that the President deemed the rejoinder insulting; and thus ends the first attempt at negotiation, and the last made by the South Carolina patriots.

Without going into an analysis of this correspondence, it is clear that the turning point of the case, and which occasioned the breaking down of the negotiation, was the change of the garrison under Major Anderson from Fort Moultrie to Fort Sumter. What would have happened, had not that occurred, no one can tell; but what did happen was occasioned by that movement.

THEIR DEMAND INSOLENT.

And now, what is here plainly involved? South Carolina claims to have "seceded," to be "out of the Union," to be a "sovereign and independent nation," self-created, "born in a day;" to have sprung like Minerva from the head of Jove, "armed in all the panoply of wisdom." For the argument's sake, grant it all. By her Ministers Plenipotentiary she complains that the soldiers of another nation are removed from one fort to another, both of which are confessedly its own. Had not the United States Government a right to order this change, without asking permission, or giving a reason to South Carolina, or anybody else? Who shall doubt it? If it had not, then the United States is not itself an independent nation. If it had, who shall complain, if the Government choose to give the order? Or, if Major Anderson took the initiative, and the Government thought fit to sustain him, the authority for the change was the same. If it be said that the United States is not a nation, but only an "agent of the Confederated States," as the Commissioners phrase it, the case is not altered; for, unquestionably, this is one of the very functions with which the "agent" is intrusted. The Government has supreme command of the army and navy, of the national forces and fortresses, of its ships and munitions of war. It cannot surrender this agency at the request or dictation of *one* of this "congeries of nations," without any regard to the will of the other thirty-three.

But the insolence of this newly-born "nation" does not stop here. It demands "the immediate withdrawal of the troops from the harbor of Charleston," and adds that "they are a standing menace which renders negotiation impossible." This is diplomacy on stilts; which, being interpreted, is this: We have come here on our own business to talk with you; evacuate your fortress, that our "nation" may take quiet possession, or we will not open our lips! And this is the *finale:* Unless this is done, the "questions" we have come to discuss will "speedily" be brought "to a bloody issue."

This is Southern statesmanship. This is South Carolina "negotiation." This is the diplomatic etiquette of chivalry. This, we suppose, is in part, at least, "the correspondence since made public," by which Dr. Smyth would make out the general charge against the Government, that the war "was provoked, threatened, perfidiously *commenced*, and openly proclaimed by the North;" and by which he would establish "the *defensive* character of the war of the South."

WHAT PRESIDENT BUCHANAN INTENDED.

But before we admit this aspect of the issue which Dr. Smyth presents, let us look a little more closely at this diplomacy. Dates here are important. The letter of the Palmetto Commissioners to President Buchanan, bears date, "Washington, Dec. 29, 1860." The President's reply was written the next day. He states that on hearing that Major Anderson had gone to Fort Sumter:

My first promptings were to command him to return to his former position; * * * *but before any step could possibly have been taken in this direction*, we received information that the "Palmetto flag floated out to the breeze at Castle Pinckney, and a *large military force went over last night* (*the* 27*th*) *to Fort Moultrie.*" Thus the authorities of South Carolina, without waiting or asking for any explanations, and doubtless believing, as you have expressed it, that the officer had acted not only without but against my orders, on the very next day after the night when the removal was made, *seized, by a military force, two of the Federal Forts in the harbor of Charleston*, and have covered them under their own flag instead of that of the United States. * * * On the very day, the 27th inst., that possession of these two Forts was taken, *the Palmetto flag was raised over the Federal Custom-House and Post-Office in Charleston.* * * * In the harbor of Charleston we now find three Forts confronting each other, over all of which the Federal flag floated only four days ago; but now, over two of them, this flag has been supplanted, and the Palmetto flag has been substituted in its stead. IT IS UNDER ALL THESE CIRCUMSTANCES THAT I AM URGED IMMEDIATELY TO WITHDRAW THE TROOPS FROM THE HARBOR OF CHARLESTON, AND AM INFORMED THAT WITHOUT THIS, NEGOTIATION IS IMPOSSIBLE. THIS I CANNOT DO—THIS I WILL NOT DO. * * * At this point of writing, I have received information by telegraph from Captain Humphreys, in command of *the arsenal at Charleston, that "it has to-day* (*Sunday, the* 30*th*) *been taken by force of arms.*" It is estimated that the munitions of war belonging to this arsenal are worth half a million of dollars.

HYPOCRISY OF THEIR PEACEFUL PRETENSIONS.

Now we have the *true altitude* of the diplomatic seat taken by the South Carolina envoys. Writing to the President on the 29th of December, they of course knew, as the whole community did, by telegraph, the occurrences of the 27th, at Charleston; and by private telegrams to themselves, undoubtedly, they knew a great deal more. They knew that Forts Moultrie and Pinckney, and the Custom-House and Post-Office, had all been "seized," by the employment of a "large military force" as far as necessary, and that the Stars and Stripes had been pulled down and the Rattlesnake flag run up, and the latter now floated over each of those structures owned by the United States; and they no doubt knew what was to happen the next day, when the arsenal would be "taken by force of arms," and the reptile banner cover that too.

Thus forewarned and forearmed, they propose to "negotiate" on behalf of the Palmetto "nation" which at home has adopted these little customary preliminaries to peaceful diplomacy, *provided always* the President will now on his part add to them one little item more which they deem indispensable; that is, cause "*the immediate withdrawal of the troops*" from the only remaining Fort in the harbor. "Negotiation" is absolutely "impossible" without this; and, unless this is done,—and here is the grand and amicable outcome,—"a bloody issue" will "speedily" result!

The ridiculous figure cut by these Falstaffian gentlemen and one of the "Great Powers" which they represent, as the world beholds it, ought to be in itself a sufficient castigation for their insolence; but when we see the studied and persistent attempt to substantiate the charge, in the face of such facts, that the Government sustained by the North was the aggressor, and the South was acting purely on the "defensive," the whining hypocrisy of such pretensions deserves the scorn of all honest men.

IRREFRAGABLE POSITION OF THE PRESIDENT.

Passing by the "ground and lofty tumbling" of the South Carolina envoys in the *rôle* of diplomats, the President presented an argument in his communication to them which was conclusive of the whole case. They had come as the representatives of a Foreign Power, to "negotiate." He told them he had no authority to meet them in that character, and he could only treat them and their mission accordingly. He refers them to his Annual Message to Congress, presented a short time before, at the beginning of the session, in which he says:

> Apart from the execution of the laws, so far as this may be practicable, the Executive has no authority to decide what shall be the relations between the Federal Government and South Carolina. He has been invested with no such discretion. He possesses no power to change the relations hitherto existing between them, much less to acknowledge the independence of the State. This would be to invest a mere Executive officer with the power of recognizing the dissolution of the Confederacy among our thirty-three sovereign States.

The Southern leaders, in Church and State, rest the strength of their case, in attempting to show their peaceful and the North's warlike disposition, upon the fact that the Government would not "negotiate;" that is, would not at once acknowledge their "secession," and recognize their independence of the United States. This was all they wanted. They "seceded," and only asked to be "let alone." They sent Commissioners from South Carolina, the leader in secession, to "negotiate" a partition of the public property of the Union. As above related, we have seen how this mission failed, and the immediate occasion of the failure.

Passing these incidents by, and coming to the root of the matter, what the South sought, *in the way* they sought it, could not be granted; for the President truly says he had been invested with no such authority. Nor had Congress. The Constitution gives no such power either to the Executive or Legislative branch of the Government; nor to both combined. The position of President Buchanan was therefore conclusive of the whole matter, as between the South Carolina Commissioners and the Government of the United States to which they were accredited.

There was but *one* conceivable way to reach the end sought by the secessionists, if they meant *peace.* Any other course than that one, was rebellion, revolution, and war. We shall speak of that one way, after noticing further negotiations which were attempted. All we need to say just here is, that *the Southern leaders never took one step toward the only possible way for a peaceful solution of the question of separation.*

FURTHER NEGOTIATIONS—CONFEDERATE COMMISSIONERS.

After seven States had seceded, the "Government of the Confederate States of America," as they styled it, was formed at Montgomery, Alabama.

After the inauguration of President Lincoln, that Government sent Commissioners to Washington. They were Messrs. Forsyth and Crawford. They arrive, and under date of "Washington City, March 12, 1861," they address a letter to Mr. Seward, the Secretary of State, in which they say: "The undersigned have been duly accredited by the Government of the Confederate States of America, as Commissioners to the Government of the United States;" and through the Secretary, they "make known to the President of the United States, the objects of their presence in this Capital." They proceed to state, that "seven States of the *late* Federal Union" have "*withdrawn* from the United States," and "have formed a Government of their own;" and they declare, that "the Confederate States constitute an independent nation, *de facto* and *de jure*, and possess a Government perfect in all its parts, and endowed with the means of self-support."

After giving this official information, they announce the great object of their mission thus:

> With a view to a speedy adjustment of *all questions* GROWING OUT OF *this political separation*, upon such terms of amity and good-will as the respective interests, geographical contiguity, and future welfare of the *two nations* may render necessary, the undersigned are instructed to make to the Government of the United States, overtures for the opening of negotiations, assuring the Government of the United States that the President, Congress, and people of the Confederate States, earnestly desire a peaceful solution of these great questions.

It can scarcely be supposed, for a moment, that these Commissioners, or the "Government" they represented, expected "negotiations" to be opened with them by the Government of the United States, based upon any acknowledgment, open or tacit, of the political status which they assumed to exist. After the failure to negotiate with Mr. Buchanan, on the ground which he announced to the South Carolina Commissioners,—that he had no authority in the case,—Messrs. Forsyth and Crawford could not have anticipated a different result with the Administration of President Lincoln, unless, possibly, they supposed the Government might be frightened into a recognition of their *de facto* and *de jure* "nation," by reason of the more formidable proportions which the rebellion had now assumed. But if such was their expectation, they soon learned their mistake.

Mr. Seward took respectful notice of their letter, in a "Memorandum" he penned and sent to them, though not signed officially or in any other way, but dated at the "Department of State," March 15, 1861. He declines their request for an official interview, saying it is, "upon exclusively public consideration, respectfully declined." He states that "he understands the events which have recently occurred, and the condition of political affairs," &c., "very differently from the aspect in which they are presented by Messrs. Forsyth and Crawford. He sees in them, not a rightful and accomplished revolution and an independent nation, with an established Government, but rather a perversion of a temporary and partisan excitement to the inconsiderate purposes of an unjustifiable and unconstitutional aggression upon the rights and authority vested in the Federal Government." The Secretary then says to those gentlemen that "he looks patiently but confidently for the cure" of existing evils, "not to irregular negotiations," prosecuted "in derogation of the Constitution and laws, but to regular and considerate action of the people of those States, in co-operation with their brethren in the other States, through the Congress of the United States, and such extraordinary Conventions, if there shall be need thereof, as the Federal Constitution contemplates and authorizes to be assembled." He then refers them to President Lincoln's Inaugural Address, from which they would perceive that he could not admit the political status they assumed,—"that the States referred to by them have, in law or in fact, withdrawn from the Federal Union,"—"or that they could do so in the manner described by Messrs. Forsyth and Crawford, *or in any other manner than with the consent and concert of the people of the United States, to be given through a National Convention*, to be assembled in conformity with the provisions of the Constitution of the United States." He closes his "Memorandum" by saying that the President "coincides generally in the views it expresses, and sanctions the Secretary's decision declining official intercourse with Messrs. Forsyth and Crawford."

PEACEFUL SOLUTION DECLINED.

The case was thus a plain one, as between war and peace. There was *one* course open for peaceful negotiations recognized by the Constitution. To that, the Government of the United States *was shut up;* but into that, though invited, the secessionists *would not enter.* If a possibility existed of a *peaceful* separation, through "negotiation," it was in the way the Secretary of State mentioned, and which the President in his Inaugural Address suggested,—through a National Convention of the people of all the States,—*and there was no other way under the Constitution.*

It is true, that the Constitution does not contemplate the disruption of the Union in any manner; does not provide for even *considering* the question of separation, or "secession;" it says nothing about it; and it may be that a National Convention, held under the provisions of the Constitution, would have no authority to entertain the question in any shape. It has been insisted, however, that, as the people in a National Convention made the Constitution, and the people of the several States ratified it, the people of the United States and of the several States have the power, through the same process, to undo the work of their hands, to take down the edifice they erected, and to dissolve the Union. If this be so, it is a *peaceful* mode of separation. But whether there be any Constitutional mode of separation or not,—and if there be, this seems to be the only one inferrible from the instrument itself,—*this was the course* to which the Administration in power was willing to resort, for the consideration of all grievances between the Government and the complaining States; and it was a measure of *peace.* But the Southern leaders *never took one step, or expressed any desire,* for a National Convention, but always spurned every suggestion of the subject.

Nor did they propose any other measure for a peaceful solution of the vital issue between them and the Government; that issue which was regarded as underlying all other questions in debate. But they took the ground, openly and defiantly, that they were "out of the Union" by their own act; that they were separated already from the jurisdiction of the United States; that they had "seceded," and that was the end of controversy. Suppose they were in fact right,—that "secession" was their proper remedy,—but yet that they could not convince the opposite party, the Government of the United States, of the truth of their position. There were then two parties to the case. The Government did not and could not agree with them. How, then, do honest men, *disposed to peace,* act, when they cannot agree? Before resorting to extreme measures, they exhaust every possible effort for a peaceful settlement. Did the South do this? Who could be an umpire, for a peaceful solution, between them and the Government? Only the whole people, represented in a National Convention. Did they agree to this? *They spurned it.* Did they propose any other measure? *None whatever.* Nothing short of a direct, full, immediate, unconditional *yielding* to them of the *whole case in controversy,* as one of the parties, would satisfy them. Does this carry on its front the compelling conviction that they were for *peace,* and the Government was for *war?*

Were this simple question submitted to any disinterested body of twelve men, in any nation under heaven, they would give a verdict against the rebel pretension.

UNJUSTIFIABLE REASONS FOR REFUSAL.

It may possibly be said, in answer to this, that the assembling of a National Convention would have been useless; that the majority of the people were no doubt against "secession," and with the Government, and therefore the South would not have obtained "their rights" in that manner.

To this we reply, *first*, that such an opinion could not justify a refusal to make the trial. Those who, if any, entertained it, might have found themselves mistaken. Our own conviction is, that had the whole people, represented in a National Convention, been brought face to face with the alternative of *some* peaceful settlement or civil war, one of two things would have occurred: either, propositions of "compromise" would have been agreed upon, satisfactory to the vast majority of the South,—which the Southern leaders no doubt feared,—or, a proposition for an amicable separation would have passed. We do not say that a "compromise," if subsequently ratified, would have been well. It would only have postponed the evil day. Nor do we say it would have been wise to dissolve this one nation and make two. It might have saved us the present strife, and its untold horrors, but numerous and bitter wars would no doubt have followed. All we mean to say, is, that we believe the people, compelled to face this "rugged issue," would have chosen the peaceful side of the alternative, in one of these two modes.

But, *secondly*, even if the Southern people had failed in Convention, either to gain a satisfactory "compromise" or an acquiescence in their "secession," and had thereupon felt compelled to withdraw from the Convention and enact and carry out "secession" in the way they are now doing, they would, in that case,—if able to exhibit a clear record of unendurable wrongs,—have made a far better showing, and would have had a deeper sympathy from the civilized world, than is now possible; and more especially so, in the matter of showing a disposition for *peace.*

But as the facts now stand, it is the baldest of all possible pretensions, the most naked and monstrous proposition ever penned by sober and Christian men, to assert that *they* were all the while for *peace*, while the *Government* was all the while for *war.* The Government was *driven* into war, to save its authority, to recover its property, to maintain its honor, to preserve its existence; and the Administration, constitutionally put in power by the people, could do no less, under its oaths of office, than to guard and defend these interests to the last. But the conspirators against the Government could not be *coaxed* or *goaded* into any measure for peace; but to be "let alone," after they had stolen all they could grasp, and would subvert forever the authority of the Government throughout half the territory of its jurisdiction, was the least of their modest demands.

THE COMMISSIONERS DEFIANTLY COURT WAR.

If any further evidence be desired to show the determination of the South for war, we find it officially certified, by the Confederate Commissioners. In reply to Mr. Seward's "Memorandum" of March 15th, 1861, they address him a long and their final note, dated April 9th. They assert that the people of seven States "have *rejected* the authority of the United States and established a Government of their own." Mr. Seward had referred them to a National Convention as the only Constitutional method for negotiation. Notwithstanding this, they complain, that, while they had come "with the olive-branch of peace," the Government,—which the Secretary of State had assured them had no authority in the premises,—would not treat with them, nor "recognize the great fact of a *complete and successful revolution.*"

To show whether the leaves of this "olive-branch" were fresh or withered, observe what they further say:

The undersigned would omit the performance of an obvious duty, were they to fail to make known to the Government of the United States, that the people of the Confederate States have declared their independence *with a full knowledge of all the responsibilities of that act*, and with as firm a determination to maintain it by all the means with which nature has endowed them, as that which sustained their fathers when they threw off the authority of the British crown. * * * The President of the United States knows that *Fort Sumter cannot be provisioned without the effusion of blood.*

That is, if the United States shall deign to send provisions to its starving garrison, they will, if possible, prevent it by force. This is the kind of "peace" in the interest of which these gentlemen present the "olive-branch," and for which they stand ready to "negotiate" if the President will but receive them.

A DIPLOMATIC QUIBBLE.

There is one feature of this diplomatic note which exhibits true Southern chivalry. The Commissioners say to the Secretary of State, that they understand him to decline any interview:

Because, to do so, would be to recognize the independence and separate nationality of the Confederate States. This is the vein of thought that pervades the memorandum before us. The truth of history requires that it should distinctly appear upon the record, that the undersigned *did not ask* the Government of the United States to recognize the independence of the Confederate States. They only asked audience to adjust, in a spirit of amity and peace, *the new relations springing from a manifest and accomplished revolution in the Government of the* LATE *Federal Union.*

How humiliating it is to see the Plenipotentiaries of a "first-class Power" resort to such miserable quibbling. In their first note, they declare at the opening, that they "have been *duly accredited* by the Government of the Confederate States," and they ask at the close, a day to be appointed, "in order that they may present to the President of the United States the *credentials* which they bear, and the *objects of the mission* with which they are charged." In their second and final note, they say to Secretary Seward, at its opening: "You correctly state the purport of the *official note* addressed to you by the undersigned on the 12th ult." They close this note by saying: "The undersigned, *Commissioners of the Confederate States of America*, having thus made answer to all they deem material in the memorandum filed in the Department on the 15th of March last, have the honor to be," &c. And throughout the body of both notes they assert the *nationality* of the "Confederate States" they represent, both *de facto* and *de jure*, and formally declare the grounds on which they assert such claim. And yet, in the face of all this, they declare that they "*did not ask* the Government of the United States to recognize the independence of the Confederate States."

What a paltry piece of finesse for "chivalric" gentlemen! Suppose they "did not ask" this, *in terms*, did not the whole proceeding on their part imply that such was their demand? And had the United States Government held any intercourse with them, without an express disclaimer, would it not have been pleaded as a virtual recognition? This is on a par with their pretension that they bear "the olive-branch of *peace*," while they threaten the Government with an "effusion of *blood*." It is like every thing else connected with "secession" from first to last,—a lie and a cheat; mendacity and hypocrisy, diplomatically combined.

It is further noticeable here, that these Commissioners had got beyond the "secession" stage of the fever, which is always claimed to be a *peaceful* type of this Southern malady. They speak of "seven States" having effected "a complete and successful *revolution*;" and of an "accomplished *revolution*," &c. They use these terms, not with reference to any aspect of the case occasioned by their failure to negotiate with the Government, nor in consequence of the hostile attitude which they charge the Government with having taken; but they claim this as the *status* of the seceded States from the first. "Secession," then, when defined by themselves, is "revolution;" and this revolution, like most others, was begun and has been carried on till now by acts of war. "Revolution," says a distinguished writer, "always implies rebellion, and rebellion is war."

PUBLIC FACTS DECIDE THE CASE.

But take any view of the case which the *facts* disclose; trace the history of the movement from the first demonstrations immediately after the Presidential election, November 6th, 1860, to the attack upon Fort Sumter, April 12th, 1861; call to mind the seizures of every description of the property of the United States, made at every stage between these dates, within rebel reach, upon land and water; note the pulling down of the United States flag from every place where it floated, on Custom-Houses, Post-Offices, Arsenals, Mints, Forts, and Vessels of War, and the unfurling upon them instead, the flags of the respective States where this public property was located, from the Potomac to the Rio Grande, and from the Missouri to Cape Sable; estimate the thousands of troops called out, mustered, organized, drilled, and equipped with all the munitions of war, in every State which seceded; observe the formation of the Confederate States Government, and the adoption of a Constitution other than that of the United States, and the establishment of the offices and the exercise of all the functions of an independent nationality; bear in mind that the seizures of this United States property and the organizing of these armies, first undertaken by the separate States, and afterwards sanctioned and adopted by the Government of the Confederate States, was for the purpose of maintaining the independent authority which this new Government had assumed; and then, having pondered the case well, let any honest man ask himself if all this means *peace?*—or, if this be not *revolution*, and these the movements which were undertaken to maintain and defend this revolution, by all the appliances of *war?*

That is one side. The other is equally clear, and more briefly told. The first act of war undertaken by the Government of the United States was on the 15th of April, 1861, in the calling out of the first body of troops; and that was done simply to repel the open assaults of its enemies, to recover its stolen property, and to maintain its rightful authority; with, even then, "twenty days" given, which might have prevented collision. No Government on earth, called as an umpire, could give any other judgment between the parties upon the simple question of peace and war.

REBEL CONDITIONS OF PEACE SINCE THE WAR BEGAN.

The rebels have talked much of a desire for peace, ever since the war has been in progress. To show on what terms they would conclude peace, we insert the conditions given in the *Richmond Enquirer*, of the 16th of October last. That paper says:

Save on our own terms we can accept *no peace whatever*, and must fight till doomsday rather than yield an iota of them; and our terms are: 1. Recognition by the enemy of the independence of the Confederate States. 2. Withdrawal of the Yankee forces from every foot of *Confederate ground, including Kentucky and Missouri*. 3. Withdrawal of the Yankee soldiers from *Maryland*, until that State shall decide by a free vote whether she shall remain in the old Union or ask admission into the Confederacy. 4. Consent on the part of the Federal Government to give up to the Confederacy its proportion of the Navy as it stood at the time of Secession, or to pay for the same. 5. Yielding up all pretension on the part of the Federal Government to that portion of the old Territories which lies West of the Confederate States. 6. An equitable settlement, on the basis of our absolute independence and equal rights, of all accounts of the public debt and public lands, and the advantages accruing from foreign treaties. * * * These provisions, we apprehend, comprise the *minimum* of what we must require before we lay down our arms. That is to say, THE NORTH MUST YIELD ALL —WE NOTHING. The whole pretension of that country to prevent by force the separation of the States must be abandoned, which will be equivalent to an avowal that our enemies *were wrong from the first;* and, of course, as they waged a causeless and wicked war upon us, they ought in strict justice to be required, according to usage in such cases, *to reimburse to us the whole of our expenses and losses in the course of that war.* Whether this last proviso is to be insisted upon or not, certain we are that *we cannot have any peace at all* until we shall be in a position not only to demand and exact, but also to enforce and collect treasure for our own reimbursement out of the wealthy cities in the enemy's country. In other words, unless we can destroy or scatter their armies, and *break up their Government, we can have no peace;* and if we can do that, then we ought not only to extort from them our own full terms and ample acknowledgment of their wrong, but also *a handsome indemnity* for the trouble and expense caused to us by their crime. * * * Once more we say, IT IS ALL, OR NOTHING. This Confederacy or the Yankee nation, one or the other, goes down, down to perdition. That is to say, one or the other must forfeit its national existence, and lie at the mercy of its mortal enemy. * * * As surely as we completely ruin their armies,—and without that, is no peace or truce at all,—so surely shall we make them pay our war debt though we wring it out of their hearts.

All *loyal* men will of course cheerfully accept the alternative here presented, that "one or the other" of these "nations" "goes down;" and that there can be peace in no other way. It has been our opinion from the beginning, that there is no other road to "peace" but to "conquer" it; to crush the military power of the rebellion, which means to crush the *leaders*. They will fight as long as they can keep their armies together; but the time may come when *the people*, who have been their dupes, will rise up and themselves dispose of them.

These "terms of peace" are instructive to two classes,—the truly *loyal* and the "peace" men. These "terms" undoubtedly express the views of the rebel leaders. They show to the loyal the utter hopelessness of any conditions emanating from the South, which can for a moment claim serious consideration; and they thus show the paramount duty of every citizen, in sustaining the Government in its efforts to crush the rebellion, that peace may be attained. They show to that class who are always crying "peace," and who are mourning over the grievous burdens of the Government, to what a repast of taxation and plunder they are invited by their Southern friends.

THE REBEL PRESIDENT AND REBEL CONGRESS ON PEACE.

These "terms" also explain what has been meant by the rebel President and his Congress when they have spoken of "peace," and when they have attempted to make capital for foreign consumption out of their complaints against the United States Government, that the precious boon could not be obtained by them.

In an "Address of Congress to the People of the Confederate States," issued from Richmond in February last, it is said:

> This cruel war has been waged against us, and its continuance has been seized upon as a pretext by some discontented persons to excite hostility to the Government. Recent and public as have been the occurrences, it is strange that a misapprehension exists as to the conduct of the two Governments in reference to peace. Allusion has been made to the unsuccessful efforts, when separation took place, to procure an amicable adjustment of all matters in dispute. These attempts at negotiation do not comprise all that has been done. In every form in which expression could be given to the sentiments,—in public meetings, through the press, by legislative resolves,—the desire of this people for peace, for the *uninterrupted enjoyment of their rights* and prosperity, has been made known.

We know what they regard as "their rights," and therefore know what kind of "peace" they have desired and manifested in all these modes. They are set forth in the "terms" above given.

Then the Address of this Congress goes on to say that President Davis has joined in this pervading "desire," and many times expressed it in his State papers:

> The President, more authoritatively, in several of his messages, while protesting the utter absence of all desire to interfere with the United States, or acquire any of their territory, has avowed that the "advent of peace will be hailed with joy. Our desire for it has never been concealed. Our efforts to avoid the war, forced on us as it was by the lust of conquest and the insane passions of our foes, are known to mankind."

And having thus spoken of their President, of themselves, and their people, they speak of the Government of the United States, as follows:

> The course of the Federal Government has proved that it did not desire peace, and would not consent to it *on any terms that we could possibly concede.* In proof of this, we refer to the repeated rejection of all terms of conciliation and compromise; to their recent contemptuous refusal to receive the Vice-President, who was sent to negotiate for softening the

asperities of the war; and their scornful rejection of the offer of a neutral power to mediate between the contending parties.

THEY MISREPRESENT THE CASE.

If the gentlemen composing the Congress that issued this Address, or Mr. Davis in his Message, can seriously believe that any person who understands the case will be duped by such representations, it is evidence that rebel infatuation has gone deeper into their souls than we had supposed. To protest, as they do, that there is in them an "utter absence of all desire to *interfere* with the United States, or acquire any of *their territory*," and to charge that "the lust of *conquest*" is the motive of the United States in prosecuting the war, is to assume the whole matter in dispute. They make it a *condition precedent* to negotiation for "peace," or even to negotiation "for softening the asperities of the war," that the United States shall *give up the vital point* at issue between the parties. If they will but do that, at the *outset*, then the door will be *open* for settling all matters of detail.

The whole question in issue is one involving *nationality*, and hence of territorial jurisdiction. The United States claim jurisdiction over the whole country. The Confederates claim jurisdiction over a part of it. Which claim is just, is not now material; nor is it material, here, which party began the war. The parties are *at* war, to determine the claim; the South fighting for their independence, the United States for maintaining their rule intact over the whole country.

These being the facts, the point in hand is, Which party is bent on war, and which is burning with a desire for peace? The "Confederate States" charge the United States with a wilful indisposition to peace, and a ferocious thirst for war; and insist, before all the world, that they are anxious for peace, and they only. The solution is simple. Our amazement is, that men, in their official acts and manifestoes, should not admit the truth in so plain a case. That the "*desire* for peace" is mutual, is unquestionable. The *determination* for "war" is also mutual, and the alternative on which its prosecution rests is the same with both parties; the "Confederate States" determined to prosecute it until they gain their independence, and establish their nationality unmolested over a part of the country, and the United States determined to prosecute it until they regain their rule over the whole country. So far as declarations and corresponding acts go, this mutual determination is as plain as terms can make any proposition. What the final result will be,—which party will carry out its determination to the end, and triumphantly, or whether either will,—are matters foreign to the present point.

Now in view of these indisputable facts, it is worse than idle for either party to monopolize *all* the "desire for peace," as the case now stands, and to charge the other with possessing the sole passion for "war." Both the desire and the determination mentioned are mutual, when we consider the ends at which the parties are aiming. We are, therefore, somewhat surprised that sensible men,—and Mr. Davis and his Congress claim to be sensible,—should make so lame an attempt, in official documents, to mislead the world on so plain a point; to charge that the United States are ferocious, while they are so lamb-like. The United States are ready for peace at any moment, *on their terms;* and the rebels are ready for peace *on their terms;* and, at present, both are determined for war, until their respective terms shall be granted.

This is *the whole case* as it now stands; and he who represents it otherwise, writes himself down a falsifier of the plainest public facts.

THE REAL QUESTION IGNORED BY THE REBELS.

While the question of *nationality* plainly underlies the whole contest, and while to settle it the war is prosecuted, the rebels constantly attempt to ignore this question. Mr. Davis does this in his Message above quoted, when insisting that the United States are prosecuting a war of "conquest." The rebel Congress do the same in their Address, as seen in their illustrations to prove the charge that the Federal Government "did not desire peace." They refer, as an example, to the "contemptuous refusal to receive the Vice-President, who was sent to negotiate for softening the asperities of the war." Why was he not received, and why is the "refusal" deemed "contemptuous?" Look at the facts.

Mr. Stephens was in James River, on a "Confederate steamer" called the *Torpedo,* with a "Confederate flag" flying. From that vessel, under a flag of truce, he sent a letter to an officer of the United States Navy, asking permission to come up to Washington in his vessel, and deliver his credentials, embracing a letter from Jefferson Davis, "President of the Confederate States," to Abraham Lincoln, President of the United States, and as a Minister of one Government to open negotiations with the other. This was in July, 1863. That is to say—*He was there in his official character as Ambassador, upon a national vessel of the Confederate States, bearing official dispatches from his Government to that of the United States, to negotiate upon matters of the highest national concern, namely, of peace and war.* This is the rebel view of the case.

Had he been received, in the manner sought, it would have been equivalent to a concession of all the rebels claimed on the simple issue of *nationality;* hence, his mission was declined. Because it was declined, the rebel Congress take it in high dudgeon, and pronounce it a "contemptuous refusal." The contempt consisted in not at once virtually acknowledging their nationality.*

Why not fight it out, gentlemen, as the question has been referred to the sword? Or, if tired of that, why seek to gain your end by a trick of diplomacy? If it was simply *Mr. Stephens* whom you wished to intrust with the negotiation,—an acknowledged statesman, of high character, and a man as likely to be received by the Government as any other prominent rebel leader,—why not send him *simply as* Mr. Stephens? But, plainly, it was Mr. Stephens as "Confederate States" *Ambassador*, whom you insisted should make his august approach to Washington. You would thus, if possible, gain the whole case by diplomacy, which might not be gained by the sword; and you would have the point acknowledged by the United States Government *at the start*, in order that negotiation might begin, or else you would pour complaints into the ears of all the earth.

* Mr. Davis's Letter of "Instructions to Mr. Stephens" is dated Richmond, July 2, 1863. He gives him also a "Letter of authority to the Commander-in-Chief of the Army and Navy of the United States," and it is "signed by me," Mr. Davis says, as "Commander-in-Chief of the Confederate Land and Naval forces." In the former document, Mr. Davis says: "If objection is made to receiving your Letter on the ground that it is not addressed to Abraham Lincoln as President, instead of Commander-in-Chief, &c., then you will present the duplicate Letter, which is addressed to him as President, and signed by me as President. To this Letter, objection may be made on the ground that I am not recognized to be President of the Confederacy. In this event, you will decline any further attempt to confer on the subject of your mission, as such conference is admissible only on the footing of perfect equality." With these documents in his pocket, Mr. Stephens sailed down James River, and addressed a note to Rear-Admiral Lee, of the United States Navy, dated, "Confederate States steamer Torpedo, on James River, July 4, 1863," in which he says: "I desire to proceed directly to Washington in the steamer Torpedo, commanded by Lieutenant Hunter Davidson, of the Confederate States Navy, no person being on board but the Hon. Mr. Ould and myself, and the boat's officers and crew." (Signed) "Alexander H. Stephens." These documents show the ground on which the respective parties were placed by the Richmond authorities, and what was required to be conceded by the United States Government, *antecedent* to the opening of negotiations.

When the question had been debated for two whole years, with powder and shot and shell, and the discussion was still going on in that manner, truly these kind gentlemen were very sensitive, if *such* "contemptuous" conduct could disturb them seriously.

REBEL OFFICIAL MENDACITY.

But there is something more serious here than this rebel charge of contempt. When these sensitive gentlemen charge that "the Federal Government would not consent" to peace "on any terms" that they "could possibly concede," and say, "in proof of this we refer to the repeated rejection of *all terms of conciliation and compromise*," the charge attains a seriousness which claims consideration. It is nothing short of the most deliberate and direct official mendacity. Do they, in their long and labored Address, *specify* any "terms of *compromise*," to which, they say, "we refer?" None whatever. Were there any such "terms" extant to which they *could* "refer?" None whatever. Did their authorities ever, in any shape, *propose* ANY "terms of conciliation and compromise?" Never, in a single instance. Let him who denies it, show it. Much less is the Federal Government guilty of "the repeated *rejection*," or even *one* "rejection" of any such "terms;" for, none such *were ever once made*. This is well known.

The whole question, as we have said, respects the claim of the Federal Government to the *entire* territory of the Union, and that of the "Confederate Government" to a *part* of it. The Federal Government has never proposed to "compromise" that question, and undoubtedly it never will. On the other hand, is it pretended that the rebel authorities have ever presented, in any way, even indirectly, "terms" that did not embody their claim to an independent nationality over a portion of the territory claimed by the Federal Government? No honest man will pretend this. What, then, have they proposed to "compromise," a rejection of which warrants them in charging that the United States "would not consent" to peace? *Nothing under heaven.* There has been no "compromise" on either side offered, touching the question of territorial jurisdiction,—the radical point at issue,—the only question which has broken peace, and the only question which continues war. We therefore speak plainly, but truly, when we say that this rebel charge is nothing short of an official and deliberate falsification of the truth; and no persons know it better than the rebel Congress who adopted this Address.

So, also, on another point, these chivalric gentlemen show an equal disregard of truth, where the plainest historical facts confront them. They say in this same Address: "Allusion has been made to the *unsuccessful* efforts, when separation took place, to procure an amicable adjustment of *all matters in dispute;*" and for this result, they hold the United States Government responsible. They of course allude in the phrase, "when separation took place," to the time and the "efforts" of the South Carolina Commissioners who corresponded with President Buchanan, and to those of the "Confederate States" Commissioners who corresponded with Secretary Seward, both of which cases we have already noticed. But, so far from those Commissioners proposing to negotiate upon "*all* matters in dispute," the matter which one party regarded as *the whole* question at issue,—the right of jurisdiction, in the Federal Government, over the whole territory of the Union,—neither set of those Commissioners opened, or would open, at all. They did not regard it, in any sense, as an open question, but in every sense as a question settled forever by the sole action of *one* of the parties, the authorities they represented. When the Secretary of State referred them to a National

Convention as the only tribunal for negotiation upon that question which the Federal Government regarded as the vital one, and as underlying "all matters in dispute," the Confederate Commissioners replied in a style which shows that diplomacy and negotiation were at an end. They say to the Secretary, in their final note:

> Persistently wedded to those fatal theories of construction of the Federal Constitution always rejected by the statesmen of the South, and adhered to by the Administration school, * * * you now, with a persistence untaught and uncured by the ruin which has been wrought, refuse to recognize the great fact presented to you of a *complete and successful revolution;* you close your eyes to the existence of the Government founded upon it, and ignore the high duties of moderation and humanity which attach to you in dealing with *this great fact.*

It thus appears, that in each and every instance of attempted negotiation, beginning with the South Carolina Commissioners and Mr. Buchanan, and coming down to the proposed visit of the Rebel "Vice-President," in July, 1863, and to the time of putting forth this Address by the Rebel Congress in February, 1864, the rebel authorities have uniformly adhered to their claim of nationality; and yet, in the face of all this, they pretend to have repeatedly offered "terms of conciliation and compromise," and directly charge the Federal Government with "the repeated rejection" of such terms.

In all the instances of plain, deliberate, unvarnished falsehood, both official and unofficial, which have characterized the leaders in this rebellion,—and they have been neither few nor far between,—this case of the Rebel President and the Rebel Congress is among those which are noteworthy; first, on account of its perfect stark nakedness, having not the least shadow of a basis to rest upon; and secondly, because it is a hypocritical whining to make an impression that they are the most peaceful and meek creatures upon earth.

The case is a simple one. The facts show that the South are responsible for beginning the war, as they are responsible for beginning the rebellion. They also show that both parties are ready for peace, when their terms can be granted; and that they are equally bent on war, in the hope that their ends may be gained.

ANOTHER EFFORT FOR PEACE.—NIAGARA FALLS CONFERENCE.

We have already seen that every movement, official and unofficial, on the part of the rebels, for peace, has been based on a dismemberment of the Union, and the recognition and establishment of the Southern Confederacy as a *separate nation*. From the beginning till now, while mourning over the horrors of the war, and attempting to fix the whole responsibility for its continuance upon the Government, the rebel leaders and their presses have insisted on this condition as a *sine quâ non* in any terms of peace; and generally, too, they have taken a course which involved this condition, as *antecedent* even to entering upon negotiations.

The case is not in the least altered by the latest efforts which have come to our knowledge. Mr. C. C. Clay, Jr., formerly in the United States Senate from Alabama, and Professor James P. Holcombe, lately of the Rebel Congress, from Virginia, met at Niagara Falls with Hon. Horace Greeley, of New York, about the middle of July, and held a consultation about terminating the war and settling conditions of peace. It was at first supposed, as appears from the correspondence which has been widely published, that Messrs. Clay and Holcombe were "duly accredited from Richmond, as the bearers of propositions looking to the establishment of peace." That impression was in some way made upon the mind of Mr. Greeley, and as he had been requested by them through a third person to obtain for them a safe-conduct to Washington, he communicated their desire to the President of the United States; and, thereupon, Mr. Greeley and the President's Private Secretary were promptly authorized to go to Niagara to consult with them, and to "tender" to them the President's "safe-conduct on the journey proposed," provided their character and mission were such as Mr. Greeley had imagined. It turned out, however, that they were not authorized by the Rebel Government. They wholly disavow any official character in which to conduct negotiations "looking to the establishment of peace," but declare that they are "in the confidential employment of their Government, and are entirely familiar with its wishes and opinions on that subject," and think, if they can be allowed to go to Washington and to Richmond, that they, or other gentlemen, "would be at once invested with the authority" to negotiate.

Mr. Greeley thereupon determined to "solicit fresh instructions" from the President. He immediately obtains them; and the President announces the terms on which he will receive and consider a proposition for peace "which comes by and with an authority that can control the armies now at war against the United States." No terms had been intimated, by Messrs. Clay and Holcombe, on which "their Government" would make peace, though they claimed to be "familiar with its wishes." Among the terms named by the President as a basis for negotiations, is that which has always lain at the bottom of the strife, and to maintain which the Government has been at war from the first, viz.: "the integrity of the whole Union." This has always been deemed the great and unalterable condition,—the maintenance of our *nationality*.

At this point, this conference on the part of the "confidential" employés of the Rebel Government breaks down. Jefferson Davis "controls the armies now at war against the United States," as the head of that "Government" with whose "wishes and opinions" on peace they "are entirely familiar." Knowing that "their Government" is unalterably determined on maintaining independence against "the integrity of the whole Union," they declare that their rulers "have no right to barter away their *priceless heritage of self-government.*" They also say for their people at large: "While an ardent desire for peace pervades the people of the Confederate States, we rejoice to believe that there are few, if any among them, who would purchase it at the expense of liberty, honor, and self-respect. If it can be secured only by their submission to terms of conquest, the generation is yet unborn which will witness its restitution." And so the affair terminates.

It thus appears from this last semi-official effort, conducted by these "confidential" gentlemen, that the rebel authorities and people, although anxious for peace, and anxious to throw the whole responsibility of continuing the war upon our Government and people, still insist, as the only possible basis for peace, on a total dismemberment of the Union, and a complete establishment of the Southern Confederacy as a separate nation.

MISSION TO RICHMOND.—PEACE AGAIN.

About the time that the Niagara Falls conference was in progress, a mission was undertaken by two gentlemen to the rebel capital, which has generally been understood to have some connection with movements for peace; or, at least, to ascertain, if possible, the temper of the Richmond authorities on that subject.

Whatever its object may have been, it is known that

Colonel Jaques, commanding an Illinois regiment in the Federal army, and Mr. James R. Gilmore, of Boston, made a visit to Richmond in July, and after having intercourse with the Rebel President and other officials, returned within the Union lines. Their mission was authorized or permitted by the Government at Washington, and they were passed through the lines of the army by General Grant. They were kindly and hospitably received, as they report, during their brief stay in Richmond, and had an opportunity to gain valuable information.

All that bears upon our immediate subject, so far as the object of this mission has been made public, is found in a letter of Mr. Gilmore, under date of July 22, 1864. Referring to the Niagara Falls conference, between Messrs. Greeley, Clay, and Holcombe, he says:

It will result in nothing. Jefferson Davis said to me last Sunday,—and, with all his faults, I believe him a man of truth,—"This war must go on till the last of this generation falls in his tracks, and his children seize his musket and fight our battle, *unless you acknowledge our right to self-government.* We are not fighting for slavery. We are fighting for *Independence*, and that, or extermination, we *will* have."

This statement shows, that the position taken by Mr. Davis as late as Sunday, the 17th of July, is *precisely the same in terms*, upon peace, as that declared by Messrs. Clay and Holcombe, in their final note to Mr. Greeley, under date at Niagara of July 21st. The great point which divides the parties is the same now as in the beginning, and is that which led to the war; the rebels determined on dividing the Union, destroying our nationality, and claiming "self-government and independence;" and our Government determined on maintaining our nationality and preserving "the integrity of the whole Union."

Whatever Mr. Davis,—who is indorsed by Mr. Gilmore as "a man of truth,"—may find it convenient to say at this late period, for private or public effect, for domestic or trans-Atlantic consumption, about their "not fighting for slavery," the world well knows,—the proof comes from the rebels themselves, and we have given it in full,—that "slavery" was the prompting cause which led them first to "secede" for "independence," and then to "fight" in order to establish it.

Our main purpose, however, in referring to these late movements upon peace, is to hold up the fact that it is *our nationality* which is at stake in the war; that the rebels will not *make* "peace," though they may constantly *clamor* for it, except on the condition of a total *destruction of the Union.* This is their *ultimatum*, and it has been their position from the first. We are free to say, that as to maintain "the integrity of the whole Union" was the position taken by our Government and people from the first, we hope this position will be held to the end. If on that issue the rebels, in the words of their President, court "extermination," then let them be exterminated.

We have said, as simply indicating our opinion, that we believed there would be no peace till it was *conquered* by a destruction of the rebel armies, and resulted in the complete triumph of the Government and the re-establishment of the national authority over every foot of the Union. This has been our conviction from the first, and it is our conviction still. And yet, we have many times seen it illustrated since the war began, that it is safest not to prophesy. It is possible that the leading conspirators may be willing to submit to the Government before their military power is totally overthrown, but we doubt it; and it is among the possible eventualities which may occur, as the result of the pending Presidential canvass, that the people may be willing, in order to spare the effusion of blood, to submit to a settlement on the basis of a recognition of the Rebel Confederacy; but we have much mistaken what we believe to be their fixed purpose if this shall be finally achieved. We shall therefore adhere to our earliest and present opinions, until the event shall prove them erroneous.

CHAPTER V.

RESPONSIBILITY OF THE SOUTHERN CHURCH FOR THE REBELLION AND THE WAR.

In charging the full responsibility for the rebellion upon the South, we must go back of the public actors on the political arena to find a proper lodgment for a large share of it.

Immediately upon the result of the Presidential election of 1860 being made known by the electric flash, the treasonable work began.

Upon the sixth of November (the day of the election) [says Dr. Palmer, speaking of the people of the seceded States generally], these masses went to bed as firmly attached to the Union as they had ever been, and awoke on the seventh, after Mr. Lincoln's election, just as determined upon resistance to his rule. The revolution in public opinion was far too sudden, too universal, and too radical, to be occasioned by the craft and jugglery of politicians. It was not their wire-dancing upon party platforms which thus instantaneously broke up the deep foundations of the popular will, and produced this spontaneous uprising of the people in the majesty of their supremacy; casting party hacks aside, who shall have no control over a movement not having its genesis in their machinations.

The substantial truthfulness, in good part, of what is here related, suggests the most painful and humiliating feature which the three years' progress of the rebellion exhibits. The above was published in April, 1861, in the *Southern Presbyterian Review*, of Columbia, South Carolina, before the attack upon Fort Sumter. At that time the secession of seven States had occurred. As stated in a former chapter, it is well known that a majority of the people in nearly every one of the seceded States was at first against secession; that in fact many of the States were carried out by violence, and in direct opposition to the will of the people; and that, as regards the most of them, their ordinances of secession were not submitted to a popular vote. Dr. Palmer's language is therefore altogether too sweeping, as to the suddenness and universality of the change in the popular sentiment of even the seven States to which he refers. It did not become "universal" and "radical" for secession till long afterwards, even if there has not always been, as indeed facts assure us, a strong Union element in the seceded States. Writing in the spring of 1861, he gives the impressions which things then occurring about him made upon his enthusiastic nature, rather than the facts as they existed immediately after the Presidential election.

The Gulf States had then seceded; the Provisional Government at Montgomery had been inaugurated; the batteries of his own native Carolina were thickly gathering around beleagured Sumter; their opening upon the devoted fortress was anxiously awaited, to bring the Old Dominion and other States into the ranks of treason; and already Southern orators were painting the visions of coming glory which would soon burst in full-orbed splendor upon the great Slave Empire of the Gulf. The eloquent divine was too much dazzled by that bewildering present and its glowing future to be a safe chronicler of the events of even the then recent past.

But admitting substantially what he declares on this point (only with abatement as to *time*), and freely conceding that "the revolution in public opinion" was by no means "occasioned by the craft and jugglery of politicians," we are then led to inquire, what mysterious and potent agency it was which "broke up the deep foundations of the popular will," and which, if it did not assume, by "casting party hacks aside," absolute control over a movement not having "its genesis in their machinations," did at least furnish the intellectual and moral pabulum upon which the popular appetite was feasted, and the popular strength nerved for the dark deeds which were before it? We would know who is to be held *chiefly responsible*, when we are told that "the deep foundations of the popular will" were broken up in a single night, and that the great popular heart, hitherto "firmly attached to the Union," was so suddenly, by a "spontaneous uprising of the people in the majesty of their supremacy," brought to abjure the Union, and to love all that was treacherous and perjured and vile!

There must have been some powerful cause for this, of which he does not inform us. The people never act without leaders, in a revolution or in any other great movement. We have no difficulty in finding the secret which perhaps Dr. Palmer's modesty would withhold. His own teachings, in good part, and the teachings of others of his own profession, furnish the mournful answer to these astounding questions.

[The real truth of the case deliberately and solemnly holds the Southern Church and the Southern ministry,—or the Southern ministry, with a few influential laymen, leading the Southern Church, and they together leading the more influential portion of the Southern millions,—to a vastly higher responsibility for the inception, advocacy, progress, and the consequences resulting, of this treason and rebellion, than any other class among the Southern people; and, in asserting this, we but agree with Southern statesmen, whose testimony, to be given in due time, corroborates what the palpable facts so fully and lamentably declare.]

EARLY AGENCY OF LEADING DIVINES.

To substantiate this grave indictment, it is only necessary to notice events in the order of their occurrence, at the beginning of the rebellion and for the few months which immediately succeeded. The Presidential election occurred on the sixth of November, 1860, and the ferment in South Carolina commenced immediately after, and soon spread into other States. The State authorities of South Carolina,—who, we presume, are included by Dr. Palmer among those that on the sixth of November "went to bed as firmly attached to the Union *as they had ever been* (for thirty years at least), and awoke on the seventh, after Mr. Lincoln's election, just as determined upon resistance to his rule,"—were not at least then so taken up with "their wire-dancing upon party platforms," that they could not think upon their schemes with what we must charitably suppose was some little serious concern; and so they appointed a State Fast for the twenty-first of November, just fifteen days after the election. We have the sermon which was preached on that day by Dr. Thornwell, at Columbia, the State capital.

REV. JAMES H. THORNWELL, D. D., AIDS THE REBELLION.

All who have known the preacher, and the reputation he had, know that he was a man of master mind and commanding influence. He combined logical acuteness, strength in argument, perspicuity of style, and oratorical power, as they are found in but very few men. He was idolized and honored both in and out of the Church, in his native State and elsewhere, for his great natural abilities, profound attainments, and ripe scholarship. We cannot detract from his fair fame in any of these respects, nor have we the least disposition to do so. He was in all respects a very eminent man. In the South he was called "the Calhoun of the Church." He had been President of the State College at Columbia, had often preached before the South Carolina Legislature, at their request, and was, at the time the rebellion began, a Professor in the Theological Seminary of the Presbyterian Church at Columbia.

As his work is done on earth, and he has departed this life, we cannot say any thing disparaging to his memory, further than a condemnation of his sentiments and great influence, as giving early and efficient aid to a most wicked rebellion, may be construed as doing so. We know of no principle in ethics, however, which would justly condemn a candid examination at the present time of what he wrote and published, and the holding of the influence which he exerted in favor of the rebellion to its just measure of responsibility, which would not also condemn the animadversion of the historian a hundred years hence. In what we say, therefore, here and elsewhere, we shall exhibit no squeamishness in dealing with his views. We admired him when living, and for the same qualities we admire him now, dead; and simply of the *man* we can sincerely say, *Requiescat in pace.* But his published sentiments upon the rebellion, as upon every other subject, are the property of the public.

This sermon of Dr. Thornwell, preached so soon after the Presidential election, and only wanting a day of one full month before the secession of the State of South Carolina and the assembling of her Convention, enters into and urges the whole doctrine of secession on the ground of Constitutional right, the alleged encroachment upon slavery being given as the justifying cause. We need not say that this work was done with ability. It could not be done otherwise, when the preacher attempted to lay out his strength. We give only a sentence or two from this discourse, the object being simply to show his *position* rather than his argument, as our only aim here is to present the simple fact of *responsibility*, as seen in the order of time. An article published soon after, to which we shall subsequently refer, presents his *argument* for secession more fully, justifying it on the same ground here assumed, the alleged encroachments upon slavery.

HIS FAST-DAY DISCOURSE, NOV. 21, 1860.

In his sermon he says:

> The Union which our fathers designed to be perpetual, is on the verge of dissolution. A name once dear to our hearts, has become intolerable to entire States. Once admired, loved, almost adored, as the citadel and safeguard of freedom, it has become, in many minds, synonymous with oppression, with treachery, with falsehood, and with violence. The Government to which we once invited the victims of tyranny from every part of the world, and under whose ample shield we gloried in promising them security and protection—that Government has become hateful in the very regions in which it was once hailed with the greatest loyalty.

The cause of this feeling in the South is thus stated:

> There is one subject, however, in relation to which the non-slaveholding States have not only broken faith, but have justified their course upon the plea of conscience. We allude to the subject of *slavery*. They have been reluctant to open the Territories to the introduction of slaves, and have refused to restore fugitives to their masters. * * * I shall restrict myself to our dealings with the institution which has produced the present convulsions of the country, and brought us to the verge of ruin. [And near the close he warns his hearers, that, for the sake of "the institution," they may have to meet the horrors of war and carnage—prophetic, and awfully true:] Even though our cause be just, and our course approved of Heaven, *our path to victory may be through a baptism of blood.* Liberty has its martyrs and confessors, as well as religion. The oak is rooted amid wintry storms. * * * Our State may suffer; she may suffer grievously; she may suffer long. Be it so: we shall love her all the more tenderly and the more intensely, the more bitterly she suffers.

The foregoing sentences, to which many in a similar strain might be added, show the key-note thus early struck. How eloquent and earnest men become,—and the ministers of religion, too,—when pleading for "slavery" in the name of "liberty," and braving all the miseries of war for its sake!*

HE VINDICATES THE SECESSION OF SOUTH CAROLINA.

South Carolina seceded on the 20th of December, 1860. Immediately after, Dr. Thornwell wrote his elaborate vindication of the act, reviewing the "Ordinance" and "Declaration of the Immediate Causes," &c., put forth by the Convention. It was published in the *Southern Presbyterian* (Quarterly) *Review*, for January, 1861. It was regarded by Southern statesmen as by far the ablest paper written on the subject, and several editions were published and sown broadcast over the South. In this article he says:

* An event showing Dr. Thornwell's *animus* about secession, occurred still earlier. The Presidential electors in South Carolina are chosen by the Legislature instead of by the people. The Legislature met on the day of election (Nov. 6th, 1860) to choose electors. Dr. Thornwell opened the session with prayer. We have this prayer, at length, as taken at the time from a Southern paper. In the midst of much that is excellent, these sentences are found, which, considering the time, occasion, and circumstances, are significant of what soon after became open treason and rebellion: "O God! the destiny of this country may turn upon the events of a few short hours." "Give wisdom to all our assemblies; give the spirit of a sound mind to the members of this Confederacy, and grant that Thy name may be glorified. If it be Thy will that a different destiny awaits us, we ask Thy blessing upon our Commonwealth." "We beseech that Thy favor may rest upon all those States that have a common interest with us. We beseech Thee that they may be bound together in the holy ties of truth, justice, and love. Give us, we beseech Thee, an honorable name among the nations of the earth." Dr. Thornwell avowed himself for rebellion even earlier than election day, by at least some six months. When the General Assembly of the Presbyterian Church was sitting in Rochester, New York, in May, the news of Mr. Lincoln's nomination at Chicago, just then made, became a topic of conversation. Dr. Thornwell declared that if either Mr. Lincoln or Mr. Douglas were elected, the Southern States would inevitably secede; that neither was acceptable to the South; that secession was a foregone conclusion; and that the South would not and ought not to acquiesce in the election of either.

South Carolina has now become a separate and independent State. She takes her place as an equal among the other nations of the earth. This is certainly one of the most grave and important events of modern times. It involves the destiny of a continent, and, through that continent, the fortunes of the human race.

This fixes the writer's own estimate of the responsibility which he and his fellow-clergymen assumed in taking the lead in a matter so momentous.

He then proposes to declare "the causes which have brought about this astounding result;" declares, "that there was a cause, and an adequate cause, might be presumed from the character of the Convention which passed the ordinance of secession, and the perfect unanimity with which it was done;" that "it embraced the wisdom, moderation, and integrity of the bench, the learning and prudence of the bar, *and the eloquence and piety of the pulpit*;" and then says, showing the cause to be what we have before stated, that it was "the universal sentiment of all, that the Constitution of the United States has been virtually repealed, and that *every slaveholding State has just ground for secession*." He then, in view of the fact assumed, "that the Constitution, *in its relations to slavery*, has been virtually repealed," says: "If this point can be made out, *secession becomes not only a right, but a bounden duty*." Such is the burden of the argument which pervades the entire article.

OPEN RESISTANCE COUNSELLED.

The following sentences will show still further, from the same article, how *open resistance* to the Government was urged at this early period by this stanch Churchman, and the responsibility which he, as an influential leader of God's people, thus voluntarily assumed:

Now, we say that this state of things is *not to be borne*. A free people can never consent to their own degradation. * * * If, therefore, the South is not prepared to see her institutions surrounded by enemies, and wither and decay under these hostile influences; if she means to cherish and protect them, *it is her bounden duty to resist* the revolution which threatens them with ruin. The triumph of the principles which Mr. Lincoln is *pledged to carry out*, is the death-knell of slavery.*

More exhortations to open resistance are found in this article:

[If the South could be induced to submit to Lincoln, the time, we confidently predict, will come when all grounds of controversy will be removed in relation to fugitive slaves, by expunging the provision under which they are claimed. The principle is at work and enthroned in power, whose inevitable tendency is to secure this result. *Let us crush the serpent in the egg.* * * * We know it to be the fixed determination of them *all* (the slaveholding States), *not to acquiesce* in the principles which have brought Mr. Lincoln into power. * * * The evil day may be put off, but it must come. *The country must be divided into two people*, and the point which we wish now *to press upon the whole South*, is the importance of *preparing at once for this consummation.* * * * Conquered we never can be. * * * *To save the Union is impossible.* * * * We prefer peace—*but if war must come*, we are prepared to meet it with unshaken confidence in the God of battles.]

CHARGE OF TREASON ESTABLISHED.

The foregoing is sufficient to show the influence which the powerful pen of Dr. Thornwell gave to secession, when it was yet in its embryo state, with the exception of South Carolina. If these utterances are not,—morally and before God, and by the Constitution and laws,—*instinct with treason*, then it is difficult to define the term. The Constitution of the United States ("to which," even Dr. Thornwell admits, "these States swore allegiance") says:

* We have shown in previous pages, by documentary proof, that so far from Mr. Lincoln having been "pledged to carry out" any "principles" which would interfere with the rights of the States over slavery, he was "pledged" to do just the contrary; by all the speeches he made and letters he wrote when a candidate, by the platform of the party that nominated him, by his letter of acceptance, by his Inaugural Address, and by all else he said and did.

"Treason against the United States shall consist only in levying war against them, or in adhering to their enemies, giving them aid and comfort." Dr. Thornwell's writings and speeches show an adherence to the "enemies" of the Government, and were a powerful incitement to the "war" now raging; were so used, and thus gave the most substantial "aid and comfort" to rebels in arms,—that of *moral* countenance and earnest support, the most essential element of success, and without which powder and lead and all other "aid" are worthless.

But how civil tribunals would regard such a case, is not with us the chief question. By the doctrines of religion, and before the bar of God, he was guilty of one of the highest crimes against the State,—God's own ordinance,—which any man can commit. That he was sincere, we do not doubt, but that does not relieve his criminality. He was a minister of the Gospel, of the highest ability and influence. He is largely responsible for bringing *the Church*, —one of the most powerful elements of society,—to "aid" in the horrid work of treason, rebellion, and war.

DRS. THORNWELL, LELAND, AND ADGER, UPON THE STUMP.

[In addition to the power of his pen, Dr. Thornwell gave his eloquent voice to the cause of treason, at a meeting held at the capital of South Carolina, to ratify her secession.]

In the *North Carolina Presbyterian*, of January 5, 1861, is found a letter from "a student of Columbia Seminary," detailing the proceedings of "the great ratification meeting," held at Columbia, "which was called to indorse the action of the Convention." He says: "Many of the clergy were called on to express their views in regard to this important matter. Rev. Drs. Thornwell, Leland, Adger (all Professors in the Theological Seminary), and

Reynolds, and Rev. Messrs. Mullaly and Brecker, addressed the meeting." This shows how early, and how extensively, *the clergy of the South* became the open advocates of treason and rebellion. The writer then gives an account chiefly of Dr. Thornwell's speech, as follows:

> Dr. Thornwell spoke at some length. He said that he had foreseen, and some time ago predicted, the course which our affairs would take, in case that Lincoln, or any other man with his avowed principles, was elected President. As to the right of secession, he said that he held that the election of Lincoln is equivalent to presenting a new Constitution to the States, and asking them to subscribe to it. Secession is only refusing to abolish the old and adopt the new Constitution now presented to us by the Black Republican party. The avowed principles of this party are not constitutional, and its success in electing the President of the United States upon principles which, if carried into effect, will subvert the National Constitution, and trample it under foot, and set up a sectional one in its stead, is equivalent to putting the question to the States, Will you submit to this new Constitution or not? Secession is the refusal to submit, and is therefore not unconstitutional. The Constitution to which these States swore allegiance has been wrested from us, and something else, gotten up by a sectional party, is presented to us in its stead. He advised that the State act with calmness, caution, and decision, and so demean herself towards her sister Southern States, as to secure, if possible, their co-operation with us. He believed that all our sister Southern States would co-operate with us, and that we would be permitted to withdraw peaceably from the United States. He hoped to see two Republics standing side by side, and becoming all the greater, by the honest rivalry that would exist between them. Rashness and temerity on our part would repel our sister States from us, which are one with us,—one in race, one in institutions, one in interest, and we believe that they should be one in a separate, Southern Confederacy. All the other speeches were of a similar tone, and breathed the same spirit. I think I can safely say, that this report expresses the sentiment of the people of this State.

Dr. Thornwell admits that "the *States* swore allegiance to the Constitution;" then they *violated* that "allegiance" by *secession*.

EARLY AID OF REV. B. M. PALMER, D. D.

The influence of Dr. Palmer was publicly given in favor of secession only eight days after Dr. Thornwell's Fast-Day discourse was preached. On the day of the State Thanksgiving in Louisiana, the 29th of November, 1860, he preached in New Orleans a discourse (before quoted), in which he vehemently urged secession, justifying it on the same ground taken by Dr. Thornwell, the apprehensions of governmental interference with slavery.

DR. PALMER AND THE MISSION OF SENATOR TOOMBS.

We have heard related an occurrence of singular significance connected with this Thanksgiving service. We cannot personally vouch for its truth, but its authority is said to be the Hon. Miles Taylor, a member of the United States House of Representatives of the Congress of 1860–61, and among the last of the Union members from Louisiana to give up his seat after the secession of that State. The case strongly illustrates the estimate which Southern statesmen had of the ability of the Church to aid the rebellion, the necessity they felt of enlisting the Christian portion of the community in leading the way, and the ready compliance of an eloquent divine with their wishes.

It is well known that a strong Union sentiment existed in Louisiana, and especially in New Orleans, long after secession had carried over other States, and that the vote of the people of Louisiana, when it was finally taken, was actually against secession, and was never officially declared. So important was it deemed to have New Orleans move in the matter early, that Mr. Robert Toombs, of Georgia, still holding his seat in the United States Senate, and occupying it long afterwards, was sent with other distinguished gentlemen on a mission to that benighted city, to stir up its sluggish waters. He went and surveyed the ground, canvassing the matter with leading citizens privately, but met with little success. He was about to abandon the field of his missionary enterprise in despair.

At length, it was agreed that Dr. Palmer should be sounded by some of his friends, and it was found that he was willing to break ground publicly. He entered on the work *con amore*, and preached on Thanksgiving Day. The result is known. Previous to the 29th of November, Mr. Toombs, in the *rôle* of a missionary, was likely to prove a sad failure. True, indeed, his native abilities, education, long course of training, and other qualifications for the peculiar work in hand, were of a high order, but he could make no headway, and could scarcely get a congregation to hear his discourses. He had only mistaken his field. He had come among a people where the heresy of fealty to the Union was too deeply rooted for *him* to eradicate. They abjured *this* kind of "political preachers." They must first hear the new Gospel, founded on slavery as the chief "corner-stone," from the pulpit rather than the rostrum. Dr. Palmer supplied what Mr. Toombs lacked, and the effect was sudden and wonderful. Mr. Toombs had sown some seed, but Dr. Palmer gathered an immediate harvest. It was found, after the delivery of his sermon, that the secession mania spread like fire in a prairie; a great revival of the spirit of latent treason occurred, and conversions to the new faith were greatly multiplied.

Dr. Palmer's congregation, by far the largest and most influential in the city, were mostly taken by surprise, and some among its leading men at first strongly dissented. But his eloquence, always of a high order of a certain kind, carried the mass of his hearers captive, and the dissentients at length for the most part yielded. His discourse was immediately published, not only in New Orleans, but in Georgia and South Carolina, and spread over the South far and wide. We have in our possession copies of it from several different editions. This was the work of November, 1860.

SPECIMEN OF HIS THANKSGIVING DISCOURSE.

A few passages from this discourse are here given, simply to show *the lead which the Church took*, through her ablest ministers, at the earliest moment, and before the secession of a single State. His treasonable exhortations are found in the introduction, and pervade every part of his discourse. We give a sample of them:

In the triumph of a sectional majority, we are compelled to read the probable doom of our once happy and united Confederacy. * * * The hour has come. At a juncture so solemn as the present, with the destiny of a great people waiting upon the decision of an hour, it is not lawful to be still. *Whoever may have influence to shape public opinion*, at such a time must lend it, or prove faithless to a trust as solemn as any to be accounted for at the bar of God.

Truer words were never spoken, both as to the *duty* and the *responsibility*. Dr. Palmer had such influence; but how disastrously did he use it! But hear him further:

Is it immodest in me to assume that I may represent a class whose opinions in such a controversy are of cardinal importance—the class which seeks to ascertain its duty in the light simply of conscience and religion, and which turns to the moralist and the Christian for support and guidance? The question, too, which now places us upon the brink of revolution, was, in its origin, a question of morals and religion.* It was debated in ecclesiastical councils before it entered Legislative halls. * * * The right determination of this primary question will

* Why cannot Prof. Christy, and all that class of Northern "allies" of the South, as Jefferson termed such men in his day,—who are ever declaiming, when the Church takes action upon slavery, that she is meddling with that which does not properly concern her,—learn a lesson here from their friends? Dr. Palmer allows *slavery*, the "question" to which he here refers, a place within the domain of "morals and religion;" but they call it "politics."

go far towards fixing the attitude we must assume in the coming struggle.

How clearly does he recognize the fact that the people of God, and the mass of the community too, look to their religious teachers for guidance; and how momentous must be the guilt if they lead them astray,—into treason, rebellion, and war, against lawful authority embodied in a Government which their own ablest statesmen declared, *during the very month* when Dr. Palmer preached, had done the South no manner of harm!*

* Mr. Stephens, the rebel Vice-President, in a speech before the Georgia Legislature, November 14, 1860, says: "The first question that presents itself is, Shall the people of the South secede from the Union in consequence of the election of Mr. Lincoln to the Presidency of the United States? My countrymen, *I tell you frankly, candidly, and earnestly, that I do not think they ought.* * * * To make a point of resistance to the Government; to withdraw from it, when a man has been constitutionally elected, puts us in the wrong. We are pledged to maintain the Constitution. Many of us have sworn to support it. * * * Let not the South, let us not be the ones to commit the aggression. We went into the election with this people. The result was different from what we wished; but the election has been constitutionally held. Were we to make a point of resistance to the Government, and go out of the Union on that account, the record would be made up hereafter against us. * * * I do not anticipate that Lincoln will do any thing to jeopard our safety or security. * * * He can do nothing unless he is backed by power in Congress. The House of Representatives is largely in the majority against him. In the Senate he will also be powerless. There will be a majority of four against him. * * * Why, then, I say, should we disrupt the ties of this Union when his hands are tied, when he can do nothing against us? * * * My countrymen, I am not of those who believe this Union has been a curse up to this time. * * * *This Government of our fathers, with all its defects, comes nearer the objects of all good Governments than any other on the face of the earth. This is my settled conviction. Contrast it now with any on the face of the earth.* * * * *This Model Republic is the best which the history of the world gives any account of.* * * * Where will you go, following the sun in his circuit round the globe, to find a Government that better protects the liberties of its people, and secures to them the blessings we enjoy? I think that one of the evils that beset us is a surfeit of liberty, an exuberance of the priceless blessings for which we are ungrateful. * * * Suppose it be admitted that all of these are evils in the system, do they overbalance and outweigh the advantages and great good which this same Government affords, in a thousand innumerable ways that cannot be estimated? Have we not at the South, as well as at the North, grown great, prosperous, and happy under its operation? Has any part of the world ever shown such rapid progress in the development of wealth, and all the material resources of national power and greatness, *as the Southern States have under the General Government, notwithstand-*

RESISTANCE COUNSELLED.—THE LAST DITCH.

But to proceed with this traitorous and war-exhorting discourse. On speaking of the "trust" committed to the South, "to preserve and transmit our existing system of domestic servitude," he says:

This trust we will discharge in the face of the worst possible peril. Though war be the aggregation of all evils, yet, should the madness of the hour appeal to the arbitration of the sword, we will not shrink even from the baptism of fire. If modern crusaders stand in serried ranks upon some plain of Esdraelon, there shall we be in defence of our trust. *Not till the last man has fallen behind the last rampart*, shall it drop from our hands; and then only in surrender to the God who gave it.

This, we presume, is the true origin of the favorite phrase,—so far as the present war is concerned,—which has filled so large a space in Southern belligerent literature, of "dying in the *last ditch*." As to the "surrender" of the "trust" of preserving and transmitting slavery, for which the rebellion was undertaken, events look very much as though God had already made the demand.

WAR WELCOMED.—THE UNION DENOUNCED.

But there is more treason and war here, and so much indeed that one can almost take the sentences at random:

The moment must arise when *the conflict must be joined*, and victory

ing all its defects? * * * This appeal to go out, with all the provisions for good that accompany it, I look upon as a great, and I fear a fatal temptation. When I look around and see our prosperity in every thing, agriculture, commerce, art, science, and every department of education, physical and mental as well as moral advancement, and our colleges, I think, in the face of such an exhibition, if we can without the loss of power, or any essential right or interest, remain in the Union, it is our duty to ourselves and to posterity to do so."

While this FOREMOST STATESMAN of the South was thus truthfully portraying before the Georgia Legislature the blessings of the Union, and the great prosperity and good of every kind, to every part of the country, resulting from the action of the General Government, THE LEADING CLERGYMEN of the South, in that very month of November, were, from the pulpit and the press, striving to bring that Government into contempt in the eyes of all men, and were exhorting to treason and rebellion against it, braving defiantly all the horrors of war!

decide for one or the other. * * * Is it possible that we can hesitate longer than a moment? In our natural recoil from *the perils of revolution*, and with our clinging fondness for the memories of the past, we may perhaps look around for something to soften the asperity of the issue, for some ground on which we may defer the day of evil, for some hope that the gathering clouds may not burst in fury upon the land.

Then, after answering the objections of those who might be supposed to be not quite ready for the wicked work to which he exhorts them, and to strengthen the timid, he proceeds:

But the plea is idle. * * * I say it with solemnity and pain, *this Union of our forefathers is already gone.* * * * I throw off the yoke of this Union as readily as did our ancestors the yoke of King George III., and for causes immeasurably stronger than those pleaded in their celebrated Declaration.

Then, after replying to other objections of the wavering and the Union-loving, he urges "the Southern States" to "reclaim the powers they have delegated;" to "take all the necessary steps looking to separate and independent existence;" and "thus, prepared for every contingency," to "let the crisis come." Fearing that these exhortations may not be effective, he flatters Southern pride a little:

The position of the South is at this moment sublime. If she has grace given her to know her hour, she will save herself, the country, and the world. It will involve, indeed, temporary prostration and distress; the dikes of Holland must be cut to save her from the troops of Philip. But I warn my countrymen, the historic moment, once passed, never returns.

THE PROPHECY FULFILLED UNEXPECTEDLY.

It is a noticeable fact, and finds its illustrations all over the Southern rebel States, that the very evils which the rebels imagined were to be averted by their revolt, are the evils which their rebellion has brought upon them. Dr.

Palmer, in view of the consequences of "submitting to Lincoln," thus warns:

> Our children will go forth beggared from the homes of their fathers. Fishermen will cast their nets where your proud commercial navy now rides at anchor, and dry them upon the shore now covered with your bales of merchandise. Sapped, circumvented, undermined, *the institutions of your soil will be overthrown;* and within five-and-twenty years, the history of St. Domingo will be the record of Louisiana.

The picture here drawn of New Orleans is wellnigh true, but from "resistance" rather than "submission," and much sooner than was anticipated; and so of the South at large. We hope the horrors of St. Domingo are not to be added to what they already suffer, but if they are, posterity will blame none but the rebels themselves.

On the last page of this eloquent utterance of treason, Dr. Palmer says:

> *I am impelled to deepen the sentiment of resistance in the Southern mind,* and to strengthen the current now flowing toward a union of the South in defence of her chartered rights. It is a duty which I shall not be called to repeat, for such awful junctures do not occur twice in a century.

HIS SERMON STEEPED IN SIN, GUILT, AND CRIME.

No man who has correct ideas of the moral responsibility of a minister of the Gospel in the pulpit,—to God and religion, to society and civil government,—can rise from the perusal of this discourse, delivered at such a juncture and in such a place, without a painful sense of the great guilt of making such an utterance. Our hope is, that such men may see the sin and repent of it before they die. IT WAS A SIN, AND AN EXHORTATION TO SIN.

It will be seen from the date of the discourse, that *three weeks* before the secession of the first State, and before any public movement for secession had been made in New Orleans, and while the masses of the people there were still strongly attached to the Union, as is known by the Union meetings which were held long afterwards, Dr. Palmer threw himself into the van and made these bold utterances for treason. He mounted the very crest of the wave and became the king of the storm.

HE FURTHER VINDICATES SECESSION.

In April, 1861, Dr. Palmer published in the *Southern Presbyterian* (quarterly) *Review* his "Vindication of Secession and the South." In this article, as Dr. Thornwell had done before him in the same periodical, he argues at length in favor of the Constitutional right of secession, justifying it on the charge that the rights of slavery had been infringed and were in danger. Here, Dr. Palmer again strikes out boldly for secession, vindicating it in seven States which had already gone out, and indicating the hope and making the prophecy that all the remaining slave States would follow them. We give a brief extract from the article, where he speaks of the course of South Carolina, his native State:

> When all hope of safety had died within her, she stood calmly under the shadow of the Capitol, before the clock which silently told the Nation's hours, and which would ere long sound the knell of its destiny. No sooner was this heard, in the shout of Black Republican success, than she leaped, feeble handed and alone, into the deadly breach. History has nowhere upon her records a more sublime example of moral heroism. Ignorant whether she would be supported, even by her sister across the Savannah, relying on nothing save the righteousness of her cause and the power of God, she took upon her shield and spear as desperate and as sacred a conflict as ever made a State immortal. * * * The Genius of history has already wreathed the garland with which her brow shall be decked. Long may she live, the mother of heroes who shall be worthy of their birth!

There is the same strain of eloquent treason all through the article. But we forbear further quotations, as we have given the same sentiments, at considerable length, in his earlier utterances.

REV. THOMAS SMYTH, D. D., STRIKES THE SAME CHORD.

Among many other examples of labored essays and discourses similar to the foregoing, we give but one. Dr. Thomas Smyth, of Charleston, S. C., a distinguished ecclesiastical author, has written one of the most earnest and passionate articles which the literature of the rebellion has produced. It is found in the *Southern Presbyterian Review* for April, 1863, entitled, "The War of the South Vindicated," and is divided into four parts, as follows: "1. The war of the South is in self-defence; 2. The war of the South vindicated by the fundamental principles of American Liberty; 3. The war of the South is justified as a defensive war against fanatical abolition; 4. The Divine right of secession."

Like all Southern writers, he makes the dangers to be apprehended to slavery, the cause of secession and justifying resistance to the Government; and making slavery, in its preservation and extension, a religious duty, he thus justifies the war on their part:

> We have taken up arms for the defence of our civil and religious rights, and God, our country, and the world at large, call upon us to acquit ourselves like men, for our wives and our little ones, for our homes, our sanctuaries, *and even our religion itself.* * * * The war now carried on by the North is a war against slavery, and is, therefore, treasonable rebellion against the Constitution of the United States, and against the word, providence, and government of God.

The groundless assertions of Dr. Smyth form a striking characteristic of the article:

The Missouri Compromise, forced upon the South by the North, only to be immediately and constantly resisted and perverted, rung the death-knell of the Union. * * * The North first entrapped the South into the Union, under false pretences and hypocritical promises. * * * The sure beginning of the sad end was formally laid down in the platform of the Republican party, on whose basis the present abolition administration was *clothed with power to rend the Union,* and to involve in one common ruin the happiness of both North and South.

The total untruthfulness of what is here asserted about this "platform," we have demonstrated in previous pages.

JUDGMENT AND BLESSING.

Here is a contrast between the North and the South:

This war is a judgment upon the North, for its persistent, perjured, abolition fanaticism. Nearly severing the Union in 1790, it rung its death-knell in 1820, and has since then inflamed an irrepressible conflict, which has now destroyed the Union, and is overwhelming the North in inextricable difficulties.

Dr. Smyth thus regards attempts to destroy the Union as wicked, bringing down Divine judgment. What, then, is the South to receive for her present attempt? Only blessing, in this way:

God is working out a problem in the physical, social, political, and world-wide *beneficial character of slavery, as a great missionary agency, of unexampled prosperity and success,* which He is now demonstrating to the family of nations. In this war the South, therefore, is on God's side. She has His word, and providence, and omnipotent government, with her. And if she is found faithful to Him, *and to this institution,* which He has put under her spiritual care, then the heavens and earth may pass away, but God will not fail to vindicate His eternal providence, and defend and deliver His people, who walk in His statutes and commandments blameless.

RESISTANCE UNIVERSALLY INSTILLED.

This whole article is very much of the character of the foregoing extracts. We give its closing paragraph, as an example to show how the Southern clergy, besides being leaders in treason, *have blown the rebel war-trumpet* from first to last:

Let the spirit of resistance be infused, with its mother's milk, into the baby in its cradle. Let it mingle with the plays of childhood. Let it animate the boy in its mimic manhood; the maiden in the exercise of her magic, spell-binding influence; the betrothed in her soul-subduing trance of hope and memory; the bride at the altar; the wife in the arms of her rejoicing husband; the young mother amid her whirl of ecstatic joy; the matron in the bosom of her admiring children; and the father as he dreams fondly of the fortune and glory of his aspiring sons—let it fire the man of business at his place of merchandise; the lawyer among his briefs; the mechanic in his workshop; the planter in his fields; the laborer as he plies his pruning-hook and follows his plough;—*let the trumpet blow in Zion, and let all her watchmen lift up their voice;*—let all the people, everywhere, old and young, bond and free, *take up the war-cry,* and say, each to his neighbor, "Gather ye together, and come against them, and rise up to the battle."

These extracts would seem to show that the fervency of the clergy of the South in the rebel cause advances with the progress of events. Dr. Smyth, if possible, is more intensified with the furor and frenzy of the strife than the other South Carolina Doctors. But these things from his pen were written at a later period. Nor have we given by any means the most glowing of his sentences, as will be seen in a subsequent chapter, where we illustrate another phase of the subject.

THE CLERGY OF ALL DENOMINATIONS AID THE REBELLION.

Other ministers of every denomination all over the South joined in urging on the rebellion, and some of the more distinguished of them were as early in the work as those we have mentioned. The course of the Right Reverend Leonidas Polk, D. D., Bishop of the Episcopal Church in Louisiana, early a Major-General in the rebel army (lately killed in battle in Georgia), is too well known to need any thing more than to be named. Bishop Elliott, of Georgia, Cobb, of Alabama, Green, of Mississippi, all of the same Church,—and, indeed, nearly all the influential ministers of all the Protestant denominations in the South,—took early position and gave the whole weight of their social and official influence in direct aid of the rebellion. Names of the most distinguished could be given in great number if necessary. Drs. Mitchell, of Alabama, and Waddel, President of La Grange College, Tennessee, wrote elaborate articles in aid of the rebellion at a very early period.

Every religious newspaper of the rebel States,—and they were all edited by ministers of the Gospel,—located at Nashville, New Orleans, Columbia, Fayetteville, Richmond, and other cities, urged secession in most cases from the first step in the movement, and in all at a very early period. And the houses of worship of all denominations, from first to last, have echoed the utterances of treason and rebellion from the pulpit in all parts of the South.

LEADING CLERGYMEN IN THE REBEL ARMY.

Many distinguished ministers, after preparing those under their care for the terrible work of war in defence of the treason they had inspired, led them to the field in person. Dr. Atkinson, President of Hampden Sidney College, Virginia, became Captain of a company composed mostly of his College students, fought in the first battles of the war, was taken prisoner at Rich Mountain, Western Virginia, and was paroled. Dr. Dabney,* Professor in

* At the beginning of the movement for secession, Dr. Dabney took strong ground for peace, urging his brethren farther South to desist. In an Address to Christians "of the Southern country," dated, "Hampden Sidney, Nov. 24, 1860," he says: "Whence, too, is the great divisive question borrowed? Is it not from Christianity? *Her sacred authority is the one which is invoked to sanctify the strife.*" He here refers to that feature of Southern "Christianity,"—modern views of sla-

the Union Theological Seminary, Virginia, early became an Adjutant-General in the army, and was upon the staff of Stonewall Jackson. Dr. McNeill, for many years one of the Secretaries of the American Bible Society, and living in New York, left his post and returned to his former residence in North Carolina, joined the army as a Lieutenant-Colonel, and was seriously wounded in a cavalry contest at one of the Mountain Gaps in Virginia, just before the battle of Gettysburg. And besides these, many other ministers of distinction have had military commands in the rebel armies. Dr. Palmer, of New Orleans, after that city was occupied by the national forces, went on a mission to the rebel army in Northern Mississippi, and harangued the troops at various points; and the testimony of one of the Generals in command was, that his services were worth more to the rebel cause than a soldiery of ten thousand men. We cannot vouch for the fact, but it has been frequently stated in New Orleans within the present year, and has been published in some of the religious journals of the country quite recently, that Dr. Palmer is now a Colonel in the rebel army. It has also been published that he is a chaplain. Both are probably true.

MANY MINISTERS GO SOUTH AND AID THE REBELLION.

While an exodus of ministers took place from the South immediately after the rebellion began, either leaving voluntarily, from patriotic motives, or being driven out on account of their Union sentiments, many ministers, some of Northern and some of Southern birth, left their stations at the North and went South to give in their adhesion and influence to the Southern Confederacy. Among others of

very,—as the *cause* of "the strife;" and charges upon the *religious* portion of the community a heavy responsibility. But, a little later, despite his earnest call to peace, he took the sword himself, and mingled in "the strife."

distinction, are the following: Dr. John Leighton Wilson, leaving his secretaryship in New York, went to South Carolina. Dr. Hoge, of New York, colleague of Dr. Spring, though born and educated in Ohio, son of a former Professor in the Ohio University, at Athens, himself afterwards Professor and Pastor there, resigned his charge in New York and went to Virginia. Dr. Leyburn, of Philadelphia, and Dr. Lacy, of Frankfort, Kentucky, gave up their respective posts as Editor and Pastor and went to Virginia. And many other well-known cases occurred in various parts of the country, which many persons will remember. The motive for these movements, openly avowed, was the sympathy felt for the cause in which the rebel States had embarked.

OTHER REBEL CLERGYMEN AT THE SOUTH.

As our armies have advanced into the rebel territory, while many of the *people* have rejoiced in the deliverance thus afforded, and while in this number may possibly be found, here and there, a minister of the Gospel,—though the cases of which we have heard are remarkably few, and that, too, over the extensive regions of the Southwest where we are personally acquainted,—many clergymen have only availed themselves of the approach of the Union forces to show a deeper hatred to the Union, and have been kept partially quiet only by reluctant oaths of allegiance; while many others have gone, in advance of the armies, "farther into the Confederacy," or are now enjoying, in the loyal States, the protection of that Government whose overthrow they desire. Among these, are Drs. Palmer, Leacock, Goodrich, Mr. Hall, and others, from the single city of New Orleans; Dr. Leacock, a native of Old England, and Dr. Goodrich, a native of New England, both of whom refused to take the oath of allegiance, and were required to leave the city; Messrs. Marshall, Lord, Rutherford, and one other, of four different denominations, and some of them of Northern birth, left Vicksburg on the fall of that city, and went "into the Confederacy;" besides others, located in Nashville and Memphis, and in many of the towns of Northern and Western Virginia; and, indeed, from almost every important city and village, wherever Churches were planted, have similar exits occurred, as the national arms have recovered the country.

SOUTHERN CHURCHES ORGANIZED IN AID OF THE REBELLION.

Besides the influence which so many of the ministry in the rebel States, in the many ways mentioned, have exerted in aid of the rebellion, *the Church as a body*, and in its separate organizations, was early consecrated to the same work.

The leading ministers, and other influential men in the respective Churches of all denominations, at the earliest moment, brought all the religious bodies of the South to break their connection with those of the North,—that is, with those religious organizations which hitherto were co-extensive with the Union,—changed their formularies of Church Polity, their Prayer-Books, and Directories for Worship, so as to give in their adhesion to the Government set up by the rebels, and thus recognize it as a lawfully established Civil Power. The words "United States of America" were blotted out, and the words "Confederate States of America" took their place, in the Liturgies, Prayers, and Standards of Faith, of every Church in the rebel dominions.

It is to be especially noted here, that THE CHURCH, *as such*,—the Church in its organic capacity as a *spiritual*

body, acting through its highest corporate tribunals, and not its individual members in their capacity as *citizens*,—made these radical and formal changes BEFORE the "Southern Confederacy" had been recognized as a lawful Civil Power, or admitted into the family of nations, either *de jure* or *de facto*, by any Civil Power of the world. And not only was this done while the contest of arms, whose issue should decide the claim of the Confederacy to such consideration, was pending, but it was done at the earliest convenient moment after the opening of the strife; and, in some cases, the initiatory steps of ecclesiastical bodies, which culminated in this more general action, were taken at the very beginning; and, in some others, even before the Southern "Confederate Government" was *formed*, or the States, out of which it was at length organized, had seceded. Such facts as these, in a most striking manner, illustrate the *animus* of the Church, and show its tremendous responsibility, not only for its support of the rebellion, but for the *lead* which the Church took in the cause, under the guidance of those men whose sentiments we have given, who preached, prayed, wrote, labored, and finally fought, for it from the beginning.

As an instance of the Church's course in anticipating the State in its eagerness for secession, it may be noted for illustration, that before the secession of South Carolina, the Presbyterian Synod of that State, by the most deliberate and formal action, under the lead of Rev. Dr. John B. Adger, Professor in the Theological Seminary at Columbia, decided to cast in its fortunes with those of the State in case it should secede from the Union; thus becoming an accessory before the fact to the crime of treason, and giving the influence of the Church, and pledging its support in encouragement of politicians, to commit the highest crime known to the laws.

Rev. Dr. Yerkes, in the *Danville Review* for September, 1861, thus alludes to this proceeding on the part of the Synod of South Carolina:

If the statement made on the floor of the Assembly (at Philadelphia, May, 1861) is to be credited, that Synod approved *in advance* the act of secession which it was well known the State Convention would pass. They could not wait till the foul deed was done. They were so fondly anxious to baptize the cockatrice, that they could not wait till the cock's egg hatched. They anticipated the monstrous birth, and sanctioned it *by a decree of the Church.*

ADDRESSES OF SOUTHERN CHURCHES SUSTAINING THE REBELLION.

Besides organizing all the Southern Churches on the basis of supporting the rebellion, and changing their respective corporate titles so as to conform to the name of the rebel Government, the larger religious bodies at the South adopted formal addresses, either to their own people or to the Christian world at large, vindicating their course in sustaining the rebellion through a disruption of the Church.

THE PRESBYTERIAN CHURCH.

Among others, the largest body of Presbyterians at the South put forth an address, from which we have already quoted, entitled, "Address of the General Assembly of the Presbyterian Church in the Confederate States of America, to all the Churches throughout the Earth," in which they speak as follows:

It is probably known to you, that the Presbyteries and Synods in the Confederate States, which were formerly in connection with the General Assembly of the Presbyterian Church in the United States of America, *have renounced the jurisdiction of that body, and dissolved the ties which bound them ecclesiastically with their brethren of the North.* * * * Commissioners, duly appointed from all the Presbyteries of these Con-

9

federate States, met accordingly in the city of Augusta (Georgia), on the 4th day of December, in the year of our Lord 1861, and then and there proceeded to constitute the General Assembly of the Presbyterian Church in the Confederate States of America. The Constitution of the Presbyterian Church in the United States, that is to say, * * * were unanimously and solemnly declared to be the Constitution of the Church in the Confederate States, with no other change than the substitution of "Confederate" for "United," wherever the country is mentioned in the standards. *The Church, therefore, in these seceded States, presents now the spectacle of a separate, independent, and complete organization, under the style and title of the Presbyterian Church in the Confederate States of America.* In thus taking its place among sister Churches of this and other countries, it seems proper that it should set forth *the causes* which have impelled it to separate from the Church of the North, and to indicate a general view of the course which it feels it incumbent upon it to pursue in the new circumstances in which it is placed. * * * *A political theory was, to all intents and purposes, propounded, which made secession a crime, the seceding States rebellious, and the citizens who obeyed them traitors.* * * * The Presbyterians of these Confederate States need no apology for *bowing to the decree of Providence, which,* IN WITHDRAWING THEIR COUNTRY FROM THE GOVERNMENT OF THE UNITED STATES, *has at the same time determined that they should withdraw from the Church of their fathers.*

THE PROTESTANT EPISCOPAL CHURCH.

Another instance is seen in the action of the Episcopal Church, in the form of a "Pastoral Letter from the Bishops of the Protestant Episcopal Church, to the Clergy and Laity of the Church in the Confederate States of America," issued from Augusta, Georgia, November 22, 1862, in which the Bishops say:

Forced by the Providence of God to separate ourselves from the Protestant Episcopal Church in the United States,—a Church with whose doctrine, discipline, and worship, we are in entire harmony, and with whose action, up to the time of that separation, we were abundantly satisfied,—at a moment when civil strife had dipped its foot in blood, and cruel war was desolating our homes and firesides, we required a double measure of grace to preserve the accustomed moderation of the Church, &c. * * * The Constitution of the Protestant Episcopal Church in the

Confederate States, under which we have been exercising our legislative functions, is the same as that from which we have been providentially separated, &c. * * * The Prayer Book we have left untouched in every particular, save where a change of our Civil Government and the formation of a new nation have made alteration essentially requisite. Three words comprise all the amendment which has been deemed necessary in the present emergency. [Among several "sources of encouragement," this is given:] In our case, *we go forward with the leading minds of our new Republic cheering us on* by their communion with us, and with no prejudications to overcome, save those which arise from a lack of acquaintance with our doctrine and worship. * * *

Another source of encouragement is, that there has been no division in the Church in the Confederate States. Believing, with a wonderful unanimity, *that the providence of God had guided our footsteps*, and for His own inscrutable purposes *had forced us into a separate organization*, there has been nothing to embarrass us in the preliminary movements which have conducted us to our present position. * * * Many of the States of this Confederacy are missionary. * * * Hitherto has their scanty subsistence been eked out by the common treasury of our united Church. Cut off from that resource *by our political action*, in which they have heartily acquiesced, they turn to us and pray us to do at least as much for them, as we have been accustomed to do for the Church from which they have been separated *by a civil necessity*. * * * It is likewise the duty of the Church to press upon the masters of the country their obligation, as Christian men, so to arrange this institution (slavery) as not to *necessitate the violation* of those sacred relations which God has created, and which man cannot, consistently with Christian duty, annul. *The systems of labor which prevail in Europe*, and which are, in many respects, *more severe than ours*, are so arranged as to *prevent all necessity for the separation of parents and children, and of husbands and wives;* and a very little care upon our part, would rid THE SYSTEM UPON WHICH WE ARE ABOUT TO PLANT OUR NATIONAL LIFE, of these unchristian features.

CHRISTIAN ASSOCIATION.

The Young Men's Christian Association of New Orleans, under date of May 22, 1861, issued an Address "to the Young Men's Christian Associations of North America," in which they say, in their Circular Letter:

We wish you to feel with us, that there is a terrible responsibility now resting upon us all as Christians, in this trying time of our country. * * * We in the South are satisfied in our judgments, AND IN OUR HEARTS [their own capitals], that the political severance of the Southern from the Northern States *is permanent*, and SHOULD BE SATISFACTORY. We believe that reason, history, and knowledge of human nature, will suggest the folly and futility of a war to re-establish a political union between the severed sections. * * * Has it not occurred to you, brethren, that the hand of God MAY BE in this political division, that both Governments may more effectually work out His designs in the regeneration of the world? While such a possibility may exist, let His people be careful not to war against His will. It is not pretended that the war is to maintain religious freedom, or extend the kingdom of Christ. Then, God's people should beware how they wage or encourage it. In the name of Christ and His divine teachings, we protest against the war which the Government at Washington is waging against the territory and people of the Southern States; and we call upon all the Young Men's Christian Associations, in the North, to unite with us in this solemn protest.

THE BAPTIST CHURCH.

The Southern Baptist Convention, a body representing "a constituency of six or seven hundred thousand Christians," in session at Savannah, Georgia, May 13, 1861, "unanimously" adopted resolutions, in which the following sentences are found:

In view of such premises, this Convention cannot keep silence. Recognizing the *necessity that the whole moral influence of the people*, in whatever capacity or organization, should be enlisted in aid of the rulers, who, by their suffrages, have been called to defend the endangered interests of person and property, of honor and liberty, it is bound to utter its voice distinctly, decidedly, emphatically, &c. * * * *Resolved*, That we most *cordially approve of the formation of the Government of the Confederate States of America, and admire and applaud the noble course of that Government up to the present time.* * * * *Resolved*, That we most cordially tender to the President of the Confederate States, to his Cabinet, and to the members of the Congress now convened at Montgomery, the assurances of our sympathy and entire confidence.

With them are our hearts, and our hearty co-operation. * * * Every principle of religion, of patriotism, and of humanity, calls upon us to pledge our fortunes and lives in the good work. * * * *Resolved,* That these resolutions be communicated to the Congress of the Confederate States at Montgomery, with the signatures of the President and Secretaries of the Convention.

METHODISTS, BAPTISTS, EPISCOPALIANS, PRESBYTERIANS, LUTHERANS, GERMAN REFORMED, AND OTHER CHURCHES.

In April, 1863, all the leading religious bodies of the South, as above named, united in putting forth "An Address to Christians throughout the World," declaring the causes of the revolt, and intended to justify their course in sustaining the rebellion and the war against the Government of the United States. The Address is signed, on behalf of these various branches of the Church, by ninety-six ministers. It is a very long document, going fully into the religious and political "situation," and takes substantially the same views as are found in the extracts from other Addresses, above given.

Among other things, they set forth that "the war is forced upon us—we have always desired peace;" that "the Union cannot be restored;" that the "Confederate Government is a fixed fact;" and, assuming that the President's Proclamation of freedom to the slaves was designed to provoke an insurrection, and that it would result in "the slaughter of tens of thousands of poor, deluded insurrectionists," they thus speak further of this document, and what may result from it:

The recent Proclamation of the President of the United States, seeking the emancipation of the slaves of the South, is, in our judgment, a suitable occasion for solemn protest on the part of *the people of God throughout the world.* * * * Make it absolutely necessary for the public safety that the slaves be slaughtered, and he who should write the history of that event would record the darkest chapter of human woe yet written.

They argue at length to show the grounds on which all Christians in the world should unite with them in a solemn protest against this Proclamation, and yet, like other Southern writers, pretend to regard it, after all, but a *brutum fulmen*, a "mere political document." They heartily approve of and sustain the "Confederate Government," and the war it is prosecuting against the lawful Government of the United States, and they highly compliment the Christian character of their rulers, generals, soldiers, and people; and, in a word, throw the whole power of the Southern Church, in all its denominations, into the scale of treason, rebellion, and war.

SOUTHERN RELIGIOUS PRESS ON THE REBELLION.

One of the most efficient aids of the rebellion, early and late, has been the religious press of the South, conducted by leading clergymen. We have given long citations from Southern quarterlies. We give a sample of the weekly religious press.

AT NEW ORLEANS.

The New Orleans *True Witness*, long before the Presidential election in November, 1860, warned its readers at the North, that, in case of Mr. Lincoln's election, there would be great trouble, and disunion would be the result. Immediately upon the issue being joined between Unionists and Secessionists in New Orleans, soon after the election, it openly espoused the rebel fortunes, and from that day until New Orleans surrendered to the Union arms, it battled heartily in the cause. A single paragraph from its issue of April 27, 1861, upon the attack made upon the Massachusetts troops in Baltimore, on the 19th of that month, will serve to show its spirit, and the means used by a *religious* journal to "fire the Southern heart."

Maryland is kindling with Southern fire, while Baltimore has stood at the font of *baptismal blood, in solemn covenant* for the Confederate States; and Providence ordered that this thrilling deed, *this sealing ordinance*, should be on the anniversary of the battle of Lexington, Mass., the memorable 19th of April. Thus the same day beheld the first blood of '76 and of '61—fortunate omen of the result.

The editor of that paper, who is responsible for this transparent blasphemy, Rev. Richmond McInnis, took his seat, in May following, in the General Assembly of the Presbyterian Church, which met in Philadelphia, and "solemnly protested" against the terrible defilement of religion with politics, because the Assembly resolved to stand by the Government which he, through the encouragement thus given to treason and rebellion, was using all his might to overthrow.

AT COLUMBIA, SOUTH CAROLINA.

Another specimen of the Southern religious press is seen in the *Southern Presbyterian*, published at Columbia, South Carolina. We of course do not look for any thing else from that quarter but treason. Its utterances, however, do not outrage the solemn ordinances of religion, when commending a cowardly attack upon the country's gallant defenders. On the 15th of December, 1860, when as yet no State had seceded, it thus speaks of the contemplated Convention of South Carolina:

It is well known that the members of the Convention have been elected *with the understanding and expectation* that they will dissolve the relations of South Carolina with the Federal Union, immediately and unconditionally. *This is a foregone conclusion in South Carolina.* It is a matter for devout thankfulness, that the Convention will embody the very highest wisdom and character of the State; private gentlemen, judges of her highest legal tribunals, and *ministers of the Gospel.* * * * Nothing, at present, assumes any definite shape, except the resolve in South Carolina, in the face of all obloquy, and ridicule, and menaces, of all the wrath and contempt of those who alternately curse and jeer her, *to assert her independence.* Before we issue another number of this paper the deed may be done—the Union may be dissolved—we may have ceased to be in the United States.

Thus, we have another instance in which the religious press, controlled by the clergy, *went ahead* of any acts o the civil authority, in "aiding and abetting" the rebellion. In the same issue, this paper, in an article on "Be not deceived," and in still another, in reply to a "Boston correspondent," thus speaks of the *cause* of the "contest" upon which the "foregone conclusion" is given:

We entreat our readers to let nothing mislead them on this point. The *real* contest now in hand between the North and South, is for the preservation or destruction of *slavery*. * * * We ask our correspondent, we ask all or any of the sober men of the North, if it is not the almost unanimous resolution of the Northern people to forbid THE EXTENSION OF SLAVERY? We believe it is; and the Southern people, for a thousand reasons, must regard that as a wrong that CANNOT BE SUBMITTED TO.

AT RICHMOND, VIRGINIA.

The *Central Presbyterian*, of Richmond, Virginia, edited or mainly controlled at the time by two clergymen of Northern birth, and Pastors of large Churches in Richmond, Dr. Moore, a native of Pennsylvania, and Dr. M. D. Hoge, a native of Ohio, in connection with Rev. Wm. Brown, spoke as follows, *before* the secession of Virginia, after the attack upon Fort Sumter:

We are henceforth a divided nation. We do not now search for the causes, or the place of blame. The stupendous fact is before us, "like the great mountains" of God, deep-rooted and high—plain to the eye of the whole world and immovable. *We are a separate people.* The answer of the President at Washington to our commissioners, and his proclamation calling for an armed force of seventy-five thousand men to "execute the laws,"—that is, to subjugate the seven seceding States,—is an end of the matter. *Separation is unavoidable.* * * * The position of Virginia, so far as the act of her Convention can fix it, will soon be known. It is not our place to assume any thing in anticipation. * * * Their determination will be such as may give reason to every member of our Commonwealth for saying, in the face of the world, and of Heaven itself, "IT IS RIGHT." *Its support will then be accepted as a religious trust.*

These modest gentlemen say, "It is not our place to *assume* any thing *in anticipation;*" and yet they both assume and anticipate a large amount that is political, for a religious journal. They openly declare for separation; "assume" to know, "in anticipation," that the action of the Convention will be "right" before "every" Virginian, and before "Heaven itself;" and all this, when the Convention gave *the people* of the State some forty days to think upon the matter, before *they* should be called to vote upon the Ordinance of Secession. How valiantly these "Northern ministers with Southern principles,"—who have constantly protested against "mixing politics and religion,"—can fight with religious weapons on the arena of politics, when they become *leaders* of the people, and declare their will forty days before they are called on to express it, and seal it "in anticipation" with the signet of "Heaven!"

AT FAYETTEVILLE, NORTH CAROLINA.

So, also, the *North Carolina Presbyterian*, with no more modesty than the Virginian, and likewise *before* that State seceded, while disclaiming to "assume," does yet declare, what should be done, as follows:

What, then, shall North Carolina do? Where does she stand? On which side? Without assuming to speak for others, though we doubtless reflect the opinions of four-fifths of the clergy and membership of the Southern Presbyterian Church, we say that *the South should unite for the sake of the South*—for the sake of peace, humanity, and religion—of our soil, our honor, *and our slaves;* and that ALL THE SLAVE STATES *should make common cause in this hour of their extremity.*

And so it was with the conductors of the religious press all over the South, of every denomination which had its organs. They were among the early champions of treason and rebellion, urging resistance to the Government "in anticipation" of Conventions and votes of the people; and thus becoming open leaders, and "assuming" momentous responsibilities.

EDUCATION IN AID OF THE REBELLION.

Another item in illustration of our subject, relates to the efforts in behalf of Education in the South, on a footing which should secure its independence of Northern Colleges and Universities, and strike out a *curriculum* within which should be safely ensconced all the interests of the "peculiar institution."

The world is familiar with the fact, that for many years the South has attempted to provide itself with an expurgated literature; that nothing in the shape of books and periodicals, from the North or from across the Atlantic, suited its tastes; that nothing of this sort was deemed "safe" or "sound," from a Child's Primer up to a work on Moral Philosophy; and as for teachers of both sexes, for whom it was largely dependent on the North, and most commonly upon New England, they could "not be borne with much longer, even though Southern children should have to grow up in ignorance." Their progress in this direction was small, though of late years something was accomplished. As they supposed the time nearly ripe for national disruption, a stimulus was given to their efforts.

We aim here only to notice one recent movement of a different kind. The South has been constantly increasing the number of its Colleges, and some of them are of a high character. But since the Presidential election of 1856, a bold scheme for a Southern University of magnificent proportions was projected, which is worthy of a passing consideration. Its design will be seen to have been to "conserve and perpetuate" the educational interests of the South in behalf of Slavery.

GREAT SOUTHERN UNIVERSITY.

The plan is developed in *De Bow's Review*, a monthly, issued in New Orleans, which has been a leading organ of disunion, and one of the stoutest champions for perpetual slavery. The project is treated in several numbers, and seems to have occupied the attention of leading minds in Church and State for several years. In the number for November, 1857, is one of a series of articles advocating the plan, written by a gentleman of Georgia. It is entitled, "Central Southern University: Political and Educational Necessity for its Establishment." The editor prefaces the article, representing the author as saying:

> That the Southern people, through individual, municipal, and State action, comprising all denominations, orthodox and heterodox, Jew and Gentile, should move with one accord to secure, *for our political as well as intellectual redemption and development*, at some advantageous point, a vast Central University, towards which should radiate, to be afterwards condensed, intensified, and reflected, the emanations of our municipal and State Schools, Academies, and Colleges.

DISUNION.—FIGHTING MEN TO BE EDUCATED.

The article presents the subject in four parts. The following sentences are taken from the first, illustrating the "necessity" for such an institution, and the grounds on which it rests:

> The opinion that it is *vitally important* to the interests and general welfare of the South, for the slaveholding States to endow and organize as speedily as possible a great Central Southern University, seems to be rapidly gaining ground. * * * That there does exist a *political* necessity for the establishment of an institution of learning of the

character alluded to, an institution around which shall cluster the hopes and the pride of the South, *the teachings of which shall be thoroughly Southern, one pledged to the defence and perpetuation of that form of civilization peculiar to the slaveholding States*, will not, perhaps, be questioned, although some may entertain doubts as to the pressure of that necessity. * * * The difficulty between the South and the North *can never arrive at a peaceable settlement.* The supreme and ultimate arbiter in the dispute now pending between them, MUST BE THE SWORD! To that complexion it must come at last. The first step then which the South should take in preparing for the great contest ahead of her, is to secure harmony at home. * * * The safety of the South, the integrity of the South, not the permanence of the Union, should be regarded as the "paramount political good." No true Southerner, no loyal son of the South, *can possibly desire the continuance of the Union as it is.* * * * The University of Virginia *is not sufficiently Southern*, sufficiently central, sufficiently *cottonized*, to become the great educational centre of the South. * * * According to the census of 1850, the number of white inhabitants of the Southern States is 6,113,308. The number of *fighting men* is usually estimated at about one-fifth of the population. That gives 1,222,661 *fighting men*. Of these, at least one-fourth are of an age suitable for going to College. * * * The establishment of the University has been proposed as a measure certain to produce, by its working, unity and concord of action on the part of the slaveholding States. The young men of the South will then assemble and drink pure and invigorating draughts from unpolluted fountains. They will meet together as brethren, and be educated *in one common political faith*, at one common *alma mater*.

The writer urges, in this article, the necessity of action, on the further ground that "each of two denominations of Christians at the South proposes to establish a Central Southern University,"—the Methodist Episcopal South, and the Protestant Episcopal,—for the same general ends, of promoting the special interests of the South; and he thinks other denominations may follow suit, and hence the system may lack the power which one institution of his type would have for making "thorough Southerners." In this same number of *De Bow*, is found a brief notice of a pamphlet issued by the Bishops of the Episcopal Church at the South, exhibiting a plan for a "Southern Episcopal University;" one of the cases referred to. This institution was not to go into operation until $500,000 had been subscribed. The agreement entered into by the Southern Bishops and several distinguished laymen, all of whose names are given in De Bow, was "signed at Lookout Mountain, near Chattanooga, Tennessee, the sixth day of July, A. D. 1857."

ENDOWMENT, FIVE OR TEN MILLIONS.

In the number of *De Bow* for December, 1857, the Georgian further develops his plan for a great "Central Southern University," from which we learn something of its grand proportions:

A total, then, of *five millions* is supposed to be sufficient, both to establish the University, and to endow it in perpetuity. This is not a very large sum; and even should it be advisable or necessary to double the amount, and make it *ten millions*, that would be a very small sum to be paid by fourteen sovereign States, for the innumerable blessings and advantages which are sure to result from it. * * * The method which I suggest for raising the five millions of dollars, is to levy a tax on population, a tax on area, and a tax on property.

PROFESSORSHIP ON PATRIOTISM.

The writer then presents at length his programme for "professorships," of which he proposes forty-three, numbered in order. The eighth is devoted to "Patriotism," on which the writer thus descants:

The duty of the incumbent of this professorship should be, to instil into the minds and hearts of his pupils *a pure and undivided love of country; to vindicate the domestic institutions of the South; and to hold them up as worthy of their hearty support, their love and admiration.* He should be a man of commanding presence, of fervid eloquence, of undoubted integrity, of extensive erudition, great in historic lore, A THOROUGH SOUTHERNER.

EPISCOPAL UNIVERSITY OF THE SOUTH.

In the May number of *De Bow's Review* for 1859, we find the "Address of the Commissioners to the people of the Southern States," in behalf of the Episcopal University before spoken of, which had now taken the name of "The University of the South." This Address is dated, "New Orleans, February 24, 1859." These Commissioners are Leonidas Polk and Stephen Elliott, Bishops respectively of the Dioceses of Louisiana and Georgia, by whom, on behalf of the other Bishops and the Trustees, the Address is signed. They set forth the plans of the institution. It is to subserve the interests of slavery and Southern independence. They speak of their resources and propects thus: "Nine thousand acres of land have been given us by the Sewanee Coal Company, and by the citizens of Franklin county, Tennessee." "We have bound ourselves not to take a single step, until we have received obligations to the amount of $500,000, bearing interest, as the lowest point at which we should commence." They also say that "one million of dollars is much less than we hope to raise," and that this sum "should be subscribed for its endowment." They say further: "Thirty persons have given us, within a few weeks, over $200,000." At length, the minimum, $500,000, having been secured, their location was chosen on one of those lofty mountains near Chattanooga, where the corner-stone was laid, with great pomp and ceremony, in the presence of the Bishops and a great multitude.

But alas! for all human calculations! Before the institution had accomplished its great mission of instructing the young men of the South in the peculiar notions of "Patriotism" developed in that projected "professorship," and before even the main building had risen on that ample corner-stone, lessons of *genuine patriotism* were taught on that very spot. The Union army of the Cumberland, under Rosecrans, there fought and won a battle for *liberty*, enriching with the best blood of an heroic soldiery the soil consecrated with religious rites to *slavery*. The soldiers occupied for barracks the surrounding buildings, and that corner-stone was blown to fragments by Union powder, no more to be an "aid and comfort" to treason. We sincerely trust, that, by the grace of God, the armies of Union and of Liberty may shiver to atoms, with equal ease, in His own good time, that other "corner-stone" on which the rebel Vice-President boasts that the rebel "nation" is built.

These were *some* of the schemes,—in actual operation and projected,—by which all the appliances of Education, in its highest grades and most systematic and enlarged plans, were to aid the press, the pulpit, and the politicians, in training up a race of "Southrons" to regard *human slavery* as "worthy of their hearty support, their love and admiration," under the name of "PATRIOTISM," while they should be taught to give other illustrations of that virtue by preparing to attack and plotting to overthrow that Government which had never wronged them, which the South had most commonly controlled, and whose foundations were laid in the blood of patriots of all sections of the Union.

REBEL MAJOR-GENERAL HILL AS AN EDUCATOR.

As a fitting conclusion to our notice of the schemes for "peculiar" education at the South to foster the "peculiar institution," we present Major-General D. H. Hill, of the rebel army, in the character of an educator. He is an Elder in the Presbyterian Church, and was a member of its General Assembly which met at Indianapolis, Indiana, in May, 1859. He is a native of South Carolina, was educated for the army at West Point, fought under General Scott in the Mexican War, and rose to the rank of Major. He resigned his commission and entered on the duties of civil life; first, becoming a Professor of Mathematics in Davidson College, North Carolina, and afterwards, in 1859, taking the office of Principal of the North Carolina Military Institute, at Charlotte. In this post, if we are rightly informed, he remained until the occurrence of the rebellion, into which he threw his whole soul, and finally rose to the rank of Major-General.

HIS HATRED OF THE NORTH.

A writer who appears to understand and appreciate his character, thus speaks of him:

> General Hill is a South Carolinian in all his feelings, principles, and prejudices, and doubtless rejoices that he is such. He has nursed his hatred to the North to such a degree, that it has become as near to a passion as his cold nature permits. In the year 1860, he delivered a lecture at several places in North Carolina, in which he complained bitterly of the injustice which had been done to the South by the Northern historians of the Revolutionary War; and in which he asserted, in substance, that all the battles gained in the Revolution by Northern troops were a series of "Yankee tricks," and that the real, hard, open fighting had been done by the South. So inveterate is this enmity to Northern men and the Northern character in General Hill, that it crops out in unexpected places, and in most remarkable ways.

SECESSION TAUGHT BY ALGEBRA.

This writer goes on to declare of General Hill that which reveals the ingenuity of his intellect, the bitterness of his heart, and his zeal as an educator, in training up the young at the South to hate the Northern people, and preparing them for the work of rebellion in which they are now engaged. He thus continues:

It would puzzle the ingenuity of most men to import sectional feelings and prejudices into the neutral region of pure mathematics; but General Hill has succeeded in conveying covert sneers by algebraical symbols, and insinuating disparagement through mathematical problems. In 1857 he published a text-book, called the "Elements of Algebra," of which Thomas Jonathan Jackson (the famous Rebel General, "Stonewall," another Elder in the Presbyterian Church), then Professor of Natural and Experimental Philosophy in the Virginia Military Institute, said, in a formal recommendation, that he regarded it as "superior to any other work with which I am acquainted on the same branch of science."

SPECIMEN OF ALGEBRAIC PROBLEMS.

Here are a few examples of the manner in which General Hill taught "the young idea how to shoot," of which the present rebellion furnishes the best illustration that his teaching was not in vain:

A Yankee mixes a certain number of wooden nutmegs, which cost him one-fourth of a cent apiece, with real nutmegs worth four cents apiece, and sells the whole assortment for $44, and gains $3 75 by the fraud. How many wooden nutmegs were there? Again: At the Woman's Rights Convention, held at Syracuse, New York, composed of 150 delegates, the old maids, childless wives, and bedlamites, were to each other as the numbers, 5, 7, and 3. How many were there of each class? Again: A gentleman in Richmond expressed a willingness to liberate his slave, valued at $1,000, upon the receipt of that sum from charitable persons. He received contributions from twenty-four persons, and of these there were fourteen-nineteenths the fewer from the North than from the South, and the average donation of the former was four-fifths the smaller than that of the latter. What was the entire amount given by the latter? Again: [The year in which the Governors of Massachusetts and Connecticut sent treasonable messages to their respective Legislatures is expressed by 4 digits. The square root of the sum of the first and second is equal to 3; the square root of the product of the second and fourth, is equal to 4; the first is equal to the third, and is one-half of the fourth. Required the year.] [Again: The field of battle at Buena Vista is six and a half miles from Saltillo. Two Indiana volunteers ran away from the field of battle at the same time; one ran half a mile per hour faster than the other, and reached Saltillo five minutes and fifty-four and six-elevenths seconds sooner than the other. Required, their respective rates of travel.

Who does not perceive that treason and rebellion, and hatred and contempt for the North, would inevitably result from such appliances of education, under the direction of leading religious men? They set themselves soberly at work to prepare for this horrid business, and were training the young of both sexes for it, with a zeal and ingenuity which were truly Satanic.*

AID OF THE CHURCH INDISPENSABLE TO THE REBELLION.

We have now given sufficient proof,—to which, indeed, much more might be added,—to show that THE SOUTHERN CHURCH, through its leaders, has a very large share of responsibility to shoulder for stirring up in the beginning, and for urging on with zeal and energy through every stage of its progress, the fiendish work of treason and rebellion, and in all possible modes of action which the case admitted; in the pulpit and through the press, writing for it, preaching for it, praying for it, and fighting for it; becoming leaders in all this work, entering upon it earliest, and drawing the better and more influential classes of society along with them.

* Here is an example of what was in progress at the South to instil the same spirit into the female mind of its leading families. The following is from an advertisement of the widely-known Nashville Female Academy, under the Rev. C. D. Elliott, of the Methodist Episcopal Church, who is a native of Hamilton, Ohio: "TEACHERS.—We employ a full Faculty of Teachers in all departments. This we can do safely, since our teachers, being Southern, are willing to invest their labor in the cause of the South, and to receive pay according to the number of pupils present. The Academy will continue to wage war,—uncompromising and unrelenting,—against all Yankee teachers, teachings, tricks, isms and ideas. We hope, in one more year, to be able to say that we do not use a single book written or published, North of Mason and Dixon's line." In regard to Rev. Mr. Elliott, the Principal, a Nashville writer says: "With most indefatigable industry he has labored to fill the tender hearts of little girls with hatred of Northerners, telling them in precept upon precept, here a little and there a little, that the Yankees were thirsty for blood."

There is the clearest testimony to show that Southern statesmen deemed this aid of the clergy invaluable, indeed ESSENTIAL, going so far as to say that were it not for the clergy leading on the Church, politicians could not have succeeded in arousing the masses of the people, could not have made a successful beginning in the work. We have already instanced the failure of Mr. Toombs in the character of a missionary, and the aid rendered him by Dr. Palmer. An item of evidence on this point, which is broad in its application, may be obtained from a single source.

THIS AID ACKNOWLEDGED BY STATESMEN.

In the *Southern Presbyterian*, under date of April 20, 1861, *the indispensable aid* rendered by the Southern Church and clergy is argued. A communication appears from Macon, Georgia, entitled "The Church and the Confederate States of America." The editor introduces the writer to his readers thus: "Many of them will recognize it as written by a gentleman occupying a high civil position in the Confederacy, and an Elder in the Presbyterian Church." This high civilian and Elder is supposed to be Thomas R. R. Cobb, a General in the rebel army afterwards, who was killed in battle near Fredericksburg, Virginia, in December, 1862. In this article, he says:

This revolution has been accomplished MAINLY BY THE CHURCHES I do not undervalue the name, and position, and ability of politicians; still I am sure that our success is *chiefly* attributable to the support which they derived from the co-operation of the *moral sentiment of the country*. Without that, embodying, as it obviously did, the will of God, *the enterprise would have been* A FAILURE. As a mere fact, it is already historical, that the *Christian community sustained it with remarkable unanimity*. * * * In times like these upon which we have fallen, the opinion of the Church upon political questions, when unanimously and freely declared, is far more potent than the tricks of the demagogue, or the eloquence of the renowned orator, or the oracular instructions of the retired sage. The reason is, that our Church, being sound, has the confidence of the irreligious world *Let the Church know this, and realize her strength. She should not now abandon* HER OWN GRAND CREATION. She should not leave the creature of her prayers and labors to the contingencies of the times, or the tender mercies of less conscientious patriots. *She should* CONSUMMATE *what she has* BEGUN.

A STATESMAN'S VIEW INDORSED.

Upon the position and influence of the Southern Church in aid of the rebel cause, as set forth in the foregoing article, the editor, Rev. A. A. Porter, writes his indorsement, as follows:

We have no fears but that the Christian people of the land will prove faithful to their country, in this day of trial, to the very last. As our correspondent suggests, *this present revolution is the result of their uprising.* Much as is due to many of our sagacious and gifted politicians, they could *effect nothing* until the religious union of the North and South was dissolved, nor until they received the *moral support and co-operation of Southern Christians.*

This is quite to the point. The men who write thus,—one an Elder of the Presbyterian Church, holding a high office in the Rebel Government, and the other a minister, and an editor on the mount of observation,—know whereof they affirm. The *status* of the Southern Church and clergy is fixed, and it is acknowledged by their leading politicians; and their testimony is, that, without the early influence and powerful moral co-operation of the Church with the leading politicians, the work of treason and foul rebellion "would have been a FAILURE." The Southern Church may thus look upon "HER OWN GRAND CREATION." As they glory in what they have done, we leave them to enjoy the spectacle.

It is perceived from this, that the charge which we bring against the Southern Church, of being chiefly responsible for the rebellion, is not a Northern fabrication.

THE CHURCH LED THE POLITICIANS.

An important fact in an earlier number of the *Southern Presbyterian*, February 23, 1861, is stated in an article on "Northern Misconception," as follows:

[They (the Northern people) persist in believing this universal upheaving, this unanimous and determined protest, is a mere matter of *politics*, the movement of a few hot-headed and ambitious men; whereas, nothing is so well known among us as that *the people have driven, not been led by, the politicians;* and by their own calm, great voice, have pressed them on to carry out their will.]

Admitting the correctness of this, then, who have "driven" or "led" *the people?* The people never act without leaders; the case never was known, since time began, in a revolution, religious or political, or any other great movement; not even in a mob. The people always have *leaders.* If they were not "led" by the "politicians," no doubt they had *the clergy* for their leaders or "drivers." Their own statesmen so declare. We are willing to leave it there.

This view of the case is still further insisted on, and the opposite view resented as an insult, in an article in the same paper, of March 16, 1861. In replying to a Northern paper, the editor says:

Will he still refuse to believe that *the Churches of all denominations* and the State are AT ONE on the questions involved? that, as Christian citizens, THE WHOLE HEART *of ministers and people* is in this matter? * * * And for the Churches of the *whole South*, of every denomination, we indignantly *deny* that they have been, are now, or ever will be, "the humble and obedient *servants of politicians.*" No honest man, who knows any thing of Southern Churches, will assert it of them. It is utterly false. He finds "ministers of the South urging political men to uncompromising resistance." Just now it was politicians leading ministers! Yes! And so long as we have tongue or pen to use, *will we urge, as a duty to God and man, resistance* to this unholy crusade against what we believe God's truth, right, duty, honor, and interest.

THE PROOF CONCLUSIVE.

Thus it appears that this influential religious journal, located at the capital of South Carolina, doth "indignantly deny" the charge, as a gross slander upon their character, that the clergy of the South were the "servants of politicians" in the cause of rebellion; and it denies this, furthermore, "for the Churches of the whole South, of every denomination;" and it undoubtedly is well qualified to make the denial, from its ample knowledge in the premises. But when the counter-charge is made, that the *clergy led the politicians*, "urging political men to uncompromising resistance" to the United States Government, it does *not* deny the soft impeachment; but it says, "Yes!"—we *did* do it—"and so long as we have tongue or pen to use," we will continue the good work!

Well,—we must leave it so. If they make up such a record for themselves, and if the politicians in the highest places in the "Confederate Government" agree to it, as we have seen they do, then the clergy of the South, "of every denomination," have a most fearful responsibility upon them for the horrors of this rebellion; a responsibility claimed, gloried in, and of which they are so jealous that they will not divide it with politicians. Be it so; and let God reward them "according to their works."

This, be it observed, was the language used a month before the crisis brought on by the attack on Fort Sumter.

There can be no doubt that nothing beyond the simple truth is stated in the foregoing extracts. It would have been impossible for the political demagogues of the rebel States *to carry the people* with them into rebellion, had not THE CHURCH, at the earliest moment, under her leaders, given to it of "her strength;" and even after the work had been thus begun, "the enterprise would have been a failure," and that soon, had not the Church stood by the object of "her own grand creation."

The power, and of consequence the responsibility, of the Church of the South in aid of the rebellion, may be illustrated by contrast, and that in two respects; by mentioning what is well known concerning an early period of the strife in some of the loyal Border States, and by noting the action of the larger religious bodies all over the loyal States.

LOYAL CLERGYMEN IN THE BORDER STATES.

As illustrating the first point, take the case of Kentucky. What would have been its condition had all its leading clergymen, as in the rebel States, taken open ground for the rebellion at the beginning of the contest? Does any one suppose, in such case, that the State would not have been carried into secession, so far as the action of its own people is concerned? On the other hand, take the case as it is. Does any one doubt that leading clergymen of the State, taking open and public ground for the Union, through the press and in other ways, at the earliest and most critical period, contributed most essentially to form the public sentiment of the more influential classes of the people, to preserve the State to the Union, and to save its fair fields from becoming, far more than they have been, the scene of the most bloody and suicidal carnage?

It is stating no more than what is believed throughout the country, as we have often heard expressed, that, in addition to the valuable aid rendered by others, Kentucky's adherence to the Union is due to the influence of Dr. Robert J. Breckinridge more than to that of any other man in the State; and we only repeat what we have many times heard stated by citizens of Kentucky, that had he taken the course of the Thornwells and Palmers of the

South at that early day, the power he would have wielded in the Church and among the leading politicians of the State would have carried Kentucky out by an act of secession, and thus have made her territory the great early battle-ground of the West. We quite as confidently believe, that, had the distinguished ministers of the South taken a determined stand against secession, they would have been equally successful. It is but stating what their own politicians declare.*

LOYALTY OF NORTHERN CHURCHES.—THEIR DUTY.

The other point is illustrated in the action of the religious bodies in the two sections of the country. They have given, in their influence over the people, the most powerful aid to the respective Governments. Those in the North could, in conscience and before God, do nothing less. They did but their duty. We say nothing here

* We find the views we have taken concerning the responsibility of the Southern Church and the Southern Clergy, fully sustained by the Rev. Dr. George Junkin, in his work entitled "Political Fallacies." Dr. Junkin was, at the beginning of the rebellion, President of Washington College, at Lexington, in the Valley of Virginia, and, from his position and enlarged acquaintance, is a most competent witness. He says: "These Southern Presbyterians are either laughing at your simplicity or pitying your stupidity. For, first, it is notorious that they held the controlling power in their hands. I could name half a dozen of Presbyterian ministers who could have arrested the secession, if they had seen fit. *Notoriously, the Presbyterian ministers of the South were the leading spirits of the rebellion. It could not have been started without them.* That stupendous victory, won by ten thousand of the unconquerable chivalry, over Robert Anderson and his seventy-two half-starved soldiers, after thirty-six hours of heavy cannonading, could never have been achieved but for the encouraging shouts of Rev. James H. Thornwell, D. D., and Rev. Benjamin M. Palmer, D. D. But secondly, even in the Border States, the Presbyterian ministers alone, if they had had a moiety of the heroic martyr spirit of Robert J. Breckinridge, could have shut up the sluices of treason and turned the battle from the gates. All that was needed was to present a solid front, and the demon spirit would have cowered before them and slunk back to his own den. Had my beloved brother, Dr. White, and his twelve Union elders, stood firmly together, all the demons of pandemonium, and Charleston, too, could not have driven them from Rockbridge county, and forced treason and rebellion on a people *who had voted more than ten to one* in favor of the Union candidates for the (Virginia State) Convention."

upon the character and details of the "deliverances" and "resolutions" adopted. Some of them, in some branches of the Church, may have points of special faultiness. We now speak only of the one principle running through them all, of allegiance to the Government. To express that unequivocally, at such a time of civil war, was their manifest duty; for the same civil obligations rest upon the Church, in her corporate or organic capacity, as rest upon any other organizations of men, or upon the individual citizen, so far as they may apply to each respectively. These religious bodies, as such, are under civil protection, which the Government is bound to render; they enjoy immunities which the civil authorities grant and guard; they hold property under the laws of the land; their charters and franchises are from the State; they have the same rights and privileges at law and in equity which other corporations enjoy; and in other ways, in their organic character, do they stand related to the Government.

By virtue of their public organization, and of their relations to the civil power, these religious bodies wield a vast influence over society, and especially over its more influential classes. By virtue of these things, they owe, in their organic character, full allegiance to the civil authority. Every principle of the Word of God, of human law, of common sense, and every principle in any way entering into the welfare of society, shows this beyond dispute. It is, therefore, their manifest duty, *in their organic character as public bodies*, when the land is rent and torn by foul rebellion, striving to overthrow the Government, formally to express their allegiance to the Government before all men. If it be said that this is *political* action, we meet it with a denial. It is action which God enjoins as a duty of *religion;* and should be recognized among the demands of conscience.

DUTY OF THE SOUTHERN CHURCH THE SAME.

On the other hand, it was equally the duty of the Church in the South to stand by the Government in opposition to rebellion. Had she done this, it is the testimony of Southern politicians that they could not have succeeded in initiating civil war. But be this as it may, it was equally her duty.

What right had the Presbyterian Church in the rebel States, for example, in defiance of her civil and religious obligations, to give in her adhesion, organically, to a rebellious Power styled the "Confederate States of America," at the earliest stage of the rebellion? A time might possibly come when it would be right for her to acknowledge such a Government *de facto*. But that time had not arrived when her leading men took their earliest step. They bounded into the arena at the very beginning of the civil strife. Some of them, in their public utterances, went ahead of the politicians around them; and some ecclesiastical bodies did the same.

Was this a proper spectacle to be presented by the Church of God? It is, rather, her decent mission to adhere to "the powers" which God has placed over her, and when the issues of a bloody rebellion shall have been *determined*, then to acquiesce in the result. The case is not altered, even when, as in the South, the fires of revolution were burning around or even within her. She is still to stand to her civil as well as to her religious obligations, and abide the issue.

But this, it may be said, would have subjected her to persecution, and brought her ministers to the halter. Well—what of that? May we abandon duty for safety? Are we not to *suffer*, as well as *do*, the will of God? We do not suppose we should have been, personally, more ready for Southern martyrdom than other people, but that cannot in the least affect the vital principle here at stake. It is merely a question whether allegiance to the civil authority is a duty of the Church. If that be decided affirmatively, as it clearly must be, then it is as incumbent on the Church to discharge that duty as any other; and if God in His providence call her to suffer, it is as much her duty to suffer in defence of her civil rights and in the discharge of her civil obligations as for any others, for they are all founded on and enforced by the highest religious sanctions.

This path of duty is, too, after all, the only path of safety; for if it shall ever come to a practical question of halters, it may be found that they can be used by the lawful Government of the Union as well as by the abortive Government of the rebellion. And when the future Church historian shall record the sufferings for righteousness' sake endured in this war, he will give a high place in the niche of fame to those ministers of the South, though few in number, who have been incarcerated and hung because they would not bow their necks to treason; while the memory of those who have led the Church astray, and thus prepared an easier triumph for political demagogues, and a more ready altar for the sacrifice of thousands of their countrymen, will go down to posterity with an insupportable load of infamy.

If, for the sake of present safety and peace, the Church may even quietly acquiesce in all the horrid work of this rebellion, without raising her voice in remonstrance to even her own members who are giving all their energies to its support, then there is no duty of Scripture which she may not neglect, and no fact which gives glory to her past history which she may not ignore. Had the Southern Church taken and maintained a righteous and heroic stand,

and been subjected to persecution therefor, she would have come out of the furnace with no such odious smell upon her garments as must now attach to them, for leaping into the front rank of the hordes of treason, winning the earliest and highest honors in its apologetic literature, and leading on its armed legions to battle. We envy not the fame which these men will have in the opinion of mankind, nor the reward which will be meted out to them in the just judgment of God!

CHAPTER VI.

CLERICAL DISLOYALTY IN LOYAL STATES.

It is a phase of the general subject in close alliance with that treated in the preceding chapter, that a similar opposition to the Government is seen in marked instances among clergymen in some of the loyal States.

The great body of the clergy of all denominations in the loyal States, have unquestionably been loyal to the General Government. But not a few, and among them men of ability and influence, have shown decided sympathy with the rebellion; sometimes in overt acts, often in speech and in their writings, and through other methods; and sometimes by a reticence which has been quite as significant as any open line of conduct. Some of this description have been required to take an oath of allegiance to the Government, which they have done reluctantly. Some would not take it, or their course was such that the alternative was not offered them; and they have voluntarily left, or have been sent out of the country. Others, whose acts have been deemed more highly criminal, have been imprisoned; while still another class have been sent South beyond the lines of the Union armies, as in several instances in Tennessee and other States.

The more numerous cases of disloyalty among clergymen in the loyal portion of the country, are to be found in the Border Slave States and in the District of Columbia. We give illustrations in a few examples, from which others will be readily called to mind by those who are familiar with current events. Similar instances may probably be found in all the Border States.

CLERICAL SYMPATHIZERS IN MARYLAND.

The difficulties which Bishop Whittingham, of the Episcopal Church in Maryland, had with some of his clergy, in the early period of the rebellion, are well known. As a loyal Prelate, he observed the recommendation of the Government in its appointment of Fast and Thanksgiving Days; issued his letter to his clergy, enjoining observance, and prescribed suitable prayers for the service; but from some of the Rectors under his charge, earnest protests were made, clearly revealing their rebel proclivities. The prayers he has written, to be used during the continuance of the war, are even now omitted in some Churches, or the clergy and the Bishop have been brought into open collision upon the issue; while the customary prayer for the President of the United States, co-existent with the Church service itself, is omitted in some cases, or hypocritically uttered.

Other denominations in Maryland, especially in Baltimore, have had ministers in their pulpits who would not observe the public days and service recommended by the Government, by reason of their rebel sympathies.

Ministers in some Churches in Baltimore, as reported in the daily papers of that city, have succumbed to the demand of their parishioners that prayers should not be offered for the President, and have left their charges; while in other congregations, both Protestant and Catholic, where such prayers have been offered, open manifestations of disapprobation have been made, sometimes by worshippers leaving the house during that part of the service, and at other times by significant marks of dissent while retaining their seats. Some ministers left Maryland, by reason of their Southern sympathies, and early cast in their lot with the fortunes of the rebellion.

DISLOYAL MINISTERS IN THE DISTRICT OF COLUMBIA.

It is somewhat surprising that ministers should sympathize with a rebellion seeking the overthrow of that Government under the very shadow of whose seat of Administration they live, and whose protection makes their homes safe and their daily bread sure. But so it was, at the beginning of the rebellion, with two prominent clergymen of Georgetown, in the District of Columbia. We cannot account for it except on the principle that they had Virginia blood in their veins, of the *modern* quality. It certainly could claim no affinity with that which characterized the era of Washington and his compeers.

One of these men is the Rev. John H. Bocock, D. D., at the time Pastor of the Bridge Street Presbyterian Church, in Georgetown. On the call of President Lincoln for seventy-five thousand troops, April 15, 1861, the amiable Doctor said, that "the yellow fever, in the course of the summer, would be worth seventy thousand troops *to us*;" accompanying the remark with significant signs of satisfaction. His rebel proclivities became so demonstrative, at a period a little later, that he was obliged to go South, beyond the lines of the Federal army. He has since given in his full adhesion to the rebellion, and was at one time engaged in superintending a manufactory of the munitions of war in Richmond, where it was reported he was seriously injured by an explosion which occurred in the establishment during the summer of 1863.

The other gentleman referred to is the Rev. Dr. Norwood, Rector of an Episcopal Church in the same city, when the rebellion began. On the latter part of that mournful Sabbath on which the first battle of Bull Run was fought, July 21, 1861, the secessionists of the North, and especially those near the seat of the General Government, were in high glee. During the early part of the day, and until near its close, it was supposed the Union troops had been victorious; but when stragglers from our army poured into the capital, and wended their way through the streets of Washington and Georgetown, and the result of the contest became known, the rebel joy could no longer be restrained. The pious Rector referred to was too much elated to hold religious service in the evening of that Sabbath, and hence ordered that the Church-going bell should not be rung, and it was accordingly silent, and the Church closed. But, instead of the usual worship, so "irrepressible" was the gladness at the defeat of the Federal arms, that the good Rector and a portion of his parishioners held a sort of levee on the porch of his house; and as the flying rumors of disaster came in quick succession from the battle-field, they eagerly drank them in, and their congratulatory "responses" resounded through the balmy Sabbath evening air; and this, too, when some of the loyal citizens feared for the safety of the capital. On the announcement of one "rumor," the joy over the Union disaster seemed to reach its climax. It was reported that Colonel Corcoran, of the New-York Sixty-ninth (Irish) regiment, who was taken prisoner, had been killed. The "Thank God for that," which was uttered from the lips of feminine delicacy by a member of the Rector's family, was "applauded to the echo."

Dr. Norwood soon became too demonstrative to suit the military authorities, and he too went to "his own place"—within the rebel lines.

It is believed that in no place within the jurisdiction of the General Government, are rebel sympathies among the religious *people* more demonstrative than in the two cities at the seat of Government; a sad testimony for their religious guides.

REBEL SYMPATHIZERS AMONG KENTUCKY CLERGYMEN.

The more prominent *open* sympathizers with the rebellion, among clergymen in Kentucky, are two Presbyterian Pastors, the Rev. Thomas A. Hoyt, and the Rev. Stuart Robinson, D. D. The former is a South Carolinian by birth, and the latter an Irishman. The former is Pastor of the First, and the latter of the Second Presbyterian Church in Louisville. Though they have both been exiled from Kentucky for some two years or thereabouts, they still retain, we believe, in form at least, the Pastoral connection with their respective Churches. Why this is, we do not know, unless it be that a large portion of their congregations sympathize with them. Whether they are, for the time, "retired on half pay," or have their salaries paid in full, are private matters, and best known to those who foot the bills. We refer to them because they are representative men of a considerable class, and because their respective cases illustrate important principles involved in the struggle between loyalty and treason.

REV. THOMAS A. HOYT.

Some two years since, Mr. Hoyt was arrested in Ohio for certain proceedings alleged to be disloyal, in connection with a Presbyterian clergyman of St. Louis, and they together were for a short time imprisoned in Newport Barracks, opposite Cincinnati. On being released, Dr. Brookes, of St. Louis, as we were informed, took the oath of allegiance; and we learn that he has since been commendably loyal, and is now a warm supporter of the Government in its contest with treason. Mr. Hoyt would not take the oath of allegiance, and was sent by the military authorities away from his charge in Louisville. Why he did not return to his native South, when offered the *privilege*, was surprising to some who had the matter in charge. He was permitted to go to the "hated North." For a time, we believe, he sojourned in Canada. But New York city is understood to be his "Head-quarters;" whence, as occasion requires, not being permitted to preach in Louisville, "for his oath's sake," he can preach for his sympathizing brother Van Dyke, of Brooklyn, where it may be oaths are not required.

We have never been able to understand why a clergyman who is not permitted to remain at home and preach because of his disloyalty, or for refusal to take the oath of allegiance, should be permitted to go elsewhere within the jurisdiction of the Government with entire freedom and "exercise his gifts." If it is the principle of *criminality* for which he is exiled, he should be turned over to the rebels or exiled out of the country; for a man who will not acknowledge the first duty of a citizen, to be obedient to the Government under which he lives, puts himself entirely without the Government's protection. If it be merely to prevent the *harm* which a disloyal man may do, we think he could do less at home than abroad. The congregating of disloyal clergymen who have been exiled from New Orleans and from other Southern cities because they would not take the oath, in the city of New York, for example,—the head-quarters of rebel sympathizers,—affords greater facilities for aiding the rebellion than they would have if they were back in the Crescent City, under the watchful eye of a military police.

MR. HOYT'S DISLOYAL SERMON.

Mr. Hoyt's position was defined at an early period of the rebellion. On the National Fast Day appointed by President Buchanan, January 4, 1861, he preached in his Church in Louisville, and published his sermon in the

Presbyterian Herald, then issued in that city, January 10th. This discourse is instructive on the following points: It shows that Mr. Hoyt agrees with other Southern men, that slavery lies at the root of the strife; it is an exhortation to the citizens of Kentucky and other slave States, to resist the Government, and let the seceders go their way; and while he is one of that class who deem it sacrilege to introduce "politics into the pulpit," he here shows us what, on this question, in his judgment, is *not* "politics," by deciding the gravest matters of political duty concerning the Government, and exhorting his congregation to the most definite line of action upon them; and much more of the same sort. We here give a few illustrations.

In the following paragraph, he intimates the importance of the issues involved, in the contest then impending:

And first, we should settle in our minds that great principles underlie this whole matter; we should avoid superficial views, and strive to see the mighty issues that are pending. This is no temporary, though acute, disorder of the body politic, but a chronic distemper, now breaking out afresh and throwing the patient into convulsions. This young giant would not writhe and perish under a mere functional derangement; an organic disease preys upon the vitals. The different portions of our country could not come into such hostile and deadly collision upon the ordinary questions of public policy.

Then, under the carefully-guarded phraseology employed in the following paragraph, he means to intimate that *slavery* is the disturbing element. Nothing else of a *religious* nature can be referred to, where he speaks of "revealed truth;" and slavery is also covered up under some other phrases. The italics are his. The "one section" is of course the South:

One section of this country believes that its dearest rights are injured—the right of self-government, the right to Constitutional liberty, the right to equality in the common Government and common domain; she believes that along with these rights is implicated the *truth*, the *truth of*

God, the *revealed* truth of God; and believing that these priceless treasures are gliding from her grasp, she is struggling to regain them. If all this be true, if our liberties and our religion are in danger, what have we to do but to stand up boldly for our rights?

POLITICAL PREACHING DEFINED.

He determines against his right to "preach politics;" and shows what is involved therein, as follows:

Questions of great magnitude and difficulty arise as to the time and mode, the when and the how, of discharging our duties in this matter. But these are purely political questions, and as such cannot properly be discussed in the pulpit.

We think we see it now. The "time" and the "mode," and the "when" and the "how," in regard to "discharging our duties," make up the *political;* while the "duties" themselves are *religious*. Mark this distinction, all ye who preach the Gospel, and whose vocation it is to teach others how to preach it. This we should deem one of the latest South Carolina distinctions. After having clearly stated it, Mr. Hoyt then expatiates on the *political* and non-pulpit side of it, still further:

Born on the soil of South Carolina, and educated in her views, I have not abjured the convictions of a lifetime and professed to have received a new revelation, but I have been true to the instincts of nature, and have cherished the lessons that I drank in with my mother's milk. But what I may think as a man is of no consequence to you on this occasion and in this place; you only wish to know the *message of the Lord* at my mouth. The terms of my commission are limited—I am commanded to *teach religion*, and am allowed to touch on other topics only so far as they touch on religion. Were it otherwise, were I allowedfull scope, my natural feelings would spring forward with alacrity to discuss this whole matter. But I dare not do it; my commission forbids it. * * * For these reasons, I cannot take up those questions—they are civil, and not at all religious.

That is, the "civil" questions concerning the "time,"

the "mode," the "when," and the "how;" for he specifies no others which are *political.*

RELIGIOUS PREACHING DEFINED.

He then exhibits the *religious* side:

> But there are other aspects of the matter which rightfully fall within the scope of this day's discourse—aspects which are so strenuously urged by every dictate of humanity and religion, and which so exactly tally with the precepts of the Gospel of peace, that I feel bound to press them upon your attention. The question that lifts its solemn presence amongst us this day is, "Shall we have peace or war?"

How easily a man can deceive himself by using the phrase "Gospel of *peace,*" and how convincingly persuade a certain class of his hearers that he is not meddling with either *politics* or *war.* We have a good illustration of this before us. Mr. Hoyt abjures "politics;" but when he comes to put in practice his right to preach *religion*, he shows that it embodies the following *political* things, as exemplified in this particular discourse: Allowing him to *decide*, that the "secession" which had then taken place was "a revolution *accomplished*," and so to *instruct the people;* that the Federal Government has *no right* to employ force to maintain its authority over the seceded States; that "the whole power of the Federal Government" cannot do this; that, should it be attempted, the people of Kentucky and other Border slave States, a portion of whom he was addressing, should *resist* the Federal Government, "should rise up and hough the horses of war,"—that is, if the Government should undertake force of arms against the rebels, Kentucky and the other Border slave States should put *themselves* into an attitude of rebellion by openly opposing the Government; and then, that the seceded States must enter on war, at all hazards if need be, to maintain the doctrine of secession: all which he felt "bound to press" upon the people as their *religious* duty.

The point here is none other than this,—that these "duties" are "religious," and as such Mr. Hoyt is authorized to preach them, and exhort to their discharge; whereas, to point out the "time" and the "mode," the "how" and the "when," would be "political," and a violation of his commission.

WAR PREACHED IN THE NAME OF PEACE.

Let us see how fully the points we have made are sustained by his own language. Commencing our quotation immediately after his question, "Shall we have peace or war?" he proceeds:

The responsibility of its answer rests upon you as citizens of Kentucky, and as a portion of the middle slaveholding States, it is for them to say whether blood shall be shed. They may have delayed their answer too long, but I trust not. *These great States should rise up from their knees this day and hough the horses of war.* [That is, as appears, the *Northern* or *Government* "horses."] They should say *to the North,* You SHALL NOT attempt force towards the seceding States—THEY MUST be allowed peaceably to go out, *if they choose.* It is not necessary that you should admit the right of secession. You may regard it as a revolution, *but as a revolution* ACCOMPLISHED. You may say, if you choose, that we do not admit that our Constitution contemplated secession, and that we do not think the cotton States warranted in what they have done; but, *as they have done it,* WE WILL NOT PERMIT *them to be assailed.*

And is it not a revolution accomplished? Does a revolution ever go backward? Can force compel South Carolina to return? No! the whole power of the Federal Government is inadequate to the task. She may be overrun by invading armies; her cities may be demolished, and her fields ravaged; her churches may be deserted to the moles and the bats; her classic halls may echo the hoot of the midnight owl; her sons may perish on a hundred battle-fields; her women, and children, and old men, may fly from their burning dwellings; but she can never be conquered—never, never!

On speaking of the rights and dangers of the South, he thus enlarges upon the duty of maintaining them by force, if need be, even to the decapitation of the supreme authorities:

> If all this be true, if our liberties and our religion are in danger, what have we to do but to stand up boldly for our rights—rights that we inherit as Englishmen and as Americans; rights that began to be secured to us when the Barons wrested Magna Charta from the nerveless grasp of King John; rights that sought revenge for their violation in the royal blood of Charles I.; rights, the vindication of which hurled James II. from the throne; rights, that, rising to still grander proportions in this New World, found a champion in Washington, and an embodiment in the institutions of our country.

THE GRAND DISTINCTION—RELIGION AND POLITICS.

We have then, here, a practical illustration of what it is for the pulpit to eschew "politics" and preach "religion." It is preaching *religion* to decide high questions of State; to declare what the Government has a right to do, and what it has no authority or power to do; to settle the whole doctrine of "State rights," of which "secession," deemed "a revolution accomplished," is the culmination; to determine constructions of the Constitution, wherein statesmen differ; to decide, that in case the Government determines on asserting its authority to overthrow treason, it is the duty of the people of other great States to run into treason and rebellion likewise; and, most especially, under the specious language, "the Gospel of *peace*," to cause the Church to resound to the blast of the *war*-trumpet, to summon men to join the armies of revolt against a lawful popular Government. All this is *religion*, and in it the people are instructed by authority. To add the ingredient of *politics*, which would defile the whole service, it is only necessary to determine the "time" and the "mode," the "how" and the "when."

This is a pretty fair specimen of the value which that class of men, who are ever harping about "political preachers," place upon their own doctrine. The sentiments preached are sufficiently "religious," if they are *on their side;* but they are wickedly "political," if *opposed to their views.*

NO POSSIBLE NEUTRALITY.

We commend the outspoken frankness of Mr. Hoyt, so far as seen in contrast with another class, remarkably reticent. In a time of treason, rebellion, and devastating civil war, it is every man's solemn duty,—clergyman or layman,—to show his colors. It is a sin to do otherwise. Neutrality, at such a time, is a sin against God, and a crime against the country. But there is, in fact, *no neutrality,* regarding this contest, in the breast of any American citizen. It is an impossible thing, and every man knows and feels it. He is either for the Government in this struggle, or against it. And yet, there are men in the Border States, and elsewhere, who have at least the *form* of manhood in outward appearance,—men, too, who hold a commission, as they declare, from God, to instruct the people in their religious duties,—who, in this contest between loyalty and treason, claim to be "neutral," to have "no opinion," and to deem it best that "a minister's views should not be known." We can only utter for such the prayer of the Judge for the culprit sentenced to the gallows, "May the Lord have mercy upon their souls!"

While we admire Mr. Hoyt's candor, infinitely better than that feigned "neutrality" which many Border State ministers pretend without practising, we place him in the same list of guilty responsibility for the treason and rebellion now desolating the land, with distinguished ministers in the Rebel States; with this marked difference, that he is living within the *loyal* district covered by the Government, while giving his heart and his preaching in the line of that rebellion which is seeking its overthrow.

REV. STUART ROBINSON, D. D.

We have already spoken of Dr. Robinson as Pastor of a Church in Louisville, at the beginning of the rebellion, and still holding a formal connection with it. For some two years he has been an exile in Canada, living in Toronto. The facts about his exit from his adopted country, and taking refuge under the flag which waves over the " swate isle" in which he was born, are about as follows:

During the summer of 1862, when temporarily absent from Louisville, such was the feeling entertained toward him by the military authorities in that city, as his friends believed, that they advised him not to return. He took their advice, and voluntarily betook himself to a place without the jurisdiction of the United States, where he has since remained. We have never heard what was charged against him, nor why his friends were apprehensive for his safety, in case he should return home. It has been said by some of them, that he would not take the oath of allegiance, and hence would not return, knowing that this would be required of him. Dr. Robinson himself has admitted, substantially if not directly, in what he has since written upon this express point, that he would not take the oath of allegiance to the United States Government. It may be, for aught we know, that this is the sole occasion of his exile. Even if this is all, it is sufficient proof of disloyalty with right-minded men.

But a question lies back of this. Why was such a demand made of him? What words, or acts, or other conduct, was he guilty of, that led the authorities to deem the oath requisite in his particular case? All ministers are not required to take an oath of allegiance. But in special cases, such requisition has been deemed essential for public safety. A minister of the Gospel, above all other men, should so conduct, that he cannot even be *suspected* of being disloyal to the Government which protects him. And we venture to say, that there has been no case of arrest, or infringement, or threatening of any one's liberty or safety, in the loyal States, concerning whom there was not some good ground for the *suspicion*, at least, that he was in some way aiding the rebellion. But the simple fact that Dr. Robinson's friends thought, and his judgment and conscience approved the suggestion, that Canada was a safer place for him than Kentucky, is *prima facie* evidence that the case is against him; that his presence and influence in Louisville were deemed to be against the Government by the military authorities, and that it would be improper for him to return there without taking the oath of allegiance; all which is strengthened by the consideration that the Commander of that Military Department at the time was Dr. Robinson's particular friend, and would do him no injustice.

HE EDITS A DISLOYAL PAPER.

Our object in referring to this case at all, is, that it furnishes a striking illustration of disloyalty to the Government, and sympathy with the rebellion, in a leading minister of a Border State, which, by successive votes of its people at the polls, has determined to stand by the Government and the Union. We need not go for proof to what he did, immediately leading to his exile. Ever since he has been in Canada, he has edited a paper, which is issued in Louisville, and widely circulated in Kentucky, from which the proof of his disloyalty and sympathy with treason and rebellion is patent to all who read the sheet.

This paper is called *The True Presbyterian*. It was published for some time before Dr. Robinson left Kentucky, and edited by him, and was at one time suspended by military authority; and afterwards, through the interference of a friend, the resumption of its publication was allowed. During the last year or more, its disloyal utterances have been more outspoken than usual, though from first to last its whole tone and spirit have been pervaded with hostility to the course of the Government and sympathy with the rebellion. Its articles are spiced with a venom which is scarcely rivalled by the secular prints of Richmond.

The animating spirit of the paper is Dr. Robinson, safely housed in Toronto under the protection of the British flag, while the paper emanates from Louisville, protected in its treasonable influence by the flag of the United States. We have not the least doubt that *The True Presbyterian* is one of the most powerful auxiliaries for keeping alive the spirit of the rebellion among the secessionists of Kentucky.

In saying that this is a disloyal sheet, we do not speak at random; we shall give the proof. For the responsibility of its influence, its editors, publishers, correspondents, subscribers, and patrons, must be held to account, on any correct principles of judgment; though, as we have said, Dr. Robinson is the soul of the concern. For our individual self, as we have taken this paper from the beginning, our conscience is vindicated on the same ground that the late Dr. Emmons justified himself for purchasing infidel books. He said his library contained "the best and worst books in the world:" that it was necessary for a minister to consult infidel works such as he would not recommend to his people, for "they should know what the Devil is about." On the same principle, in this time of rebellion, we by no means confine our reading to one side of the question, either in secular or religious literature. We consult papers and books of all parties, and especially those which claim to be of the "religious" sort. For this purpose we have taken, as long as the mails were open, several of the religious papers and periodicals of the South. On the same principle, if his Satanic Majesty should escape to the earth, and set up a religious or secular journal in some metropolis of our country, we should become one of his subscribers. But we seriously doubt whether he could carry out his designs more effectually through such means than they are now being executed by some of the servants he employs; of which *The True Presbyterian* is a fair specimen of the "religious" press, and indeed the only paper of any denomination that we know of in all the loyal States that is not openly and decidedly sustaining the Government in its efforts to put down the rebellion.

ITS DISLOYAL COURSE IN GENERAL.

We do not intend to wade through the entire files of this paper for our proofs, but will take a single number of a recent date as a sample of many more.

Before quoting it, however, we will simply note the leading characteristics of the disloyalty which runs through this paper, from the first number to the last, as must be well known to every *loyal* person who reads it.

It started out on the avowed principle that it was going to maintain a high tone of spirituality; that the necessity for this arose from the fact that the religious papers of the country had become secularized and political,—the best illustrations for which were, that they spoke out boldly in opposition to the rebellion, and in support of the Government and the war for its suppression,—and that the

Churches of all denominations had become openly corrupt and utterly apostate, as seen in their resolutions and acts adopted in support of the Government. In this extraordinary state of religious degeneracy, *The True Presbyterian* was going to be strictly and purely "religious," would abjure and eschew "politics" altogether, and set a high example of what a *religious* journal should be. The mask was soon thrown off. It is, and has been from its first number, for a paper claiming to be "religious," one of the most intensely political journals in the country; and its politics are disloyal and treasonable in their spirit, tendencies, terms, and *intent.*

IT VILIFIES THE CHURCH FOR LOYALTY.

There is not a branch of the Church which has passed resolutions in support of the Government which it has not denounced and maligned in the most bitter and vile terms. There is no body of religionists in any part of the loyal States which has manifested disfavor with the Government and sympathy with the rebellion, which it has not held up for approbation; as, for example, that of a Methodist congregation in the interior of Pennsylvania, which recently passed resolutions against the loyal action of the General Conference of that large and influential Church in May last in Philadelphia, and that of a Methodist Convention held in Louisville, which took action against the proceedings of the Bishops of that Church. There is not a distinguished man in the Church who has shown his loyalty in his writings, nor a periodical that has taken the same course,—especially those in the Presbyterian branch,—that has not been blackballed by that sheet by name, in terms that would eclipse a London Fish Market; embracing such venerable names as Drs. Hodge, Spring, Breckinridge, Junkin, Musgrave, and hosts of others, including all the editors of the religious press; and not a prominent man in the Church sympathizing with treason, nor an insignificant one of that character, has escaped its commendations. On the other hand, while it has often been very earnest in its exhortations for "peace," and has continually denounced and mourned over "this cruel war *against our* SOUTHERN brethren,"—a war begun by themselves for the destruction of our nationality,—and while the ministers of the Southern Church of all branches have been the foremost in urging on the war against the National Government, the Constitution, and the Union, and many of the more prominent of them have held commissions as officers and have fought in the rebel army, no article has ever appeared in that paper whose object was to condemn the wickedness of this pious work of "our *Southern* brethren," but many paragraphs are found in its columns extenuating their course, which were well calculated and directly designed to give them substantial "aid and comfort;" while, also, some of these leading men have been especially commended by name for their exalted virtues, and held up as models worthy of imitation by all men. It sometimes waxes very warm upon the question of *Northern* infraction of "Constitutional rights," but this paper may be searched throughout for a single condemnation of the infractions of the Constitution by treason and rebellion which *Southern* men have committed, and *not one* such line of condemnation can be found.

IT ABUSES THE GOVERNMENT.

In regard to the General Government, whose flag protects the property of *The True Presbyterian,*—and under whose jurisdiction the "unclean spirit" of the paper, "walking through dry places, seeking rest," does not find it well to reside,—its course is very similar to that towards the loyal action and loyal men of the Church. There is scarcely any thing which the Government does towards putting down the rebellion which it does not condemn. We challenge the most careful reader of that sheet, whether he be loyal or a secessionist, to point to a single article it ever published, whose object was to show sympathy for the Government in its contest with treason, and that it favored putting down the rebellion *by any means whatever;* or that it ever contained an editorial or any other article, whose object was to show that the rebellion is wrong, as an offence against either man or God; or that its editor, Dr. Robinson, has ever explicitly stated in that paper, that he is *not* in favor of the triumph of the rebellion and of the dismemberment of the Union in the setting up of an independent "Confederacy" in the South, —*that he is* NOT, *heart and soul, in full sympathy with the rebels,*—although the charges that he *is* so have been frequently made against him publicly, and he has been challenged to deny them in his columns in direct terms.

While this negative view of the case is sufficient of itself to condemn any such editorial course in a time of rebellion, and to brand an editor who pursues it with public and open disloyalty, the charge cannot be evaded in this case on any plea of neutrality, and that silence is maintained for *spirituality's* sake, and because it is a "religious" journal. On the contrary, this paper speaks out openly against the Government; against almost every department of it, civil and military; against its general course and its specific measures towards the rebellion; against the acts of the Administration, and of the War Department; against the Military Orders of the Government; against the course of its Commanding Generals; against its interference with slavery in the rebel States; against, indeed, every thing which it is doing to put down the rebellion; including abuse of it for interfering with openly disloyal citizens at the North. As a fitting illustration of this, it evinces its deep sympathy for treason and traitors, by holding up as martyrs some whom the Government has laid hands upon to protect its own safety and the safety of the people at large. Mr. Vallandigham is a special object of its editorial compassion, although he was condemned by a regular Military Court, which was sustained by the United States District Court, and again by the non-interference of the Supreme Court of the United States, as well as by the Executive of the nation, and although he was repudiated by the people of Ohio. While making a martyr of one thus judicially condemned for disloyalty, it abuses most especially and repeatedly in its columns, the upright and honored Judge who declined to interfere with the regular course of lawful authority in the case.

The terms which it employs to vent its spleen at the whole administration of the Government, civil and military, are fully equal to any emanations from the secular press at Richmond, and in many respects the rebel journals of the rebel capital are left far in the rear in the effort to seek out phrases of treasonable malignity.

In giving these general characteristics of *The True Presbyterian*, every loyal reader of the paper knows that they are fully maintained by the facts, and that, if there is any difference, our representation falls below the truth. This is the kind of paper which is sustained by respectable people in Kentucky, some of whom are loyal; sustained largely by the Presbyterian Church, in which, among the ministry and people, are specimens of as rank sympathy with the rebellion as can be found in any part of the Union. Is it any wonder, with such aids *at home*, that the State is overrun with rebel raiders, under the lead of John Morgan, "the chivalrous Southern gentleman," as refined ladies style him, and that its loyal people are constantly harried and harassed in person and property?

SPECIMENS OF DISLOYALTY.—HIS POSITION DEFINED.

For an example of many, we take a single issue of *The True Presbyterian*, that of March 17, 1864. One article is specially noticeable in the fact, that while Dr. Robinson is apparently attempting to vindicate his loyalty, he abuses the Government in the same breath. Referring to the *New York Observer's* remark, that it is a "sin and shame not to be for the Government," Dr. Robinson says:

> We are not sure that we and the *Observer* "understand the case alike" here, as President Lincoln says. If he mean by "Government" the Constitution, and official acts of the Administration according to the Constitution, then we have given stronger proof of loyalty than the *Observer*. For though maligned, insulted, and robbed, by minions of the Administration, we have steadfastly withstood the temptation to swerve from our fidelity in "word or conduct" to the Government. But if, by "the Government," the *Observer* means *an Administration in the hands of cut-throat abolition infidels, setting at defiance alike the ordinance of God and the Constitution of the country*, THEN WE ARE "NOT FOR THE GOVERNMENT," *whatever "sin and shame" may be involved in it.*

This is sufficiently plain as defining his position. It embraces the essence of the usual resort of traitors, who sometimes attempt to distinguish between the "Government," and the "Administration" in which, for the time being, all the authority, dignity, and power of the Government are embodied. It qualifies this, however, by the distinction between the Government constitutionally and unconstitutionally administered,—a very palpable distinction. And then,—passing by the official and authoritative decisions of every department of the Government, Executive, Legislative, and Judicial, in which they have been *agreed* on all questions which have been acted upon by them respectively touching the rebellion and the war, —Dr. Robinson takes upon himself to be sole judge in the matter, and to decide on his individual responsibility that the Government is acting unconstitutionally, "setting aside the Constitution of the country," and therefore openly announces, "*we are not for the Government.*" If this is not disloyalty, it would be difficult to define the term.

The spur of his zeal for Constitutional *liberty*, is his devotion to negro *slavery*. To deify and sanctify the right to enslave *four millions* of human beings, who have an infinitely clearer right to liberty before the bar of justice, than he has to his personal freedom before the laws of the country he is betraying, *The True Presbyterian* is largely devoted; and he deems it God-service to abuse the Government because it has stopped the mouths of *a few* prominent men, who, like himself, were acting in sympathy with those who are in arms to overthrow it. It is not difficult, therefore, to select the term out of the phrase in which he characterizes the rulers of the country,—"cut-throat *abolition* infidels,"—which most of all expresses the depth of his soul's abhorrence.

In the same article from which we have quoted, Dr. Robinson further shows his contempt for "the powers that be," by speaking of some of the Generals in the army highest in rank as "petty military despots," and of their "rule" as being "instigated by the *canaille* of the neighborhood;" and of the head of the Department of War, as "that eminent father in God, Secretary Stanton;" and elsewhere, so exact are his rebel instincts, that he falls into rebel phraseology aptly, when characterizing General Butler as "Beast Butler," and other leading Generals of the army as "military satraps," and much more of the same sort, found in every number.

GOD'S "CURSE" WITH THE PRESIDENT.

Another instance revealing his strong rebel leanings in the paper of the same date,—for all our extended extracts are confined to one number,—is seen in an editorial in which he objects to the course of certain religious gentlemen, wherein he takes occasion to draw a comparison between preceding administrations of the Government and the present one, much to the disparagement of the latter, in this style:

> Under the thirteen preceding Presidents, God's blessing seemed to rest upon the nation from generation to generation, *while His awful curse comes with Mr. Lincoln.* We are free to say, wicked as we no doubt will seem to these holy men, that judging from the history of our country, while "we as a nation had no religion," we were far better off than now, *with all the religion that Mr. Lincoln's official piety has infused into the nation.* As "a nation with no religion," we had generally peace and quietness—faithful observance of public covenants—respect for the amenities of civil and social intercourse between all sections of the land—unparalleled success in all secular enterprise, and marvellous success in all our efforts for the advancement of Christ's kingdom. As a nation with a religion, in spite of Presidential fastings and prayers and thanksgivings, we are rapidly verging to barbarism, the land filled with rapine and blood, &c.

These comparisons are understood. Under all former administrations, "public covenants" were scrupulously kept; under the "curse" of Mr. Lincoln and his "official piety," they are broken. Under former Presidents, proper "civil and social amenities" were shown toward "our Southern brethren;" but now, poor souls, they are treated very uncivilly with shell and canister for their pious offerings on the altar of treason. Under Presidents Pierce and Buchanan, when, through their *peculiarly* "faithful observance of public covenants," slavery had a fair prospect of becoming universal in the country,—either by importing more Africans, or enslaving, as the amiable Dr. Armstrong would have it, all the "poor whites,"—we had "unparalleled success in all secular enterprise," and cotton was to reign over all nations; but now, under the "awful curse that comes with Mr. Lincoln," gold goes up and greenbacks go down, and as for the great Apostles of the rebellion among "our Southern brethren," their idol king is dethroned and they are reduced to quite an apostolic condition, as many of them have "neither gold, nor silver, nor brass, in their purses, neither two coats, nor shoes," and as for their "scrip," it has long since gone down far below zero. Under former Presidents, when it was orthodox to preach up the divinity of slavery, and when it was sin, "infidelity and apostasy," to preach or resolve against it, "Christ's kingdom" had a most "marvellous success;" but now, under "Mr. Lincoln's official piety," when the country is ready to throw off the incubus of slavery, "we are rapidly verging to barbarism." These may be entitled "The Pious Lamentations of Stuart Robinson," and will do to keep company with the "Sorrows of Werter."

THE WAR CHARGED ON NORTHERN MEN.

We give two extracts more from the same number of the paper, contributed by other writers. We cannot vouch for the correctness of the writer's quotations in the first extract, except in one instance, but we give them as we here find them. He is mourning over the war, and charging the responsibility for its sad events upon the men he names. It shows on which side *his own* heart is,—that of the rebellion or the Government:

How naturally the poor dying soldier might claim, that in a very acceptable manner he must have been serving God, while employed in butchering rebels! Could he not refer to the calmest utterances of the most eminent of the so-called conservative preachers of the land, representative men of by far the largest part of the Presbyterian Church, *that the war is, on the Federal side, a just, a necessary, and a holy war?* Did not the learned and able Rev. George Junkin, D. D., on the floor of the General Assembly, in 1862, *unrebuked by that Assembly*, declare, that "the present rebellion is a hell-born delusion, an ungodly, wicked delusion; the present war was founded in treason, in deception the most terrible that ever was on earth, except the deception in Eden?" Did not the meek and gentle Rev. S. I. Prime, D. D., editor of the *New York Observer*, write in his paper in May, 1862, that no punishment in this world or the next was severe enough for those Southern traitors? Did not the amiable and fearless Professor in the Danville Theological Seminary, even Rev. Robert L. Stanton, D. D., deliberately characterize this Southern movement—so written in the *Danville Review*,—as "the most wicked and causeless attempt to overthrow good government which has ever been made since the rebellion of the angels which kept not their first estate?" Did not the sober and earnest Rev. George W. Musgrave, D. D., long a Secretary of the Board of Domestic Missions, tell the Almighty in his public prayer, in the hearing of assembled thousands, as met at the second anniversary of the Christian Commission, in Philadelphia, January 28, 1864, that "the treason of the rebels is a crime against their country not only, but a crime against the Almighty Himself; that they are resisting His servants, His divine, established ordinances?"

The article from which the above is taken, is headed "Who slew all these?" The writer indicates *his* answer, which shows that he relieves "our Southern brethren" from the responsibility.

OUR GOVERNMENT WORSE THAN FRENCH REVOLUTIONISTS.

The only further reference we make, is to an article in which the writer draws a comparison between the French Government, in the Revolution of 1793, and the General Government of the present time, and strives to make out a case most decidedly in favor of the French. He quotes at great length from a discourse of Dr. Timothy Dwight, of Yale College, delivered in 1812, upon Infidelity. Speaking of the French, Dr. Dwight says:

They raised armies, in different years, amounting to five, seven, nine, and twelve hundred thousand men: "the strongest and most formidable body which was ever assembled on this globe." This multitude they emptied out upon every neighboring State. The life, liberty, and property of every bordering nation was consumed; and a boundless scene of desolation everywhere marked its course. It made no difference whether the nation was a friend or a foe, was in alliance with them, or at war. Whatever was thought convenient for France, was done; and done in defiance of every law of God or man; of the most solemn treaties, of the most absolute promises.

This is but a small portion of the extract, and although we have not verified it, we presume it is correctly taken from Dwight's works. Upon the whole extract, as he gives it, the writer says, referring to the course of the United States Government, and those who support it in putting down the rebellion:

In making this quotation, it is not my purpose, Mr. Editor, *to enlarge upon the similarity* of the events and doings of the French Revolution, and those of our own land and day. Were your columns the proper place (how scrupulous!), it would be no difficult task to show a *most striking resemblance* in the events and doings of the two countries and times. Indeed, it could be demonstrated, that, taking all things into consideration, the wickedness and crimes of the fanatical infidels, and their adherents of our day, *far exceed* in atrocity and enormity those of the time of the French Revolution. * * * Like their elder brethren, the infidels of France, they (the "Gospel ministers and Christians in the Northern States") have allowed an adoration of our NATIONAL UNITY, greatness and glory, equality and fraternity, to supplant in their hearts the adoration of the Prince of Peace; and principles and precepts of *corrupt humanity* to rule their actions, instead of the principles and precepts of the Gospel of God.

It is only necessary to observe, in reference to the above, that the character drawn by the graphic pen of Dr. Dwight of the ruling party in France, led by Robespierre, Danton, and their *confrères*, is held up by this writer as furnishing a good picture of the character of the Government of the

United States and its supporters in the present war against rebellion, except that "the wickedness and crimes" of the latter "far exceed in atrocity and enormity those of the time of the French Revolution."

CHARGE OF DISLOYALTY SUSTAINED.

It may be thought that we have given far too much attention to the course of a single paper. Our apology is, that it is probably the only paper claiming to be "religious," within the loyal portion of the country, which is not friendly to the Government; that it is published and mainly circulated in a State which has repeatedly voted against secession, and which is at this moment, and has frequently been since the beginning of the war, overrun by guerrillas who are laying waste the country, and that the course of this sheet is well calculated to give "aid and comfort" to this mode of rebel warfare.

And now we ask, can any candid man read the evidence we have adduced in the foregoing extracts,—all taken from a *single number* of the paper,—and say that *The True Presbyterian* is not a disloyal print?—that its editor, publishers, and correspondents, are not inimical to the Government which protects their homes, and that their innermost souls are not in full sympathy with rebels in arms who are seeking to overthrow it? No jury of twelve honest men could hesitate to bring in a verdict of guilty.

CALUMNY SELF-REFUTED.

This paper and certain secular prints from which it often quotes, denounce the Government for its tyranny and oppression, for its interference with the liberty of person, speech, and the press. Dr. Robinson says of himself, in the first extract given, that he has been "maligned, insulted, and robbed, by minions of the Administration." The reply to this is unanswerable. The simple fact that such men and such papers are permitted to live and labor to thwart the Government and to aid the rebellion, is an overwhelming disproof of its oppression. If the Government were really acting with *stern justice*, they would never more be permitted to trouble it. If they were pursuing such a course at Richmond, they would instantly have a lodgment in Castle Thunder, or be hung by the neck—or the heels. This they well know. It would be no better with them if they were doing their traitorous work in Paris or London. There is no nation under heaven, but that of the United States, where such things would be tolerated for a moment in a time of foul rebellion, while possessing the power which this nation has developed. And yet, the Government is maligned as oppressive! The very paragraph which contains the calumny is its own refutation.

THE REMEDY.—TWO EXAMPLES.

If such is the guilt, what is the remedy? We have already indicated what would be done elsewhere. But we incline to the opinion that the Government would act wisely to allow such prints to go on unmolested; though many think differently. They unquestionably exert a powerful influence against the Government, and give to the rebel cause substantial "aid" and much needed "comfort." But they serve at least two good purposes. They afford to the world the best illustration of the leniency of the Government; and they give striking examples of the depth of human depravity. Both of these may have an important end to serve in the development and final elevation of mankind.

An example may be given, however, of a remedy which eminent statesmen of a Border State approve. The Maryland Constitutional State Convention, July 19, 1864, passed the following order, by a vote of thirty-three to seventeen:

Ordered, That this Convention, representing the people of Maryland, hereby respectfully request the President of the United States, and the Commandants of Military Departments in which Maryland is included, *as an act of justice and propriety*, to assess upon sympathizers with the rebellion resident in this State, the total amount of all losses and spoliations sustained by loyal citizens of the United States resident in this State, by reason of the recent rebel raid, to compensate loyal sufferers.

It is as clear as the light, that these raiders in the loyal Border States are encouraged by the sympathizers with the rebellion therein; sometimes by secret organizations, which the President's Proclamation of Martial Law in Kentucky declares, upon the authority of military men and others, to exist in that State; sometimes by information given to them; and powerfully by the disloyal presses in the Border States. Through these means, the raiding parties, and especially those guerrilla bands that are nothing more than highway robbers and land pirates, are emboldened in their work. The Maryland Convention has expressed its solemn judgment, proposing a remedy. At the very time that State was thus suffering, and the national capital was threatened, raiding parties were laying waste Kentucky, through encouragement given by "their friends" at home. If the remedy suggested by a body of eminent statesmen, is "an act of justice and propriety" for the longitude of Maryland, it would be no less so for that of Kentucky. If the rule were applied there, many men, now rolling in wealth, who have aided John Morgan, and ladies who have kissed his hand and wept tears of joy over his photograph, would be made penniless. If, under this "act of justice," that quality were meted out in the manner proposed, and the guilty were rewarded "according to their works," the editors, publishers, and correspondents of *The True Presbyterian* would be reduced to beggary.

Another example is found in what the papers state, that Major-General Burbridge, commanding in Kentucky, has lately issued an order similar in principle to that recommended by the Maryland Convention, and even going much farther in retaliatory measures. We have not seen it, and cannot speak of its provisions; but if founded on "justice and propriety," as we presume is the case, it may turn out that editors and others who are sowing broadcast those seeds which produce such a harvest of desolation and blood through the fair fields of Kentucky, may yet receive their deserts in the visitations which will be made upon their persons and property.

GOVERNMENT ORDERS VINDICATED.

It will be appropriate, at this point, to notice one of the grossest charges which the "religious" journal above named has brought against the Government, and against every branch of the Northern Church. On application to the War Department, by the Bishops of the Methodist Episcopal Church, and by Missionary Boards of the Baptist, Presbyterian, and other churches at the North, for permission to occupy the pulpits and vacant neighborhoods of the Rebel States, that the Gospel might be preached, the Government granted these requests, regarding the commission given by these several Church authorities as a guarantee that the men sent South would be loyal, and imposing no other condition. Orders were issued to the different military commanders to give persons thus duly commissioned by the Church, all proper facilities for their work, and to put the pulpits at their disposal. The Generals in command issued their orders accordingly.

This proceeding on the part of the Government has been denounced by the above-named paper; and that the Church should seek such authority from the State, has been paraded as one of the conclusive proofs of its utter apostasy. At least one religious body, the Presbytery of Louisville, complained to the General Assembly of the Church that its Board of Missions should thus seek to have the commissions of its ministers indorsed by the State; and, in this course, it saw nothing but shame and "ruin" impending. It is in regard to these measures particularly, that Dr. Robinson speaks so contemptuously of the Secretary of War, and of the orders of certain military commanders. In the *same number* of his paper before quoted, he speaks of "Secretary Stanton's letter installing Bishop Ames as Military Pontiff in a vast district, and the infamous Norfolk order of Gen. Wild;" and also has the following:

> What though Methodist and Baptist Mohammedans grasp the sword offered them by that "eminent Father in God," Secretary Stanton, to drive back their Southern brethren into the fold out of which Northern faithlessness to covenants and semi-infidel opinions had driven them twenty years ago. * * * We had fondly hoped that so far as Churches are concerned, this disgrace might be confined to Northern Methodists and Baptists. To our mortification, and the disgrace of our own Church, we find the (Philadelphia) *Presbyterian*, a journal that will be understood to speak for Presbyterians because it once did,—for the public at large will not understand its miserable fall,—proposing that the Presbyterian Board of Missions should apply to the War Department for an order similar to the Methodist order! We have little fear that this Board will adopt the suggestion. Even should it be so run mad, the Church would be apt to stop supplies till a saner Board were put in its place.

The Board here referred to did "apply to the War Department for an order," and obtained it, and if not entirely "similar to the Methodist order," it is nevertheless based on the essential principle which underlies the whole case as between the Church and the State; and it is in regard to that principle, chiefly, that we now refer to the case. It is in reference to this latter application that the Louisville Presbytery complained; and it need only be said here, in contradiction to the above prophecy, that the General Assembly, in May last, did not elect "a saner Board," but approved and sustained its course.

The order from the War Department to the Methodist Bishops, and that of General Wild, are before us. We see nothing "infamous" in either, although both are so styled. In the first, "transportation and subsistence" are to be furnished "Bishop Ames and his clerk, when it can be done without prejudice to the service." This is mostly an affair of the Government, and is of minor consideration. In that of General Wild, it was ordered that the Churches should be "open freely to all officers and soldiers, white *or colored*," &c. Perhaps the *infamy* is found in the hue of the skin. But these, as we have said, are subordinate matters. We only desire to look at the radical principle at the bottom of these cases, as furnishing or not a just ground of complaint, to say nothing of vile abuse, both of the Church and the Government.*

* That the reader may see the two orders referred to, each of which is pronounced "infamous," we here insert them as found in *The True Presbyterian* of March 17, 1864:

"WAR DEPARTMENT, ADJUTANT-GENERAL'S OFFICE,
"WASHINGTON, *November* 30, 1863.

"To the Generals commanding the Departments of the Missouri, the Tennessee, and the Gulf, and all Generals and Officers commanding armies, detachments, and corps, and posts, and all Officers in the service of the United States in the above-mentioned Departments: You are hereby directed to place at the disposal of Rev. Bishop Ames, all houses of worship belonging to the Methodist Episcopal Church South, in which a loyal minister, who has been appointed by a loyal Bishop of said Church, does not now officiate. It is a matter of great importance to the Government, in its efforts to restore tranquillity to the community and peace to the nation, that Christian ministers should, by example and precept, support and foster the loyal sentiment of the people. Bishop Ames enjoys the entire confidence of this Department, and no doubt is entertained that all ministers who may be appointed by him will be entirely loyal. You are expected to give him all the aid, countenance, and support, practicable in the execution of his important mission. You are also authorized and directed to furnish Bishop Ames and his clerk with transportation

What is here involved? Here is no union of Church and State, as some have pretended; no subordination of the Church to the Government, out of its proper sphere, nor of the Government to the Church; no "indorsing" by the Government of a minister's "commission to preach the Gospel;" no improper position for the Church at the North to take; and no injustice to the Church at the South, so far as it is in rebellion, as to rights of property, organization, or spiritual teachers.

CHURCH APPLICATION VINDICATED BY THE FACTS.

In regard to the action of the Church at the North, its several branches have applied to the War Department for a "permit" or a "passport," that their ministers might go within the lines of the army, and occupy the vacant pulpits of the South, from some of which disloyal ministers had fled within the rebel lines, and from others of which they had been ejected by the Government. In its essence, this is all that the application involves. And what is it? It is precisely similar, and nothing more, than the permission which is sought and obtained from the War, Treasury, Navy, and State Departments, for citizens to exercise their business, trade, or profession, of a secular character,

and subsistence, when it can be done without prejudice to the service, and will afford them courtesy, assistance, and protection. By order of the Secretary of War.

"E. D. TOWNSEND, *Assistant Adjutant-General.*"

"HEAD-QUARTERS, NORFOLK AND PORTSMOUTH,
"NORFOLK, VA., *Feb.* 11, 1864.

"*General Orders, No.* 3.—All places of public worship in Norfolk and Portsmouth are hereby placed under the control of the Provost-Marshals of Norfolk and Portsmouth respectively, who shall see the pulpits properly filled by displacing, when necessary, the present incumbents, and substituting men of known loyalty and the same sectarian denomination, either military or civil, subject to the approval of the Commanding General. They shall see that the Churches are open freely to all officers and soldiers, white or colored, at the usual hour of worship, and at other times, if desired, and they shall see that no insult or indignity be offered to them, either by word, look, or gesture, on the part of the congregation. The necessary expenses will be levied, as far as possible, in accordance with the previous usages or regulations of each congregation respectively. No property shall be removed, either public or private, without permission from these head-quarters. By command of "E. A. WILD, *Brig.-General.*"

within the "seceded" States, or within the lines of the Federal army, *or to go there at all for any purpose;* the conditions being that the business, in the judgment of the Government, shall be proper in itself, and warranted by the circumstances of the case and the state of the country, and that the persons concerned in it shall be loyal.

The Church looked at the simple *facts*, that many Southern pulpits were vacant, and that others would become so as our armies should advance; that Southern ministers had abandoned and had been driven from their positions; and that the Government would not allow any but loyal men to fill their places. Besides this, tens of thousands of freedmen, women, and children, were as "sheep without a shepherd." The Gospel, therefore, would not be preached at all to multitudes of people, white and black, many of whom were loyal, and would gladly welcome it, unless the Government should open the way. Under these circumstances, was the Church doing wrong or right in asking the sanction of the Government,—obtaining a "permit," for it was no more than that, and just what is sometimes done on heathen ground,—to "go into all the South and preach the Gospel to every creature?" Looking at the facts alone, it is clear that the Church at the North has done nothing more than her duty. Had she not done it, she would have been verily guilty before God, and the blood of multitudes of souls would have been found upon her. We do not say what might or might not have been the duty of the Church, in this case, had the application been denied. It is not necessary to raise any question of the Church's duty to preach the Gospel, even in the face of opposition from the civil power. That has nothing to do with the present issue. This, however, may be said, as a principle universally applicable,—that, if the civil power is opposed to the Church's proper work, the Church should seek to conciliate rather than disregard such opposition. In this case, we simply look at the facts as they are. The Church could not send men South to preach without permission of the Government, or provoking its hostility. It was, then, its duty to ask permission to go within the lines of the army, and, if granted, to accept it, provided the work itself was proper. The actual condition of the South reveals the duty, and the application vindicates the Church in seeking to discharge it in a way not to provoke collision with the Government.

CHIEF GROUND OF COMPLAINT.

But suppose the Church, looking beyond the facts, should entertain the question, whether she might not, in this course, be conniving at a great wrong done by the Government to the Southern people; how would her conduct be affected? This brings up the other side of the case. It is no doubt here that *The True Presbyterian*, and those who agree with it, found their great objection, denying that the Government has any right to take possession of the Southern Churches, or turn them over to loyal men from the North or elsewhere; and that the Church, in asking and accepting this from the Government, is guilty of compounding a felony with the State. Dr. Robinson speaks as follows upon this point:

When the Administration, or any of its functionaries, obtrude themselves into the affairs of religion, and undertake to direct the affairs of Christ's kingdom, from which they are restrained both by the law of Christ and the Constitution of the country, we are obliged to treat them as any other false teachers and *usurpers* in the Christian commonwealth. * * * It comes to settling the powers of civil and military government over religion. * * * The people of the country will surely be slow to recognize such powers over religion in this Government; for who knows how soon the order may be extended to embrace Ohio, New York, and Pennsylvania, as well as Missouri, Tennessee, etc.?

When the cases become *similar* in Ohio, New York, and Pennsylvania, and through treason and rebellion the ministry and people of the Churches in those States turn traitors, and their pulpits become vacant, as is now the case all through the South within the lines of the Federal armies, then "the order *may* be extended to embrace" *them* also, on the ground of the most unquestionable principles of public law, as recognized among all nations. It is on this ground that the course of the Government toward disloyal ministers and people at the South is justified.

GOVERNMENT AND CHURCH VINDICATED BY THE LAW.

The laws of war regard all citizens of a hostile nation as public enemies, whether actually engaged in war or not.* When a nation is engaged in civil war, and, as in the present case, is attempting to put down a rebellion undertaken by organized States, all persons within the territory in rebellion are in like manner deemed enemies of the Government. This is settled public law among all nations;† and it has been so held in regard to the present rebellion, by the Supreme Court of the United States.

But the case immediately in hand goes far beyond this. It concerns ministers and churches that are notoriously in

* "It is understood that the whole nation declares war against another nation; for the sovereign represents the nation, and acts in the name of the whole society; and it is only in a body, and in her national character, that one nation has to do with another. Hence, these two nations are enemies, and all the subjects of the one are enemies to all the subjects of the other. In this particular, custom and principles are in accord. * * * Since women and children are subjects of the State, and members of the nation, they are to be ranked in the class of enemies. But it does not thence follow that we are justifiable in treating them like men who bear arms, or are capable of bearing them. It will appear in the sequel, that we have not the same rights against all classes of enemies."—*Vattel*, b. 3, ch. 5.

† "It is very evident that the common laws of war ought to be observed by both parties in every civil war."—*Vattel*, b. 3, ch. 18.

open rebellion, and are among the leaders in the revolt. What the Government has done is to recognize these facts, and to assume control of the property which these fugitive rebels left behind them, and which had been used against the Government. So far as this church property is concerned, the Government might have confiscated every dollar of it to its own use by the regular operation of military law; for, notoriously, these abandoned pulpits were the places which bred and fostered treason, and without which the rebellion would never have had more than an abortive birth; and they were the most powerful instigators of the war against the Government, up to the very moment its armies reclaimed the ground on which they were built.*

When Admiral Farragut captured New Orleans, he or General Butler might have taken Dr. Palmer's Church for a hospital, or for any other military purpose, and the Government might retain it forever as such, a standing monument to the infamy of his treason; for the trustees, elders, pew-holders, and all claiming an interest in the property, had permitted him from that pulpit to assail the Government with his unwonted eloquence, and to urge the people to open rebellion against its authority. All property, public or private, used in open aid of war, is liable to

* "When once we have precisely determined who our enemies are, it is easy to know what are the things belonging to the enemy (*res hostiles*). We have shown that not only the sovereign with whom we are at war is an enemy, but also his whole nation, even the very women and children. Every thing, therefore, which belongs to that nation,—to the state, to the sovereign, to the subjects of whatever age or sex,—every thing of that kind, I say, falls under the description of things belonging to the enemy."—*Vattel*, b. 3, ch. 5. "We have a right to deprive our enemy of his possessions, of every thing which may augment his strength and enable him to make war. This every one endeavors to accomplish in the manner most suitable to him. Whenever we have an opportunity, we seize on the enemy's property, and convert it to our own use; and thus, besides diminishing the enemy's power, we augment our own, and obtain, at least, a partial indemnification or equivalent, either for what constitutes the subject of the war, or for the expenses and losses incurred in its prosecution,—in a word, we do ourselves justice."—*Ibidem*, b. 3, ch. 9.

condemnation on its capture. No principle of public law is more fully laid down by all writers on the Laws of Nations and the Laws of War than this; and it applies to the vast majority of Church edifices throughout the South. By their being used as among the most powerful means for sustaining and prosecuting the war, the Government has an indefeasible title to use them if it can capture them; to eject disloyal ministers and people from them, and to appropriate them to any proper purpose in maintenance of its just authority.

But what has the Government actually done? It has preserved these Churches for religious worship, and has simply taken a course which would secure loyal men to occupy their pulpits. This is the whole case, and the Government stands justified, while in fact it might have appropriated them to other uses.

And what has the Church done? Its course is fully vindicated both by the *facts* and the *law*.

And yet a howl of indignation has come over from the city of Toronto, week after week, and has taken form in traitorous paragraphs in the city of Louisville, and its senseless bellowings are echoed through the land to frighten pious and timid women.

VINDICATED BY REBEL AUTHORITY.

If Dr. Robinson is willing to receive *instruction* touching the relations of Church and State, bearing directly upon the point in hand, we refer him to a teacher whom at least *he* ought to respect. It comes from the pen of Dr. Thornwell. It is found in the "Address of the General Assembly of the Presbyterian Church in the Confederate States of America," which was republished in Louisville with commendation, and with which Dr. Robinson probably had something to do. The following sentences from that Address are all that are necessary for our present purpose.

When the State makes wicked laws, contradicting the eternal principles of rectitude, the Church is at liberty to testify against them, and humbly to petition that they may be repealed. In like manner, *if the Church becomes seditious, and a disturber of the peace,* THE STATE HAS A RIGHT TO ABATE THE NUISANCE.

That is good doctrine, and we commend it to Dr. Robinson's acceptance. It comes from a man for whom he has always, with ourselves, had a high admiration. And besides, it is the doctrine of the whole "Confederate General Assembly," for this Address was "unanimously adopted by the Assembly." It is true, indeed, that they write their own condemnation, for no nation under heaven ever tolerated a class of men within it who were more "seditious," and were more influential "disturbers of the peace," than these same men have been during this whole rebellion; but that does not affect the matter; it is sound doctrine, nevertheless.

We insist, then, that the case shall be tried upon their own principles. The Government has done nothing more than carry out the law as here laid down. If any fact is well established, it is that the mass of the Southern Churches, led by their ministers, have gone heart and soul into the rebellion and the war against the Government. These Churches have been recruiting agents for the rebel armies, and many of their ministers are now commissioned officers in them. For this course of the Southern Church, the Government, upon their own showing, "has a right to abate the nuisance." This only is what it is doing, and the manner of the abatement is mild and gentle, infinitely more so than what simple justice would sanction, but probably dictated by sound policy. It merely forbids these "seditious" men and "disturbers of the peace" to occupy the pulpits they have profaned, and turns them over to men who will preach the Gospel instead of treason, and who will enjoin obedience to lawful authority instead of rebellion against it. Its course stands approved by the laws of God and man, as these laws are understood by the rebels themselves. It is condemned by certain men in the Border States and elsewhere, because they are hostile to the Government and in *sympathy with its enemies.*

We have now shown, in a few examples, that there is disloyalty of the rankest kind among the ministers of the Gospel in some parts of the loyal States. These cases will serve to illustrate others. That such deeds should be permitted, is proof of the leniency of the Government; that they should pursue such a course, is proof of their deep guilt, and of their utter insensibility to the prime obligations of citizenship. We shall see, in a subsequent chapter, how such things are regarded, and what punishment is justly due them, in the judgment of their Southern friends.

CHAPTER VII.

THE CHURCH, NORTH AND SOUTH, ON DISLOYALTY.

The contest in which the nation is now engaged for its life, has brought into discussion, both among politicians and churchmen, many important principles regarding men's duties and rights under civil government. Among them are the relations of the Church and the State, in the different spheres marked out for them by that divine authority on which, as organizations, they both rest; and the responsibilities and immunities of citizens in regard to their civil and religious character.

The principles involved in these branches of the general subject are always theoretically important. At the present moment, within the United States, they are more practically and vitally so than they have ever been before. They affect more numerous classes, a greater multitude of individuals, and more widely extended interests, relating to the political, social, and moral welfare of the whole people, in every section of the country, than has been the case at any previous period in our history. Personal liberty, of speech, of the press, and of action; reputation and character for good citizenship and for piety on the one hand, and a wreck of these on the other; property, and even the means of earning one's bread and educating one's family; the good or bad name which a man will consign as a heritage to his children; the punishment from the authorities of his country, if he prove false to her interests in a time of civil peril, or, if he escape that, the judgment which may overtake him from God; these are only the obvious bearings which the case presents.

It is not our purpose to go into a full discussion of this broad subject in this place. Each branch of it would require more space than we can devote to the whole. There are a few points, however, which it is essential to consider, to meet the demands of the general object which this volume is designed to serve; and these we propose to view chiefly in a practical rather than a theoretical light, and to note the principle which is sanctioned from the action which is taken upon it.

ALL MEN SUBJECT TO CIVIL AUTHORITY.

The authority of civil government extend to all men, and all organizations of men. It rests ultimately upon the fact that civil society is ordained of God. This is declared in His word. The first civil duty of every citizen, therefore, is to render obedience to the lawful government under which he lives. When he violates this duty, he puts himself without the pale of its protection, and renders himself liable to punishment. There can be no exception, in either of these aspects,—as to the duty, or the consequences of failure to discharge it,—in the case of any persons or classes of persons. These are obvious truths, and are commonly admitted.

OBEDIENCE TO CIVIL AUTHORITY A RELIGIOUS DUTY.

If civil society is ordained of God, and if civil government derives its authority from Him, then obedience to civil rulers is not only a civil but a religious obligation; and hence it follows, that any infraction of this duty, either in omission or commission, is not only an offence against the laws of the land, but is a sin against God. Here, likewise, there are no exemptions. The religious as well as the civil sanction binds all men, whether they believe in God or deny Him, whether they have religious affections or are corrupt. The obligation is perfect, and if disregarded or violated, the sin is complete; and they rest upon God's ordinance, and not upon men's views of it or their feelings in regard to it. An atheist is bound to render obedience to civil authority as really as any one else, and if he falls short of this he sins as really as any other person. His unbelief can neither destroy his obligation nor cancel his guilt.

While this is so, the weight of obligation and the heinousness of guilt may be affected by men's light and advantages. This all men admit, and this the Scriptures teach. Hence, a man who has been taught from childhood to render religious obedience to civil authority, and in whose soul dwells the power of divine grace,—who recognizes the full weight of Christian obligation in all things, and gives to it the voluntary homage of his heart,—is deemed a far more guilty man, when he commits treason against his country, than is he who commits the same crime and yet who has enjoyed none of these advantages, but has been sunk in ignorance and corrupting immoralities all his life. This doctrine commends itself to every man's common sense, and has the sanction of Scripture.

MINISTERS TO PREACH SUBJECTION.

The same doctrine holds good in the practical application of the principle to ministers of the Gospel. They with all other men are bound to render religious obedience to the civil authority. But in the sight of God, simple obedience on their part, while a high duty in itself, is at the lowest point in the scale in this class of their duties. They are not only to obey the powers that be, but they are in this to be an example to others; and, above all, they are to preach this truth to the people; to give instruction in all the principles of God's word in regard to obedience, to point out the obligation, and to hold up the guilt of violating it.

Nor are they to deal in vague generalities and abstractions on this theme, any more than upon any other doctrine of the Scriptures. They are to point out in what obedience consists, what it involves, and what it demands, in heart, word, and deed, just as in regard to any other religious duty; and they are to declare wherein it may be violated in any of these respects. They are to endeavor to make this as plain, both regarding the duty and the sin of violating it, as any doctrine of salvation, for all are alike from God; and, indeed, if duty and sin are involved herein, even salvation may be endangered or promoted by a wrong or right direction given to the judgment, heart, conscience, or conduct, in reference to this as truly as to any other subject of revelation. In a word, all that God has declared upon these themes, the minister is bound to unfold to the people.

OMISSION OF THIS DUTY A SIN.

If such be the weight of obligation resting upon a minister, under such a view of his office, his guilt must be correspondingly great if he barely omit this branch of his public duty. The failure to instruct the people upon these themes, to the full extent that they are revealed in the Scriptures, becomes, in him, a heinous sin; for he is placed in the pulpit by the authority of God for this very purpose.

It may be further true, that the time when especially this duty should be fully met, is the time when men openly set at naught these obligations,—when they turn against the authority of lawful civil rulers, and combine and conspire together for its overthrow; and more especially may this be true when so great a scandal rests upon the Church itself, when the people of God, to so great an extent, meet in His sanctuary to hear His law from the priest's lips, and then turn deliberately against that lawful Government which God in His providence has placed over them; and most conclusively must this be the time for God's ministers to cry aloud and spare not, when the members of his Church extensively engage in the work and guilt of treason and rebellion with others not only, but when they take the foremost ranks in the movement, and plead religious obligations as a justification. Then, above all times, is it a minister's duty to declare the law of God, and warn his people of sin. If he omit it, he is verily guilty. If he discharge it, he is but doing his official work.

THE CROWNING GUILT.

What, then, must be thought of that class of ministers whose guilt consists not merely in the omission of this duty, but who publicly and privately counsel open resistance to the civil authority?—who prostitute the pulpit to preaching rebellion against their civil rulers, and who become leaders in a stupendous revolution against a popular Government, and the open advocates of war upon it which is slaying millions of their fellow-countrymen, and filling the land with widowhood and orphanage?

And what shall be thought of the religious press which openly teaches such doctrines, and becomes the most powerful ally, with the pulpit, in leading the people of God into these crimes? Under the garb of religious doctrine, it teaches that which is at war with its first principles; under a pretence of piety, it openly encourages sin; with the plea of serving God, it is the most powerful agent of the devil; pretending to a regard for human life, a desire for peace, and a horror of blood and carnage, it is directly aiding those who have raised the standard of a bloody rebellion against a Government which, by the confession of their ablest statesmen, never injured them, and whose power and patronage had always been in their hands.

If guilt surpassing this has ever been committed, since time began, among so enlightened a people, and under pretence of *religion*, the case has entirely escaped our notice.

DISLOYALTY PUNISHABLE BY THE STATE.

It becomes an interesting question, What does disloyalty deserve, and who may mete out its punishment? Upon this men have disagreed, and do still.

That the civil authority may punish it, no one doubts. Treason, its highest type, is a crime committed directly against the State. It seeks the overthrow of its authority, or the destruction or usurpation of the Government. In all countries it is regarded as the highest of crimes, for it perils the Government and all it guards, and hence it is generally punishable with death, though some degrees of it with banishment or with the heaviest civil disabilities. The Constitution of the United States defines treason, and the laws enacted under it declare the penalty of death.

There is also misprision of treason, and there are other crimes which come under the general designation of disloyalty. As these, in all their grades and degrees, are crimes against the State, they may be punished by its authority.

We of course use the term "loyalty" not in any legal, but wholly in a popular sense. We are not aware that the word is found in any of our statute laws as a legal term. But this is of no consequence; all understand what is meant by it, as applied in the contest now raging in our country. Nor is it of the least moment where, how, or when, the term originated. It is amusing to see how many words have been wasted in an attempt to show that *loyalty* and *disloyalty* can have no application to the people in *our* civil war. It is of no manner of importance that "loyalty" was formerly used to express attachment to the sovereign and the reigning family in monarchical countries. It has become popularized in the United States, and at the present moment expresses attachment to the Government now imperilled and a desire for its maintenance against the rebellion seeking its subversion.

WHAT LOYALTY AND DISLOYALTY ARE.

Loyalty means faithfulness to the obligations of *law;* obedience to lawful authority. Men will differ as to whether a certain act or line of conduct is *loyal* or *disloyal*, according as they define these *terms*. The guilt or innocence of a person on trial for any crime, must be determined by the facts and circumstances of the particular case, and which may not belong to any other case; nor would full light be thrown upon the proper result by the most accurate verbal definition of the crime under which he were arraigned.

It is of little practical avail, therefore, that men differ upon the meaning of the *term* "loyalty." It is of far more importance that they agree upon the duty of manifesting it in support of the Government, even though they differ as to the manner and degree in which such manifestation should be evinced. For ourselves, we deem it a citizen's duty to sustain the Government in *putting down the rebellion* by all the power he can command; by his personal influence, by word and deed, by his purse, his sword, and his prayers. By putting it down, we mean, *destroying it root and branch*, *crushing the life out of it*, and putting it forever past the faintest hope of resurrection; and we are free to say, that we value that citizen's loyalty at a very low figure which does not come up to that point. It is worth nothing, and *may* be worth infinitely less than nothing in such perils as are now upon the nation,—yea, may be counted upon the other side,—unless it be openly demonstrative, in all proper ways, times, and places, in sustaining the Government against its deadly foe.

DISLOYALTY PUNISHABLE BY THE CHURCH.

We have seen that disloyalty is punishable by the State. It is equally clear that it is punishable by the Church. Men have differed upon this point, and do still, as they do upon other matters that are plain. We cannot expect them to agree in those things in which their prejudices are deeply enlisted, until they are willing to lay them aside. It is perfectly demonstrable, however, that disloyalty is an offence of which the Church may take cognizance.

In saying this we wish not to be misunderstood. We have indicated what, *personally*, we deem to be genuine loyalty for every citizen of the United States in this time of civil peril. We do not, however, announce that as a standard for the Church, on which she should act in ecclesiastical discipline; nor do we lay it down as a standard for other men. To his own Master each one standeth or falleth. We give it, simply, as our own view of what duty demands. It is *our opinion;* nothing more. We allow other men to have theirs.

But that disloyalty is an ecclesiastical offence which the Church may consider and judge, is something higher than mere opinion. It follows inevitably from the teachings of the word of God. What loyalty and disloyalty are, in any case that may come before the Church for adjudication, those who have to deal with it must determine; for, as before observed, each case must be settled by the facts and circumstances which are peculiar to it. But that the *principle* of disloyalty is such that it may involve an ecclesiastical offence by the word of God, is beyond doubt; and it is only to the principle that we now give any consideration.

REASONS FOUNDED ON REVELATION.

The doctrine we maintain arises inevitably from the nature and duty of obedience to the civil authority. The nature of the obedience enjoined is *religious*. It has God's highest sanctions. To violate the injunction is *sin*. Sin is to be removed by inculcating truth; and when it breaks out in open acts of scandal, it may be met by ecclesiastical supervision, trial, and censure. This is the case with every grade and kind of offence which affects private or public morals, or the welfare of society, or the influence and good name of religion among men.

Disloyalty is no exception to this. Open disobedience to rulers, when it manifests itself in disturbing or threatening the peace of society, or aims or connives at resistance to lawful authority, or subverting the Government, is a sin and a scandal by the word of God; and if committed by a member of the Church, he may be arraigned and punished for it as clearly as for any other scandal. If not, why not? Is it because this is a civil offence, and punishable by the State? So is arson, so is murder, so is fraud; and yet, will a man pretend that one may burn down his neighbor's house, or take his life in cold blood, or cheat him out of his property, and not be disturbed by the Church, because the State may take cognizance of these offences? This is in the highest degree preposterous. Nor is it enough that the State does actually punish for these crimes; the Church may also inflict censure for them, in the same case, in the person of the same individual on whom the State has inflicted its highest sentence. It would be a singular spectacle to behold a man incarcerated justly as a civil penalty for forgery, and yet the Church take no action, and he, in consequence, remain in good standing, on the ground that he was already suffering punishment from the State. Nor, on the other hand, is the Church to be governed or limited by the State in such cases. The State is not infallible. A man may be punished unjustly. If the victim of tyranny, or prejudice, or ignorance, or incompetency, be a member of the Church, the whole case may be ecclesiastically considered and decided, notwithstanding the State may have acted upon it. The Church is not bound in such case by what the State has done, so far as to be debarred an adjudication; and if, in her judgment, her member is oppressed, she may so declare. She may consider the testimony, conduct the case by her own rules of proceeding, and come to a decision independent of the State and contrary to its judgment. She cannot release from prison, nor restore to life, but she may place the man in good standing within her pale, and show the most clear reasons, it may be, for her decision; and in nothing of this does she show the least insubordination or disrespect towards the civil authority, but may be entirely submissive to it. All this arises from the fact that the respective jurisdictions of the Church and the State, though embracing the same persons and covering the same offences, have different spheres to fill, and different ends to serve, in their cognizance of the same conduct.

SPIRITUAL JURISDICTION BROADER THAN CIVIL.

But the difference between these separate ruling powers does not stop here. The spiritual jurisdiction is both deeper and broader than the civil. It embraces offences which the latter does not touch; and in those which the civil power does consider, there are moral elements which the spiritual power alone deems important. There are a multitude of offences, any one of which, habitually committed, would destroy a man's standing in the Church, and upon trial would cast him out of it; and yet, though guilty of all of them, his good standing before the laws of the land would not be affected. And there are grades of the same radical offence which the Church holds to be stamped with guilt, but which the State overlooks. A man may be guilty of "perjury," and the State will punish him; but all false swearing, or false statements under oath, are not "legal perjury." But by the laws which regulate ecclesiastical discipline, lying, deception, falsehood,—all which enter into the moral elements of perjury,—are themselves offences which the Church may consider, whether committed under oath or not. A variety of hearings and pleadings in almost any case before a Church court, which a civil court would not consider, or would rule out entirely, may be deemed important, and may be decisive of the result which is reached. The principle here involved is of the highest moment. The jurisdiction of the Church, as embracing a man's conduct, or as cognizant of any act of his life, reaches where the State cannot go, because its rule is spiritual, and deals primarily with the heart and conscience; and although in actual discipline the Church deals only with acts, there are classes of actions and elements of conduct which are deemed proper for its consideration which do not come within the civil statute.

This may be illustrated in regard to the offence of disloyalty. Who will pretend to say, that, because a man may not have committed "treason" in the technical sense of the statute, he may not have been actually guilty of it before the law of God? or that, because there may not be ground for prosecution before a civil court for that offence, it *therefore* follows necessarily that there cannot be ground for charges before a spiritual court? To decide that there cannot be, is to decide that the Church must simply follow in the wake of the State; to take the position that only offences of the same nature belong to both; to confound the jurisdictions, which are distinct, into one; to join together what God has forever separated. Any person may be safely challenged to point out where such a position is sustained by the word of God. It is, therefore, a totally erroneous doctrine to maintain that the Church cannot go beyond the State in inquiring into this or any other alleged offence; or that either is precluded, within its own proper sphere, from canvassing an offence against its own law, by reason of what the other may have done or not done.

DISLOYALTY ACTUALLY CONDEMNED BY THE CHURCH.

Passing from these abstract principles, we find that the Church has sustained them in its actual practice. Nothing is better settled in its whole history. Disobedience to the civil authority, disloyalty, treason, and misprision of treason, have always been treated as ecclesiastical offences. This is shown in the records of every Church. Members have been excommunicated, and ministers have been deposed, for such offences by the Church; and they have also, for the same crimes, been punished by the State. These things have occurred, as is well known, in every country in Christendom.

Sometimes they have occurred in times of quiet, but most commonly in times of civil war. We say nothing upon the merits of any particular case. Great injustice may sometimes have been done in ecclesiastical convictions for disloyalty; while, on the other hand, no doubt, some men may have gone "unwhipt of justice" by the Church, as some will go hereafter. All we are seeking is the sanction of the principle, and we find that abundantly sustained in the history of the Church.

Several of the leading denominations at the North, during our present civil war, have acted on the right and duty of the Church to discipline their members, and especially their ministers, for disloyalty. In some instances they have censured, suspended, or silenced them. We know nothing of the merits of these special cases, but they illustrate the principle, that disloyalty is deemed to be an offence within the proper cognizance of the Church. The secular prints, in some cases, and at least *one* "religious" journal, have made a great outcry that such proceedings were a violation of the Church's spiritual principles, and an interference with the rights of the citizen. But all such outbursts are senseless, stupid, silly, and have no other importance than that they give "aid and comfort" to rebels in arms against the Government. The Church has as clear a jurisdiction over its ministers and members, touching loyalty and disloyalty, as over their conduct touching drunkenness or profanity.

PRESBYTERIAN CHURCH.—DR. McPHEETERS.

One of the most noted cases, of recent occurrence, by which the doctrine for which we contend has been illustrated by an actual adjudication, is that of the Rev. Samuel B. McPheeters, D. D., Pastor of the Pine Street Presbyterian Church in St. Louis, Missouri. It was decided in the General Assembly of the Presbyterian Church, at Newark, New Jersey, in May last. The trial lasted several days, and the decision was given after a full discussion, in which Dr. McPheeters and a large number of members of the Assembly participated.

It is not necessary for our present purpose to go largely into this case, or to discuss its merits, or to pass judgment upon the decision. None of these are essential to the immediate matter in hand, or to an understanding of the principles we are considering. We have only to say of the decision, that as it was made by the court of last resort, by conscientious and intelligent men, and by a majority of one hundred and seventeen to forty-seven, after a full hearing, we there let it stand.

It is proper to say, however, that Dr. McPheeters was not on trial before the Assembly on a formal charge of disloyalty. Indeed, there were no charges, strictly so called, and no testimony in the usual sense, either before the Assembly or the court below, on which the case proceeded. It was a dissolution of the pastoral relation existing between Dr. McPheeters and his congregation, made by the Presbytery of St. Louis, and their forbidding him to preach, out of which the case grew, and of which Dr. McPheeters complained to the Assembly. Irregularities in the proceedings, a want of authority in the Presbytery to act in the premises, gross injustice done to his pastoral and ministerial rights, and acting without the wishes of a majority of the congregation, were among the things charged in the complaint against the Presbytery. The merits of the case thus involved many radical principles of purely ecclesiastical law, and in dismissing the complaint and sustaining the Presbytery, the Assembly overruled the grounds on which the complaint was based.

It is nevertheless perfectly clear, that Dr. McPheeters regarded himself, and was regarded by his friends, as *virtually* on trial for "disloyalty." This is the aspect given to the case by the proceedings of the Assembly, by the arguments on both sides, though not of course by the judgment. Disloyalty was the ground of dissatisfaction in a large minority of his congregation, and this alone led to the action of the Presbytery. This is a simple matter of fact, and of record. The Assembly's decision, by the large vote given, was thus deemed a virtual condemnation for disloyalty, was foreshadowed in many of the speeches as involving that consequence, and has since been so accepted by the friends of Dr. McPheeters in their animadversions upon the proceedings of the Assembly.

It then appears that the General Assembly of the Presbyterian Church, has virtually sustained the doctrine that "disloyalty" may be treated as an ecclesiastical offence by its action in the case of one of its ministers.

INDIVIDUAL OPINIONS IN THE ASSEMBLY.

It must not be supposed that the vote given in the case of Dr. McPheeters, is the criterion for determining how large a portion of the General Assembly consider "disloyalty" as a proper offence for ecclesiastical action. On the contrary, we have not observed (though, possibly, some case may have escaped our notice) that a single member took open and distinct ground that disloyalty was *not* a proper subject for Church censure. Certain it is, however, that the most distinguished ministers and other members of the *minority*, as well as Dr. McPheeters himself, directly admitted, in their arguments, that disloyalty *is* an ecclesiastical offence. We refer to a few of them.

Dr. McPheeters said in his defence:

He was prepared to admit that a man might render a *formal* obedience to all lawful requirements, and so demean himself as to avoid liability to punishment, and yet, in times like these, lead such a course as to render him a dangerous member of the community, and an intolerable citizen of an agitated State. * * * The Assembly must decide what liberty the Church will allow her pastors, whose conscientious convictions lead them to stand aloof, in the pulpit, from the civil strife now desolating the land. *This, after all, underlies the whole case.* * * * The Assembly must decide, if they do not sustain this complaint, that I cannot preach to Pine street, because, as a minister, I stand aloof from civil strife. But if not in Pine street, then nowhere; for the same principle applies everywhere. * * * *If he was disloyal* in any sense that should mar his case before this court, he was also guilty of perjury, for he had taken an oath of allegiance, and kept it too; and when he was tried, he wished it done on charges regularly tabled. He wished evidence; not in loose statements, innuendoes, and patriotic speeches, but evidence under oath. * * * Now, what he had asked as a defiance to his accusers, he demanded as a right of this Assembly, that if any statements were made or insinuations thrown out that he had been guilty of *such offences*, that you will order the Presbytery of St. Louis *to take up and issue the case.*

Dr. McPheeters thus makes the most explicit acknowledgment of the right of a Church court to try a person on charges of disloyalty. Dr. William L. Breckinridge said upon this case:

It has been attempted to thrust him out of his work among the flock, over which the Holy Ghost hath made him overseer, and to brand into him a mark of dishonor—with the allegation of that, which *on all sides is called a crime.* * * * He is called a disloyal man—not true to the country—and on this clamor it is attempted to drive him from his work in the Church.

Dr. N. L. Rice took ground that disloyalty was an offence which may be dealt with by the Church, and spoke as follows:

We have virtually a minister on trial—*virtually* on trial; visited too with the severest penalties that could result from a trial. * * * We have been told that a majority of the ministers of the Synod of Missouri are disloyal, and, *of course, immoral.* * * * The real charge brought against Dr. McPheeters was *disloyalty;* on this the opposition of the minority of his Church was based; on this the allegation of loss of usefulness was founded; on this charge the Presbytery proceeded. This is manifest in all the pleadings there, and in all the pleadings here. This was a charge affecting his *moral character; for disloyalty is a sin.* Had the Presbytery a right to punish him for *this sin*, and to fix this blot upon his character, without arraigning him, and tabling charges, and giving him an opportunity of defence? * * * They entertained this charge affecting his moral character. * * * If Presbytery believed that he was *disloyal, they should have tried him*, and given him the usual opportunity of defence. They did not go far enough, if the charge is well founded; if he was loyal, they have gone too far. * * * He (Dr. Rice) did not know whether that brother is loyal or not. * * * Prove his disloyalty, and he would go farther than the Presbytery went.

Mr. Cleland said:

If Dr. McPheeters is guilty of treason—this is the highest crime against the laws of God and of man, against the Church and the Commonwealth—*then he ought to be suspended from the Church by the Presbytery*, and from the gallows by the sheriff of his county!

All those whose remarks we have given above voted in the minority. Certain friends of Dr. McPheeters, belonging to the Presbytery that acted on his case, sent a "memorial" in his behalf to the General Assembly, in which they state as follows:

He openly announces his recognized obligations to "be subject to the powers that be," and his enemies have been challenged in vain to point to one word or one act inconsistent with those obligations. *If such word or act can be fairly pointed out*, your memorialists hereby agree to withdraw all interest and effort in his behalf, and *to consign him to his just deserts* at the hands of a Presbytery which has shown every disposition to deal with him in the utmost severity.

The foregoing extract, (together with a much larger portion of this memorial), we take as we find it embodied in the speech of Dr. W. L. Breckinridge.

It thus appears, that not only the Assembly in its virtual act, but the minority of the body, in their speeches on the case, with Dr. McPheeters and the St. Louis "memorialists," put themselves on the record in favor of the doctrine that a minister may be prosecuted in a Church court on a charge of "disloyalty," and that therefore this is an ecclesiastical offence. We trust they will be found standing there in any time of future need.

DR. McPHEETERS ON MILITARY ORDERS.

We had occasion to notice in the last chapter the malignant denunciations of *The True Presbyterian* against the Government, for not allowing the ministerial traitors at the South to occupy the pulpits from which they had preached treason. We showed that the orders of the War Department were justified, both by the law and the facts, in turning the Southern Churches over to loyal ministers; and that, even according to rebel authority, from the "Confederate General Assembly," it was admitted that "the State has a right to abate the nuisance," whenever "the Church becomes seditious, and a disturber of the peace," as was notoriously the case with the mass of the whole Southern Church of all denominations.

It is but just to allow Dr. McPheeters to be heard on this point, as his Church was taken from him by military authority. In his late speech in the General Assembly, he said:

> It was seized * * * to the exclusion of the session, trustees, and its own congregation. He had no wish to arraign or find fault with the officers of the Government. He wished to treat them fairly. He acknowledged that, in a State convulsed by armed resistance to the Government, *they would be justified in doing whatever they deemed necessary for the public safety,* Nor would he have thought them wrong in seizing his Church, banishing him from the pulpit, or dragging him from the very altar, *if he or his people had used these for fomenting treason, or in any way opposing the Government.*

We commend these just sentiments, applied here by Dr. McPheeters to himself and Church hypothetically,—but true to the letter of the Churches in the South taken possession of by the War Department,—to the serious consideration of *The True Presbyterian;* but we doubt whether its conductors are in a state of heart to learn any thing even from one for whom they manifest so deep a sympathy.

Dr. McPheeters might, furthermore, become their instructor upon the nature of the order of General Rosecrans, which they have so assiduously perverted, if, indeed, they were not callous to instruction from any good quarter. Dr. Robinson speaks of it, as "Rosecrans's impious and infamous order of Cæsar's oath as a qualification for sitting in Christ's court." But Dr. McPheeters, in his speech, while mentioning his "scruples of conscience which made that order a restraint," speaks of it as follows:

In making this statement, Dr. McPheeters said that the end aimed at by the General *was a justifiable one, one which it was necessary they should try to accomplish*, viz.: to prevent bodies of men from meeting and acting in a way injurious to the State, *if there is good reason to suspect that they will so act.*

One more point of comparison will suffice. Speaking of the proceedings of the Assembly in the case of Dr. McPheeters, Dr. Robinson says: "Others, in the very slang of Strong & Co., declared the issue to be, Dr. McPheeters's loyalty or disloyalty." But Dr. McPheeters himself, in reference to this very issue, said: "*This, after all, underlies this whole case.*" And so the mass of the General Assembly regarded it, the minority as well as the majority; and so did the friends of Dr. McPheeters, the St. Louis "memorialists."

FALSE CRITERION OF LOYALTY.

While the whole Church seem to agree that disloyalty is an ecclesiastical offence,—always excepting the Canadian exile and his paper,—it is well to note what is often resorted to as a standard of loyalty, and which is in reality no just criterion at all.

Nothing has been more common, as a defence against

charges of disloyalty, in the case of certain clergymen, than to point to their "piety." Our "Southern brethren," the rankest rebels among them, have had the shield of such defences thrown around them; and so have ministers in the Border States, and some whose homes are farther North. Such a man "cannot be disloyal; he is a lovely character, meek, devoted; his piety is a disproof of the charge." Many persons are disposed in this manner to shield disloyalty under the garb of piety. This was one of the views presented in the General Assembly in vindication of Dr. McPheeters; and Dr. Robinson, in his paper, speaks of "the universally admitted character of Dr. McPheeters for piety, prudence, and meekness." Nor do we call this in question. We judge no man's piety. Our object in referring to this feature of the case, is to present a *Southern* standard, that we may perceive how these men are judged *by their friends.* We shall see how clearly the "Confederate General Assembly," by the pen of Dr. Thornwell, "unanimously" write the condemnation both of the patriotism and the piety of certain clergymen in the Border States and elsewhere.

In the Address of that Assembly "to all the Churches throughout the earth," they formally, solemnly, and "unanimously" declare:

> We cannot condemn a man in one breath as unfaithful to the most solemn earthly interests of his country and his race, and commend him in the next as a loyal and faithful servant of his God. *If we distrust his patriotism, our confidence is apt to be very measured in his piety.* The old adage will hold here as in other things, *falsus in uno, falsus in omnibus.*

What a withering condemnation is this, of many a minister within the loyal States, whose piety should be subjected to such a test! From the stand-point of the nation at large, indeed, it equally condemns the very men who wrote and published it; for their "patriotism" may not only be "distrusted," but they are in open rebellion against their "country," and are waging a traitorous war against their "race." But, without allowing that ethics are to be determined or applied by lines of latitude, how pointedly does this consign to hopeless disrepute both the "piety" and the "patriotism" of many Border State men, and of some farther North. "Distrust" of their "patriotism" rests upon multitudes, while in others disloyalty is proved by their deeds; and this is the "Confederate" standard for their "piety." How must "our Southern brethren" regard such men?

Take the Border States, for example. They have stood by the Government, by overwhelming majorities, in all their elections. And yet, many citizens within them,—embracing religious men and some ministers,—are decidedly in *sympathy* with the "Southern Confederacy," and others hesitate not to *declare* it, and some *labor* for its success. Can "our Southern brethren" do any thing less than despise them for their want of "patriotism?"—and more heartily for their *pretension* to it? Can the "Confederate General Assembly" do any thing less than despise their "piety," and abhor their *professions* of it? They have done both already. If they are honest, they mean what they say.

That, as a general rule, both politicians and clergymen in the Rebel States, heartily despise those of their class at the North who manifest sympathy for them and a desire for their success,—and who are in an underhanded, cowardly way, working for it, in opposition to the Government under which they live,—is most unquestionable, both from the well-known facts, and from the common principles of human nature. They would *trust* a hated "Abolitionist" sooner. They may love the treason, but they are certain to despise the traitor, just as the English did Benedict Arnold. We hope all Northern "sympathizers" will take comfort from the estimation in which their "patriotism" and their "piety" are thus held by "our Southern brethren."

GENERAL ROSECRANS'S ORDERS.

It has appeared to us a little remarkable that certain military orders of this General, and one in particular, should have called forth a condemnation from the religious press which we have seen visited upon no other Federal Commander. We notice it here, because it stands connected with the subject we are illustrating. We of course looked for nothing more nor less from Dr. Robinson and *The True Presbyterian.* But we did not expect to find every religious paper of the Presbyterian Church (we now call to mind no exception), and possibly some of other denominations, join in this *special* hue and cry at the time the order in question was issued.

What was the purport of this condemned order? It was issued at a time when the Department of Missouri, of which General Rosecrans was in command, was extensively infested with guerrillas and threatened with rebel invasion; when, in certain parts of the State, and in and about St. Louis, citizens claiming to be loyal, and others known to be disloyal, were aiding and ready to aid the invaders; when, notoriously, some even of the ecclesiastical bodies, when assembled, would so act, as the authorities feared, as to endanger the public safety, as for example, the Methodist Episcopal Church South, and others; when certain religious men were suspected of infidelity to the Government, and felt the requisition of an oath of allegiance to be an indignity and a burden; and when thousands felt that their property, and the peace and lives of themselves and families, were at stake. It was under these circumstances that the General Commanding issued an order, which, from our recollection, was to this effect: prescribing an oath of allegiance to the General Government, as a condition precedent for sitting and transacting business in any religious court, conference, or convocation, of any Church. This was the essence of the order.

This order was attacked at the time by religious loyal journals, and was condemned by certain speakers in the late General Assembly of the Presbyterian Church at Newark, as interfering with religious freedom, as allowing the *State* to determine the qualification for sitting in a court of *Christ*. This was urged in discussing the case of Dr. McPheeters before the Assembly. It was said that the Presbytery that acted in his case "could not be a free Presbytery," because of this required oath.*

To say that this order "prescribes a qualification for a seat in an ecclesiastical court," is one of those statements which may convey both a truth and a falsehood. It does not prescribe such qualification in any improper sense. The Government may at all times do what is essential to the public safety; and especially is this true in a time of rebellion and civil war, and within the immediate sphere of military rule, when the Government is contending for its life against enemies within and without. Of *what is* essential in any emergency, the Government and its agents must be the sole judges. Nor can they know any distinc-

* Dr. Rice, with his accustomed caution, said: "He would not go into a discussion of the military order, requiring men to take a certain oath, *in order to qualify for a seat in ecclesiastical bodies.* It was certain that many good men could not take that oath. Had he been there, he *might* have taken it; but when he went to Presbytery, he was bound by a *previous* oath to go into Presbytery by our *Book.* One principle involved in this case is the validity of a Presbytery and of its action, when a majority of the body were not there through restraint. Wise and good men could not take the oath *as a qualification to attend Presbytery;* they thought it compromised their rights of conscience."—*Phila. Presbyterian.*

tions among citizens by their professions, business, or other circumstances; they can know and deal with two classes of persons only, friends and foes, the loyal and disloyal. Nor, if they would save what is at stake, can they always wait for treason to develop itself in overt acts. They may act on reasonable grounds of apprehension, with regard to individuals and bodies of men. He who denies this, denies the most settled principles of public law and the most common usages among all civilized nations.

Now, how do these rules apply to the present case? General Rosecrans believed that ecclesiastical convocations within his Department needed watching,—might act, or counsel, or concoct disloyalty, or in some way add to the perils with which the people and the Government were environed. Any man, having but half an eye open to what has occurred in the history of this rebellion, must see that there may be ample reason for such apprehensions. What, then, does he do? Does he forbid the *meeting* of ecclesiastical bodies? By no means. He might even do *that*, if in his judgment the facts should warrant it. But he allows *all* to meet when and where they please, and sit however long, Protestant and Catholic, Jew and Gentile; only prescribing that they shall take *an oath.* What! the *State* prescribe a religious test for the *Church!* How dreadful! He prescribes an oath of allegiance to the Government of the United States; that Government which *protects* their assembling by its civil and military power; and, even then, allows a dispensation to all who had previously taken the oath prescribed by the State *civil* authority, the Convention of Missouri! This is the whole of the dreadful thing.

We should like to know, on what principle of Scripture, public law, reason, or common sense, those individual men composing a body calling themselves "the Presbytery of St. Louis," can claim exemption from such a requisition? It was just that which might be made of a body of merchants, shoemakers, or any other class of citizens proposing to assemble. The order regarded religious bodies simply as *citizens*. It could regard them in no other character. It specified them by their ecclesiastical names, —Conferences, Associations, or whatever terms were used, —simply as descriptive terms of certain bodies of citizens; just as it might have said of others, Knights of the Golden Circle, Red Men, or "Anacondas."

If the members of the Presbytery of St. Louis, or any other ecclesiastical body in that military department, cannot take the oath prescribed, so much the worse for them. We respect their tender consciences, but they need a more enlightened conscience. Without any disparagement of them personally,—for they are mostly strangers,—conscience, in these times, like some other mental and moral qualities brought into action, is affected by latitude, particularly where it respects taking an oath of allegiance to the Government. But be that as it may, it cannot be taken as a rule of public duty for the Government, nor be made a criterion by which it is to be condemned.

"HONOR TO WHOM HONOR."

One word with the religious press. As we have already said, so far as we have seen, the religious press, with one accord, condemned this order of General Rosecrans at the time it was issued. In every instance of this condemnation that we saw, the fact was prominently brought out that General Rosecrans was a Catholic, and a brother of the Roman Catholic Bishop of Cincinnati. This was dwelt upon as an important ingredient, as was believed, leading to the issuing of the order. The fact, also, was mentioned in at least one religious journal in a Metropolitan city, that while commanding the army in Tennessee, General Rosecrans never disturbed a Catholic Church, while Protestant Churches were freely taken for military purposes.

Let us do justice to the patriot-soldier. Let us honor the man, if honor is his due, who took the demoralized army of General Buell, and led it in triumph over the terrific fields of Stone River and Murfreesboro', and finally planted it in Chattanooga. We claim, personally, as strong an adherence to the Protestant faith as any of our brethren of the religious press, and yet we honor the brave, whether commanding an army or standing in the ranks, who perils his life to put down this rebellion, and save the national flag from disgrace, without inquiring of what religious faith he may be.

As to the reports from Tennessee, about the distinction which General Rosecrans made between the Churches, we know nothing, one way or the other. But certain things which were noticed in the secular prints, just after the issuing of the order of which complaint was made, occurred in the Department of Missouri, and which we searched diligently for in the religious papers, but searched in vain. It was stated that General Rosecrans had reprimanded or suspended two Catholic priests in Missouri for their disloyalty, and that he had, for the same reason, forbidden the circulation within his Department of the well-known Roman Catholic journal, the Metropolitan Record. This is quite enough to relieve him of all suspicion that he was impelled by any sectarian considerations in giving an order which has called forth the strictures of religious journals and Church courts.

Let all men be honored according to their merit, of

whatever religion or nation, whether Jew or Gentile, Greek, Barbarian, or Scythian, bond or free, who will help us to save the nation by putting down the most godless rebellion the sun ever shone upon.*

DOOM OF TRAITORS.—SELF-CONDEMNATION.

We close this chapter by an extract from Dr. Thornwell's Fast-Day Discourse, preached in Columbia, South Carolina, Nov. 21, 1860, upon the National Crisis then impending. It will be another good lesson for disloyalists. We commend it to their serious consideration. If it is "preaching politics;" if it presents before "traitors" an awful doom, and pronounces their "damnation;" if it seals the destiny of him who penned it, and of multitudes of his co-laborers in the South; if it embraces those in the loyal States, who, though they have not taken up arms against the Government, are doing every thing they dare do to aid those who are in arms and in rebellion; all we have to

* After this chapter was written, and the stereotyping was nearly completed, the *Biblical Repertory* for July came to hand (received July 30), in which we are glad to find one for whom we entertain so profound a respect as Dr. Hodge uttering himself so decidedly, and sustaining the propriety of General Rosecrans's order. On reviewing the proceedings of the General Assembly in the case of Dr. McPheeters, and referring to the reasons for non-attendance in the St. Louis Presbytery, resulting from that order, he says: "To us it seems that these unfortunate scruples are founded in error. *There was no just ground of complaint against General Rosecrans's order.* There was nothing therein inconsistent with the independence of the Church or true allegiance to Christ. Suppose the small-pox had been prevalent in that region, and the authorities of the city had issued an order that no one should attend any public meeting, ecclesiastical or secular, who did not produce evidence that he had been vaccinated. Would this be an interference with the liberty of the Church? Not at all—because the object sought (viz., the public health) was a lawful object; and because the thing demanded (vaccination) was something the authorities had a right to demand. So in General Rosecrans's order, the object sought, the public safety, was a legitimate object; and the thing demanded, allegiance to the Government, was admitted to be obligatory. In our view, therefore, the order in question presented no lawful or reasonable objection to a free attendance on the Presbytery." And more than this, too: "the thing demanded, allegiance to the Government," *was* "obligatory," whether "*admitted* to be" or not.

say is, that it comes from South Carolina, and from one of the ablest divines in any branch of the Church. Though the original application was different with the preacher from that now given it, the truth it contains applies none the less pointedly to all who are disloyal to the General Government.

In reference to our position as a nation before the rebellion occurred, to our power and destiny among the nations of the earth and upon the welfare of the human race, and to the guilt of destroying the hopes of mankind in this nation by rebellion, the eloquent divine thus says:

> The day of small States is passed, and as the federative principle is the only one which can guarantee freedom to extensive territories, the federal principle must constitute the hope of the human race. It was the glory of this country to have first applied it to the formation of an effective Government, and, had we been faithful to our trust, a destiny was before us which it has never been the lot of any people to inherit. It was ours to redeem this continent, to spread freedom, civilization, and religion, through the whole length of the land. Geographically placed between Europe and Asia, we were, in some sense, the representatives of the human race. The fortunes of the world were in our hand. We were a city set upon a hill, whose light was intended to shine upon every people and upon every land. To forego this destiny, to forfeit this inheritance, and that through bad faith, *is an enormity of treason equalled only by the treachery of a Judas*, who betrayed his Master with a kiss. Favored as we have been, we can expect to perish by no common death. *The judgment lingers not, and the damnation slumbers not, of the reprobates and traitors*, who, for the wages of unrighteousness, have sapped the pillars and undermined the foundations of the stateliest temple of liberty the world ever beheld. Rebellion against God, and treason to man, are combined in the perfidy. The innocent may be spared, as Lot was delivered from the destruction of Sodom; but the guilty must perish with an *aggravated* doom.

We trust that for decency's sake nothing may be said, henceforth, about what Northern men may think should be done with "traitors," when Dr. Thornwell dooms those whom he regards as such to something a little more disagreeable than such a shower of fire and brimstone as came down upon the cities of the plain.

We of course understand what is couched under the glowing phrase, that "it was ours to redeem this continent, to spread *freedom, civilization, and religion*, through the whole length of the land." We have shown this in a previous chapter, when speaking of the Slavery Propagandists among whom Dr. Thornwell was a High Priest; that to "redeem" the continent was to convert it into slave territory; that "freedom" means the relation of master and slave, the slave to come from Africa if he could be obtained; the master to be a white man if "rich," or to be a slave if "poor;" that the "civilization" was to be universally of this type; and that the "religion" was to be that which should sanction all this as "divine," and any thing preached in opposition was to be "infidelity" and proof of "apostasy."

Patriotism and treason are also understood. To be a "patriot" was to give heart and soul, tongue, pen, purse, and ballot for such a "destiny" to one's country; and to be a "traitor" was to oppose such a destiny, or, if living at the South, to hesitate and falter about aiding to bring it about. And then so glorious to us and so philanthropic to mankind was such a destiny, and so correspondingly deep was the guilt of all who were "reprobates and traitors" to it, that their "judgment lingers not" and their "damnation slumbers not," but is rapidly approaching in the form of a shower-bath like that which came upon Sodom!

Well, gentlemen, all we have to say, is, that when the actual trial and doom of "traitors" shall come, we hope you will stand up to it like men, and let justice take its course.

CHAPTER VIII.

SOUTHERN PROVIDENCE IN THE REBELLION.

The doctrine of a Divine Providence in the affairs of men is a tenet of both natural and revealed theology. It has been the common belief of all nations and all times. It has been taught by the priests of every sect in religion, received by the sages of every school in philosophy, and sung by the poets of every age of the world. The bard of Avon has but expressed the sober judgment of mankind when uttering a sentiment which we may take in its utmost latitude of application,—

> There's a divinity that shapes our ends,
> Rough-hew them how we will.

GOD'S PROVIDENCE EXTENDS TO NATIONS.

This providence has been conceded to extend to nations as truly as to individual men. Without the light of Scripture, this has been an accepted truth; in that light, we read it on every page. It is concerned in the birth of nations, in their progress, and in their downfall. It attends them in peace and in war, gives them their rulers, awards their prosperity and glory, and brings them to honor or ruin. In the rise of nations, in their career, in their permanent endurance or in their passing away to give place to others,—an unceasing round through all the cycles of time,—God is but accomplishing His eternal purposes, in the execution of which "He doeth according to His will in the army of heaven and among the inhabitants of the earth."

ITS DESIGNS TOWARDS THE UNITED STATES.

It has been the common belief, through every period of the comparatively short career of the American people, that this doctrine of providence had a special significance in its application to this nation, as bearing upon its own well-being and that of other nations of the world. The time of the discovery of the American Continent, the circumstances of its colonization, the character of its early settlers, the planting here upon a broad basis of the doctrine of civil and religious liberty, the formation of a system of popular government under a written constitution, the freedom of the right of suffrage, the universality of the means of education, the unrestricted protection to the various forms of religion, the wide domain and unlimited resources of a country extending through twenty degrees of latitude and fifty-five of longitude, and the unsurpassed material prosperity which has been developed in the departments of agriculture, manufactures, commerce, trade, inventive skill, and the mechanic arts; all this, which had placed the United States, with her more than thirty millions of people, in the front rank among the most favored nations of the earth, in an age of unparalleled progress, had contributed to the fond anticipation, indulged down to the period of the rebellion, that God had given us a high destiny to fill, of honor to ourselves and of good to mankind. When foul treason plotted the overthrow of the Government, the hearts of many failed them. They were led to think they had wholly misinterpreted the purposes of God, however plainly they had supposed them indicated in the remarkable facts of our history.

There may have been much of national vanity indulged in these glowing prospects; but many were led to hope for their realization, prompted by the purest impulses.

THE DEAD FLY IN THE OINTMENT.

In all the phases of our history, there was one subject which gave pain and apprehension to many of the more sagacious and reflecting. That in a Government consecrated by the blood of martyrs to liberty, and founded on the principle announced in its earliest records,—the freedom and equality of rights of all men,—there should be incorporated into its supreme organic law a concession in several specifications to the bondage of millions of human beings, was an anomaly so monstrous as to provoke the jeers of foreign despots, and bring down upon the Model Republic the daily growing scorn of the Christian world.

However men may view the case from our present historical stand-point, we are not now disposed to bring any reproach upon those great men who founded our National Government, for admitting that element into its structure. Surrounded by the perils which succeeded the Revolutionary War, and under the practical failure of the Articles of Confederation, they found that "a more perfect union" was essential to national existence, and at that time union in one nationality could only be secured by the Government they formed. But it is as clearly written upon the history of those times as is any other fact of the period, that many of the leading statesmen, North and South, who were concerned in forming the Constitution of the United States, disapproved of slavery as an institution, and confidently counted on and desired its termination. King Cotton was then in his infancy, or scarcely born, and it was not then dreamed that he would ever come to the throne and usurp so wide a dominion.*

* For proof of what is above asserted, that "leading statesmen," in the era of the formation of the Constitution, "disapproved of Slavery," and "counted on and desired its termination,"—and that this was "the common sentiment" of that day,—we refer to the speech of the rebel Vice-President, quoted on page 49. Mr. Stephens's

THE IRREPRESSIBLE CONFLICT.

As in our history we advanced from step to step; as slavery became more profitable and more expanded; as under its profits, and under the change in sentiment regarding its character, it became more and more exorbitant in its demands, the anxiety concerning its effect upon the destiny of the nation became daily more intense. Under the later developments of the character and tendencies of the institution, that sentiment which has sometimes been attributed to the President, and again to the Secretary of State, and for which much reproach has been heaped upon them by the rebels and their "allies,"—that it were impossible for this nation to continue half slave and half free,—was but the utterance of what a far-reaching sagacity saw to be inevitable. It was no incendiary tenet, as shallow-brained demagogues have termed it. It was the simple announcement of a great fact whose certain coming already cast its shadow before. It was but the prediction of an "irrepressible conflict" which even some of the *fathers of the Revolutionary era feared*, and which was sure to occur in God's own plan. Its undoubted existence in the womb of time, the throes and convulsions which its issuing forth would occasion, would have been all the same if they had not foreseen and declared it. They did not create it. They were not responsible for it. It was an inevitable outgrowth of the system of Government our fathers formed.*

testimony will be deemed valid, and save the trouble of quoting from the original sources.

* Thomas Jefferson announced the "irrepressible conflict." We at present state it on the authority of the Rebel Vice-President. In his speech at Savannah, Georgia, March 21, 1861, Mr. Stephens said: "African Slavery as it exists among us—the proper *status* of the negro in our form of civilization—this was the immediate cause of the late rupture and present revolution. Jefferson, in his forecast, had anticipated this, as 'the rock upon which the old Union would split.' He was

THE DIFFICULTY BEYOND HUMAN WISDOM.

But with all these apprehensions, the wisdom of no man in Church or State was equal to grapple with the subject. Slavery had so interwoven its power with every element of our politics, had so completely subsidized every department of the Government, that the nation stood appalled at the threatening danger, while no one could see our way out of the labyrinth of difficulties by which we were environed. Slavery had become a universal theme for discussion; its character, bearings, dangers, extortions; but no one could solve the problems it presented. It had become the *pons asinorum* in politics and religion, for statesmen, philosophers, divines. We quite agree with Dr. Palmer, in his Thanksgiving Discourse in New Orleans:

> It is not too much to say, that if the South should, at this moment, surrender every slave, the wisdom of the entire world, united in solemn council, could not solve the question of their disposal.

This is a sentiment to which probably, at the time it was announced, the mass of his countrymen would have subscribed. But God can easily do what man cannot, and that too through man's reluctant agency; bringing to mind another truth in the same discourse:

> Baffled as our wisdom may now be, in finding a solution of this intricate social problem, it would, nevertheless, be the height of arrogance

right. What was conjecture with him, is now a realized fact." Those declaimers who deem Mr. Lincoln or Mr. Seward awfully guilty for uttering "that hideous sentiment," should vent their wrath upon Mr. Jefferson, and other statesmen of our early history. We can excuse some stump orators for their ignorance; but it is a sign that the schoolmaster *ought* to be abroad, when the Legislature of Jefferson's own State can commit the blunder of ascribing this saying to Mr. Lincoln as its author. The *Richmond Enquirer* of July 4, 1864, publishes an Address from the Legislature of Virginia to the people of that State, in which this sentence occurs: "Mr. Lincoln was the author of that hideous sentiment, that the States of the Union could not remain part Free and part Slave States—that they must be wholly Free or wholly Slave."

to proncunce what changes may or may not occur in the distant future. In the grand march of events, *Providence may work out a solution undiscoverable by us.* * * * If this question should ever arise, the generation to whom it is remitted will doubtless have the wisdom to meet it, and Providence will furnish the lights in which it is to be resolved.

How little did the eloquent divine think, when he was uttering this pregnant sentence, so profoundly true, and its realization not reserved for "the distant future," but apparently so near at hand, that he was but as Balaam before the hosts of Israel, with a blessing on his lips instead of a curse, and that, as God's unwilling Prophet, he was to bear so distinguished a part in unravelling the mysteries of His inscrutable providence, and in "working out a solution" which had so long "baffled the wisdom of the entire world."

HOPES DASHED AND RAISED AGAIN.

When the rebellion occurred, as we have said, the hopes of many regarding our national destiny died within them. They verily believed we were now to be dashed in pieces as a potter's vessel, and to be blotted out and known no more as a great people. They looked upon the war as the scourge of God for our great iniquities, and so far undoubtedly they were right; for war is always a judgment for sin. But it began early to be believed that God's ultimate design was our purification and preservation, and that to this end He would in His own way terminate the institution which had been seized upon as the occasion of our strife, and that when this were accomplished the nation would emerge from this furnace, and be prepared for a higher career than were otherwise possible. How this was to be done, by whom, when, and where a beginning was to be made, were problems involved in darkness; but as events have been developed, as the necessities of the war have arisen, as time has rolled on, as the reverses and successes of our arms have alternated,—even though "the end is not yet,"—we think it is not rashly interpreting God's purposes to say, that in His providence slavery will be removed from the land entirely, as the result of that very treason and rebellion, darkly concocted and persistently pursued, for the express purpose of its more firm and expanded establishment. If our Saviour spoke the truth when He said, "All they that take the sword shall perish with the sword," then, as slavery unsheathed the sword to war upon lawful authority, we believe it will perish by the war made in the Government's defence.

And yet, we freely admit that the result may be quite different from this. Secret things belong to God only. Slavery may be yet longer preserved, to be a scourge to the nation. What scheming politicians may plot, what timid statesmen may yield, what the people may be willing to concede for the sake of ending the war,—and what God's real plans may be, to be reached through all these schemings and plottings and concessions,—we presume not to know; and still, our faith is strong in the ultimate result stated, that slavery will, as a consequence of the rebellion, be removed, to curse the land no more.

PROVIDENCE FROM A SOUTHERN STAND-POINT.

But it is not our purpose to canvass this subject at present. We shall consider it at some length in a succeeding chapter, when we come to speak directly of God's providential designs in the rebellion. Our object now is to look at providence from a Southern stand-point; to note some remarkable things in Southern literature upon this theme, which the rebellion and the war have developed.

The leaders of the rebellion have from the first claimed for their cause a high character for righteousness, and they have exhibited in its behalf much religious zeal and devotion. They have always claimed that God was on their side, and that the initiatory and subsequent steps of the movement were undertaken by His direction. When recounting their military successes (and they have claimed a victory on nearly every battle-field), it is wonderful to note how their journals, especially the religious, have ever found in current events striking evidences of God's favoring providence.*

We should suppose that at least religious men, before making such a wholesale appropriation, would wait to see the outcome; for God often gives temporary or apparent success, where the final upshot is an utter overthrow. But so elated have they been at present results, that they have often predicted certain triumph; and they have frequently so put the case as to be willing that their cause should be judged by the determination of the contest. Here again they are ethically at fault, for success is not necessarily a criterion of merit, nor does virtue always conquer; and yet, without admitting the principle, we are almost willing to rest the present case on that issue. We are doubtful, however, whether, with all their boastings, they will so readily abide the judgment which the result may furnish. Already, as the contest progresses, we see signs of misgiving, and less confidence expressed in the favor of God than formerly. What the bearing of this may be, even

* In the winter of 1861-2, after the campaign of the first season of the war was over, an "Address to the People of Georgia" was issued, signed by Howell Cobb, R. Toombs, M. J. Crawford, and Thomas R. R. Cobb, in order further "to fire the Southern heart." This passage on providence will illustrate what we have said above: "We have faith in God and faith in you. He is blind to every indication of providence who has not seen an Almighty hand controlling the events of the past year. The wind, the wave, the cloud, the mist, the sunshine, and the storm, have all ministered to our necessities, and frequently succored us in our distresses. We deem it unnecessary to recount the numerous instances which have called forth our gratitude. We would join you in thanksgiving and praise. 'If God be for us, who can be against us?' We have no fears of the result—the final issue."

as modifying their ethics, no one can foretell. That they need a modification, not merely upon current events of the war, but upon matters which underlie the whole structure of human life, is easily made apparent.*

The providence of God has been so much dwelt upon by them in their public journals, debates, and discourses, and especially by the clergy, that it becomes a fruitful theme for meditation, as furnishing a marked feature in the moral phases of the contest.

IT UPSETS THEIR THEOLOGY.

One of the most noted things about the views of the clergy among the rebel leaders, is seen in this,—that while their devotion to treason, in the interest of slavery, has blinded them to the demands of duty to their country, the same devotion has unsettled the foundations of some of the prime articles of their religious faith. Their elaborate

* No one familiar with the early events of the war, can forget how the rebels exulted that the fleet sent to Charleston, at the time the last effort was made to provision Fort Sumter, was dispersed by a storm, so that it could not enter the harbor. This gave the rebels an opportunity to complete their plans, and to capture that fortress without opposition from the fleet. Its dispersion, they said, was "no accident," but the very "finger of God was in it," and a sign of His favor to them. We accept the doctrine; God "was in it," but possibly for a different purpose than they supposed. And so they have exulted almost ever since. Observe, however, one among many signs which have occurred more recently, where serious disappointments are laid to the account of "accident," and where hope in "Providence" is waning. Remarking upon the "invasion" of Maryland and the threatening of Washington in July last, the *Richmond Enquirer* says: "It is said that a *lucky accident alone* saved Washington. Canby's Corps, from New Orleans, arrived at Fortress Monroe on Saturday night, *the very day on which the battle of Monocacy was fought, and which revealed to the enemy the magnitude of the danger that threatened Washington.* Ordered by telegraph to that city, it arrived there on Monday in time to prevent the capture of the city, and to hold the defences until the arrival of additional corps from Petersburg had rendered the storming of the works useless. *The accidental arrival of Canby saved the city.* Had he passed up to Grant, *or been delayed in his arrival one day longer*, Washington would have been captured. However great the disappointment may be, yet much has already been and much more will be accomplished." No storm delayed Canby "one day longer." God "was in it." The *Richmond Examiner* thus refers to the same inva-

discoursings upon providence furnish a striking illustration.

We of course admit, that while the whole world agree in holding to a doctrine of providence, men often differ as to the doctrine itself; as to its extent, whether general only or particular, or both; whether it is concerned only in the great affairs of the world, the marked and unusual occurrences, or extends to all events alike, great and small; whether it controls and works through the free volitions of men, or only reaches outward things; whether its ends are accomplished through wicked agents as directly and efficiently as through the good and holy, or only through the latter; and a thousand other questions, which theologians and metaphysicians have discussed more or less from time immemorial. We do not name these differences to enter into any examination of them. Our present business is more simple. The divines who are foremost in the apologetical literature of the rebellion, so far as this has come more immediately under our observation, and from which we cite examples, are of the same school in theology with ourselves. They have received the same standards of faith, and when adopting them received the doctrine of providence therein set forth, which substantially is that received by nearly the whole Christian world. We doubt whether they ever would have so widely departed from it under any other influence than that of this rebellion,

sion: "It must be confessed that our 'invasion' just at this moment looks like one of the most paltry affairs of the war. Washington was not taken. Baltimore was not taken. The Yankeeized population of Martinsburgh has embraced their townsman Hunter again. Not a bridge of the road between Washington and Baltimore was burned. The road itself was unbroken. What has been done then? What has yet been obtained by these opportunities,—Lynchburg and Washington,—*the like of which Providence has not vouchsafed since the first year of the war?* One house has been burned; two thousand head of cattle brought off; Major-General Tyler and Major-General Franklin were taken prisoners and both permitted to escape. * * * *Let us hope, and pray, and trust,* that the story still is left half told."

which with them has overturned some of the fundamental principles in morals as well as theology.

THE TRUE DOCTRINE OF PROVIDENCE.

That doctrine of providence is thus concisely expressed: "God's works of providence are His most holy, wise, and powerful preserving and governing all His creatures; ordering them, and all their actions, to His own glory." This is simple, comprehensive, and unquestionably founded on the teachings of Scripture. Its purport is plain. It sweeps the universe. It leaves nothing without the control of God. Not a sparrow can fall to the ground without His notice, nor is a hair of any head unnumbered. It embraces men, angels, demons, races of men, nations, families, and the concerns and interests of each and of all; and directs all things for great purposes of good to those who love God, and for glory to His great name. If the Ruler of the Universe is indeed GOD, then He will do His pleasure in heaven and upon earth, and no being or thing can thwart His plans.

SOUTHERN EXPOSITION OF IT.—DR. PALMER.

Now observe how some of the high priests of the rebellion preach upon this doctrine. We will let Dr. Palmer lead the way, in his Thanksgiving Discourse before referred to. He sets out with the undoubted truth, that nations have a special destiny to fulfil in the designs of God; that "a nation often has a character as well defined and intense as that of an individual;" that "this individuality of character alone makes any people truly historic, competent to work out its specific mission, and to become a factor in the world's progress." He says, also, concerning the crisis then reached, that, "in determining our duty in this emergency, it is necessary that we should first ascertain the nature of the trust providentially committed to us." Having ascertained, as he supposed, what the special trust of the South was in the plans of God, he then declares it, and gives assurance of providential security in its execution, as follows:

> The particular trust assigned to such a people becomes the pledge of Divine protection, and their fidelity to it determines the fate by which it is finally overtaken. What that trust is, must be ascertained from the necessities of their position, the institutions which are the outgrowth of their principles, and the conflicts through which they preserve their identity and independence. If, then, the South is such a people, what, at this juncture, is their providential trust? I answer, that it is *to conserve and to perpetuate the institution of slavery as now existing.*

PROVIDENCE FRUSTRATED.

The announcement in the last sentence, declaring what the providential trust of the South was understood to be, is the substratum of the whole discourse. We do not, just here, propose to dispute so remarkable a proposition. We have only given this passage as opening the way for exhibiting some views of providence which are quite as remarkable; indicating that the preacher supposes it within the power of man to *frustrate* God's plans, and betraying an excited fear not merely that He might do so in matters then undeveloped, but charging directly that it had already and most grossly been done, as seen in the election of the Chief Ruler of a great nation, and in the special bearings of that election upon God's providence, showing a positive interference by the electors with "the particular trust assigned" to the South, in the execution of which they had "the pledge of the Divine protection." But let the preacher speak for himself:

> All that we claim for them (the slaves) and for ourselves is liberty to work out this problem, guided by nature and God, without obtrusive interference from abroad. These great questions of providence and his-

tory must have free scope for their solution; and the race whose fortunes are distinctly implicated in the same, is alone authorized, as it is alone competent, to determine them. *It is just this impertinence of human legislation, setting bounds to what God only can regulate,* that the South is called this day to resent and resist. * * * * * The Most High, knowing His own power, which is infinite, and His own wisdom, which is unfathomable, can afford to be patient. But these self-constituted reformers *must quicken the activity of Jehovah,* or compel His abdication. * * * *It is time to reproduce the obsolete idea that Providence must govern man, and not that man should control Providence.* * * * * * These fierce zealots undertake to drive the chariot of the sun; working out the single and false idea which rides them like a nightmare, *they dash athwart the spheres, utterly disregarding the delicate mechanism of Providence;* which moves on wheels within wheels, with pivots, and balances, and springs, which the great Designer alone can control. * * * * * *Such an issue is at length presented in the result of the recent Presidential election.* * * * The decree has gone forth, that the institution of Southern slavery shall be constrained within assigned limits. Though nature and Providence should send forth its branches like the banyan-tree, to take root in congenial soil, *here is a power superior to both, that says it shall wither and die within its own charmed circle.* What say you to this, to whom this great providential trust of conserving slavery is assigned?

SOUTHERN THEOLOGY REBUKED BY SCRIPTURE.

How is it possible to explain that a sincere believer in the doctrine of providence,—and Dr. Palmer is unquestionably a believer,—can utter sentences of such impassioned earnestness against what he just as sincerely believes, in the events specified, to be direct infractions of God's providential prerogative? Admit, if you please, every specific thing over which he laments,—the act, the design, the tendency, the motive, the result,—and still, is it not all a part of God's comprehensive plan? But, more especially, can any event occur among men which is more clearly providential, and as such more stupendously grand, than the election of a Chief Ruler by thirty millions of people to preside over one of the greatest nations of the earth? Does Scripture point out any event as more specifically providential? "The lot is cast into the lap; but the whole disposing thereof is of the Lord." "God is the Judge; He putteth down one, and setteth up another." "He removeth kings, and setteth up kings." Or does the Word of God declare any thing to be more strictly within the purview of His providence than human legislation? "By me kings reign, and princes decree justice. By me princes rule, and nobles, even all the judges of the earth." Or can the sentiment that God claims directly to govern nations, by His providence, and does actually so govern them through the lawfully constituted rulers of the world, be more definitely and broadly declared than it is; and that upon this ground, therefore, as well as upon other grounds, it is a heinous sin to resist their authority? "Let every soul be subject unto the higher powers; for there is no power but of God: the powers that be are ordained of God." Or, on the other hand, can any thing be found in Scripture which militates against the position that God works just as freely and efficiently, in accomplishing all the designs of His providence, through the folly of men as through their wisdom; through their imbecility as through their energy; their wickedness as their holiness? Is it not, rather, directly declared everywhere in His Word, that He works through and by all these characters and agencies; indeed, that He makes every thing bow to His will, in heaven, earth, and hell? "When He giveth quietness, who then can make trouble? and when He hideth His face, who then can behold him? whether it be done against a nation, or against a man only." "All the inhabitants of the earth are reputed as nothing: and He doeth according to His will in the army of heaven and among the inhabitants of the earth; and none can stay His hand, or say unto him, What doest thou?" "Our Lord is in the heavens: He hath done whatsoever He hath pleased." "I am the Lord, and there is none else; there is no God besides me: I girded thee, though thou hast not known me; that they may know from the rising of the sun, and from the west, that there is none besides me. I am the Lord, and there is none else. I form the light, and create darkness: I make peace, and create evil: I the Lord do all these things."

PROVIDENTIAL RULE SUPREME.

What unspeakable folly is it, then,—unless His providential rule is reduced to that of a mortal,—to talk about the "impertinence of human legislation," in great matters of state or in small, interfering in any manner with "what God would regulate." Such legislation, and all other, lies directly in the line of His providence. And what consummate folly is it to talk about man, or a political party, or the rulers of a people, or the whole nation, or all the creatures of God combined, "dashing athwart the spheres, utterly disregarding the delicate mechanism of Providence; as though any power in the universe, short of Omnipotence, could interpose the obstacle of a hair to obstruct the perfect working of that "delicate mechanism!"

When these great providential events had occurred, in the mighty movings of the people of a powerful nation, it would have exhibited a sounder theology and a more reverential piety, and contributed to a brighter fame to both, had Dr. Palmer bowed to these events, and detected in their occurrence some unsoundness in his own providential theory, and the dogma of a "divine trust to perpetuate slavery," on which it was founded; instead of making God's plain workings the occasion of lashing himself into a tempest of indignation, and misleading his flock not only on the Scriptural doctrine of providence, but openly urging resistance, instead of teaching obedience, "to the higher powers;" and, as a result, giving his great influence to plunge the people into troubles which time can never cure. This is said not merely in view of events as they now appear. The errors which Dr. Palmer proclaims lie upon the very surface of his discourse, and are in conflict with the tenor of the whole Word of God.

AN EXPLANATION NEEDED.

How can such a phenomenon be explained? How could a minister of the Gospel, sound in the faith, make such an inexcusable perversion of the truth? This is just as easily answered as would be a similar question upon any other part of his discourse; touching his urging an open disruption of the Union, at the declared risk of war, and openly braving and defiantly courting, if need be, all its horrors; or touching the cause for which all this should be done and braved, in order to discharge "the trust providentially committed" to them, "of conserving and transmitting the system of slavery with the freest scope for its natural development and extension;" or touching the time when these utterances were made,—the 29th of November, 1860,—when as yet politicians had not matured their plans, and his own city and people for a long time afterwards, many of them, were strongly for the Union. If any one can resolve these points satisfactorily, we can explain all the difficulties about his utterances upon providence.

There is probably some common ground on which these theological vagaries, and much else that is apparently puzzling in his sentiments and course, may be solved.

A SOLUTION PROPOSED.

We think there is no difficulty in solving any of the points of the case. The theory about slavery, which is at the bottom of the whole,—the "corner-stone" of the entire structure,—had stultified in the Southern leaders every thing it touched. It rooted out their loyalty to the Union as soon as they discovered the Union could be no longer serviceable to their demands. It blasted their sense of obligation to "be subject to the higher powers," just as soon as they saw they were no longer to be under their own control. It confused their perception of moral distinctions, perverted the doctrines of religion, and gave false glosses to Scripture, whenever slavery was the topic of consideration. The emanations from the system had become so ground into their very natures, intellectual and moral, and in some cases literally into their *blood*, that they could stake all upon the issue they forced upon the country—loyalty, honor, glory, historic memories, righteousness, truth, life!

A PROVIDENCE OF MAN'S DEVISING.

This led them to form to *themselves* a theory of providence,—a path for God to walk in,—which exactly chimed in with their plans. They had fondly persuaded themselves that this was *God's* providence instead of *their own*. They had determined for themselves the special "divine trust" which, under this providence, they were to execute, and which was committed to them for their great mission as a people. They had brought all their abilities and attainments, which indeed no one can well despise, to fortify their convictions and religious fervor in the full faith of these dogmas, in spite of the sentiments of the whole Christian world. And then, when they imagined on false grounds that their cherished plans were about to be invaded, through a course of events as grandly providential as God ever controlled,—they failed to see the pointing of the Divine finger, but rose in wrath to invoke upon the land all the wild terrors of civil war. The world nowhere presents, all things considered, a case of infatuation which can equal this.

If our solution is not satisfactory, we can only vary it in other words, which, however, are but an embodiment of all we have said: God smote them with judicial blindness; and, "for this cause,"—the cause which lies at the bottom of the trouble in the land,—He sent upon them "strong delusion that they should believe a lie," *that slavery might be destroyed.*

SOUTHERN PROVIDENCE FURTHER ILLUSTRATED.—DR. SMYTH.

The peculiar views of providence which we have presented are by no means confined to Dr. Palmer. They are those commonly entertained by the clergy of the South who have been leaders or supporters of the rebellion. We give an example or two more.

Dr. Smyth claims God's providence in their favor from the beginning of the rebellion, and during every step of its progress. Our quotations are from the same source often here referred to, the *Southern Presbyterian Review*, April, 1863. Dr. Smyth, referring to the great change he supposes to have been wrought in the "character and conduct of such men as Drs. R. J. Breckinridge, Spring, Hodge, Jacobus," and others, says:

> To this blind, fervid fanaticism, the South must oppose the only invincible shield, and that is faith, faith in God, faith in His word, faith in His omnipotent providence, faith in the righteousness of a cause sustained by His immutable and everlasting truth. * * * God's mani-

fest presence and providence, in the bloodless and yet triumphant victory of Sumter; in the electric sympathy with which eleven States rushed into each other's arms; in the peaceful, prayerful unity with which a Constitution and a Confederation were ratified on earth, *and sealed in the chancery of Heaven:* all this seemed to be the evidence of God's presence with us. *God seemed* thus *to* COMMAND His people in these Southern States, to whom, as the divider of nations, He had apportioned their inheritance, and imposed upon them the solemn trust of an organized system of slave labor, for the benefit of the world and as a blessing to themselves, while imparting civil, social, and religious blessings to their slaves; *now that His word and providence were denied*, and covenanted rights and immunities were withheld, and the annihilation of that system of labor was made the basis and cohesive bond of a dominant mobocratic and sectional party, inaugurated as the Government of the United States, and invested with absolute power, *God now spake as with a voice from heaven, saying,* "COME OUT OF THE UNION, MY PEOPLE. From such withdraw thyself, for all the men of thy Confederacy have brought thee even to the border; the men that were at peace with thee have deceived thee, and prevailed against thee; they that ate thy bread have laid a wound under thee; there is none understanding in them." The heart of the South was bowed before the Most High, the Lord God omnipotent that reigneth, and with one voice they cried unto Him and said unto Him, "If thy presence go not with us, carry us not up hence; for wherein shall it be known that we, thy people, have found grace in thy sight? Is it not in that thou goest with us? So shall we be separated from all the people that are upon the face of the earth." Then came up from millions of hearts the shout, "GO FORWARD! FOR GOD IS WITH US OF A TRUTH." *But* ABRAHAM LINCOLN *neither heard nor heeded this voice that spake so audibly from heaven, in the otherwise inexplicable events that were occurring around him. He hardened his heart, and stiffened his neck, and would not let the people go.*

BLASPHEMY AND FANATICISM SUBLIMATED.

The reader will make his own reflections upon the "blind, fervid fanaticism," which must have prompted such remarkable passages from an able, scholarly, and accomplished divine. The transparent blasphemy of this writing is in a high state of sublimation; deeming the whole Southern people "the chosen of God" as the Israelites were, and on that ground applying to them those words of Scripture which were applied to His ancient people. The likening of the President of the United States to the king of Egypt,—and of course regarding Jefferson Davis as a second Moses,—are essential to complete the conception.

The most satisfactory solution which we can give of the mental and moral state of a man of Dr. Smyth's well-known abilities, under such an exhibition of them, is that previously given in reference to Dr. Palmer, and applies to the mass of Southern writers upon the rebellion. Their views of the "peculiar institution," and of the "trust" concerning it "providentially committed" to them, present every thing relating to the contest in which they have embarked for its sake, to their minds and hearts, in an aspect so very "peculiar," that they alone, of all mankind, are able to perceive things as they see them. There is at least one peculiarity between their present condition and that of God's ancient people, which is true in fact: "their minds are blinded;" and "the veil is upon their heart."

THE PROVIDENTIAL CLIMAX.—DR. STILES.

We give but one more sample of this remarkable religious literature of the South. In some respects it exceeds all that has gone before it. It is from a discourse of the Rev. Joseph C. Stiles, D. D., a Georgian by birth, but who was formerly settled for a short time over a Church in Cincinnati, and subsequently was Pastor of the Mercer-Street Church in New York, and then Pastor of a Church in New Haven. He also spent several years of ministerial life, previous to these several Northern settlements, in Kentucky. He was a slaveholder by inheritance, and removed to Kentucky for the purpose of preparing his slaves for freedom, and at that time deemed freedom better than slavery both for himself and them. We believe he emancipated them all.

On the breaking out of the rebellion, he joined the rebel leaders, and has since given the power of his unwonted eloquence and fervent prayers to the attempt to erect that treasonable "nation" whose "corner-stone" is slavery. The discourse to which we refer, came to light in the summer of 1863, and is entitled, "National Rectitude the only true Basis of National Prosperity; an Appeal to the Confederate States," founded on the text, "Righteousness exalteth a nation."

THE SOUTHERN CONFEDERACY TO USHER IN THE MILLENNIUM.

Dr. Stiles holds to the doctrine of a "good time coming," believes in common with all branches of the Church that a millennial day will yet dawn upon the world; and as in his view this is to be providentially accomplished through national instrumentality, some one nation taking the lead, he is firm in the faith that this high honor is to fall upon that "nation" which glories in human bondage. But let him speak for himself:

> Why should it seem a thing incredible to you, that God should raise *this* nation from the dead, and raise her now! A *freer* nation, the sun does not shine upon, *and you know it,* though she has never been blatant about free thought, free speech, and free soil. A nation of simpler, purer Christianity, thank God, earth does not hold, and you believe it, though she has never been as boastful as some whose religion bears many a sad mark of corruption. Why should not God distinguish this nation, *which has so decidedly distinguished herself in His behalf?* Why should not God draw nigh to a people who are wont to draw nigh to Him, not in the worship of established ordinances only, but whose Constitution itself approaches God with a reverence, you believe, never similarly expressed by any other people? Do you not know that the interpreta-

tions and calculations of the soundest Christian learning justify the faith that ere long the approach of the Millennium must begin to show itself in appropriate premonitory changes, both in the political and Christian world? And is it not reasonable to suppose that God will inaugurate this glorious era of the Church, *by wheeling some one nation out of the ranks of the world, to take ground for God and man under the banner of the Gospel?*

We have but little doubt that, in the course of God's providence, at least *one* thing here predicted by Dr. Stiles will prove true, though not in the sense he intends nor for the object he states; and that is, that this rebel "nation" will ere long be *literally* "wheeled out of the ranks of the world" and be known as a "nation" no more. That God had selected that "nation," however, which boasts of standing on an ebony "corner-stone" on which no other nation "in the history of the world" ever stood, as His grand instrumentality, and Jefferson Davis as his Vicar-General, in ushering in "the Millennium," is something we had not before supposed was recorded in ancient prophecy.

Of course, this glowing prospect opened up to rebel vision by this modern Daniel, who puts all the "astrologers, the magicians, and the soothsayers" of the Church to flight, furnishes a basis on this "interpretation of the dream," for a most earnest and pious exhortation to the people to come up to the help of the Lord against the "atrocious;" and thereupon Dr. Stiles implores them as follows:

And now, at a period when the atrocious opposition of a powerful nation would seem to *invite the interposition of God in our behalf*, tell me, why should not every man who loves God or his country, to the uttermost of his ability, preach, pray, and work, to arouse our population to seize *this one great niche of time in the history of the world, and occupy that national position?*

REBEL VICTORIES BY MIRACLE.

Certainly; why should they not "preach, pray, and work," as never before; and especially, when the prospect is so good for counting on the direct "interposition of God" in their behalf? As the circumstances of their extremity "would seem to *invite* the interposition," can God withhold it from those whom Dr. Smyth regards as his "chosen people," and from that "nation" here specially selected "to take ground for God AND MAN under the banner of the (Southern) Gospel," and to usher in the "Millennium" of universal negro-slavery, a "nation" that has "so decidedly distinguished herself *in this behalf?*" God cannot withhold it; He certainly will interpose by the direct might of His omnipotence. See how it is to be done, as pictured by Dr. Stiles:

> Oh, how far you live from the light! Why, let the North march out her million of men on the *left*, and array upon the *right* all the veteran troops of England, France, Russia, and Austria; and bring up the very gates of hell in all their strength to compose the *centre* of her grand invading army. What then? Why, *every thing in God and from God assures us* that these Confederate States would hear a voice from heaven: "The battle is not yours but *mine.* Stand ye still and see the salvation of the Lord." If they dared to advance one step, a righteous and an angry God would fire off upon the aliens terrible thunder that angel ears never heard, and shoot out upon them vengeful fires and lightnings that cherubic vision never saw, and fling down upon them cataracts of angry power that hell herself never felt, and if necessary to our deliverance, shake the very earth from under their feet!

A NEW SIEGE OF JERICHO.

It is somewhat difficult, but we finally recover our breath again!—and being able to speak once more, we have a suggestion or two to make to those Southern Christians and to their preacher, founded upon his own words: "Oh, how far you live from the light!"

Our first suggestion is this: If "every thing in God and from God *assures*" you of such an easy and complete victory over your foes, and by such means, why don't you lay aside such expensive and cumbrous things as shot and shell and canister, and imitating your prototypes, God's *ancient* chosen people, march out with "rams' horns" as they did at the siege of Jericho? You would be saved an amazing amount of "transportation," and the whole thing would be done in a single week, and then we should have "peace," for which we all sigh.

You of course, as you read your Bibles, know how it was done in the olden time. "Seven priests" were commanded by Joshua to "bear before the ark seven trumpets of rams' horns." Let General Lee, your modern Joshua, select Dr. Stiles to head the list of "priests," with Drs. Palmer, Smyth, Sehon, Fuller, Adger, and Moore; we should certainly name Bishop Polk and Dr. Thornwell, had they not gone to their final account. The "ark" will of course contain a copy of the Constitution of the "Confederate States of America" which founds your nation on the "corner-stone" of human bondage. As the whole thing would have failed at Jericho had not the priests taken the "ark" into which God had previously commanded "the testimony" to be put, so it is essential that your "ark" should contain "the testimony" which you have given to the world in your Constitution. The ancient "ark" was "overlaid with pure gold within and without." As gold may be scarce with you, it may be covered and lined with "Confederate Scrip" of the latest issue.

Thus prepared, let the Confederate armies "compass" the camp of their enemies, followed by the priests, "bearing the ark and blowing the trumpets," once a day for six days, and on the seventh day go round seven times; and having done this, you may be able to hear the voice from heaven, which Dr. Stiles said you would, and be able to witness the destruction of all the Yankee armies by those "cataracts of angry power" of which he spake. It may be—have you ever thought of it?—that the reason why you have not already been completely successful over them, is, that you have counted on God's "interposition" without using God's means. Beware of such presumption, hereafter. We recommend this amendment in your "strategy." But one thing, especially, bear in mind. Don't "shout" the victory too soon. This was a point on which the people were particularly cautioned at the taking of Jericho under the ancient Joshua.

THE CONFEDERATE ARMAGEDDON.

We have another suggestion, which will still further illustrate the good policy of your adopting this ancient mode of warfare. As "every thing in God and from God assures" you that you can whip all mankind and Satan's hosts into the bargain,—with the United States composing the "left" wing, the great European Powers the "right" wing, and "the gates of hell" the "centre" of the grand army,—why not call the "priests," get the "rams' horns," and make a final end of all your enemies at once? You will then have a fair field for your Slavery Propagandism. You can then carry out universally, the "Christian Slavery" which is so pleasing to the mind and heart of Drs. Armstrong, Thornwell, Palmer, and the rest of "our Southern brethren" who mourn and pray over "free society;" making masters of whites who are "rich," and slaves of whites who are "poor."

And there is another element of encouragement. There would unquestionably be a wholesale desertion to the Confederate standard. The moment the rich music of the blast from the trumpets of the priests carrying the new "corner-stone" faith in the "Confederate ark," should reverberate along the line, the entire "centre" *would go over to you in a body*. They are one with you now, in heart, and only want the opportunity, to be arrayed with you bodily. You would *then* have a triumph which would cast all the Jerichos of the world into oblivion. Would it not be the battle of the Millennial Armageddon?

One of your preachers, you know, the Rev. Mr. Baldwin, wrote a volume, a few years ago, entitled "Armageddon." He imported the plain of Esdraelon from Palestine, and located the scene of the battle in the Mississippi Valley. According to Scripture, God's "chosen people" are to fight this battle, and against them are to be arrayed all infidel nations and all the corrupt ecclesiastical hierarchies of the world. Now, as you are the "chosen people," as you regard your nation the only righteous one among men,—"whose Constitution itself approaches God with a reverence never similarly expressed by any other people," especially the "corner-stone" article, as Mr. Stephens claims,—as you regard all other nations "infidel" and all other Churches "apostate," because they are wedded to "free society," and as you are to bring in the Millennium, you undoubtedly believe you are to fight the battle of Armageddon. The "terrible thunder," and the "vengeful fires and lightnings," and the "cataracts of angry power," of which Dr. Stiles speaks, exactly corresponding with the imagery of the Seer of Patmos, and the "direct interposition of God" which is claimed, all show that the great Millennial battle is meant by the preacher. Only amend your "strategy," then, in the manner here respectfully suggested, and,—*with the desertion to your ranks of the "centre" in a body*,—you undoubtedly will triumph.

Then the whole earth will rejoice that the long-wished-for Millennial Day has dawned!—with universal slavery for the "poor," mastership for the "rich," all Yankees destroyed, the Confederates everywhere triumphant, and Jefferson Davis God's Vicar-General over the world!

But seriously,—Do we need any better evidence that the leaders of the rebellion are demented, than that here furnished, in such religious rhapsodies as these leading divines indulge in? If these were emanations from ordinary men, they might be passed by as idle breath; but they come from the greatest intellects and the ripest scholarship among Southern Churchmen. That they are uttered to "fire the Southern heart" is undoubtedly true; and yet, that these men are sincere we as little doubt. That they have had more influence over the more serious portion of society, in urging on and keeping up the spirit of the war, than any other class, is confessed by Southern politicians and patent to the world. Our solution of the matter is, that they are judicially blinded; given over to strong delusion to believe a lie, yea, even a legion of lies; and that, through their delusions, the God of universal providence is working out great purposes of good to mankind and glory to His name.

CHAPTER IX.

PROVIDENTIAL DESIGNS IN THE REBELLION.

We have given in the previous chapter the doctrine of Divine Providence, and the remarkable perversions which are made of it by writers interested in the cause of perpetuating human bondage by a wicked rebellion. We propose here to set forth what we regard as some among the true purposes of God, now in process of being wrought out, by the stupendous events which are occurring in this nation.

If we speak with confidence, it is only because our convictions are strong and our faith abiding. At the same time, we claim no infallibility, in judging of events, either present or future. We say here, once for all, that we only utter our *opinions* upon what we regard as God's designs. To them we are entitled. We allow others the enjoyment of theirs. We aim only to *interpret* rather than *predict*, and give merely our best judgment of some things which we think the present contest is likely to work out.

The true doctrine of providence, as entertained by the common consent of Christendom, embraces, among others, these elements: it includes all beings and all things; and through all, God is working out great purposes of ultimate good to the world and glory to Himself.

If these positions embody the truth, they may be applied to the rebellion now in progress, and to the efforts made for its suppression. God is controlling all agencies and events at work in the contest, and out of all He will bring good to mankind and glory to Himself. No doubt great errors may be committed in attempting to interpret God's providence, so as *certainly* to declare, beforehand, what He specifically intends in a given event, or in a series or long course of events. We think that here Southern writers have deceived themselves, and have gone counter to one of the sound canons for interpreting God's will, whether referring to certain portions of His word or to His providence. It is a principle of prophecy, that rarely, if ever, is it so plain that it can fully be determined before its fulfilment. It is so with providence; we must wait for the issue, in most cases, before being able to comprehend fully the design. But as in certain prophecies there are way-marks which may guide the sincere inquirer to an approximately true interpretation before their fulfilment, and lights which cast a glimmer of truth along the path he would travel, and thus he is profited in their study and enabled to enter the vestibule of the temple which is ultimately to be opened to the full view of all men; so in providence, the honest and devout student, aided by God's word and Spirit, may be able to indicate with some approach to truthfulness, some, at least, of the grand results which the providence of God, as illustrated by daily occurring and consecutive events, is designed to reach.

While we would guard against the folly of committing the same error into which Southern writers have fallen, there is a marked difference in the position they assume upon the grand designs of providence as applied to the present contest, and that which we propose to take, which may aid in their solution, even though we should occupy precisely the same ground with them, or they with us, in reference to the canon of interpretation to which we have adverted. The sum and essence of the "trust" which they regard as "providentially committed" to them, and the design of God contemplated in their secession,—to "conserve and perpetuate" human bondage,—we regard as monstrous and diabolical, and such an application as but little if any thing short of blasphemous. On the other hand, as regards this particular element in the case, we interpret God's providence as tending to just the contrary result,—one of good,—of freedom and elevation to the negro race, instead of designed to render their bondage more secure, and their freedom and elevation utterly and forever hopeless.

As we differ in our interpretation, and as those who disagree with us claim as much ability to ascertain God's will as ourselves, we know of no better umpire to decide between us than this : for the present, the common judgment of Christendom ; and at length, the final issue of the contest. There we most willingly leave it, and are willing to abide the issue.

SLAVERY TO BE TERMINATED.

This preliminary course of thought brings us to notice this point first, as among the designs of God in His providence. It is quite proper that it should have this place, as for the sake of perpetuating slavery the rebellion was undertaken, and as a means for its suppression the Government has decreed the destruction of slavery. The point now is to inquire, on which side of the contest the purposes of God are arrayed. This can only be determined, at the present historic point, from the principles which are involved, and from the events which have occurred and are now in process of being wrought out. In taking the position that God designs the termination of slavery in this land, as one result of the rebellion, we mean that He designs its termination forever; and in giving what we deem the evidences which support it, we would construe them in proper subordination to the canon we have stated.

It is our opinion that the termination or the perpetuation of slavery, is by no means necessarily connected with the result of the war. In any event we believe the doom of slavery sealed.

If the Union shall be preserved in the complete triumph of the national arms, slavery will be ended. It needs no seer to declare the foregone conclusion of the American people upon this point. They will admit no compromise; it is beyond the reach of party jugglery; the great party of *the people* will say, and adhere to the saying, that on the reinstatement of the national authority over the territory of the entire Union, that element of our national life which has wrought such havoc, shall die the death. They will never permit the possibility of a repetition of so foul a treason in its name. Once in a thousand years,—or, once for all time,—is quite sufficient for such an issue within the bounds of the same nation. The memorials of the rebellion which the current age will embalm, and the materials out of which the future historian will elaborate the truth, will present a record in such hues of the deeds done for the sake of slavery, that the memory of them will be wrought too deeply into the soul of each successive generation to admit of its being possible that negro slavery can ever be reinstated within the domain of the Union. At least, this is our *opinion.*

MANNER OF ITS TERMINATION.

The precise manner in which the institution will be universally terminated, and its termination maintained, in the event of the preservation of our nationality, it is not material here to dwell upon, though we do not doubt the ultimate point which will be reached. It will be by an amendment of the Constitution of the United States. Although that measure has been for the present defeated in the House of Representatives, and may not be passed till a new Congress shall be elected, or possibly may be even longer deferred, it cannot admit of doubt that when the people shall have determined on prohibiting the institution forever, the form and substance of the prohibition will be embodied in the supreme organic law, the most sacred depository of the popular will.

In the mean time, and while waiting for this consummation, it may be accomplished in all the Rebel States by an Act of Congress; or it may occur simply under the Proclamation of the President already issued; or it may end through the measures which the civil power may take for receiving the revolted States to their proper standing in the Union. Whatever may be the course of the civil authorities, however, looking to that end, no measure which they may adopt, during the continuance of the war, will be effectual, except as backed up by military force; and it may be that while the war continues, no effective measures will be adopted, but such as are embraced within and may be carried out by the war power of the Executive; and even after the war shall have ended, in the complete success of the Union arms, and the civil authority shall have erected its barriers, we do not anticipate a ready acquiescence on the part of the entire Southern people to a parting with slavery. Whatever *status* may be given to the institution by the law,—even a prohibition of it forever, and that by the Constitution, and a requisition that similar prohibitions shall be inserted in each State Constitution in the rebel dominions,—this may not of itself, for many years, be sufficient. A military force may be requisite, in many parts of the South, to maintain the Constitution and the laws. But if so, it will be furnished;

even if it require a perpetual standing army. If Southern slaveholders so elect, such will be their condition; they will be kept in order by the troops of the United States, formed out of the materials they have held in bondage, just as the Government is now employing such troops to reduce them to subjection to the Constitution and the laws. It is among the clearest of all propositions, as reasonable, that the people who sustain the Government in prosecuting the war, who have endured and are enduring its untold sacrifices, will shrink back from no burden and no measure, when the war shall have ended in triumph, which may be essential to make good their determination to destroy the cause of the rebellion, that it may trouble their children or their children's children no more forever.

ACTION IN CERTAIN BORDER STATES.

We have spoken thus far of the termination of slavery in the Rebel States only, and on the supposition of the complete suppression of the rebellion and restoration of the national authority. The remaining slave States, with, we believe, but one or possibly two exceptions, have recently taken measures within themselves to terminate slavery by State Constitutional authority. Maryland is now engaged in altering her Constitution so as to abolish it within that State, and the sentiments of her people are well known to favor the measure by a large majority.* West Virginia, a new State formed from Virginia, has already abolished

* The *Baltimore American* of June 27th, brings an important announcement from the proceedings of the Constitutional Convention of Maryland. It gives the twenty-third article of the Bill of Rights, as follows: "Hereafter, in this State, there shall be neither slavery nor involuntary servitude, except in punishment of crime, whereof the party shall be duly convicted; *and all persons held to service or labor as* SLAVES, *are hereby declared* FREE." Upon this, the *American* says: "This article, after a protracted debate in the Constitutional Convention, in the course of which it was sustained in a masterly manner by the advocates of Anti-Slavery, was passed by a vote of fifty-three yeas to twenty-seven nays." This lacks

slavery. Missouri has not yet accomplished that result, but it is well known that the mass of her people are in favor of it, the main or only difference among them being whether it shall be immediate or gradual. There are so few slaves in Delaware, and the territory they occupy is so small, that practically the matter is of little consequence in its bearings upon the national question. We do not know whether any measures have been taken since the war began, to remove slavery from that State; but in any event it is fair to conclude, that when slavery shall have been removed from the other Border States, and shall have been overthrown in the rebel States, it will not long continue to infest the soil of Little Delaware. Tennessee was not embraced in the President's Proclamation declaring the freedom of the slaves in States that had rebelled; but it is well understood from the sentiments of her leading loyal men of all former political parties, that the masses of the people desire the institution to cease among them, and public Conventions of the people have so declared; but in consequence of the presence of war within her borders, and the disorganization of the

but one vote of being *two to one*. The people will of course ratify it by a large majority, for the Convention, so recently elected, but reflects in this act the popular will. It was upon this question that the election turned. It makes Maryland a free State, by *immediate emancipation*, and that *without compensation*. "My Maryland," thus stands erect. She has the honor of being the first of the loyal States which has voluntarily made "all men free" within her borders. The *American* further says: "The regeneration of a Commonwealth like ours is not an every-day occurrence. It is hard to estimate this work at its full value. But we shall see and know it better hereafter. All we know now is that the vestiges of a great evil are cleared away; that the canker of a great iniquity is extirpated, root and branch; that to our posterity no compromise is bequeathed which may be a fruitful source of discord hereafter. Races are forgotten, and humanity is honored. We have joined the train of rejuvenated States in the march of Freedom. We have torn away the mask from the deformity of Slavery, and we have wrenched the rod from the oppressor. We look to the future with hearts full of hope and trust, confident that Providence in its own good time will work out for us a brighter destiny. We offer our hand to our sister States and ask their congratulations. We ask them to join us in the prayer, *God preserve the Commonwealth of Maryland.*

civil authorities by the rebellion, no determinate action has yet been taken. The District of Columbia has been instantly changed from slave to free territory by an Act of Congress, since the outbreak of rebellion; and by the same authority freedom has been secured to all the Territories of the United States.

Kentucky is the only remaining slave State. She has taken no action upon slavery since the rebellion began. This may be owing to the fact that such are the provisions of her Constitution, that no measures of a legislative character, looking to its removal, even by a gradual process, could reach their decisive point, short of some six or seven years from their inauguration by the Legislature. Many citizens of Kentucky believe, and so express themselves freely, that long before that period can arrive, slavery will be terminated in that State and throughout the whole country, by the course of events inevitably resulting from the action of the Government in putting down the rebellion.

SIGNS OF ITS TERMINATION.—THE LOYAL STATES.

We present, then, as the first palpable indication which we notice, in the course of providence, that God's design, in this rebellion, is the removal of slavery from the country entirely, the events to which we have referred.

The simultaneous action of the States of so large a territory as is embraced in the broad belt of the Border States, for the freedom of thousands of slaves, taken in connection with the pervading sentiment in favor of the removal of slavery in the other loyal slave States, and the actual removal of slavery from the District of Columbia, and its prohibition in all the Territories of the Union, are events of such importance, that, were they not overshadowed by the excitements immediately attending the war, they would occupy a prominent place in the public thought of the world.

These unexpected and extraordinary events are the *direct result of the rebellion;* among the "first-fruits" which it has immediately brought forth. It is difficult to believe they could have occurred so extensively, and occurred within so short a period, and at the same time, had not the rebellion taken place. No such change in public sentiment could have been brought about, within such a period, nor such action inaugurated, by any method of mere discussion, even confined within the respective States. And had Congress undertaken, at any time within twenty years, to free the slaves in the District of Columbia, or to engraft upon every Territorial bill a prohibition of slavery, as it has done within the last three years, it would have convulsed the nation; it would have inaugurated rebellion, which was in fact undertaken in the apprehended fear that such measures might possibly occur.

We cannot understand how a believer in providence can interpret events so unlikely to occur under ordinary circumstances, so palpably occasioned by the rebellion, in any other manner than that God designs to remove slavery from the vast regions mentioned, and that the rebellion,—in which He makes the wrath of man to praise Him,—is the agency through which He aims to accomplish it.

FUGITIVE SLAVE LAW REPEALED.

There is another important fact in the line of providence and bearing directly upon the termination of slavery, a fact which has a special influence upon the continuance of slavery in the Border States, and which more or less affects it in the whole slave portion of the Union. The present Congress has repealed the Fugitive Slave Law, both the Act of 1793 and that of 1850; so that now there is no law of the United States for the reclamation of slaves escaping from their masters. The Canada line, in its previous bearings upon slavery, is now the Ohio and the Potomac. Even if the Border States had taken no action for abolishing slavery, the effect of this repeal would soon be very visible upon the institution within them, as well as upon the whole slave region.

Here is another important measure, *the fruit of the rebellion.* Congress could not, at any period since 1850, and before the rebellion, have repealed the Fugitive Slave Act of that year, without producing a revolution. The members from the South would very likely have carried out their oft-repeated threat, and withdrawn in a body from both Houses. Those threats were once thought to be only idle breath, Southern bluster; but no special credulity is now required to believe that they would have been put in execution.

SLAVES FREED BY THE WAR.

Another event disastrous to slavery, and which has been occasioned by the rebellion, is the influence which has resulted from a state of war and the presence of the army. We speak now particularly of the Border States. With the Federal armies traversing those States, and with the usages of war in former times,* and the orders of the War Department and the decision of the Executive, and the Acts of Congress, in revising the Articles of War, the point was early reached that all slaves coming within the lines of the army should be deemed free, and not returned to their masters.

Besides this, the action of the Government, under Ex-

* We shall show, on a future page in this chapter, that the United States authorities, military and civil, have, in former wars, recognized the freedom of slaves coming within the lines of the United States army.

ecutive authority, in enrolling negroes, free and slave, as soldiers, and securing to the latter their freedom; and finally, the Act of Congress providing for their enrolment in all the States, guaranteeing to the slaves their freedom, and to loyal masters compensation; these are among the measures which have had a great influence in rendering the institution comparatively worthless, even in the loyal Border States. In Maryland and Kentucky, where great opposition has been made to the Enrolment Act, in hundreds of cases the slaves have not waited either for the enrolment or draft, but have gone to the camps and enlisted, and under the orders and decisions of the Government have become thenceforth free; so that, in every way, from the presence of the army, and from a state of war, the institution of slavery in the loyal States, where there was no disposition on the part of the Government to interfere with it in itself considered, has become thoroughly demoralized, almost wholly worthless, and is rapidly melting away, leading to the feeling entertained by a large number of those most interested in the institution, that the sooner it is finally terminated the better it will be for all persons and interests concerned.

ALL TRACEABLE TO THE REBELLION.

Such are the facts passing before our eyes. Whatever may be thought of this course of events,—whether they afford matter for rejoicing or lamentation,—one thing is most clear: *they are the fruits of the rebellion.* If any lament, they must hold the rebellion responsible; while those who survey them justly, must behold in them "a Divinity that shapes our ends," operating through the "rough-hewn" aims and deeds of a foul conspiracy.

We say again, that we cannot understand how it is that any person who holds to the doctrine of providence, that

God works out His purposes through the agency of man,—the wicked and the good alike,—can note carefully and candidly passing events, and not come to the conclusion that God designs, as one result of the rebellion and the war, the removal of slavery from the land. Besides the facts mentioned, it is the *desire*, as founded in justice and good policy, seen in the opinions of leading men in these States, which we shall give hereafter, that slavery should be removed; and it is likewise their *belief*, that "the fulness of time" for this grand consummation has at length come.

TERMINATION OF SLAVERY IN THE REBEL STATES.

Many of the same causes which we have mentioned, operating to the removal of slavery from the Border States, have the same effect upon the States farther South. The repeal of the Fugitive Slave Acts, the removal of slavery from the District of Columbia, its prohibition in all the Territories, affect all the States alike, though not to the same extent. So, also, the action of the Border States, and the sentiments of many of their leading men, in favor of abolishing slavery therein, are not without their moral effect in the same direction upon the other States.

Another sign of great significance is the development already of antislavery sentiment and action in the remotest Gulf States and others, as they have been restored by the Union arms. Louisiana is revising her State Constitution, purging it of slavery, and has already inaugurated a State Government upon an antislavery basis. Arkansas has done the same. Tennessee has taken steps in the same direction, and will soon stand erect, organized, and purged of slavery. All these States will soon be fully represented in Congress; possibly in the next session of the present Congress.

Other States will follow in the same direction when reconquered to the Union, and when there can be an opportunity for the true sentiment of *the people* to be heard. Undoubtedly the mass of them have preferred slavery, and perhaps would prefer it still as a system of labor, in itself considered, for they have known no other; but as the arms of the Union advance, and they see that there is no hope of realizing their dreams of a Slave Empire, and as they reflect on the prosperity they once enjoyed and the woes with which they are surrounded,—all brought upon them by "secession" for the security of slavery which they were assured would be "peaceful"—they will, as they love peace better than war, and as they prefer prosperity, stability, certainty, and quiet, to an endless strife over slavery, submit to the necessities of the case and abandon their idol to its fate. We look for a rapid development of this feeling, and for corresponding results, in North Carolina, Georgia, and some other States, whenever they shall have been completely possessed by the armies of the Union, and the danger of a repossession by the rebel forces is past.

In large districts of the South slavery will die hard. Powder and shot, and shell, war, blood, and carnage, have been invoked for its security and expansion; these are the weapons which will work its death, while the victims of its bondage will prove the sentinels which will watch over its grave.

We may see what the march of armies is doing for slavery in the daily events of the war. Into every slave State where the Union forces move, the institution gives way. Many are driven off and huddled together in regions farther South; thousands are enlisted into the ranks; and what remains of the institution becomes useless to masters, of no avail to the country, and its victims look to the hand of the Government for their daily bread. Such will be the condition of things, substantially, all over the South as the country is reclaimed.

When the conquest is complete, and the war ended, slavery will be terminated in every Rebel State by the course of measures already mentioned. The security for this will be the military power of the Union, just as long as it may be necessary. When the people get tired of this, and think it best to submit to the authority of the Government, give up their love of slavery, and employ their former slaves as free laborers, and treat them properly, they can be released from their own bondage; but until they do this, the military rule will undoubtedly continue.

SLAVERY DOOMED THOUGH DISUNION TRIUMPH.

We have already said, in this chapter, that the termination or the perpetuation of slavery is by no means necessarily connected with the result of the war; that, in any event, we believed its doom was sealed. We will now explain what is meant by this.

We have presented considerations thus far to show that providential designs, read in the light of passing events, point to the termination of slavery; but we have considered these events only as connected with the complete overthrow of the rebellion and the re-establishment of the national authority. That the nation will eventually triumph, we have never doubted; and that with its triumph by its military power will come the eternal doom of slavery, we have as little doubt. We regard it as decreed of God. But whether our nationality shall perish or survive, we view the doom of slavery as written in the clearest light; and for this we will present what we deem satisfactory reasons.

INTERNAL CAUSES OF ITS DESTRUCTION.

The main one, and which is the germ of all, is, that the rebellion has completely demoralized the institution throughout the whole slave region. So thoroughly has this been done, and will it be done by the further prosecution of the war, that it will be impossible to restore it to its former condition, so as to be safe and profitable as before, by all the power which the "Confederate States," if established and recognized, can muster for that object.

That an exertion of power for that end, not requisite hitherto, would be demanded in the case supposed, is too plain for doubt. The slaves can never again be made contented with their condition in bondage. It is idle to tell us that they have been entirely contented with that condition hitherto. Having lived more than fifteen years of our professional life in two of the Gulf States, and travelled extensively over several others in the extreme South; having seen the system in city and country, at work and in recreation, upon the plantation and in the household, in the cabin and in the church, at home and abroad—we know something of its character and workings, and have very little that is new about it to learn. The stringent police system universal in the South, and a thousand facts and aspects of the case with which we will not weary the reader, but which are well understood by all who have lived where slavery prevails, especially in the Rebel States, establish the certainty that far more discontent has always existed—creating an anxiety often ill-concealed—than slave-owners were generally willing to admit.

But, passing the former discontent and its immediate occasion by, the case is now materially changed. The influence of the rebellion has invaded every plantation of the rebel dominions. All the slaves believe that the war is waged for the continuance of their bondage on the one hand, and for their freedom on the other. That they desire the latter condition is unquestionable. However little they may have desired it hitherto, that desire is now universal. Witness the multitudes that have flocked to the Union armies as far as they have penetrated slave territory, men, women, and children. They no doubt have very crude and erroneous notions of freedom; in thousands of instances they will find their lot a hard one, on gaining their liberty, owing to the distracted state of the country; in thousands of cases more, owing to the same cause, have they died of disease and neglect, and many will die hereafter; and, undoubtedly, arising from these hardships, will many sigh for their former homes, and some perhaps, if possible, may return to them; but, after all, it is still true, that the desire for this new condition is universal, and that it prompts them to action to gain it, and try the experiment as soon as an opportunity is given by the presence of a coat of blue.

ILLUSTRATIVE INCIDENT.—COLONEL DAHLGREN.

A fact sustaining this view, confirmed by a thousand instances, is well known. It is the universal testimony from our armies, that the slaves give true information of the country and of the enemy, and often at the greatest risk of life, while it is a rare thing for the whites to do this. In all our reading about the rebellion, we can call to mind but one instance to the contrary; that in which the slave of Mr. Seddon, the rebel Secretary of War, misled a portion of the forces of the lamented Colonel Dahlgren, on his approach to Richmond. Some have doubted the deception practised in this case; but, if true, it is the exception which confirms the rule.

FACTS, AND THEIR LESSON.

Two facts are sometimes mentioned, one of a negative and the other of a positive character, to confront the view we have given. We admit them both, but deny the conclusion drawn from them. It is said, if the slaves are so desirous of freedom, why have they not shown it by rising upon their masters universally? Many supposed this would be the case on the issuing of the President's Proclamation of Freedom, 1st of January, 1863. We were not of the number. Our acquaintance with the South led to a different opinion, and the result has verified its correctness.

That the Proclamation is known and understood by them as extensively as any other specific and important measure of the Government we do not doubt. But three causes, to name no more, are sufficient to prevent, at the present time, a wide insurrection for gaining their freedom. The first is, their powerlessness, while the whole Southern country is armed, and they are guarded by a more strict police than ever. With all their ignorance, they know such attempt to be hopeless, and that it would end in their indiscriminate slaughter.* The second is, that they would have first to conquer and destroy the women and children upon the plantations, in addition to the police, to prevent their giving information, and to dispossess them of the arms which many of them have. *This would operate* as a restraint upon many, even though they saw freedom before them; for, whatever else may be said, a very strong attachment exists, very extensively, between them and the *personnel* of the household. But

* The testimony that a universal slaughter would result from insurrection, is given in the "Address to the Christian World," by ninety-six Southern clergymen of all denominations, quoted on page 183, in Chapter v.

the third cause is sufficiently powerful to overcome the temptation which might impel them to violence. They believe the day of their deliverance is near, and that they have only to wait in order to realize it. They believe that their freedom will be secured by the Union armies, in the suppression of the rebellion, and that they must wait for their coming. That their Day of Jubilee is at hand, is with them a conviction as strong as death.

The other fact relied on to show that they are contented with their lot, and not desirous of freedom, is the alacrity they display in serving their masters in the camp, and in other positions connected with the rebel service. This is easily explained. They are entirely under military control, and infinitely more in the army than on the plantations, although few of them have been placed in the rebel ranks. Their lot is to obey, or forfeit life.

WAR EDUCATING SLAVES FOR FREEDOM.

Another important consideration, bearing on the destruction of slavery, even though the Confederacy should at length be established, is the education which the rebellion, more or less extensively, is diffusing among the slaves. It is making them acquainted with war; giving many of them habits of military discipline, and an acquaintance with many important details of the military art. We have already stated, what is well supported by the facts, that the reason why so few comparatively of the slaves are put into the rebel armies, is owing to the fear of the consequences which would result from making them soldiers. But enough has been done to make the experiment dangerous, should peace result and leave them in bondage. This leaven would be diffused, and the knowledge improved and extended.

We have no manner of doubt, that, if the rebellion should triumph, and its leaders should determine to realize their idea of building a great Empire on the "corner-stone" of slavery,—securing its perpetuity, extension, and stability against all dangers,—the slaves, seeing that their longings and hopes were about being destroyed, would become even more demoralized than now, so far as employment is concerned, and would then rise and assert their freedom to the extent of their power, even though they should deem the issue doubtful and destruction probable. We might then look for a repetition of the scenes of St. Domingo, a servile war with terrible atrocities, and for the negroes, possibly, at the end—freedom; but certainly not a continuance of negro slavery, in a great Empire of the Gulf, of which that element should be the "corner-stone."

EXTERNAL CAUSES OF ITS DESTRUCTION.

We have only considered the causes which would operate within the Confederacy for the destruction of slavery, in case its independence were acknowledged. There are powerful causes which would operate outside of it for the same end.

In no treaty which could possibly be made with the United States would any immunity be granted to slavery. No Fugitive Slave Law will ever again ornament the Statutes at Large of the Union; nor would any other concession to the system be made. The party that should attempt it would be hurled from power and doomed to infamy. The Administration that should propose or agree to it would provoke a revolution. The people have had that chalice pressed to their lips for the last time. They have drunk it in blood, the blood of their sons and brothers. They will drink of it no more forever.

Without such guarantees, how long could slavery exist in a Southern Confederacy? The line between freedom and slavery would steadily march South, first placing the Border States behind it, then the next tier, and so on steadily, by the escape of slaves; until the States, from the paucity of labor, and in sheer self-defence, would adopt the free-labor system in order to maintain the cultivation of the soil.

Besides this, every possible effort would be made by those in the old Union who are violently opposed to slavery, to interfere with it; by publications, by underground railroads, by John Brown raids, and by any and every other means within their power. Nor would they be at all restrained, but rather stimulated to this, by what they have already sacrificed in a war for which slavery is responsible; and should an insurrection occur in the South, it would be aided freely. Nor could any legislation prevent such course of action, should it be attempted. We say nothing of the propriety of any of these measures, but only speak of what would inevitably occur, taking human nature as it is. How long, under this state of things, could slavery endure?

ENVIRONED BY ENEMIES.

But this is not all. Such a nation would bring down upon it the wrath of the world. It has been about as much as the United States could bear with a good grace, to withstand the odium of universal Christendom, with a portion of its territory burdened with slavery merely under toleration; but when a nation should have consummated the consecration of that system as its "corner-stone," through a ceremonial of treason, blood, and carnage, and should attempt to carry out its new Gospel to the results designed by its founders, it would become insufferable among men; and should it open the African slave-trade to replenish its fields with laborers, as was a part of the original plan of its leaders, it would be dealt with as a pirate among the nations, just as individuals are now treated who engage in that execrable traffic.

It is not easy to perceive how the "Confederate States of America," thus beset by millions of enemies within, each feeling that he is personally wronged in the deprivation of his manhood, and beset by enemies of such power and number in the nations of the world without, each feeling that it had a duty to discharge toward the oppressed and in behalf of humanity, could long rest securely on its favorite "corner-stone." The stone would crumble under such blows, and the whole edifice would fall and perish.

COTTON DREAMS VANISHED.

It is quite too late in the day to affirm that such a nation would be countenanced by other nations *from necessity;* and to admit, with Dr. Palmer, that to "conserve and perpetuate slavery" was a duty they owed "*to the civilized world*," even though it be true that "the blooms upon Southern fields, gathered by black hands, have fed the spindles and looms of Manchester and Birmingham not less than of Lawrence and Lowell." All such dreams are of the past, so far as they relate to *slavery;* for nothing is more certain than that those "blooms" can equally well be "gathered by black hands" that are *free.* Nor is it at all needful that those "hands" should be "black;" much less that "the blooms" they gather should be from "Southern fields" alone. The necessities growing out of this rebellion have demonstrated that the throne of King Cotton is not immovably built on Southern plantations, and that his daily attendants may be found among other people than the dark-hued sons of Africa. The mills of Manchester and Birmingham have already learned this practical lesson, and those of Lowell and Lawrence are quite as apt scholars.

The dream of Dr. Palmer, however, is none other than that which filled the watches of the night and the hours of the day of all the Southern leaders. "Strike a blow," says he, "at this system of labor, and *the world itself* totters at the stroke." And with a patriotism which is quite cosmopolitan, he exclaims: "Shall we permit that blow to fall? Do we not owe it to *civilized man* to stand in the breach and stay the uplifted arm? If the blind Samson lays hold of the pillars which support the arch of *the world's industry*, how many more will be buried beneath its ruins than the lords of the Philistines?" And with a complacency which is quite edifying, he applies the words addressed to Queen Esther, to the people of the South, with only this difference, that while she was merely desired to prefer a simple "request" to save the Jews from apprehended evil, they are exhorted to treason and rebellion to save "the world itself" from absolute "ruin:" "Who knoweth whether we are not come to the kingdom for such a time as this?"

But we presume that if the world were really driven to the extremity, as it existed several thousand years before the discovery of the cotton-gin, it probably could continue awhile longer if the cotton-plant should be completely exterminated; though we have no fear that such a catastrophe will occur, or any opinion that the world would be much the loser, if the "Confederate States" and all they contain should be blotted from its map forever.

SLAVERY DOOMED AND THE UNION MAINTAINED.

But the doom of slavery is not dependent, as we believe and have said, on either result of the war. No result of the bloody issue joined in its favor can save it. In a separate nation it perishes under its own weight. With our nationality maintained, it dies by the same blow which brings the rebellion to the block.

As we have said, however, we do not doubt the alternative to which God's providence points, and which His decree has made sure. It is, in our judgment, "fore-ordained,"—and we say it with no other light than that which is vouchsafed to others, but we think every available consideration warrants the position,—that this nation is to stand, that its enemies are to be overthrown, that the rebellion is to be crushed, and the "Confederate States of America" blotted out; and just as surely as that is done, the same decree of God, executed by the American people, will terminate negro slavery in this land. This, at least, is our *opinion.*

If any persons hesitate to accept these conclusions, we can only ask them to defer their opinion until the case is decided. This is safe. They might tell us to do the same. We are quite willing to wait; but we will, as briefly as may be, give "a reason for the hope that is in us," and we trust not without "meekness and fear."

Under God, it is a question of means, and a question of endurance. There is a sense in which the remark of the great Napoleon is true, that "the providence of God is with the strongest battalions," and there is a sense in which it is false. We accept the true sense, and apply it to the present case. Another remark we accept, that "the age of miracles is past," and we apply it now to war. And yet, we hold rigidly to the true doctrine of providence, that God works in, through, by, and controls, *all* that takes place, educing evil out of good, and exalting His great name. While the Omnipotent and the Omniscient thus works out His purposes through means, there is generally an adaptedness of the means to the end, an adaptedness which a close observer can often perceive, and the course of which he can often trace with clearness and declare the result.

Now, apply these general principles to the case in hand, and we say that the issue of this war between lawful Government and a foul rebellion is merely or mainly a question as to which of the parties can hold out the longest. We take it for granted, at the outset, that neither intends to *compromise* the question which underlies the whole contest, the question of *nationality.* The Government will not surrender its authority of rule over the whole Union, but upon one condition,—that it is compelled to this by the total defeat of its armies. No party or administration would dare do this. *The people* will not allow it. It is the people's Government, and *the people* are carrying on the war to sustain it. On the other hand, we have no idea that *the leaders* of the rebellion will ever give up the contest, except upon one of two conditions,—that their independence as a nation is recognized; or, that the rebellion itself is crushed, which means the destruction of its military power. Such being the case, the war must go on until one party or the other is completely overthrown. It is then a question of endurance, a question of means and of power. This, upon the ground we have assumed, is the *sole issue.*

REASONS FOR THIS POSITION.

What, then, is the relative strength of the parties? In answering this, we cannot go into a full examination, but will present some general considerations which are fundamental, and which substantially embrace the whole case.

With the rebels, the issue, leaving out other resources, is chiefly one of *men*, and that in comparison with men on the other side. That the rebels can "get along," and fight long and vigorously without *money*,—or rather, with that only which is worthless, except to themselves, and which may become well nigh or totally so, even to them, —is unquestionable. Nations have frequently done this. England has prosecuted her gigantic wars, during a long period, with her currency at a very low ebb; and France has fought just as vigorously with her *assignats* down at zero at the stock-boards of other nations, and worthless, for the time, upon the Bourse of Paris. The Confederate "nation" may also fight on, with a worthless currency, or with none at all; and for a circulating medium, or without one, the people can come back to *barter*. As for their bogus Government, it can get its necessities for the army, by "taxation in kind," and by arbitrary "impressment," phrases which have a place in rebel "law," and which with the people have a meaning. Those necessities which they must have from abroad, they gain by their cotton which runs the blockade; and as they have obtained supplies hitherto, we admit, for the sake of the argument, that they may gain in that way what they may need hereafter. We therefore leave all this out of the account, and come back to the simple element of *men* out of whom to make *soldiers;* and how stands the account on this score?

STRENGTH OF THE PARTIES IN SOLDIERS.

The census of 1860 answers the question. The eleven Confederate States, including Tennessee and Arkansas, and excluding Missouri, contained, by that census, *one million and a quarter* of white males between fifteen and fifty. The remaining States contained something over *five millions* of white males between fifteen and fifty. The total white population of these respective portions of the country, was, in the former, five millions and a half, and in the latter, twenty-one millions. No account is here taken of the large districts in these eleven States which are within the lines of our armies, and from which the rebel armies cannot be recruited; as, for example, the whole of Tennessee, a large portion of Arkansas, large portions of Virginia, Mississippi, Louisiana, and indeed a part of each one of the eleven. In the comparison, we give the totals of each section, as shown by the census, thus allowing a great advantage to the rebels. Admitting that three-fourths of the number between fifteen and fifty years of age,—whether it be too great or too small, probably the former, is of no consequence in the comparison,—are physically qualified for the army, there are about *nine hundred thousand* men out of whom to make soldiers in the eleven rebel States, and *thirty-seven hundred thousand* in the remaining States. This was about the proportion of fighting men within the range of the parties at the beginning of the rebellion.

How does the case as to men stand now, in the fourth year of the war? It is probable that the losses on each side have not much changed the proportion, if any. If it be said that the Union armies have lost more in killed, as the rebels have generally acted on the defensive, this is fully or more than compensated by the fact that we have, by many thousands, a large excess of prisoners; and also from the consideration that our well-organized Sanitary and Christian Commissions, and the abundant supply of every thing requisite in the Medical Department of the Union army, have contributed to the recovery of a larger proportion of our wounded than theirs, as the records from the battle-field and the hospital, and our knowledge of their lack of medical supplies, fully confirm. Upon the estimate, then, made largely from official data, that there have been killed and disabled, in the Federal armies, *half a million*, and upon the supposition that the rebels have lost *the same number*, the latter have now left for military service but *four hundred thousand* white men, while the Government of the Union has *thirty-two hundred thousand* white men, from whom to recruit their armies.

NEGRO SOLDIERS—THEIR NUMBER UNLIMITED.

The foregoing calculation relates only to the material for *white* soldiers. President Lincoln states in his letter to Colonel Hodges, of Frankfort, Kentucky, under date of April 4, 1864, that there were then in the Federal service "quite a hundred and thirty thousand soldiers, seamen, and laborers," of African descent. What proportion of this number carry a musket we do not know; but from an official report made by Adjutant-General Thomas, on his return from Mississippi in the summer of 1863, and from the rapid recruiting of negroes since, it is safe to say that there are now in the ranks of the Union armies as fighting men, at least one hundred thousand of this description.

But be this estimate about negro soldiers as it may, the facts upon this branch of the subject, present and prospective, are momentous as regards this question of the military strength of the respective parties. The rebels *dare not*, to any large extent, make soldiers of their slaves; while, into every rebel State where our armies penetrate, the recruiting office is opened, and thousands are soon enrolled and drilled to fight for the Union cause; and that negroes will fight bravely, and when they have had sufficient discipline will fight as well as white men, is too well attested by official reports from the highest commanders in our armies, for any persons who fully examine the case to doubt.

It is true that a large number of white men are required at the North to do the work of agriculture, which in the

South is done by slaves. But so far as this affects the relative strength of the material for soldiers of the two sections, it is far more than counterbalanced by the vastly larger total number of white men at the North than at the South, and by the fact just mentioned, that, while the Union armies can be indefinitely recruited, and are daily being enhanced by that very laboring population of the South,—the slaves,—the rebels *dare not*, except to a very limited extent, put their slaves into the ranks of their armies. The proof of this is sufficiently seen in the discussions which, from time to time, have taken place in the Rebel Congress on this very question.

WHITE SOLDIERS SUFFICIENT.

Taking, then, the facts of the past, based upon the material of *white men* for the war, and from them drawing the military horoscope of the future, and the case is undeniable,—leaving out of view negro soldiers altogether,—that the loyal States can stand the brunt of battle much longer than the States in rebellion; and as the rebels now have, from the estimates given, but *four hundred thousand* white men, all told, fit for military service, while the United States now have, of the same description, *thirty-two hundred thousand*, the war, at the rate of loss of life thus far, need not continue as long as it has been raging in order to bury or disable *every rebel* capable of bearing arms; while the loyal section would still be left with twenty-eight hundred thousand men, or nearly *three millions*, fit for military service, with imillions more growing up at home, and tens of thousands annually coming in from Europe of whom we have taken no acconnt, to attend to any of the little details concerning such questions as the "Monroe Doctrine" and Maximilian, or other minor matters which the emergencies of the future may present.

NATIONAL RESOURCES AND CREDIT.

There is one element which we have not adverted to on the side of the United States, which is regarded as the "sinews of war." Many are appalled at the debt we are accumulating. A recent official statement from the Secretary of the Treasury, makes the debt at the end of three years of war, to be seventeen hundred and nineteen millions. Admit that it will be doubled in three years more, or in round numbers will amount to thirty-five hundred millions, before which it will be seen the war must end, from the loss of rebel life, and still it will by no means equal the debt which Great Britain had contracted by her wars fifty years ago; and yet, Great Britain then had, as a means of revenue for a taxable basis, less than half the population that the United States now have, and her other resources then as compared with ours now were far below them. With all this burden, Great Britain has been steadily advancing in greatness, power, and prosperity, as a nation, and to-day stands in the front rank of European Powers. The national credit of the United States,—based upon our unbounded resources, to a large extent yet undeveloped, resources within ourselves with which no nation of Western Europe can compare,—may have a great pressure upon it, but it will be found able to endure it. That we have been able to endure three years of such expenditures, and have kept up our credit to the point which has been maintained, without going to Europe to borrow money, has astonished the financiers of the Old World.

The people will have pecuniary burdens without doubt, and so will our children; but when it is a contest for national life,—a contest for law, order, popular government, freedom, and humanity, against treason, rebellion, anarchy, slavery, and eternal war,—that man has a soul that is craven, or is in sympathy with rebellion, or beset with childish fears, or is ignorant of the issues at stake, who is croaking about *pecuniary* burdens. While our fathers, sons, and brothers, are pouring out their hearts' *blood*, it is but a poor sacrifice we make to sustain the Government in whose cause they are engaged—with our money.

THE RESULT.

We repeat, then, that we have confidence that the Union cause will triumph, and that the rebellion will be crushed; not merely because we have greater resources and power, but that God in His providence will operate through them to maintain the right and overthrow the wrong. In that overthrow, slavery, which is at the bottom of the strife, will perish forever from this land. The guns opened upon Fort Sumter, in April, 1861, sounded its death-knell; and not many more April suns will rise and set before patriot soldiers will exultingly discharge their trusty rifles over its grave. Such we believe to be the firm determination of the AMERICAN PEOPLE, led and sustained in the great and good work by the PROVIDENCE OF GOD.

GOVERNMENTAL DETERMINATION CONFRONTED.

But at this point we are confronted. Rebel leaders, among politicians and divines, boldly declare that the Government in its present purposes against slavery, and the Northern people in sustaining it, are sinning with a high hand; not only sinning against their rights as a people, but directly sinning against "the word, providence, and government of God," and are in "rebellion against the Lord God Omnipotent who ruleth!"

This is rather a serious view of affairs. We must look at it. We are always disposed to give men the largest liberty in the statement of their opinions; and never more so than when they profess to set forth the will of God. As this is a grave indictment brought by one of the Lord's servants, it deserves examination. We will let Dr. Smyth, of Charleston, South Carolina, make the presentment in full. In the article from the *Southern Presbyterian Review* for April, 1863, before referred to, he says:

> But the argument is lifted up to a far higher platform, when we consider slavery in reference to the word, providence, and government of God. That God's providence is holy, wise, and powerful; that it extendeth to all things and all events; our enemies themselves profess to believe, even in their catechisms. Slavery, therefore, whether as a form of temporal, political, organized society, it is good or evil, is like other similar forms of evil, providential; and as such, is under God's holy, wise, and powerful government, and to be acted upon only in accordance with the principles of His word and gospel, that by them God may, as it pleaseth Him, continue, remove, ameliorate, or modify it, as it seemeth to Him wise and good.

We wish we could say that Dr. Smyth, in other parts of this article (given in the preceding chapter), had taken views of God's "providence" no more in disagreement with His word than are found in this extract. He is right in saying that it "extendeth to all things." He admits also that one of its bearings upon slavery, may be to "remove" it, provided this shall seem to God "wise and good." We are disposed then to inquire, What hinders him from conceding that to "remove" it *is* "wise and good;" and that the "things" now occurring within this nation tending to that end, "all" of which are embraced in God's providence, are *proper* agencies for such a result? It is not difficult to answer this question. He is a believer in the modern doctrine, that negro slavery is an "ordinance of God," that it is *in itself* "wise and good," and is a "blessing" to all concerned; and therefore that it is "in accordance with the principles of God's word and gospel," to perpetuate it, to vindicate its righteousness, and to labor for its security and indefinite expansion. He thus does not deem it right to interfere with it by any measures whatever; for, as it is "to be acted upon only in accordance with the principles of God's word and gospel," and as His word is declared to be totally silent about emancipation, there are no such "principles" "in accordance with" which it can be terminated. It must therefore continue. It can never "please" God to "remove" it through the agency of man upon "the principles of His word," if it be true, as is claimed, that there are no such "principles" which meet the case. Nor is it even within the power of simple omnipotence to "remove" it "by them," if there are none. If, then, it shall ever be removed, it must be by miracle; or upon "principles" not revealed; or in utter defiance of the Almighty.

There is, indeed, an apparent concession in this extract, —perhaps a real one,—that there are *some* "principles of God's word," "in accordance with" which slavery *may* be removed. But nothing is more sure than that all Southern writers, and Dr. Smyth among them, insist that the "Gospel" is *utterly silent* upon emancipation; that there is nothing in the New Testament about the thing or the process. All his talk then about its removal upon such "principles" is idle. His *real* position, as his whole article shows, is that which we have given: that slavery is a divine institution, an "ordinance," to be vindicated, expanded, perpetuated.

OPPOSITION TO SLAVERY FIGHTING AGAINST GOD.

Dr. Smyth is therefore utterly opposed to any action whatever for the removal of slavery; and especially does he regard the measures of the United States Government impious and abhorrent to the last degree. But let us hear him upon this point, and then examine his reasoning and conclusions. The foregoing extract makes up his premises. In the next words immediately following the above quotation, and as a deduction from them, he continues as follows:

> And to wage a war of extermination against slavery,—a war in itself wicked and unconstitutional [what a becoming and sincere regard these rebels have that the *Constitution* shall not be violated!], and carried on in a spirit of diabolical perfidy and inhumanity,—is to fight against God, and to run against the thick bosses of the Almighty. It is rebellion against the Lord God Omnipotent who ruleth. To participate in it, is to join in conspiracy against the throne and empire of Heaven. And did not the South come up to the help of the Lord against the mighty, she would involve herself in the divine malediction with which the inhabitants of Meroz were cursed.

Upon the foregoing we offer a few considerations. The position in which the Government of the United States and the people who sustain it in prosecuting the war against rebellion are here placed, would be regarded of little consequence did such effusions emanate from the secular press of Richmond or Charleston; but coming as they do from a clergyman of high position and influence at the South, and addressed as they are to the more serious-minded portion of those in rebellion, they call for an examination.

THE GOVERNMENT VINDICATED IN DESTROYING SLAVERY.

All argument upon "slavery in reference to the *word*" of God, we defer to a succeeding chapter. We say, however, here and now, that we admit that slavery is "to be acted upon only in accordance with the principles of His word and Gospel,"—so far as there are any which bear upon the case, or at least not upon any "principles" which contravene any thing which God has revealed in His "word,"—and we are quite willing to hold the Government, in its present attitude towards slavery, strictly to this test.

In regard, then, to the chief matters contained in these extracts, our position is, that while we admit in the main, and for the argument's sake, Dr. Smyth's premises in the former about "providence," we deny his conclusions in the latter concerning the course of the Government and the people who sustain it.

There is no ground for dispute with Dr. Smyth about the *justice of war*. A nation may engage in war in a just cause as acceptably to God as it may serve Him in any other way. The civil magistrate is armed with the sword by God's express authority. Furthermore, in a just war, it may be as clearly the duty of an *individual* to engage, as to pray; and God may accept the service. Dr. Smyth of course admits all this, for he exhorts the South to war. We do not now argue with Quakers or other non-combatants.

The only points in question are two: Is the United States Government *now engaged* in a just war? Is its present attitude *towards slavery*, in this war, justifiable? These two points cover the whole case. We take them separately.

ITS RIGHT OF SELF-PRESERVATION.

I. Is this a just war on the part of the United States?

We aim, on both points, only to give a synopsis of the arguments by which the affirmative may be sustained, and not to exhaust the subject or to go into it at length.

1. If God's word teaches any thing that is plain, it is this: that a nation may justly draw the sword to maintain its authority against all evil-doers, even in the execution of its ordinary legislation; and especially may it do this to put down an armed rebellion, seeking to overthrow

its supreme authority, and to subvert lawful Government, which is an ordinance of God. If a man denies this, he denies the very letter and spirit of Apostolic teachings, and admits a principle under which it would be impossible to maintain civil Government at all; he lands in anarchy; and, therefore, we cannot now have any controversy with him. Dr. Smyth admits this as a Scriptural *principle.* The South *act* upon it; punishing with severity, even with death, those whom they adjudge guilty of treason in rebelling against *their* rebellion.

2. Nothing is more certain in point of fact than this: that the people of the South are now openly resisting the supreme authority and lawful Government of the United States; even resisting "the Constitution, to which," as Dr. Thornwell says, "these States *swore allegiance.*" It is perfectly immaterial to the immediate issue in hand, whether that resistance be called "rebellion," or "revolution," or by the apparently softer term, "secession." The Southern orators and papers have called it each by turn, as it suited their purpose It may be one, or the other, or all, but it amounts to the same thing. It is, in fact, *armed resistance to lawful Government.* It was that at the first instant of the movement. It is that still.

If those concerned complain of being called "rebels" and "traitors," and their work "rebellion,"—as Dr. Smyth and all the rest loudly do,—let the justice of such complaints be tested by their own standard. Those who have claimed the right of States to "secede" from the Southern Confederacy,—as has been done in the Rebel Congress by disaffected members,—and who have said that they would put that right in practice in certain contingencies, have been denounced in that Congress and in the Richmond journals as "traitors;" and even the utterance of such sentiments has been stigmatized in that body as "treasonable;" and any "overt act" which should be taken in that direction has been denounced as worthy of death. Such States, it was said, should be "restrained by the bayonet." If, then, to "secede from the Southern Confederacy," where the principle of "secession" is acknowledged as fundamental, and out of which that Confederacy originated, be justly deemed "treason" and "rebellion," then *a fortiori*, with much stronger reason is it "treason" and "rebellion" for the Southern States to "secede" from the United States, where no such principle is acknowledged. Laying aside then the main and conclusive considerations on which the charge of rebelling against the lawful authority and Government of the United States may be sustained against the Southern States and people, the charge is amply sustained when tried by their own standard.

As the Southern rebellion has taken the form of armed resistance and is making war, the Government assailed has the right to overcome this resistance by the same means, and is making war for this purpose and to maintain its authority. As a *right*, therefore, a right *by the word of God*, the Government of the United States is carrying on a lawful war to maintain its lawful authority.

DESTRUCTION OF SLAVERY A LAWFUL MEANS TO THIS END.

II. Is the Government justified, in order to its success in putting down rebellion, in aiming to destroy slavery?

We of course now speak of slavery in the Rebel States only, and of the action of the Government as confined to its operations in war. As the result of the rebellion, or occasioned by it, we have already stated that Congress undoubtedly will, ultimately, amend the Constitution and prohibit slavery in the whole land forever. By its war measures and war power, the Government are striking at slavery in the whole rebel dominions, and aim to destroy it root and branch. Is this right?—or, as charged, Is this "to fight against God," a "rebellion against the Lord God Omnipotent who ruleth," and a "conspiracy against the throne and empire of Heaven?" We sustain the Government in this determination, and will give our reasons.

The grounds of our vindication are these: A nation in a just war may adopt any measures for its success which are deemed *necessary*, provided they are not inconsistent with the principles of justice, and are sustained by the laws and usages of war among civilized nations. Those laws and usages permit a nation to attack slavery and free the slaves of an enemy, and use them against the enemy, in order to its success in war; and of the necessity of these measures the party adopting them is to be the judge. This applies to war between "nations" proper—to foreign war; much more, on the same authority, may these means be resorted to in putting down rebellion.

The justification or condemnation of such measures, as properly belonging or not to the code of war, cannot be settled by an appeal to Scripture, for the word of God says nothing whatever on the subject. It is worse than idle, therefore, to arraign the Government before the bar of Revelation, on a matter where Revelation is utterly silent. The only standard by which the case can be determined, is the one already mentioned: the laws of war as illustrated in the usages of civilized nations; and to give the case the fairest chance, we are quite willing to take our examples from those nations of modern times where Christianity has the greatest influence. Taking these principles for our guide, and scanning the facts which the course of the Government has developed, and it will be seen that the Government has not only kept within the limits of its authority, in reference to this simple issue, as determined by the criterion mentioned, but has conducted with a forbearance toward slavery in the Rebel States which has excited the wonder of other nations, and upon which history will record its judgment for remarkable leniency.

Before citing the authorities to sustain the positions taken, let us note the course which the Government has pursued.

FORBEARANCE OF THE GOVERNMENT WITH SLAVERY.

We have given the proof, and the South universally admit the fact, that their resistance to the Government,—their "secession,"—was to establish more securely the institution of slavery, which they imagined to be in peril from the Government. Slavery is thus, in a sense well understood, the cause of the rebellion and the war. The President and the party that put him in power were publicly pledged, previous to his election, and also in his Inaugural Address, not to interfere with slavery where it was lawfully established. The whole South *knew* of these pledges. They were kept inviolate. The proof of all this we have given. When the rebellion had proceeded so far as actually to fire upon the flag and vessels of the United States in the harbor of Charleston, and when the Government called out forces to put it down, the President and Congress still maintained the principle of non-interference referred to, and uniformly took the ground, and declared by acts, resolutions, and proclamations, the doctrine, that the war was "*not* waged for any purpose of overthrowing or interfering with the rights or established institutions of the States [meaning thereby, especially, *slavery*]; but to defend and maintain the supremacy of the Constitution, and to preserve the Union, with all the dignity, equality, and rights of the several States unimpaired."*

It was found at length, that, instead of being an element of weakness, as at first supposed, slavery was an element of great strength to the rebellion; indeed, its vital support, as the rebels themselves declared. It was believed, that, as slavery in the Rebel States was in open conflict with the Government, one or the other must be destroyed in the region over which the rebellion held sway. It was then resolved to strike the rebellion in its most efficient support, and thus save the Government from its most deadly enemy. As the Government was clothed with God's authority to sustain itself and put down the rebellion, it was clothed with God's authority *to use all necessary and lawful means to that end.* It was, from the nature of the case, constituted, for the time being, the sole judge of the essential means, being responsible to God and the people.†

* These words are from the resolutions passed *unanimously* by the House of Representatives, July, 1861, offered by Mr. Crittenden, of Kentucky.

† We do not of course entertain any question that may be raised here, as between the simple power of the President, by Proclamation or otherwise, as Commander-in-Chief of the Army and Navy, and Congress, touching the jurisdiction of the Executive and Legislative branches of the Government over matters of war. It is by no means essential to the sole point in hand. When we speak of the *Government* in its attitude toward slavery under the laws of war, we speak simply of the *authority of the United States* to put down rebellion, whether the particular measures of the war are determined by the President, as Commander-in-Chief, or by the Executive and Legislative branches of the Government together. As a fact, however, Congress has substantially sustained, either tacitly or by direct legislation, all the acts of the Executive in regard to slavery. In a speech made in Chicago, July 14, 1864, by the Hon. Isaac N. Arnold, a member of the present Congress, he says: "On the 13th of January, 1864, I introduced the following bill, which has been embodied substantially in another which passed Congress: '*Be it enacted, &c.*, That in all the States and parts of States designated in said Proclamation as in rebellion (the Proclamation against slavery, January 1, 1863), the re-enslaving or holding, or attempting to hold in slavery, any person who shall have been declared free by said Proclamation, or any of their descendants, otherwise than in the punishment of crime, whereof the accused shall have been duly convicted, is and shall be forever prohibited, any law of any State to the contrary notwithstanding.'" The Executive and Legislative branches of the Government are thus united in support of that measure.

EMANCIPATION PROCLAMATION.

When the Government determined to strike at slavery, by the Proclamation of September 22, 1862, the war had been going on for a year and a half with varying success. The measure was deemed a necessity, and was adopted, not for the purpose of interfering with slavery, in itself considered, but to put down the rebellion, and as a means solely to that end; the President stating, in this Proclamation, "that hereafter as heretofore, the war will be prosecuted for the object of practically restoring the constitutional relation between the United States and the people thereof in those States in which that relation is, or may be, suspended or disturbed." In this Proclamation, one hundred days were allowed to the people of the States in rebellion to lay down their arms and save the institution harmless; and loyal persons in rebel districts were promised compensation "for all losses by acts of the United States, including the loss of slaves;" a promise which any Congress would have felt bound to redeem. On the non-acceptance of these terms, all slaves in rebel districts to be designated on the 1st of January, 1863, were to be declared free. The terms proposed not having been accepted, the President issued a Proclamation of this date, declaring all slaves within such districts "henceforward free." He here states as before, this, "as a fit and necessary *war measure* for suppressing the rebellion." He enjoins "upon the people so declared to be free, to abstain from all violence, unless in necessary self-defence," and exhorts them to "labor faithfully for reasonable wages;" declares that "such persons of suitable condition will be received into the armed service of the United States;" and concludes thus: "And upon this, sincerely believed to be an act of justice, warranted by the Constitution, upon military necessity, I invoke the considerate judgment of mankind and the gracious favor of Almighty God."

Upon the principles laid down in justification of the Government for attempting the overthrow of slavery as a means for suppressing rebellion, its wonderful forbearance is illustrated in this, that what it finally did on the 1st of January, 1863, after eighteen and a half months of war, it might have done on the 15th of April, 1861, when the President issued his first Proclamation for troops for the same purpose.

ITS FINAL DETERMINATION JUSTIFIED.

We have now to see whether competent authorities sustain the position we have taken. The issue made is reduced to this: to destroy slavery in the Rebel States, in order to overthrow rebellion and restore and maintain the national authority. Is the destruction of slavery a lawful means to that lawful end? Dr. Smyth will not pretend that on this point we have any express revelation in "the word of God." For him, therefore, to assert, that "to wage a war of extermination against slavery," is "*in itself* wicked," and is "rebellion against God," is to assume the whole case.

The present object,—to maintain the complete authority and jurisdiction of the Government,—is, by "the word of God," a lawful object; and war, as a means to that end, is, by "the word of God," lawful. But upon the special measures of war for such a purpose, "the word of God" is silent. There is, then, no other course to be taken,—no other safe criterion of judgment,—but to fall back upon the laws of war, as seen in the usages of civilized and Christian nations; those principles and usages which they regard as founded in the soundest reason and justice. Here the authorities to sustain the United States Government in its present course toward slavery in the Rebel States are overwhelming.

These authorities may be reduced to the following points: General principles of the laws of war, as laid down by writers on the laws of nations; the usages of the most enlightened nations under these laws; decisions of national authorities on cases submitted; the practice of military commanders, sustained by their respective Governments; the course of the United States Government in former wars; the opinions of eminent statesmen, and among them statesmen of our own country, uttered in former times, concerning the possible occurrence of just such an emergency as that in which the United States Government now finds itself placed.

The amount of this testimony bears upon two points, all that are essential to the present case: that a nation at war may *emancipate the slaves* of another nation with which it is at war, as a means to its military success; and that it may *use those thus emancipated in its military service.*

SUSTAINED BY THE LAWS OF WAR.

In regard to the Laws of War, the general principles to which we refer are sufficiently comprehended in the following points: Standard writers declare, that "war, when duly declared or officially recognized, gives to one belligerent the right to deprive the other of *every thing which might add to his strength, and enable him to carry on hostilities.*" This "general right" is limited by the "law of nations;" and the limitations, with many things embraced within them, are specified by all standard writers; but among these, *slaves are not mentioned.* They come under that general designation of "property" which a belligerent may take and use against the enemy. The laws and usages of nations, ancient and modern, deem them liable to capture.*

So well settled was this principle under the Roman law,—and the same principle obtains among other nations where slaves are recognized as mere "property,"—that the "captor holds by a title which will become complete by the return of peace, without any treaty stipulation prescribing the contrary; but until that time the title is liable to be lost by *recapture*, and the application of what is known in law as the *jus postliminii*." This latter feature of the Roman law was to this effect: Under it certain persons and certain things, captured in war, were restored to their former condition, "on coming again under the power of the nation to which they formerly belonged;" as, for example, the son came again under the power

* Upon the general principles of the Laws of War referred to, are the following authorities, from which it will be seen, that this important principle in addition to those mentioned is laid down, that *all persons* belonging to "hostile States," are made "legal enemies" by war,—thus, in its application to the case in hand, giving the Government authority over all the slaves in the Rebel States: "It has already been stated, that war, when duly declared or officially recognized, makes legal enemies of all individual members of hostile States; that it also extends to property, and gives to one belligerent the right to deprive the other of *every thing which might add to his strength, and enable him to carry* on hostilities. But this general right is subject to numerous modifications and limitations, which have been introduced by custom and the positive law of nations. Thus, although, by the extreme right of war, all property of an enemy is deemed hostile and subject to seizure, it by no means follows that all such property is subject to appropriation or condemnation; for the positive law of nations distinguishes, not only between the property of the State and that of its individual subjects, but also between that of different classes of subjects, and between different kinds of property of the same subject." "All implements of war, military and naval stores, and, in general, all movable property belonging to the hostile State, is subject to be seized, and appropriated to the use of the captor." "There is *one* species of movable property, belonging to a belligerent State, which is *exempt*, not only from plunder and destruction, but also from capture and conversion, viz., State papers, public archives, historical records, judicial and legal documents, land titles," &c. "The reasons of this rule are manifest: *their destruction would not operate to promote, in any respect, the war.*" "It would be an injury done in war, *beyond the necessity of war*, and therefore illegal, barbarous, and cruel."—*Halleck's Int. Law, and Law of War*, Ch. XIX. secs. 1, 7, 9.

of his parent, and the recaptured slave came into possession of his former master, instead of becoming the property of the State.

The principle is thus well and universally established, that *slaves*, coming into possession of a belligerent or captured from an enemy in war, are subject to the captor's disposal, unless recaptured. This is settled by the laws of war, as understood alike among ancient and modern nations. They differ on one point. In ancient times, the captor might sell them, or make any other disposition of them, as with other captured "property;" or he might free them. In either case, whether regarded as property or as freedmen, he could employ them against the enemy in any capacity, just as any other property or freemen under his control might be thus employed. But the laws of war as seen in the usages among nations of modern times, with rare exceptions, restrict the disposition of slaves captured in war to giving them their freedom; that is, do not allow their re-enslavement.

SUSTAINED BY EXAMPLES OF SEVERAL NATIONS.

The right by the laws of nations, and the actual practice under the laws of war, *to emancipate the slaves* of an enemy, is unquestionable, and is illustrated by many examples; and the cases very fully sustain the position that *no other proper* disposition can be made of captured slaves than to give them their freedom.

This right, as a war measure, has been often exercised in modern times: as, for example, by Great Britain, in the war of the Revolution with her American Colonies, and in that with the United States in 1812;* by France, in the

* The Proclamations of Lord Dunmore, Lord Cornwallis, and Sir Henry Clinton, are well known. In the war of the Revolution, they received thousands of slaves into the British army, giving them their freedom. By the Treaty of Peace in 1783,

Island of St. Domingo, in 1793–94; by Spain in Columbia, South America, through Generals Murillo and Bolivar; and by the United States, in some of its wars, through Generals Jesup, Taylor, and Gaines, whose acts were sustained and approved by Congress, and by several Presidents.

ILLUSTRATED BY CASES IN THE UNITED STATES.

In regard to the United States, the practice of the Government in former wars has been to consider slaves captured in war as *prisoners of war*, and to *declare and insure their freedom.*

In 1836, General Jesup employed certain "fugitive slaves" as guides, and for their services gave them their freedom and sent them to the West to enjoy it. His conduct was approved by the administrations of Presidents Van Buren and John Tyler. The case of Louis, which occurred in the same year, is in point. He was the escaped slave of Pacheco, and had fought against the United States. On his being captured, and while held as a prisoner of war, his master demanded him as his property: but the demand was refused, and Louis was declared

the British Government promised to take no slaves out of the country, but a great many went with them. On the complaint of General Washington for such violation of the Treaty, and a demand for their return, Sir Guy Carleton admitted that his Government was bound to make compensation, but insisted on the absolute freedom of those taken away, declaring that "His Majesty" did not allow his officers to take from "these negroes *the liberty of which he found them possessed.*" Certain adjudicated cases by the British authorities go even beyond this. Certain slaves on board the American brig *Creole*, destined from Hampton Roads to New Orleans mutinied, killed a slave-owner, and compelled the crew to take the vessel into Nassau, a British port. The authorities examined the case, found nineteen concerned in the murder, but gave the rest their liberty. The British Government, "on grounds of comity," made compensation for the released slaves, *but refused to return them.* A decision of Chief-Justice Best, of England, upon the rights of negroes, in the case of Admiral Cockburn, upon whose vessel escaped slaves had taken refuge, is important. He declared: "He was not bound to receive them upon his ship in the first instance, but having done so, he could no more have forced them *back into slavery* than he could have committed them to the deep."—*Cited in Phillimore's International Law.*

16

free. The course of General Jesup was sustained and approved by the President and his Cabinet; and at a subsequent period, when Pacheco laid his claim for compensation for the loss of Louis before Congress, that body sustained the Administration by rejecting a bill for such purpose.

In the year 1838, General Zachary Taylor captured certain persons, during the war in Florida, who were claimed as fugitive slaves. Certain citizens of that State demanded their release and restoration. Old "Rough and Ready" told them that he had none but prisoners of war. They wished to see them, to ascertain if he had their slaves in his possession. He would not grant their request, and bid them depart. On this being reported to the War Department, his course was approved by the President; and the slaves were declared free and sent to the West.

Another case occurred in 1838, in the Southwestern Department of the Army, which is very broad in its relations to the present war, and the *status* of the slave in regard to the laws of war. A large number of fugitive slaves and Indians, who had been captured in war in Florida, had been ordered West of the Mississippi. Some of the former were claimed at New Orleans by their owners, and the case was brought into Court. General Edmund P. Gaines was then in command of that Department. He refused to give up the fugitives on the demand of the sheriff, and made his defence in court in person. His reasons for refusal were as follows:

That these men, women, and children, were captured in war; that, as Commander of that Military Department, he held them subject only to the order of the National Executive; that he could recognize no other power in time of war, as authorized to take prisoners from his possession. He asserted that in time of war, *all slaves were belligerents as well as their masters.* The slave-men cultivate the earth and supply provisions. The women cook the food and nurse the sick, and contribute to the maintenance of the war *often more than the same number of males.* The slave children equally contribute whatever they are able to the support of the war. The military officer can enter into no judicial examination of the claim of one man to the bone and muscle of another, as property; nor could he, as a military officer, know what the laws of Florida were while engaged in maintaining the Federal Government by force of arms. In such a case, he could only be guided by the laws of war; and whatever may be the laws of any State, they must yield to the safety of the Federal Government.—*House Doc. No.* 225, 25*th Congress.*

The result in the foregoing case was, that it was dismissed, the slaves were sent to the West, and became free.

ANOTHER CASE.—EMPEROR ALEXANDER.

A case of great importance was decided, growing out of the war of 1812, in which the United States and Great Britain were parties; one point of which was referred for adjudication to the Emperor Alexander of Russia. The British, acting according to the laws of war, had captured a large number of slaves. The Treaty of Ghent, which fixed the terms of peace, required that compensation for *some* of those then in their possession should be made; but it was for *those only* that were, at the time of the ratification of the Treaty, within the districts *to be delivered up* to the United States. The Government, under President Madison, did not claim that those who had been *set free*, and sent during the war beyond the limits of the United States, *should even be paid for;* much less that they should be delivered up to their masters, to be again remitted to slavery. Here was a clear acknowledgment on the part of the United States, that, by the laws of war, *slaves captured in war are free, thenceforward and forever;* and that they are not even to be paid for, except upon special stipulation between the parties at war. The point which was submitted to the Russian Emperor grew out of the construction of the Treaty. The British Government contended that the Treaty did not include, for compensation, slaves who were still on British vessels which were lying, at the time of the ratification, in American waters. The Emperor decided against the British interpretation, and gives the grounds of his decision thus: "It is upon the construction of *the text* of the article as it stands, that the arbitrator's decision should be founded." The British Government objecting, the Emperor adds: "The Emperor having, by mutual consent of the two plenipotentiaries, given an opinion founded solely upon the sense which results from *the text* of the article in dispute, does not think himself called upon to decide any question relative to what *the laws of war* permit or forbid to belligerents." This setting of "the text of the article" construed over against "the laws of war," in this manner, leads to the conclusion that the Emperor, at that time "the largest slave-holder in the world," deemed that these laws allowed the emancipation of slaves captured in war, and that when so emancipated they could not be recovered.

These numerous cases show conclusively that the United States Government has maintained the doctrine, in its military and civil administration, that, by the laws of war, slaves captured in war are, *ipso facto*, thenceforward and forever FREE.*

OPINIONS OF EMINENT STATESMEN.

The general doctrine maintained in these examples by the United States, accords with the sentiments of her most eminent statesmen. Thomas Jefferson, when complaining

* To this there is an exception; but, as an exception, it serves to confirm the rule otherwise so fully established and illustrated by actual cases. Our Government maintained the opposite doctrine against Great Britain in 1820, when John Quincy Adams was Secretary of State; but that great statesman has left it on record, that while he faithfully represented his Government on that point, he totally dissented from the doctrine itself. He says: "It was utterly against my judgment and wishes: but I was obliged to submit, and prepared the requisite dispatches."

of the acts of Lord Cornwallis, in the Revolutionary war, admits the principle that slaves may be taken from an enemy in war, and that when taken may be freed. In a letter to Dr. Gordon, found in his works, he says:

> From an estimate I made at that time (1779), on the best information I could collect, I suppose the State of Virginia lost, under Lord Cornwallis's hand, that year, about thirty thousand slaves. * * * He used, as was to be expected, all my stock of cattle, sheep, and hogs, for the sustenance of his army, and carried off all the horses capable of service. * * * He carried off also about thirty slaves. *Had this been to give them freedom, he would have done right;* but it was to consign them to inevitable death from the small-pox and putrid fever then raging in his camp.

In a debate in the House of Representatives in 1836, John Quincy Adams announced what it would be competent for the Government to do with slavery, under precisely the circumstances that now exist. As a statesman, his views, uttered in the following sentence, command respect:

> From the instant that your slaveholding States become the theatre of war, civil, servile, or foreign, from that instant the war powers of Congress extend to interference with the institution of slavery in every way in which it can be interfered with, from a claim of indemnity for slaves taken or destroyed, to the cession of the State burdened with slavery to a foreign power.

Again, in the House of Representatives, in 1842, after stating that slavery was abolished in Colombia, South America, first by the Spanish Military Commander, General Murillo, and then by the American General Bolivar, simply by *a military order given at the head of the army*, and that its abolition *continued to this day*, Mr. Adams says:

> In a state of actual war, the laws of war take precedence over civil laws and municipal institutions. I lay this down as the law of nations. I say that the military authority takes for the time the place of all

municipal institutions, *slavery among the rest;* and that, under that state of things, so far from its being true, that the States where slavery exists have the exclusive management of the subject, *not only the President of the United States, but the commander of the army, has the power to order the emancipation of the slaves.* * * * When your country is actually in war, whether it be a war of invasion or a war of insurrection, Congress has power to carry on the war, and must carry it on according to the laws of war; and, by the laws of war, an invaded country has all its laws and municipal institutions swept by the board, and martial law takes the place of them.

If we choose to go back to the times of our Revolutionary war, we find legislation in abundance by the States, both South, North, and by Congress, for recruiting the army of Washington from among slaves; and this legislation provided that those slaves should receive the *boon of freedom* for their services;* and this course was sustained by the most eminent patriots of that era.

* Among other instances of legislation, "In Congress, March 29, 1779," it was "*Resolved*, That it be recommended to the States of South Carolina and Georgia, if they shall think the same expedient, to take measures immediately for raising three thousand able-bodied negroes; that the said negroes be formed into separate corps, as battalions, according to the arrangements adopted for the main army;" and "that every negro who shall well and faithfully serve as a soldier to the end of the present war, and shall then return his arms, *be emancipated*, and receive the sum of fifty dollars." Many of the States acted without any recommendation from Congress. The General Assembly of Rhode Island adopted the following: "*Whereas*, History affords us frequent precedents of the wisest, the freest, and bravest nations having liberated their slaves, and enlisted them as soldiers to fight in defence of their country. * * * *Resolved*, That every slave so enlisting, shall, upon his passing muster, &c., be immediately discharged from the service of his master or mistress, and be *absolutely free*, as though he had never been encumbered with any kind of servitude or slavery." In Virginia, certain slaveholders sent their slaves to the army, with a "promise" of *freedom*, but after the war attempted to re-enslave them; showing some *bad faith* in Old as in Modern Virginia. But perhaps this *bad blood* did not then run in the veins of the "first families," as it has since done, for the General Assembly of that State, by solemn enactment, rebuked such perfidy, in 1783, in "An Act directing the *Emancipation of certain slaves who had served as soldiers in this State*, and for the Emancipation of the slave Aberdeen." The depth of this perfidy is seen in two or three facts stated in this Act: that "*many persons* in this State had caused their slaves to enlist," they "having tendered such slaves" to the recruiting officers as "*substitutes*" for their own dear selves, "at the same time representing to such recruiting officers, that the slaves, so enlisted, were

Alexander Hamilton, in a letter to John Jay, in 1779, speaking of these measures, says: "An essential part of the plan is to *give them their freedom* with their muskets." This, he said, would "have a good influence on *those who remain*, by opening a door to *their emancipation*."

James Madison, in a letter to Joseph Jones, in 1780, advocating the policy of arming and freeing the slaves, says:

I am glad to find the Legislature (of Virginia) persist in their resolution to recruit their line of the army for the war; though without deciding on the expediency of the mode under their consideration, *would it not be as well to liberate and make soldiers at once of the blacks themselves*, as to make them instruments for enlisting white soldiers? It would certainly be more consonant with the principles of liberty, which ought never to be lost sight of in a contest for liberty.

Thus, the most eminent statesmen of the early days of the Republic took the ground that slaves might properly be employed in the armies of the Union, and that all such should be voluntarily emancipated.

freemen," and that "the former owners have attempted again to force them to return to a state of servitude, *contrary to the principles of justice, and to their own solemn promise*," thus backing up this bad faith with very bad falsehoods. As "many persons" were here concerned, it would be strange if some of the "first families" were not involved. But the Legislature enacted that all such persons "shall, from and after the passing of this act, *be fully and completely emancipated*, and shall be held and deemed free, in as full and ample a manner as if each and every of them were specially named in this act; and the Attorney-General for the Commonwealth is hereby required to commence an action, *in formâ pauperis*, in behalf of any of the persons above described, who shall, after the passing of this act, be detained in servitude by any person whatsoever;" and the act directs that "a jury shall be impannelled to assess the damages for the detention" of persons so declared free. In Massachusetts, many negroes were enrolled in the army, though slavery had been abolished in 1776. The Judiciary of that State held that the Declaration of Independence was an edict of emancipation. In New York, the Legislature in 1781 provided for the enlistment of slaves, and enacted that any one "who shall serve for the term of three years, or until regularly discharged, shall, immediately after such service or discharge, be, and is hereby declared to be, a free man of this State." Other States passed similar acts.

VINDICATION COMPLETE AGAINST IDLE DECLAMATION.

In view of the testimony now given, from all the foregoing sources, can any thing be more idle, absurd, and fanatical, than the outcry, that the determination of the Government to overthrow slavery in the Rebel States, in order to save itself from destruction, is "in itself wicked and unconstitutional," and a "conspiracy against the throne and empire of Heaven?"

If it be said that the acts of the Executive, in giving freedom to the slaves *by proclamation*, do not come within the strict line of the authorities given, it is only necessary to say, that we presume no one supposed that the President intended to effect their liberty by that measure alone. It was a simple notification to rebel masters of the war policy of the Government; an opportunity extended to return to loyalty and save slavery, if they chose; and a warning of the consequences for continued rebellion. Slavery, if overthrown in the Rebel States by the Government, will be subverted by *actual war*, under the *laws of war*. On that simple point, it is most conclusively sustained.

SUSTAINED AGAINST THE REBEL CONGRESS.

After consulting the authorities given, and among them the numerous cases where our own Government has vindicated the right of slaves to freedom, when taken in war, it is somewhat edifying to read what the Rebel Congress say on this point, in an "Address to the People of the Confederate States," issued in February, 1864. Among other things, they say: "Emancipation of slaves, as a wise measure, has been severely condemned and denounced by the most eminent publicists in Europe and the United States." They here refer to the President's Proclamation. Whether this may be a "wise measure," men may differ.

The rebels declaim against it, because of its inhumanity; but this Address calls it "a mere *brutum fulmen*," a harmless threat. If they mean to say that all these "publicists" deem "emancipation of slaves" in war, an *illegal* "measure," the authorities we have cited show how much such assertions are worth. In view of these authorities, the following from this Address will be appreciated at its true value: "Disregarding the teachings of the approved writers on international law, and *the practice and claims of his own Government*, in its purer days, President Lincoln has sought to convert the South into a Saint Domingo, by appealing to the cupidity, lusts, ambition, and ferocity of the slave." And all this is to occur from "a mere *brutum fulmen!*"

In this Address, the Rebel Congress endeavor to press into the service the instance we have previously referred to, as an exception,—where our Government say that "the emancipation of enemy's slaves is not among the acts of legitimate warfare,"—and make this exception *the rule* in the case, when, notoriously, it stands against the whole course of the Government, as seen in its whole history. Mr. Adams admits that he "prepared the dispatches" which announced this doctrine, but that it was "against his judgment and wishes." The real wonder is, that, with the General Government, as Mr. A. H. Stephens says, for sixty-four years out of seventy-two, under Southern control, there should not have been found more such doctrine taught and practised upon. But as "one swallow does not make a summer," so one such case does not make a rule of law, nor even a precedent. The whole current of the testimony of the United States is the other way, *in actual cases determined;* and that of other nations is the same; and the whole combined is to this effect: that, by the laws of war, as recognized by the practice of the most

16*

renowned nations of the present day, it is perfectly legitimate for a nation at war to emancipate an enemy's slaves and use them against him; and that the proper *status* of such slaves, so emancipated, is *perpetual freedom.*

SUSTAINED BY SOUTHERN MEN.

To save the Government, this doom of slavery,—not only in the rebel but in the loyal States,—is called for by *Southern* men, when the issue is fairly made between the destruction of the Government and the destruction of slavery; and that man has no claim to loyalty, who can hesitate when such an issue is joined. Observe a few declarations to this effect among a thousand, equally pointed and satisfactory.

Governor Bramlette, of Kentucky, in his "Galt House Letter," dated "Frankfort, 7th November, 1863," says:

> Is it not better, should such issue be forced, that we preserve our nationality, *even with loss of slavery,* than lose both our nationality and slave property? It is certain that we, at least, in Kentucky, can never hold slave property, when this Government is broken up.

Hon. Green Clay Smith, of Kentucky, in a speech in the House of Representatives, at Washington, in January last, said:

> Having witnessed for the last two years or more the operations of the armies of the country, and, to some extent, the effect of ordnance and small arms upon the enemy, I feel it to be my duty upon this occasion to say, that while there is power in these, and while the Government must, through these, execute its laws and vindicate its integrity, *there remains behind this rebellion that which gives it strength and power which must be overthrown and destroyed* on the other side, while our armies and our ordnance move in front. * * * Their forces in arms against the Government are maintained and fed by, and their very life-blood is drawn from, *African slavery in the South.* * * * Whenever you sap the foundation of this accursed rebellion, and tear from under

the rebels that which has given them strength and power, you destroy the rebellion, and your artillery is effectual. * * * When a man has evinced a hatred to this Government, when he has voluntarily taken up arms against this Government, and when he has brought his artillery to play upon its Constitution and its principles and its liberties, he can demand of me, as a legislator for the people of this country, no privileges in horses, cattle, land, or negroes. We will take them, when we come to them, by any means we can, and by all means. The bulwark which prevented the American people, by its army, from moving down to the South and exercising jurisdiction there,—that bulwark supported by four million slaves,—*must be removed;* and the evidence that we have a right to remove it is, *that we have a right to crush the rebellion. It is the duty of the Government to do it.* The Government would have failed in its duty to itself, and to all future generations, if it did not, in its power and majesty, *sweep away that bulwark of slavery.* I thought it my duty, under the circumstances in which I am placed, coming from the country I come from, *representing the loyal people who feel as I do, and whose opinions have been expressed time and again to me,* as mine to them, to make this statement.

Mr. Lowry, a member of the Kentucky Legislature, during the last session, said, in a speech before that body:

If the protest against them meant on account of slavery, all I have to say is, that no man felt more sorry than I, when the first gun was fired on Sumter. *That was the death-knell of slavery on this continent,* and I am not going at this late day to bring about any antagonism with the Government on account of it. I want to see the *Union man who will do so.* I want to see the Union man who wants to hurl Kentucky into the whirlpool of rebellion on account of the thing. I am not willing to do a single thing to place Kentucky in the same situation as Tennessee and other Southern States, for the sake of saving slavery, and I do not believe that there is a *patriotic* man in Kentucky that would.

Hon. E. W. Gantt, of Arkansas, in a speech in Brooklyn, New York, said:

He defied any man to show him any cause for this war other than negro slavery. Negro slavery had deluged the land in blood and draped it in mourning, and now, when the Government in its might thrust the institution from it, politicians would stick it back into the heart of the Government, that new desolations might spring from it, but they could not do it. *The people of the South, the Union men there, were determined, by the help of God, to purge the body politic of negro slavery, and let the Government stand.*

Governor Hamilton, in his Address to the people of Texas, says:

If, then, you believe, as I do, that the institution of slavery has merited and invited its own destruction, and that its doom, pronounced by the sovereign power of the nation, is an act of justice,—more than human justice, attesting the presence of that Omnipotent Hand,—then speak and act as men who deserve freedom for themselves and their posterity. The day is near at hand when the name of Abolitionist will cease to be a reproach, even in the South, and when children, now daily the subjeets of attempted insult on account of its application to their fathers, will thank God that they were so reviled.

The position of Dr. Robert J. Breciknridge, of Kentucky, on the issues before the country, is well known. In an elaborate paper published in the *Danville Quarterly Review* for December, 1862, in which he dissents from the President's Emancipation policy, as foreshadowed in his Proclamation of the previous September, he thus speaks incidentally upon the simple issue between slavery and the Government:

We admit,—nay, we assert,—that it is inconsistent with the honor and dignity of the nation, that slaves once accepted and used in its military service, or given the protection of its flag, should afterwards be returned to slavery. * * * We believe that this civil war will probably, in a legitimate prosecution of it, greatly weaken the political power of the slave States, relatively considered; that it will demoralize the institution of slavery to a fearful extent; and that results from it may be reached concerning slavery, in opposite directions, far beyond our ability to foresee. And, finally, we do not believe that the existence of slavery is so serious an obstacle to our triumph, as to justify any apprehension, or any resort to unusual or illegal acts; *while, on the other hand, its total* *destruction, in the due, vigorous, and legal prosecution of the war, ought not to hinder us from putting the doctrine and practice of secession forever at rest.*

In the Kentucky State, Convention, at Louisville, May 25, 1864, Dr. Breckinridge is reported as saying:

I received, the other day, a letter from my old friend, Reverdy Johnson, of Baltimore, who has made a speech [in the United States Senate] in favor of amending the Constitution. He asked me to write what I thought about it, and I will give you the substance of my reply: "Taking the posture of the negro question as it is, and the nation as it is, my conclusion is, that the Government of the United States is absolutely bound, by every consideration of statesmanship and of safety, to do one of two things: It is bound to use its whole power, both of war and of peace, to put back the negro, as far as possible, into the condition he occupied before the war; *or it is bound to exterminate the whole institution, by all the powers the Constitution gives it, or that can be obtained by an amendment of that instrument.* If I were a pro-slavery man, I would say: Put back the negro to his former position. *But, as I am an antislavery man, I say,* USE THE WHOLE POWER OF THE GOVERNMENT TO EXTINGUISH THE INSTITUTION OF SLAVERY, ROOT AND BRANCH.

Dr. Breckinridge again expressed similar sentiments, on taking his seat as President of the National Union Convention, which assembled in Baltimore on the 7th June, 1864. He is reported as then saying as follows:

I do not know that I would be willing to go so far as probably the excellent chairman of the National Committee would. But I cordially agree with him in this: I think, considering what has been done about slavery, taking the thing as it now stands, overlooking altogether, either in the way of condemnation or in the way of approval, any act that has brought us to the point where we are, but believing in my conscience and with all my heart, that what has brought us where we are in the matter of slavery, is the original sin and folly of treason and secession, —because you remember that the Chicago Convention itself was understood to say, and I believe it virtually did explicitly say, that they would not touch slavery in the States;—leaving it therefore altogether out of the question how we came where we are, on that particular point, we are prepared to go farther than the original Republicans were prepared to go. We are prepared to demand not only that the whole territory of the United States shall not be made slave, but that the General Government of the American people shall do one of two things,—and it appears to me that there is nothing else that can be done,—either to use the whole power of the Government, both the war power and the peace power, to put slavery as nearly as possible back where it was,—for, although that would be a fearful state of society, it is better than anarchy; or else, *to use the whole power of the Government, both of war and peace, and all the practical power that the people of the United States will give them,* TO EXTERMINATE AND EXTINGUISH SLAVERY. I have no hesitation in saying for myself, that if I were a proslavery man, if I believed this institution was an ordinance of God, and was given to man, I would unhesitatingly join those who demand that the Government should be put back where it was. But I am not a proslavery man—I never was; I unite myself with those who believe that it is contrary to the highest interests of all men and of all Government, contrary to the spirit of the Christian religion, and incompatible with the natural rights of man; I join myself with those who say, *Away with it forever:* and I fervently pray God that the day may come, when, throughout the whole land, every man may be as free as you are, and as capable of enjoying regulated liberty.

Such are the sentiments of leading men in the Border and more Southern Slave States. They believe the time fully come when that institution which underlies the strife now raging throughout this nation, should cease in the land forever. This, we doubt not, will be found to be a sentiment which will extend, as the war goes on, to the entire people, so far as they are *truly loyal to their country.*

THE SUM OF PROVIDENTIAL INDICATIONS.

We have now given a bare summary of the reasons which lead us to the conclusion, that it is the design of God, in His providence, to make use of the rebellion to terminate forever the institution of slavery in the United States, and thus cause the wrath of man to praise Him.

We have already said that considerable time may elapse before the end is reached; that it may be, not till some subsequent Congress shall take that necessary step for an amendment of the Constitution, which, when ratified by the people, will give the finishing stroke to the work; and that then it may require, for a time, a military force to make even that measure practically effective. But that that end will be reached before we can have permanent peace, we believe to be as certain as that God reigns.

It is said that revolutions never go backwards. The truth of the aphorism depends on its application. The South apply it to the treasonable work in which they are engaged, and faith in the sentiment nerves their courage. It is, however, our own conviction, that that revolution will be rolled back and entirely fail. But another revolution is in progress among the loyal people. The change in their sentiments regarding slavery, in some of the developments made since the rebellion began, is remarkable. The advance which has been made by the Government respecting the institution, beginning with what it was at first supposed the Government might and might not do with it, of *right*, in putting down the rebellion; proceeding to what seemed to be a necessity, and carrying out its intentions by Congressional and Executive acts, and by military orders and power; the sentiments of the people, at first of such a character as probably would have produced a revolution at the North, if certain steps had been taken earlier; their present approval or acquiescence; the extensive belief that the destruction of slavery is now a necessity of our national existence, on a basis of permanent peace; the remarkable change in the Border States, not only among leading individuals, but among the people, as evinced in the voluntary action of these States, looking to the speedy removal of Slavery; the legislation of Congress, bearing upon its termination, to the whole extent to which it has direct civil jurisdiction; these,—every one of which has grown out of the rebellion,—are among the well-known indications of a revolution in the ideas of the Government and people. Considering the mere lapse of time, the extent of this change is remarkable; though, under the causes which have impelled it, the change is natural. *This* is one of those revolutions which we believe will not go backwards. It is one of those mighty movings in the hearts of a great people, in the right direction, which will have no rest until its glorious and ultimate goal shall be reached.

How can any believer in God's providence, which extends to *all* things,—in whose hand are the hearts of all people, —fail to see in these events the inevitable designs of God? How can he fail to read in them the doom of slavery?

We had intended to consider other designs of God's providence in the rebellion, but the extent of this chapter compels us to desist. If slavery is purged from the land, the only serious element of our national strife is removed. We can then become a homogeneous and truly *united* people. It may take time to remove the alienation and bitterness which the war has engendered, but the great *cause* being extinct, we may at length become ONE in a sense otherwise impossible of attainment. Then, by the favor of God, we may have before us a career of *true* prosperity; then, our land may indeed be the asylum for the oppressed of all lands; then, as a people, we may be prepared to fulfil our mission to the world! May God speed the day—and to Him be the glory!

CHAPTER X.

THE CHURCH AND SLAVERY.

THE relation of the Church of God in the United States to American slavery as an institution, and the sentiments of ecclesiastical bodies and leading divines upon its character, as entertained formerly and at the present time in different sections of the country, and the bearing of the whole upon the rebellion, are matters of vast moment. Some of these things have a connection as cause and effect, either directly and immediately or more or less remotely, which it may be interesting and instructive to trace.

The subject naturally presents itself under three aspects: the sentiments which generally prevailed in the early period and during the greater portion of our history, both North and South; their subsequent modification at the North, and total revolution in almost the whole of the extreme South; and the general state of the public mind at present in both sections, consequent upon the rebellion. We do not propose in this chapter to go over the ground presented in each of these periods, but it is well to note the fact in this place which a full examination would verify, that a survey of the whole field properly presents the subject under this three-fold aspect.

THREE PERIODS OF OPINION HISTORICALLY.

The first of these periods, though not separated from the second so palpably that its termination can be fixed at a precise point of time, begins at a very early day or near the dawn of our history as a people, and comes down to about the year 1835, during which the antislavery sentiment was generally prevalent. That the common opinion of the whole country in the early days of the Republic, both before and after the Revolution, and down to a comparatively recent day, was against the institution on grounds of policy and principle, is undeniable. Statesmen, divines, ecclesiastical bodies, the people at large, both North and South, with rare exceptions, regarded slavery as founded in wrong, condemned it as an institution, and desired and expected, and to some extent labored for, its removal. These are propositions so clear and certain, and so well known to all men, that it is superfluous to attempt to add any thing to make the case plainer.

It is equally true and well known, illustrating a second period of opinion, that a change occurred in the South, beginning indeed before, but becoming more marked at about the time indicated, and finally developing into the sentiment of sanctioning slavery in the highest and fullest sense, and on every ground, social, economical, political, moral and religious; and that, during this same period, while a small fraction of the Northern people, the "abolitionists proper," as they have been termed, took extreme, and, to the South, offensive ground and action, and while another portion maintained the original antislavery sentiments which prevailed from the first, still another and a very large portion of the Northern people, embracing many who were still not friendly to slavery, practically abandoned the early prevalent sentiments, became intensely "conservative," and took such a course of action, illustrated by the writings and speeches of men both in Church and State, as gave the modern Southern views a direct and intended, or a *quasi*-practical sanction and encouragement. These phases of sentiment, and their consequences, are susceptible of the clearest proof.

The third period dates from the beginning of the rebellion. In the South we see no special change among the rebels concerning slavery, except a reiteration of their former arguments in its favor more vehemently, and their determination, if possible, to make good by the sword what they have failed to do by rhetoric. But among loyal men at the South, as our arms advance, the most marked changes in sentiment appear. They denounce slavery as the cause of all their woes, and some of them outstrip Abolition itself in heaping upon it their anathemas as a wicked and monstrous institution, now that they see what use has been made of it by demagogues. This is a little remarkable for serious men, as in principle it has always been just what it now is. But men's views of moral questions are often affected by matters which really have nothing to do with their moral status and relations, or which concern them only incidentally. And this ethical feature of the case is illustrated quite as strikingly at the North. The views of the institution which many now entertain arise mainly or wholly from what the rebellion has developed, while its character as a system is unchanged. There have been substantially but two classes among the Northern people since the rebellion began. Those who in heart were antislavery, but in action conservative, are now united with all those who have opposed the system in any form, in two things: agreeing that slavery has caused the rebellion and the war; and that its just doom is to perish. They regard it an evil in a sense, and put themselves in opposition to it in a form, to which they have been brought, not by the character of the institution itself, but by what it has attempted; and looking at it now from a new stand-point, some of this class are frank to confess their former position wrong. The other phase of sentiment in the loyal States is substantially one with that of the rebels. It is seen in Church and State. There is a class of men in the Church in the loyal States who take the same ground for slavery as do the rebels, defending it as divine, and desiring it to be perpetual. They of course, like a certain class of politicians, are arrayed against the Government. They are opposed to putting down the rebellion by force of arms, or in any other way. They are in sympathy with the rebels concerning the institution which caused the war, and they are therefore against the war and for the perpetuity of slavery. These phases of present Northern sentiment,—or rather, sentiment in all the loyal States,—illustrate and confirm the declaration of the Hon. Green Clay Smith, of Kentucky, in the resolutions offered by him and passed by the present House of Representatives, that "there are now but two classes in the country—patriots and traitors."

We have already said that we cannot go over the ground covered by these three periods, so as to exhibit *in full* the evidence of these several phases of opinion upon slavery. We shall, in this chapter, confine our examination to the first two periods, and of these we can take but a cursory view, reserving to a subsequent chapter, entirely, a notice of modern Southern opinion. Our design will lead to a summary sketch of the state of opinion from early times to the present day, simply to show, in the result, how it illustrates the working out of the rebellion. We shall look chiefly at the state of sentiment in the Church, though it will be found that this corresponds with that entertained by the people generally.

THE CHURCH LARGELY RESPONSIBLE FOR OPINION.

It is undoubtedly true that the more intelligent classes in society—statesmen and others of the highest abilities, who are not connected formally with the Church, as well as the mass of her members,—have their opinions formed or modified, in a good degree, upon the moral and religious aspects of this and many other questions, by the views which the Church takes; by the formal action of its ecclesiastical assemblies; by the writings of its distinguished ministers, and by the discussions of the pulpit. This, to a great extent, is no doubt true of the general opposition felt toward slavery in the early period of our history; to that opposition as moderated or intensified at a later period; and to the total change in sentiment upon the character of slavery which occurred among the people of the extreme South. It will thus be seen, in so far as this agency in forming men's opinions is justly attributable to the Church, as illustrated in the views which the American people have entertained concerning slavery, that the responsibility of the Church in this regard is overwhelmingly great; and if it shall appear that the Church led the way, statesmen but following in her wake, in the change of Southern opinion upon the character of slavery (proof of which will be given in another chapter), and which culminated in the rebellion, it will furnish an additional item of the most momentous importance in fixing upon those who thus took the initiative, the tremendous burden of that tide of blood which is now rolling over the land.

We record the facts which bear upon such a result with no satisfaction; rather with mortification and sorrow. But if they are a part of the veritable history of these "perilous times," if they illustrate a most important phase in a great moral movement of the age, directed by the providence of God, though it be in violence and carnage, through the agency of his own Church, it may prove a valuable lesson to her and to all men, and stand as a beacon to warn and to guide in days yet to come.

PRESBYTERIAN CHURCH ILLUSTRATIVE OF OTHERS.

To avoid prolixity, we shall not collate the sentiments upon slavery of the several branches of the Church. The views published from time to time by the Presbyterian Church will probably show the opinions substantially of the Churches of all denominations in the country,—at least for the first period, and to a great extent for the second,—as explicitly as any other testimony. It was formerly among the largest in the United States, and extended into all parts of the country. It was divided into nearly equal portions in 1838, not upon any geographical line, nor upon the subject of slavery. Both branches, commonly known, after the separation, as Old and New School, were still spread over the whole country, and had each its General Assembly, in which the entire body of each respectively was represented.

In 1857, a schism occurred in the New School Church, purely upon slavery, by a large portion of the delegates from the South voluntarily withdrawing, and the Churches they represented subsequently forming a separate organization. The New School Church, however, continued to embrace Churches in the Border slave States, and its jurisdiction still extends there.

The Old School Church maintained its jurisdiction intact down to the time of the rebellion. Its highest judicatory, assembling annually, might then have been composed of commissioners from every State in the Union except Vermont and Rhode Island. When the rebellion occurred, the Churches, Presbyteries, and Synods, in the seceded States, cut loose from the "General Assembly of the United States," and formed a "General Assembly of the Confederate States." The former still extends its jurisdiction to the Churches formerly in its connection throughout the loyal States, while it has never, by any formal act, renounced its jurisdiction to the Churches of the seceded States.

It is essential that these facts should be borne in mind, in order to understand the testimony which this large body of Christians has maintained upon the subject under consideration.

FIRST PERIOD.—EARLY TESTIMONY OF THE CHURCH.

Going back to the year 1774, we find that in the highest judicatory of the Presbyterian Church (then the Synod of New York and Philadelphia) "the subject of negro slavery came up to be considered," and that "much reasoning on the matter" occurred, resulting in the appointment of a committee to make a report; but no further action appears to have been taken at that meeting. In 1787, the Synod took their first formal action. A committee made a report, in which these words occur:

> It is more especially the duty of those who maintain the rights of humanity, and who acknowledge and teach the obligations of Christianity, *to use such means as are in their power to extend the blessings of equal freedom to every part of the human race.* From a full conviction of these truths, and sensible that the rights of human nature are too well understood to admit of debate, *Overtured*, That the Synod of New York and Philadelphia recommend in the warmest terms, to every member of their body, and to all the Churches and families under their care, to do every thing in their power, consistent with the rights of civil society, *to promote the abolition of slavery*, and the instruction of the negroes, whether bond or free.

After full consideration, the body "came to the following judgment," which we give in part:

> The Synod of New York and Philadelphia do highly approve of the general principles of universal liberty that prevail in America, and the interest which *many of the States have taken in promoting the abolition of slavery.* * * * They earnestly recommend it to all the members

belonging to their communion, to give those persons who are at present held in servitude *such good education as to prepare them for the better enjoyment of freedom.* * * * [They also "recommend that masters" would give their slaves] a *peculium*, or grant them sufficient time and sufficient means of *procuring their own liberty* at a moderate rate, that thereby they may be brought into society with those habits of industry that may render them useful citizens; and, finally, they recommend it to all their people to use the most prudent measures, consistent with the interest and the state of civil society, in the counties where they live, *to procure eventually the final abolition of slavery in America.*

In 1793, "this decision was republished" as the act and judgment of the General Assembly—that body having been formed in 1787.

POLITICS AND RELIGION.—A PROPHET.

The Constitution of the United States was submitted to the people of the several States for ratification in 1787. Its relations to slavery were canvassed by the people of all classes, as they had been in the National and were in the respective State conventions. We give a single testimony, among many, showing the views of prominent divines.

Rev. Dr. Hopkins, of Newport, Rhode Island, wrote to Rev. Dr. Hart, of Preston, Connecticut, on the subject, under date of January 29, 1788, as follows:

The new Constitution, you observe, guarantees this trade (the slave-trade) for twenty years. I fear, if it be adopted, this will prove an Achan in our camp. How does it appear in the sight of Heaven and of all good men, well informed, that these States, who have been fighting for liberty, and consider themselves as the highest and most noble example of zeal for it, cannot agree in any political Constitution, unless it indulge and authorize them to enslave their fellow-men! I think if this Constitution be not adopted as it is, without any alteration, we shall have none, and shall be in a state of anarchy, and probably of civil war. Therefore, I wish to have it adopted; but still, as I said, *I fear.* And perhaps civil war will not be avoided, if it be adopted.

Verily, among the "giants in the earth in those days," there were some prophets. Dr. Hopkins, like a true seer, "smelleth the battle afar off." But he prophesied further. The historian cannot more truly depict the scenes which these latter days have witnessed in Congress, than they are graphically drawn by that sagacious divine of nearly a hundred years ago:

> Ah! these unclean spirits, like frogs,—they, like the Furies of the poets, are spreading discord, and exciting men to contention and war, wherever they go; and they can spoil the best Constitution that can be formed. When Congress shall be formed on the new plan, these frogs will be there; for they go forth to the kings of the earth, in the first place. They will turn the members of that august body into devils, so far as they are permitted to influence them.

He seems to have foreseen also, or at least feared, what would come upon the Church as well as upon the State; though here, the reality has far exceeded, in these "last times," the apprehensions expressed: "I suppose that even good Christians are not out of the reach of influence from these frogs. 'Blessed is he that watcheth and keepeth his garments.'"

This is the same Dr. Hopkins, who, in conjunction with Rev. Dr. Stiles, made "a representation," in 1774, to the Synod of New York and Philadelphia, which led to the "first notice of the subject, the slavery question," taken by the Presbyterian Church in the United States in her highest court. The Minutes say: "The representation and request relative to sending negro missionaries to Africa, was taken into consideration, in consequence of which the subject of negro slavery came to be considered."

ACTION UPON A CASE SUBMITTED.

In 1795, the General Assembly of the Presbyterian Church took further action upon an overture from the

Presbytery of Transylvania, in Kentucky. The case was that of "a serious and conscientious person," who viewed "the slavery of the negroes as a moral evil, highly offensive to God, and injurious to the interests of the Gospel," and who lived among those "who concurred with him in sentiment upon general principles, yet for particular reasons held slaves, and tolerated the practice in others;" and he wished to know whether he should "hold Christian communion with the latter."

The Assembly exhorted the man, and others similarly situated, to "live in charity and peace according to the doctrine and practice of the Apostles," and adds: "At the same time, the General Assembly assure all the Churches under their care, that they view with the deepest concern *any vestiges of slavery which may exist in our country*, and refer the Churches to the records of the General Assembly, published at different times," as given above.

The Assembly also address "a letter to the Presbytery on the subject of the above overture," in which they exhort to peace, and say that "the commissioners from the Presbytery of Transylvania are furnished with attested copies" of the Assembly's "decisions, to be read by the Presbytery when it shall appear to them proper;" and also, that "the General Assembly have taken every step which they deemed expedient or wise, *to encourage emancipation*, and to render the state of those who are in slavery as mild and tolerable as possible."

ANOTHER CASE ACTED UPON.

In 1815, the Assembly adopted another paper, founded upon "the petition of some elders who entertained conscientious scruples on the subject of holding slaves," and upon another petition from "the Synod of Ohio concerning the buying and selling of slaves." The paper of the Assembly contains these sentences:

> The General Assembly have repeatedly declared their cordial approbation of those principles of civil liberty which appear to be recognized by the Federal and State Governments in these United States. They have expressed their regret that the slavery of the Africans, and of their descendants, still continues in so many places, and even among those within the pale of the Church, and have urged the Presbyteries under their care to adopt such measures as will secure at least to the rising generation of slaves, within the bounds of the Church, a religious education, *that they may be prepared for the exercise and enjoyment of liberty,* when God in His providence may open a door *for their emancipation.*

The Assembly then refer the petitioners to the previous action in 1787, 1793, and 1795.

THE MOST ELABORATE TESTIMONY.—1818.

The paper adopted by the General Assembly of 1818 is more frequently referred to and perhaps more generally known than any other, as containing a more full and pointed condemnation of the system than had been previously enacted. It was introduced by the presentation of the following resolution: "*Resolved,* That a person who shall sell as a slave, a member of the Church, who shall be at the time in good standing in the Church and unwilling to be sold, acts inconsistently with the spirit of Christianity, and ought to be debarred from the communion of the Church." The record then proceeds: "After considerable discussion, the subject was committed to Dr. Green, Dr. Baxter, and Mr. Burgess, to prepare a report to be adopted by the Assembly, embracing the object of the above resolution, and also expressing the opinion of the Assembly in general as to slavery." This committee made a report which the record says "was *unanimously* adopted." The report is a long document, and although well known, we here give several paragraphs, to show the views of the Assembly upon the character of slavery *as a system*. The report begins as follows:

We consider the voluntary enslaving of one portion of the human race by another as a *gross violation of the most precious and sacred rights of human nature; and as utterly inconsistent with the law of God*, which requires us to love our neighbor as ourselves, and as *totally irreconcilable with the spirit and principles of the Gospel of Christ*, which enjoin that "all things whatsoever ye would that men should do to you, do ye even so to them." *Slavery creates a paradox in the moral system;* it exhibits rational, accountable, and immortal beings in such circumstances as scarcely to leave them the power of moral action. It exhibits them as dependent on the will of others, whether they shall receive religious instruction; whether they shall know and worship the true God; whether they shall enjoy the ordinances of the Gospel; whether they shall perform the duties and cherish the endearments of husbands and wives, parents and children, neighbors and friends; whether they shall preserve their chastity and purity, or regard the dictates of justice and humanity. Such are some of the consequences of slavery—consequences not imaginary, *but which connect themselves with its very existence*. The evils to which the slave is always exposed, *often take place in fact, and in their very worst degree and form;* and where all of them do not take place, as we rejoice to say in many instances, through the influence of the principles of humanity and religion on the mind of masters, they do not,—still the slave is deprived of his natural right, degraded as a human being, and exposed to the danger of passing into the hands of a master who may inflict upon him all the hardships and injuries which inhumanity and avarice may suggest.

From this view of the consequences resulting from the practice *into which Christian people have most inconsistently fallen*, of enslaving a portion of their brethren of mankind,—for "God hath made of one blood all nations of men to dwell on the face of the earth,"—it is manifestly *the duty of all Christians* who enjoy the light of the present day, when *the inconsistency of slavery, both with the dictates of humanity and religion, has been demonstrated, and is generally seen and acknowledged*, to use their honest, earnest, and unwearied endeavors, to correct the errors of former times, and *as speedily as possible to efface this blot on our holy religion, and to obtain the complete abolition of slavery throughout Christendom, and if possible throughout the world.*

We rejoice that the Church to which we belong commenced as early as any other in this country, *the good work of endeavoring to put an end to slavery*, and that in the same work *many of its members* have ever since been, and now are, *among the most active, vigorous, and efficient laborers.* We do, indeed, tenderly sympathize with those portions of our Church and of our country where the evil of slavery has been entailed upon them; *where a great and the most virtuous part of the community abhor slavery, and wish its extermination as sincerely as any others*—but where the number of slaves, their ignorance, and their vicious habits generally, render an immediate and universal emancipation inconsistent alike with the safety and happiness of the master and the slave. With those who are thus circumstanced, we repeat that we tenderly sympathize. At the same time we earnestly exhort them to continue, and if possible *to increase their exertions to effect a total abolition of slavery.* We exhort them to suffer no greater delay to take place in this most interesting concern, than a regard to the public welfare truly and indispensably demands.

As our country has inflicted *a most grievous injury upon the unhappy Africans, by bringing them into slavery*, we cannot indeed urge that we should add a second injury to the first, by emancipating them in such manner as that they will be likely to destroy themselves or others. But we do think that our country ought to be governed in this matter by no other consideration than *an honest and impartial regard to the happiness of the injured party, uninfluenced by the expense or inconvenience which such a regard may involve.* We, therefore, warn all who belong to our denomination of Christians, *against unduly extending this plea of necessity;* against making it a cover for the love and practice of slavery, or a pretence for not using efforts that are lawful and practicable to extinguish this evil. And we, at the same time, exhort others to forbear harsh censures, and uncharitable reflections on their brethren, who unhappily live among slaves whom they cannot immediately set free; *but who, at the same time, are really using all their influence, and all their endeavors, to bring them into a state of freedom, as soon as a door for it can be safely opened.* Having thus expressed our views of slavery, and of the duty *indispensably incumbent on all Christians to labor for its complete extinction*, we proceed to recommend, and we do it with all the earnestness and solemnity which this momentous subject demands, a particular attention to the following points.

The foregoing embraces the chief portion of the report. Thus, the most eminent men of the Presbyterian Church, in her highest court, including many of the most renowned of that day from the South, who lived in the midst of slavery, and knew whereof they affirmed, speak of slavery *as a system*, of what it was before their eyes: regarding it as opposed both to humanity and religion, to the "law" and "gospel" of God; the wrong of which, to their view, was "demonstrated," and was "generally seen and acknowledged;" the "inconsistency" of which, as a "practice," among Christians, was manifest; and, therefore, as involving the inevitably resulting duty, to seek its "extinction" and "extermination," just "as speedily as possible."

The recommendations above referred to are: *First*, that the American Colonization Society (for colonizing free blacks in Africa) be encouraged, and they "exceedingly rejoice to have witnessed its origin and organization among the holders of slaves, as giving an unequivocal pledge of their desire to deliver themselves and their country from the calamity of slavery." *Secondly*, they recommend to all "to facilitate and encourage the instruction of their slaves in the principles and duties of the Christian religion." *Thirdly*, they "enjoin it on all Church Sessions and Presbyteries, under the care of this Assembly, to discountenance, and as far as possible to prevent, all cruelty of whatever kind in the treatment of slaves, especially the cruelty of separating husband and wife, parents and children," etc.*

* The authorship of this celebrated report on slavery, of 1818, has been controverted, some attributing it to Dr. Baxter, and some to Dr. Green. The point is easily settled, *first*, from the testimony of Dr. Green, the Chairman of the Committee; *second*, from the testimony of Mr. Burgess, the only member of the Committee still living; *third*, by Dr. J. D. Paxton, a member of that Assembly; all of whom agree. Dr. Green, in his autobiography, makes the following statement on the point: "I was a commissioner this year (1818) to the General Assembly." "Among other things, I penned the minute on the subject of slavery, which is yet referred to by those who are hostile to African slavery." In a recent letter from Mr. Burgess to the writer, is found some interesting items in the history of this paper. Though the

CHARACTERISTICS OF THE PAPER OF 1818.

Some things regarding the foregoing document should here be noted, which strikingly illustrate the sentiments of the Church and of the country, at that period, upon the institution of slavery as a system.

1. It will be difficult to find in the English language a more direct and decided condemnation of the system than is here given. Even the most ultra abolitionists have never expressed themselves more emphatically. They have used harsher language, and they have had no such bowels of compassion as the Assembly felt, in view of the practical difficulties which beset the whole subject in any attempt to rid the country of the institution; but upon the simple matter of disapprobation of the system, and of the duty of endeavoring "to obtain the complete abolition of slavery throughout Christendom, and if possible throughout the world," the General Assembly here go as far as the farthest.

2. This paper was adopted *unanimously.* The Church was well represented from the South, and there were pres-

letter is a private one, he takes the liberty of quoting from it. Mr. Burgess, it will be seen, introduced the subject to the notice of the Assembly, and thus "occasioned" its action. He says: "I was a member of what was then the Presbytery of Miami, when I presented the paper against slavery. The Committee which reported the paper, commonly called the paper of 1818, were Dr. Green, Dr. Baxter, and myself. Drs. Green and Baxter made out the report before consulting me on the subject; so that I am not responsible for the report at all, except that I occasioned it." He further says: "I was sent to the General Assembly, where I presented my paper, having first consulted Dr. Joshua L. Wilson, of Cincinnati, also Dr. Robert G. Wilson, of Chillicothe, Dr. Hoge, of Columbus, and Dr. Mathew Brown, then President of Washington College, Penn. When I laid in my paper before the Committee of Bills and Overtures, it was not reported. Then I took an appeal, agreeably to the advice of President Brown, and Rev. John Thompson, and others. My appeal was sustained, and thus the paper was brought before the Assembly. Dr. Green moved that the subject be given to a Committee of three ministers." Dr. Paxton, who was a member of the Assembly of 1818, and also of the Assembly of 1864, bears the same testimony, in a letter we have seen, to the authorship of the paper, ascribing it to Dr. Green.

ent in the Assembly the following distinguished persons, among the clergy: Drs. Coe, Romeyn, Green, Janeway, Ely, Chester, and Jennings, from the North, and Drs. Edgar, Witherspoon, and Leland, from the South, all of whom have at some time been Moderators of the Assembly; and also from the North, Drs. Fitch, Lansing, McClelland, Geo. C. Potts, Cathcart, Matthew Brown, Duffield, and Messrs. Burges, and Dickey, and from the South, Drs. Paxton, Baxter, Speece, Morrison, McIver, Nathan H. Hall, and Mr. James K. Burch, besides many others from both sections, of no doubt equal ability.

3. While this paper expressed the solemn judgment of the Church in all parts of the land, it also expressed the opinions substantially which were entertained by the most distinguished statesmen of every portion of the country, and by the people generally. This is too well known to be questioned.

4. It is no doubt true, also, that this is a fair representation of the views of all other denominations of Christians. It would be quite remarkable that so large and influential a body as the Presbyterian Church, extending at that time into nearly every State and Territory of the Union, should express, through its highest court, a unanimous judgment in terms of such pointed condemnation of slavery, and at the same time not exhibit in such action the general sentiment of other denominations.

SECOND PERIOD.—MORE "CONSERVATIVE" VIEWS.

We come now to the second period in the history of opinions on the subject of slavery. We find them first officially brought to view, so far as the action of the General Assembly of the Presbyterian Church is concerned, in the year 1836. The reader will have noticed a complete uniformity in sentiment from 1787 to 1818, embodying disapprobation of the system in each of the several instances in which a judgment was expressed, the main difference being in the more extended expression of views in the paper adopted 1818. The Church appears to have been satisfied with this judgment for many years, for we find no further action of any kind upon the subject till the year 1836; so that, in round numbers, we may say that such had been its views for a period of fifty years; though, undoubtedly, the transition had been in operation for some time.

The modification of these opinions in the Church at the North, which we have said presents a characteristic of the second period, is in an opposite direction to that commonly supposed.

No statement has been more frequently made since the beginning of the rebellion than this: that the Northern Church has plunged the country into this civil war; that "political preachers have abolitionized the Church and the people;" that, during the last thirty years, the Northern mind had, under their tutelage chiefly, been educated up to a point of unbearable hostility to slavery; that this has been the course of action in the judgments expressed by leading ecclesiastical bodies; so that the South were actually pushed into their present attitude in pure self-defence; and that, to defend themselves against modern opinions, led to the disruption of ecclesiastical bodies, and finally to secession and war. These charges have formed the staple of a certain style of oratory upon the stump and in Congress, both from the North and the South, and the substance of many editorials in a certain class of public journals.

Now it so happens that the facts are the precise reverse of this, so far as the action of many of the large bodies of Christians and the opinions of many of the leading men in every branch of the Northern Church are concerned. Whether it be a matter for rejoicing or mourning, the fact is undeniable,—as shown by official documents of religious bodies, and by the formal utterances of leading divines,—that during this very period of the last thirty years previous to the rebellion, instead of the Church and these influential classes of the people becoming, as charged, "more and more abolitionized," there was a very marked abatement in their opinions and in their course of action in opposition to slavery,—judged from the stand-point of 1818,—and a disposition frequently manifested to concede to the South, in both sentiment and action, that which placed the Church, in the judgment of Southern divines, in decided antagonism to the whole current of its former testimonies.

ACTION POSTPONED.—1836.

The proof is indisputable. The first example we take from the action of the Presbyterian Church. Its testimony of 1818 had become practically a dead letter. "The subject being pressed on its attention by various memorials," the General Assembly, in 1836, adopted this minute:

> Inasmuch as the Constitution of the Presbyterian Church, in its preliminary and fundamental principles, declares that no Church judicatory ought to pretend to make laws, to bind the conscience, in virtue of their own authority; and as the urgency of the business of the Assembly, and the shortness of the time during which they can continue in session, render it impossible to deliberate and decide judiciously on the subject of slavery in its relations to the Church; therefore, *Resolved*, That this whole subject be indefinitely postponed.

What a marked contrast appears between this action and that of former years; and wherefore? The "fundamental principles" of the Presbyterian Church were the same as formerly. The Assembly had just as much "authority to make laws" and "to bind the conscience" as they ever had, and the institution on which they were called to speak was the same in character; at least it had not improved, though it had extended its borders and was becoming a mighty power in the land. It is no doubt true that "the urgency of the business" was great. It was just then that the disputes between the Old and New School were culminating. But the length of "time during which" they could "continue in session" was within their own keeping.

There is something very significant in the statement that it was "impossible to deliberate and decide *judiciously* on the subject of slavery in its relations to the Church." What was there which demanded special circumspection just then, lest they should pronounce unadvisedly? Were not their previous testimonies most explicit? If they deemed them *right*, how much "time" would it have taken simply to refer the memorialists to them as still their sentiments, as representatives of the Church, as had been done several times before? This would have required fewer words than were employed to justify indefinite postponement. If their previous action was *wrong*, it should have been revoked, however much time might have been required, for it touched and decided a most radical question in morals and religion. Granting what was of course true, that the Assembly had no authority "to make laws," they could certainly declare *the law of God* on the subject, and this was all that was requisite.

The truth is, that the views of the whole subject entertained by many in the Assembly representing the Southern section of the Church had undergone a change. Some were in a transition state, and some had totally reversed their opinions; so that, at this time, the doctrines of 1818 began to be odious to Southern men. They were not ready to make open war upon those doctrines in the

Assembly, as they were beginning to do through the Southern press, but it would have been hazardous to attempt at that time a reaffirmation of them.

FORMAL "CONSERVATIVE" ACTION OF 1845.

The next formal declaration of sentiment made by the General Assembly was in 1845.* Seven years before this

* The committee to whom were referred the memorials on the subject of slavery, beg leave to submit the following report:

(*a*) The memorialists may be divided into three classes, viz.: 1. Those which represent the system of slavery, as it exists in these United States, as a great evil, and pray this General Assembly to adopt measures for the amelioration of the condition of the slaves. 2. Those which ask the Assembly to receive memorials on the subject of slavery, to allow a full discussion of it, and to enjoin upon the members of our Church, residing in States whose laws forbid the slaves being taught to read, to seek by all lawful means the repeal of those laws. 3. Those which represent slavery as a moral evil, a heinous sin in the sight of God, calculated to bring upon the Church the curse of God, and calling for the exercise of discipline in the case of those who persist in maintaining or justifying the relation of master to slaves.

(*b*) The question which is now unhappily agitating and dividing other branches of the Church, and which is pressed upon the attention of the Assembly by one of the three classes of memorialists just named, is, whether the holding of slaves is, under all circumstances, a heinous sin, calling for the discipline of the Church.

(*c*) The Church of Christ is a spiritual body, whose jurisdiction extends to the religious faith and moral conduct of her members. She cannot legislate where Christ has not legislated, nor make terms of membership which he has not made. The question, therefore, which this Assembly is called to decide, is this: Do the Scriptures teach that the holding of slaves, without regard to circumstances, is a sin, the renunciation of which should be made a condition of membership in the Church of Christ?

(*d*) It is impossible to answer this question in the affirmative, without contradicting some of the plainest declarations of the word of God. That slavery existed in the days of Christ and His Apostles is an admitted fact. That they did not denounce the relation itself as sinful, as inconsistent with Christianity; that slaveholders were admitted to membership in the Churches organized by the Apostles; that whilst they were required to treat their slaves with kindness, and as rational, accountable, immortal beings, and, if Christians, as brethren in the Lord, they were not commanded to emancipate them; that slaves were required to be "obedient to their masters according to the flesh, with fear and trembling, with singleness of heart as unto Christ," are facts which meet the eye of every reader of the New Testament. This Assembly cannot, therefore, denounce the holding of slaves as necessarily a heinous and scandalous sin, calculated to bring upon the Church the curse of God, without charging the Apostles of Christ with conniving at sin, introducing into the Church such sinners, and thus bringing upon them the curse of the Almighty.

(*e*) In so saying, however, the Assembly are not to be understood as denying that the division into New and Old School had occurred, and therefore the action of which we now speak was that of the latter body only. Both still extended into the Southern States, though the Old School had much the

there is evil connected with slavery. Much less do they approve those defective and oppressive laws by which, in some of the States, it is regulated. Nor would they by any means countenance the traffic in slaves for the sake of gain; the separation of husbands and wives, parents and children, for the sake of "filthy lucre," or for the convenience of the master; or cruel treatment of slaves, in any respect. Every Christian and philanthropist certainly should seek, by all peaceable and lawful means, the repeal of unjust and oppressive laws, and the amendment of such as are defective, so as to protect the slaves from cruel treatment by wicked men, and secure to them the right to receive religious instruction.

(*f*) Nor is the Assembly to be understood as countenancing the idea that masters may regard their servants as mere property, and not as human beings, rational, accountable, immortal. The Scriptures prescribe not only the duties of servants, but of masters also, warning the latter to discharge those duties, "knowing that their Master is in heaven, neither is there respect of persons with Him."

(*g*) The Assembly intend simply to say, that since Christ and His inspired Apostles did not make the holding of slaves a bar to communion, we, as a court of Christ, have no authority to do so; since they did not attempt to remove it from the Church by legislation, we have no authority to legislate on the subject. We feel constrained further to say, that however desirable it may be to ameliorate the condition of the slaves in the Southern and Western States, or to remove slavery from our country, these objects, we are fully persuaded, can never be secured by ecclesiastical legislation. Much less can they be attained by those indiscriminate denunciations against slaveholders, without regard to their character or circumstances, which have to so great an extent characterized the movements of modern abolitionists, which, so far from removing the evils complained of, tend only to perpetuate and aggravate them. The Apostles of Christ sought to ameliorate the condition of slaves, not by denouncing and excommunicating their masters, but by teaching both masters and slaves the glorious doctrines of the Gospel, and enjoining upon each the discharge of their relative duties. Thus only can the Church of Christ, as such, now improve the condition of the slaves in our country.

(*h*) As to the extent of the evils involved in slavery, and the best methods of removing them, various opinions prevail, and neither the Scriptures nor our Constitution authorize this body to prescribe any particular course to be pursued by the Churches under our care. The Assembly cannot but rejoice, however, to learn that the Ministers and Churches in the slaveholding States are awaking to a deeper sense of their obligation to extend to the slave population generally the means of grace, and many slaveholders not professedly religious favor this object. We earnestly exhort them to abound more and more in this good work. We would exhort every believing master to remember that his Master is also in heaven, and, in view of all the circumstances in which he is placed, to act in the spirit of the golden rule: "Whatsoever ye would that men should do to you, do ye even the same to them."

larger membership there, and its Churches were located in every part of the South.

As our purpose here is chiefly historical, and as we aim merely to show a change in sentiment in the Church, we need not stop to discuss *the merits* of this or any other paper which the Assembly has from time to time adopted. This paper shows, however, marked concessions to the extremists of the South, as compared with the Assembly's earlier action, and has uniformly been so interpreted by Southern members.*

In view of the above stated principles and facts,

Resolved, 1. That the General Assembly of the Presbyterian Church in the United States was originally organized, and has since continued the bond of union in the Church, upon the conceded principle that the existence of domestic slavery, under the circumstances in which it is found in the Southern portion of the country, is no bar to Christian communion.

2. That the petitions that ask the Assembly to make the holding of slaves in itself a matter of discipline, do virtually require this judicatory to dissolve itself, and abandon the organization under which, by the Divine blessing, it has so long prospered. The tendency is evidently to separate the Northern from the Southern portion of the Church; a result which every good citizen must deplore, as tending to the dissolution of the Union of our beloved country, and which every enlightened Christian will oppose, as bringing about a ruinous and unnecessary schism between brethren who maintain a common faith.

The yeas and nays being ordered, were recorded. [Yeas, 168; nays, 13; excused, 4.]

* Referring directly to the Act of 1845, the "General Assembly of the Confederate States," in their "Address to all the Churches throughout the Earth," written by Dr. Thornwell, and "adopted unanimously by the Assembly," say: "The Presbyterian Church in the United States has been enabled, by divine grace, to pursue, for the most part, an eminently conservative, because a thoroughly Scriptural, policy in relation to this delicate question. It has planted itself upon the word of God, and utterly refused to make slaveholding a sin, or non-slaveholding a term of communion." This explicit reference to the Act of 1845 was made at Augusta, Georgia, December, 1861. To show how the Act of 1818 is regarded at the South,—an Act *excepted* from the above commendation by the words, "for the *most* part,"—we refer to the *Southern Presbyterian Review*, April, 1861, which says: "It was during this period that the various religious bodies made their deliverances on the subject of slavery, and among them the General Assembly of the Presbyterian Church adopted, in 1818, a series of resolutions looking very earnestly toward the gradual emancipation of the slaves. These resolutions were drawn up by Southern men, who were themselves slaveholders, and they were passed by the votes of Southern ministers and elders. With reference to other denominations, a rigid adherence to the modes of thought and feeling of those days has led to the disruption of the Churches; while the Old School Presbyterian Church, commonly

This characteristic of the paper may be seen at a glance. The strongest expressions which it contains against slavery as a system are these:

In saying so, however, the Assembly are not to be understood as denying that there is evil connected with slavery. Much less do they approve those defective and oppressive laws by which, in some of the States, it is regulated. Nor would they by any means countenance the traffic in slaves for the sake of gain; the separation of husbands and wives, parents and children, for the sake of "filthy lucre," or for the convenience of the master; or cruel treatment of slaves, in any respect. * * * Nor is the Assembly to be understood as countenancing the idea that masters may regard their servants as mere property, and not as human beings, rational, accountable, immortal. * * * As to the extent of the evils involved in slavery, and the best methods of removing them, various opinions prevail, and neither the Scriptures nor our Constitution authorize this body to prescribe any particular course to be pursued by the Churches under our care.

CONTRAST.—ACTION OF 1818 AND 1845.

The reader need only compare these tender sentences with the *great burden* of condemnation in the paper of 1818, to see that here is a most noticeable modification from that expressed twenty-seven years before. The two papers are very nearly of the same length, and present the following striking points of contrast:

1. In the paper of 1818, the Assembly speak in *positives.* They deal with *the system*, and pronounce it "utterly inconsistent with the law of God," and as "totally irreconcilable with the spirit and principles of the Gospel of Christ;" and say, "Slavery creates a paradox in the moral system," and that "the slave is deprived of his natural right, degraded as a human being," etc. These

regarded as so tenacious of the past, and even reproached as a fossil Church, and her doctrines derided as fossil Christianity, has had the wisdom given her to understand *the progress of events, and to keep fully abreast of the age.* The action of 1818 still stands upon her records, *not as the law*, BUT THE HISTORY OF THE SUBJECT; and Southern Presbyterians are well content that it should *so* stand."

positives condemn *the thing in its essence*, and assert a radical deprivation in the concrete as attaching to "the slave" in person, and that too in every case, as shown by the exceptions referred to. In the paper of 1845, in speaking of *the system*, the Assembly deal in *negatives;* and so far as they find any thing to disapprove, it is not at all in *the thing*, but wholly in what they deem its mere *adjuncts.* The farthest they can go is to wish "*not* to be understood as *denying* that there is *evil connected with* slavery." They utter no direct condemnation of the "oppressive laws" of slavery, but are content with saying, "much less do they approve" of them. They do not *positively* condemn even "the traffic in slaves for the sake of gain,"—which always has been the life, soul, and power of the whole system,—nor even "the separation of husbands and wives, parents and children, for the sake of 'filthy lucre,' or for the convenience of the master; or cruel treatment of slaves, in any respect;" but the utmost they feel called upon to say about these crying evils is, "*nor would* they by any means *countenance* them!" The whole style of dealing with the institution shows that they were bent on giving "a soft answer" to the memorialists, as it "turneth away the wrath" of Southern extremists.

2. The paper of 1818 styles "enslaving a portion of their brethren of mankind" as a "*practice* into which Christian people have *most inconsistently fallen*," and declares that "the inconsistency of slavery both with the dictates of humanity and religion has been demonstrated, and is generally seen and acknowledged." The paper of 1845 admits the consistency of this "practice" with Christian character, asserting that the denial of this position is against "some of the plainest declarations of the word of God."

3. The Assembly of 1818, starting from their position last noticed, declare that "it is manifestly the duty of all Christians who enjoy the light of the present day," "to use their honest, earnest, and unwearied endeavors, * * * to obtain the *complete abolition of slavery* throughout Christendom, and if possible throughout the world." The Assembly of 1845, starting from their own position, arrive as naturally at an opposite conclusion. They have *not even a single "soft" word for emancipation*, but some that are not so soft against "the movements of modern abolitionists," charging them with "indiscriminate denunciations."

4. The Assembly of 1818 believed that *the Church could do much* towards ridding the country and the whole world of slavery; hence they urge action to this end upon their members. They moreover "rejoice that the Church" they represented "commenced as early as any other in this country the good work of endeavoring to put an end to slavery, and that in the same work many of its members have ever since been, and now are, among the most active, vigorous, and efficient laborers;" and they "earnestly exhort" their members in the South "to continue, and, if possible, to increase their exertions to effect a total abolition of slavery." The whole drift of the paper of 1845 is to afford *palliatives to the system*, to make those concerned in it contented with their lot, and not the remotest wish is directly and positively expressed that the Church or the country may ever be rid of it, but rather *the efforts of the Church to remove it are positively discouraged.* This will be seen from the only sentence in which emancipation is in any manner alluded to: "We feel constrained further to say, that however desirable it may be to ameliorate the condition of the slaves in the Southern and Western States, or to remove slavery from

the country, these objects, we are fully persuaded, can never be secured by ecclesiastical legislation."

We have already said that our object here does not lead us to examine the merits of these papers, to determine which is more consonant with the word of God. We aim in this comparison simply to show their contrariety, and to present it as one of the items of evidence to prove that the Church *had greatly abated* in its opposition to slavery, during the very period with which she is charged with having provoked the South by her abolition sentiments. A great deal of discussion has taken place upon these papers, and some have attempted to show that they maintain the same bearing towards slavery. This dispute may be continued till doomsday, and it will still be true, as long as there is any force in language, that in the latter there is evinced a great *letting down in the feeling of opposition* to the system, as compared with the former.

This comparison of the language,—along with the fact that the paper of 1818 passed unanimously, while that of 1845 had only thirteen nays, with four excused from voting, against one hundred and sixty-eight yeas, and the further notorious fact that the South always claimed this as a triumph,—shows that at this time the Presbyterian Church had gone far in yielding to the wishes of extremists among Southern divines; just as Northern statesmen had gone in yielding to the statesmen of the South.

ACTION OF 1846.—DECLARATION OF AGREEMENT.

We of course notice the action of subsequent Assemblies, to see what view was entertained by them of the respective papers of 1818 and 1845. So manifest was it to a large portion of the Presbyterian Church, both North and South, that the interpretation we have given is correct, that the Assembly of 1846 was besieged to make a deliverance, by "a collection of petitions and memorials on the subject of slavery." The following report was made:

Our Church has from time to time, during a period of nearly sixty years, expressed its views on the subject of slavery. During all this period it has held and uttered substantially the same sentiments. Believing that this uniform testimony is true, and capable of vindication from the word of God, the Assembly is at the same time clearly of the opinion that it has already deliberately and solemnly spoken on this subject with sufficient fulness and clearness. Therefore, *Resolved*, that no further action upon this subject is at present needed. * * * * The following amendment was offered and laid on the table, viz.: "Except to say, that the action of the Assembly of 1845 is not understood by this Assembly to deny or rescind the testimony that has been uttered by the General Assembly previous to that date." The question was then taken on the report, when the ayes and noes were called for, and are as follows: ayes, 119; noes, 33.

Subsequently, it appears, the same gentleman who offered the amendment which had been tabled, presented the following resolution, which "was adopted without division:"

Resolved, That in the judgment of this house, the action of the General Assembly of 1845 was not intended to deny or rescind the testimony often uttered by the General Assemblies previous to that date.

Those who are at all acquainted with deliberative bodies, know that they, as truly as individuals, are subject to moods and humors, and that it is often difficult to divine the motive for their votes, or the influences at work to produce them. An illustration is before us. It is not easy to understand why the Assembly should table so important an amendment, and afterwards pass it in precisely the same words, so far as its essence is concerned. It does not appear from the Digest (from which our extracts are taken), at what stage of the proceedings the resolution passed. It may have been near the close, when, as often observed, business is pressing, members are inattentive, or many have retired from the body, or when some are bent on carrying some special measure of their own, and are using the lever employed among politicians in "log-rolling;" circumstances under which, in all deliberative bodies, ecclesiastical not excluded, important measures are sometimes "put through."*

But put any construction which is allowable upon these proceedings, including the original report (which, however, had a large minority against it), and the most remarkable thing of all is, that the Assembly should have deemed the sentiments uttered "on the subject of slavery" "during a period of nearly sixty years" as "substantially the same;" and, therefore, not disagreeing with those expressed in 1845—provided that is what indeed they meant. A declaration, however, to that effect, does not make it evident, even though made by the General Assembly. The terms, palliatives, tone, spirit, negations, omissions, of the paper of 1845, *and the regard paid to it universally in the South*, all serve to show, as does the judgment of a vast number in the North, that it embodies principles in conflict with those so plainly declared in 1818. The case is clear, if the language in these respective papers is not to be taken in a sense wholly diplomatic. But there is a far more conclusive proof, if the action of the Assembly is to be taken as

* "We all know and admit that a vote of the Assembly does not always express even the settled conviction of that body itself. Such votes are often given hastily, without due consideration, or from motives not affecting the principle involved in the case decided. At the end of the session, to avoid discussion, or to save time, things are often passed, or passed over, which, under other circumstances, would have met a different fate. It is also to be considered, that all who vote for a particular measure do not commonly do so for the same reasons. A vote to lay a resolution on the table is not decisive evidence that those who joined in it sanctioned the arguments of the speakers by whom the measure was advocated."—*Princeton Review on the General Assembly of* 1859.

decisive, that these papers are materially discordant. Before referring to it, however, (1863), we must examine other deliverances in their order.

ANOTHER CONTRAST.—1818 AND 1849.

The next paper adopted by the General Assembly was in 1849. It originated in three memorials, one praying the Assembly "not only to declare slavery to be a sin, but to enjoin upon all inferior courts a course of discipline which will remove it from our Church;" a second, "asking the Assembly to appoint a committee to collect and report to the next Assembly, statistics on this subject, and digest a plan of abolition to be adopted by our Church;" and the third, "asking the Assembly to alter sundry terms and passages in the act of 1845, relating to slavery." Upon these memorials, the Assembly adopted the following paper:

(1.) That the principles of the Presbyterian Church on the subject of slavery are already set forth in repeated declarations, so full and so explicit as to need no further exposition. (2.) That in view of the civil and domestic nature of this institution, and the competency of secular Legislatures alone to remove it, and in view of the earnest inquiry and deep agitation on the subject, which we now observe in one or more commonwealths of our country where slavery exists, it be considered peculiarly improper and inexpedient for this General Assembly to attempt or propose measures in the work of emancipation. (3.) That all necessary and proper provision is already made, for the just exercise of discipline upon those who neglect or violate the mutual duties of master and servant; and the General Assembly is always ready to enforce these provisions, where the unfaithfulness of any inferior court is made manifest, by record, or appeal, or complaint. (4.) We rejoice to believe that the action of former Assemblies, so far from aiding or allowing the iniquitous oppression of man by his fellow-man, has been steadily promoting amelioration in the condition of slaves, by winning the confidence of masters, in our freedom from fanaticism, and by stimulating the slaveholder and his pastor alike, to labor in the religious instruction of the blacks. (5.) That it be enjoined on Presbyteries situated in slaveholding States to continue and increase their exertions for the religious instruction of slaves, and to report distinctly, in their annual narratives to the General Assembly, the state of religion among the colored population.

A careful examination will show that this paper presents points of decided contrast to that of 1818. It indeed says that "the principles" of the Church on this subject as previously "set forth" are "so full and so explicit as to need no further exposition;" but this is very different from explicitly adopting them. If, however, it be maintained that this is equivalent to an approval, it is very plain that other "principles" are here introduced directly antagonistic to those of the earlier paper; or, at the very least, discouragements are presented to the most important action which that paper urged upon the Church. For example, in 1849, "the civil and domestic nature" of slavery, "and the competency of secular Legislatures *alone* to remove it," appear to have been discovered, and are deemed obstacles to emancipation. But its "nature" and its civil status were always the same; and while it was true that "secular Legislatures" *alone* could remove it as a whole from their respective *States*, it was also true that individuals might at any time remove it from *themselves*, and from *the Church*, had they chosen to make the sacrifice. If the laws required emancipated slaves to be removed beyond the precincts of the State, it was only a question of dollars and cents where there was a disposition to emancipate. On the well-known ground of individual ability, even under sacrifices,—as well as the influence of the Church, if rightly directed, to bring about emancipation in the State at large,—emancipation is urged in 1818, and members are exhorted to it, "uninfluenced by the expense or inconvenience" which it "may involve;" and they are warned "against unduly extending this plea of necessity," and "against making it a cover for the love and practice of slavery, or a pretence for not using efforts that are lawful and practicable to extinguish this evil."

A PROTEST.—ACTION OF 1845 EQUIVOCAL.

By what vote the paper of 1849 passed, we do not know; undoubtedly by a very large one, as we find a protest to the action recorded, signed by only four members. If this expresses the full strength of the minority, then it presents palpable evidence that the abatement from at least some of "the principles" announced in 1818 largely pervaded the Church, and completely overthrows the position taken by extremists of the South and their Northern sympathizers,—so far as this large and influential body of Christians is concerned, spread over the entire country,—that the Church is mainly responsible for "abolitionizing the country;" for, during the very period in which it is charged that abolition was growing, so as to extenuate the crime if not to justify the South in ultimate rebellion, the Church was decidedly more "conservative" in its leaning towards Southern opinion, and far more lenient towards its members for their neglect of what was deemed a solemn duty, thirty years before, concerning the whole subject of emancipation.

This protest has another value in reference to the question immediately in hand. It states what no member of the Assembly ventured to deny, what indeed was notorious, what has been verified to the last, and what constituted the ground of "asking the Assembly to alter sundry terms and passages in the act of 1845," viz.: "The true position of our Church, in regard to this subject, which is evidently one of overwhelming importance, is not known with certainty either by all its ministers or members, or by the world at large; some affirming that the Church sanctions slavery as an institution having the moral approbation of God; and others, that it condemns it."

This fact is as clear and true as any other fact before the public: that there has been a very prevalent opinion in the Church, both North and South,—the South rejoicing in it, a portion of the Northern members lamenting it, another portion rejoicing in it for the South's sake, and others conceding it for the sake of peace,—that the paper of 1845 was a large concession to the South from the previous stand taken by the Church. So much is undeniable, *as a simple fact.* Now it would be quite remarkable if all these classes and persons were mistaken about the bearing of that paper. It would be equivalent to mistaking their own positive convictions. As the passage of the Kansas-Nebraska bill was regarded as a political triumph to the South by Southern statesmen, so the adoption of the paper of 1845 was hailed as an ecclesiastical triumph by Southern divines. This ought of itself to be conclusive. An examination of the document shows that this opinion was well founded.

ACTION OF 1861.—SYNOD OF SOUTH CAROLINA.

Passing by the action of 1850, the next in the order of time, in which the Assembly simply declare that their "previous and repeated declarations are such as to render any action unnecessary," we come down to the Assembly of 1861. This Assembly made no formal deliverance upon slavery, but referred certain memorialists "to all the deliverances of the General Assembly on this subject from 1818 to the present time." We find, however, in the proceedings of this Assembly, proof of an official character that the Synod of South Carolina regarded the act of 1818 as "virtually rescinded" by the act of 1845. This, as we have said, was but the common opinion of the South. The Synod put this, in form, into their records, and this declaration was made the basis of an exception to their approval by the Assembly.

ACTION OF 1863.—REPUDIATION OF 1845.

The next action upon slavery was by the Assembly of 1863. It furnishes the most incontrovertible testimony to the position which we have maintained,—founded in the direct and formal action of the Assembly itself,—that a wide difference, in their judgment, was manifest between the acts of 1818 and 1845; that, in fact, the latter was a concession to Southern opinion, or an abatement from former testimonies, which they could not approve. This Assembly made a deliverance upon slavery in response to "a request" from a single Presbytery in Illinois, containing but eight ministers. Under the remarkable circumstances of the times, when slavery had demonstrated its character and aims, and had plunged thirty millions of people into a civil war, which has no parallel in history,—then raging for two years,—all for the purpose of "perpetuating and extending" the institution, and founding a Government of which it should be the "corner-stone,"—and when all the members from the rebel States had withdrawn from the Church, so that the members in the loyal States had all the power in their own hands,—the utmost that the Assembly of 1863 found it in their hearts to do, and all they actually did, and all that any Presbytery in the whole Church requested them to do, and that too a solitary and a small one, was to "reaffirm the testimony of 1818;" simply to set forth anew those very principles in terms on which their fathers had planted themselves forty-five years before, and to say no worse things of the system which had wrought out such terrible results than those venerated men had authorized by their example.

Nor was the action of 1863 taken "unanimously," as was that of 1818. There was a minority of several votes against it, and some of this minority were from the free States; thus showing, that even in the midst of civil war caused by slavery, the Church in the loyal States was not as "radical" as were the fathers of the Church in the whole country in 1818, and showing therefore the utter baselessness of the charge that the rebellion was provoked by "abolitionizing the Church."

Now observe how the Assembly of 1863 regarded the paper of 1845. They say:

> The Assembly has, from the first, uttered its sentiments on the subject of slavery in substantially the same language. The action of 1818 was taken with more care, made more clear, full, and explicit, and was adopted unanimously. It has since remained that true and Scriptural deliverance on this important subject, by which our Church is determined to abide. It has never been repealed, amended, or modified, but has frequently been referred to, and reiterated in subsequent Assemblies. And when some persons fancied that the action of 1845 in some way interfered with it, the Assembly of 1846 declared, with much unanimity, that the action of 1845 was not intended to deny or rescind the testimony on the subject previously uttered by General Assemblies; and by these deliverances we still abide.

This is rather plain language, and very much like that of 1846, from which alone we might erroneously be led to infer that they regarded the paper of 1845 "substantially the same" in its principles as all the previous deliverances. But a practical test as to whether they meant this was at hand, and the result was decisive. In the last words, which were a clincher to the whole utterance,—"and by these deliverances we still abide,"—some ambiguity might be supposed to rest. It was therefore moved to insert the word "all" before "these," for the express purpose of embracing the paper of 1845. The minutes record this motion "lost." It was then "moved to lay the whole subject on the table." This too was "lost." The minutes say: "The report was then adopted, without amendment."

No clearer testimony than this could well be given that this General Assembly *did not* regard the paper of 1845 with favor; *did not regard it as agreeing with previous action.* No other explanation can be given for voting down the proposed amendment. They did not wish, in express terms, to indorse it, as they did, in express terms, indorse the paper of 1818, and thus to include it among those deliverances by which they declared they would "still abide."

REVIEW OF TESTIMONIES.—1787 TO 1863.

We have now brought down the testimony of the Presbyterian Church on slavery from the earliest period to the action of the Assembly of 1863. The action of 1864, we shall notice in its place.

This is among the largest ecclesiastical bodies in the United States, and, until the outbreak of rebellion, extended into all parts of the country. For learning, ability, and influence, its ministers and its people stand second to no denomination of Christians in the country. The sentiments they have from time to time uttered upon slavery, *pro* and *con*, in the pulpit, in ecclesiastical judicatories, through their religious newspapers, monthlies, quarterlies, and volumes published,—and they have spoken frequently, from the hebdomadal to the huge octavo,—have probably had as great an influence in forming the public opinion of the country, both North and South, upon this vexed question, as has emanated from any other equal number of persons; and we believe that a fair criterion of these sentiments, at least as regards those persons who have always wielded most influence in the denomination (with the exception of the ultra opinions more recently adopted in the extreme South), is to be found in the deliverances of its supreme judicatory, the General Assembly.

What, then, in the main, is the teaching of the facts which we have collated from all these official sources, upon the question immediately in hand? It is substantially and plainly this:

1. That from 1787 to 1836, or about fifty years, public testimony was borne by the Presbyterian Church against slavery as a system, in the most decided terms, the most explicit declaration being the act of 1818.

2. That from 1836 to the period of the rebellion and the withdrawal of the Churches in the rebel States, in 1861, or about twenty-five years, there was gradually developed within the denomination that which grew into a more decided proslavery sentiment, or, to use a favorite term, an intense "conservatism;" to that degree, at least, which embraced many of the leading minds in the body, and other influential classes who controlled its higher judicatories; as evidenced particularly, though mildly expressed, in the act of 1845; and which, during this period, prevented any contrary action by the General Assembly, though certain individuals and Presbyteries frequently attempted to secure it.

3. That during the former period of fifty years, the highest judicatory of the Presbyterian Church made formal declaration, six specific times, or in each deliverance enacted during the period, IN FAVOR OF THE "ABOLITION OF SLAVERY," *and urged the Churches under its care to labor for that end*, viz., in 1787, directly; in 1793, by republishing the action of 1787; in 1795, by expressing "the deepest concern" that "any vestiges of slavery" remained in the country; in 1815, directly; and in 1818, directly and

most urgently: while, on the other hand, during the second period of twenty-five years, NOT ONCE IS EMANCIPATION RECOMMENDED IN ANY FORM, nor is any positive disapprobation whatever expressed of *the system;* but in the two more extended deliverances of this period, those of 1845 and 1849, the *difficulties of emancipation* are suggested, and thus, so far forth, was the work discouraged. The paper of 1845 urges Christians to seek "the repeal of unjust and oppressive laws, and the amendment of such as are defective," but sounds no note, in any form or manner, for emancipation.

4. That after the rebellion had been in progress two years, in 1863, when the Assembly was composed of persons from the loyal States only, the Church simply took its stand upon the platform of its earlier sentiment, as expressed in the act of 1818.

5. That it therefore appears,—so far as this large, extended, and influential body of Christians is concerned,—that during the very period in which it has been alleged that the Church was becoming abolitionized, and the country being educated up to a point of opposition to slavery which justified or extenuated a disruption of the Church and of the Union, the contrary sentiment prevailed and the contrary action was taken in all the deliverances of the highest court of this body; and so marked and decided was what was termed the "healthy conservatism" of this period, operating as a "breakwater against abolitionism" in other quarters, that the author of the paper of 1845 exultingly referred to it "as constituting our Church emphatically the bond of union to these United States;" and many others no doubt believed what a distinguished *millionnaire*, who in writing publicly pledged on a certain contingency a hundred thousand dollars to the General Assembly in 1859, was understood to express, that "the two strongest hoops

which held the Union together were the Democratic party and the Old School Presbyterian Church."

CORROBORATIVE TESTIMONY TO THESE POSITIONS.

There are certain special facts in great number which might be produced, further illustrating the truth of the second and fifth of the foregoing points. We will barely note a few of them.

The act of 1818, originally passed, as has been stated, *unanimously*, not a single vote being cast against it from the remotest South. When this act was reaffirmed in 1863, after the seceders had withdrawn, and there were none in the Assembly but from the loyal States, there was a minority against it; how many, we do not know, as the ayes and noes were not taken. Nor were all of this minority from the Border slave States. Several were from different parts of the free States. This is significant. The Church was not as decidedly antislavery even in 1863, in the midst of the rebellion, as in 1818.

In the Assembly of 1859, a resolution was offered recommending the American Colonization Society to the patronage of the Churches, a measure that had been passed some dozen times before, at different periods; but now it was vehemently opposed by Dr. Thornwell and other leading men of the South, on the ground that "the Church is exclusively a spiritual organization, and possesses none but spiritual power," and therefore this would be a perversion of her functions. Thus the very mildest possible form of expression adverse to slavery,—even if there was intended any thing more than a simple approval of that philanthropic enterprise on its own merits,—could not be tolerated by Southern men. The argument was, that this was bringing the Church, "a spiritual body," to commend a "secular enterprise," though philanthropic,—*a new* *doctrine in the Church*,—and the purpose was believed to be to erect a barricade, in this restriction of the Church's functions, behind which slavery should ever be safe from assault.*

* The position taken in the Assembly of 1859, by Dr. Thornwell and other Southern men, referred to above, was pronounced by Dr. Hodge, in the *Princeton Review* for July of that year, a "new doctrine" in the Church; and this is admitted, also, in the *Southern Presbyterian Review*, of Columbia, S. C., for October of that year. This "new doctrine" is again referred to by Dr. Hodge, in the same periodical for July, 1864. On reviewing the case of Dr. McPheeters before the General Assembly, he says: "We think Dr. McPheeters committed some very grave mistakes, which were the source of all his difficulties. In the first place, he adopted the *new* exaggerated doctrine as to the *spirituality of the Church*, and the limited range of her prerogative as a teacher. He says he had always resisted the introduction of what he calls 'politics' into the house of God, and on this ground opposed all deliverances on the part of Church courts touching the present rebellion, and the introduction into the services of the sanctuary of any thing which implied a decided opinion as to the controversy which now rends the country. In the year 1859, Dr. Thornwell opposed the recommendation of the Colonization Society, on the principle above stated. *In private, if not in public, he took the ground that the division of the country was a certain event.* [This confirms what we have said in a Note, page 158, of Dr. Thornwell's declaration at the Assembly at Rochester, in May, 1860.] He, however, wished to prevent the division of the Church as consequent on the division of our national Union. To secure that end, he said, it was necessary to adopt the principle that the only duty of the Church as a teacher, was to preach the Gospel, to labor for the salvation of men. He said in his public speech that if the Government choose to reopen the slave-trade, the Church would have no right to open her lips against it. *This new doctrine* excited great attention and feeling. When the Assembly met in 1860, the subject was again brought up, and caused for a time great anxiety. A resolution was prepared and presented by the Committee on Bills and Overtures, affirming the directly opposite doctrine [drafted by Dr. Hodge], and asserting that the Church, as God's witness on earth, *is authorized and bound to reprove all sin and to support all truth and righteousness.* This resolution was adopted by a *unanimous vote* of the Assembly. * * * Politics, in the wide sense of the word, includes the science of Government, the policy of States, and the duties of citizens. The plain principle which determines the legitimate sphere of the action of the Church, is, that it is limited to *teaching and enforcing moral and religious truth;* and to such truths as are revealed and determined by the sacred Scriptures. The Bible gives us no rule for deciding the litigated questions about public improvements, a national bank, or a protective tariff, or State rights. *But it does give us rules for pronouncing about* SLAVE LAWS, THE SLAVE-TRADE, OBEDIENCE TO MAGISTRATES, TREASON, REBELLION, AND REVOLUTION. *To shut her mouth on these questions, is to make her* UNFAITHFUL TO HER HIGH VOCATION. The authors of this new theory soon repudiated it; and while *those who agreed with them at the North were protesting against Church courts saying a word against the rebellion*, the pulpits, Conventions, Synods, and Assemblies, at the South, were resounding with exciting appeals to inflame the spirit of rebellion. We think that a great part of Dr. McPheeters's

At other times, a portion of the people being aware that the Presbyterian Church, so far as the manifestations in her highest court were concerned, had been for a long time drifting away from her earlier position, desired for many years a reaffirmation in direct terms of the act of 1818. This was, in some instances, proposed to the Assembly; it was discussed, and several times acted upon, in Presbyteries and Synods, and canvassed in religious journals; but the prevailing influence always discountenanced such reaffirmation, and it is believed that there was but one religious journal in the Church that favored it. At the same time, the South were violently opposed to its reaffirmation, because they regarded it as *totally erroneous.* Their religious journals plainly indicated that it would be the signal for disruption. It could scarcely be tolerated by them unrepealed; never would it have been, if reaffirmed. Southern ministers expressed through Northern journals what would be the consequences of a re-enactment of the paper of 1818, and warned the Northern portion of the Church against such a step. Many at the South declared that it had been "virtually repealed" *by the act of* 1845. The Synod of South Carolina so declared by formal enactment. Others insisted that the act of 1818 remained on the record, not as indicating the Church's present judgment, but only as a matter of *history*, showing the opinions of a bygone and unenlightened age on the character of slavery. The men of

difficulties have arisen from his adopting a principle which prevented him from uniting with his brethren in CONDEMNING THE REBELLION." Elsewhere, Dr. Hodge says, of the duty of a pastor, when speaking of the case of Dr. McPheeters: "He is the organ of the people in presenting their prayers and thanksgiving to God. They have the right to have their hearts' desires for their country brought before His throne. If the pastor's principles or feelings prevent him from doing this; *if he cannot pray for the success of our arms, and for the suppression of the rebellion; if he cannot heartily thank God for the victories He may grant our armies,* he cannot satisfy the just demands of the people."

the South took their position *openly and defiantly* on the ground of deeming that paper as teaching *a totally false doctrine of the word of God.*

PROOF AND ILLUSTRATIONS.

Let us, at this point, give the proof of this. It is found in the action of Southern Church judicatories, and in their religious journals and periodicals. For the sake of greater brevity, we take our illustrations chiefly from two or three sources among many.

The *Southern Presbyterian Review* for April, 1861, says: "The action of 1818 still stands upon her records (of the General Assembly), not as the law, but *the history of the subject;* and Southern Presbyterians are well content that it should *so* stand." This *Review*, conducted by the Professors in the Theological Seminary which was supported more than any other Seminary by the Church in the Cotton and Gulf States,—or by South Carolina, Georgia, Alabama, Florida, Louisiana, Texas, and Mississippi,—may well be supposed to represent the general sentiment of the Church in that vast region.

The Southern Presbyterian, a weekly religious journal, which was also deemed to represent the Church in several Synods in those States, thus speaks, in several successive numbers, on the points of the case stated:

It will be *manifestly impossible* for the Presbyterians in the Confederate States to maintain their connection with those in the United States, while the position of the latter on the subject of slavery is dubious, or *if it is the fact that the declarations and recommendations of the Assembly of* 1818 *are* NOT "virtually repealed." (Feb. 23, 1861.) As to the act of 1818, I agree with you, 1st. That much of its language could not be now understood except in an abolition sense. 2d. That it could not now be adopted, or authoritatively delivered, *by our Church united.* (April 6, 1861.) We have said that we think our Northern brethren owe it to us, candidly and explicitly, to let us know what are THEIR views about slavery, *and especially as to the meaning and effect of the act of* 1818, *and whether or not it has been virtually repealed or reversed.* WE DO THINK SO. * * * *The South* wants no action at all on the part of the next or any future Assembly. *We* are perfectly contented with the position of the Old School Presbyterian Church on the subject of slavery. The Synod of South Carolina *said unanimously*, that "from our brethren of the whole Church, annually assembled, we have received nothing but justice and courtesy." This sentiment is not peculiar to the South Carolina Synod, *but is the sentiment, we suppose, of the whole South.* There is no danger, therefore, of the *South* asking for the repeal of the act of 1818. WHAT THE ASSEMBLY SAID IN 1845 SATISFIES US. Southern men never did agitate the Assembly on this subject—*they* never were the unruly spirits. *And having been* PERFECTLY CONTENTED FOR SIXTEEN YEARS *with the position of the Church*, why should they now ask for any change? (April 13, 1861.) We have further said, in as intelligible terms as we could, that, if the act of 1818 is to be regarded as NOW the "opinion," or the faith, or the law, of the Presbyterian Church in the United States, *it would be* IMPOSSIBLE *for the Presbyterians in the Confederate States to bear it;* and that we thought it due to the South that we should not be left in any uncertainty on this point. * * * It has been the *impression of the South* that this act had been *virtually reversed by subsequent decisions of the Assembly.* So the Synod of South Carolina affirmed last December. Under this impression, Southern Presbyterians have been *content and quiet*, believing that our Northern brethren held *correct and Scriptural views on the subject.* It has been our joy and pride to think that *the errors of our fathers had been corrected*, and the minds of Northern Presbyterians kept pure from the follies of modern abolitionists. The act of 1818 was regarded in the South as only the opinion of the men composing the Assembly *then in session*, and not as the authoritative *permanent* judgment of the Presbyterian Church. * * * THE ACT OF 1845 WAS SUPPOSED BY THE SOUTH TO BE A DECISION IN OUR FAVOR. * * * If this is not so, then we hesitate not to say that Southern Presbyterians have been MISLED AND BETRAYED. * * * In our humble opinion, any Church in these Confederate States that affiliates with those who maintain the act of 1818, * * * will, in a very little while, find themselves in a position where they will have abundance of reason for repentance. * * * We are aware that certain schemers and wire-workers in our ecclesiastical affairs at the North, are making diligent use of their peculiar opportunities and *special talents* in that line, to engineer the Southern part of the Church into quiescence; BUT THEY WILL FAIL, and must meet the fate which invariably awaits those who resort to such methods to secure selfish ends (April 27, 1861.)

Here, then, is the most incontestable proof,—in the judgment of those who were most deeply interested in the subject as a *practical* matter,—that the Church had swerved from her ancient position, and substantially indorsed, or at least tacitly acquiesced in, the Southern views; that she had repudiated the doctrines of 1818 by the act of 1845; and therefore *the whole South* had "been *perfectly contented for sixteen years* with the position of the Church."

THE INEVITABLE EFFECT.—NORTHERN RESPONSIBILITY.

The men of the South were undoubtedly honest and sincere in this judgment of where the Church stood. The acts in question, which they compared, sustained them. Their relations to the subject, as affecting their position at home, would not lead them to over-eagerness in adopting such an opinion; but would naturally lead them in an opposite direction, unless they felt sure of their *ground* and of their *friends*. We can somewhat, therefore, enter into their surprise when assured, in the winter of 1861, from the atmosphere of Chicago, that, after all, the acts of 1818 and 1845 were in sentiment the same! "The act of 1818 *was* regarded in the South" (says *The Southern Presbyterian*, of April 27, 1861) "only as the opinion of the men composing the Assembly then in session, and not as the authoritative permanent judgment of the Presbyterian Church." But, "we are *now* told, however, that the later deliverances of the Assembly on this subject are *not* to be understood as differing from that and preceding decisions. No less authority than Dr. N. L. Rice, *who has been regarded in the South as our* BEST FRIEND AT THE NORTH-

and who, if we mistake not, drew up the act of 1845, which was supposed by the South to be *a decision in our favor*, tells us that we must not interpret that as reversing former acts."

In all the seriousness and fervor of our condemnation of the wicked deeds of the Southern clergy in bringing on the rebellion, we confess to some sympathy for men under the circumstances in which this Northern blast found them, when, counting on the support of their quondam friends, they had possibly gone too far to retreat with safety. We can imagine something of the bitterness of anguish with which the pen traced the words, founded on the assurance of the identity in sentiment of these acts by the author of the latter: "*If this is so*, then we hesitate not to say, that Southern Presbyterians have been *misled and betrayed*."

But, so far as the *responsibility* for the position of the Church is concerned, as this position was understood universally at the South, the Church herself must bear it; while, unquestionably, the leaders of the Church, in her courts, and in other posts of influence where her public sentiment is manufactured or reflected, have the chief burden on their shoulders. There *were* those who *remonstrated* against this position which the South claimed the Church to have taken, but they were always overruled; Southern influences under Northern compliance dominated; a reassertion of her early testimonies was impossible; men who were dissatisfied with her position, found effort useless, and were content to bide their time; and thus the Church stood for "sixteen years;" and now, as the result of this, and corresponding influences at work in the State, we are daily "making history," in deeds which crimson a hundred battle-fields with patriot gore!

We have a very decided opinion on this whole subject, and we have very little concern whether it be deemed wise or otherwise by the responsible actors in the case. It is well supported by the facts, and by the acknowledged principles of human nature everywhere prevalent.

Looking at matters from the stand-point of the rebellion and several years previous to it, so far from the position of the Church during this second period mentioned, or from about 1836 to 1861,—a position of departure from the testimony of the fathers, and to which the Church has since returned,—being a cause for exultation, as it has been with some, it is with us the reverse. So far from this position having contributed, as the distinguished author of the paper of 1845 and his distinguished friend believed, to hold the Union together, it is a solemn judgment to which a large portion of the people have arrived, that such concessions by the Church, and similar concessions by the civil authorities, only hastened its disruption. To use a well-understood illustration, the leaders of Southern opinion, in both Church and State, had become like spoiled children. The repeated concessions of Northern politicians, yielding the principles held by the fathers of the Republic, made Southern politicians more exorbitant in their demands, until they came to believe that verily the whole country was theirs. The repeated concessions of the Northern Church, culminating in the Presbyterian body in 1845 and sticking there immovably under all remonstrances, produced a similar state of mind in Southern divines. If both classes had stood firmly, during all our history, by the teachings of the fathers, and to which the mass of both in the North have since returned, the rebellion never would have occurred.*

* If Presbyterians of the Old School Church desire to know THE CAUSE of the withdrawal of the Southern Presbyteries and Synods, and of the formation of the "General Assembly of the Confederate States of America," in December, 1861, they may find evidence which is conclusive that THE LEADERS of the Church in the South were *not led to this step by the action of the General Assembly at Philadelphia in May,*

ACTION OF THE GENERAL ASSEMBLY OF 1864.

We come now to the last exhibition of sentiment on the subject of slavery, made by the General Assembly of the Presbyterian Church in the United States. It is the

1861, *upon the state of the country.* They had taken their position MONTHS BEFORE THAT ASSEMBLY MET, and had determined on a division of *the Church* in consequence of the course of things in *the State;* thus chaining the Church of Christ to Cæsar's war chariot. While, therefore, it may be true, as Dr. Hodge says of Dr. Thornwell, in a previous note (page 401), that in 1859, "he wished to prevent the division of the Church *as consequent upon the division of our national Union,*" subsequent facts show, as will be seen, that after the Presidential election of 1860, and during the winter of 1861, *the leaders* of the Church in the South (and Dr. Thornwell, beyond a doubt, among them) *took other ground,* and determined on a disruption of the Church, "as consequent upon" what had *then* taken place in the "secession" of several States. It may be further true, that the reason why the "resolution" presented by Dr. Hodge in the General Assembly of 1860 (declaring contrary to the "new" Thornwell theory of the power of the Church), "was adopted by a *unanimous* vote."—even Dr. Thornwell not voting against it,—was, because the leaders had at that early day determined to divide the Church if the Union should be divided; and that they expected the latter event to occur beyond doubt, is seen in what Dr. Thornwell and others said at the Assembly in 1860, as stated in a previous chapter (Note, page 158). The facts which show the disruption on that ground are (1.) Several Presbyteries that had already appointed commissioners to the Assembly at Philadelphia, called, in April and May, special meetings and *revoked these appointments.* Notices of those meetings and of their action are found in Southern religious papers that are now before us. Some Presbyteries, and those from the *extreme South,*—as from Mississippi, Louisiana, and Texas, and other points most remote from Philadelphia,—were represented; proving conclusively that it was *not the apprehension of war* which necessarily kept members away. Many in Virginia, the Carolinas, Georgia, and other less remote points, did not attend because their commissions had been revoked, or they were persuaded by those who *lead* the Church not to go. (2.) The unstinted abuse which the Southern religious press heaped upon Southern Commissioners who *did* sit in that Assembly, is another item of proof of the foregone determination for division. The speeches and the votes of these men *against* the Spring resolutions, *did not shield them* from abuse. They "should not have appeared *there at all,*" these papers declared. Did space permit, we might verify this by quotations. (3.) The fact that the Synod of South Carolina sent up its records for review, is no proof of a willingness still to continue ecclesiastically connected with the North. They had not been sent *for several years;* and there is ample ground for believing that the *motive* for then sending them was to draw forth from the Assembly just the action it took, viz.: a *disapproval* of the Synod's action, declaring the act of 1818 on slavery "virtually repealed." This was an argument the Synod wished to use "to fire the Southern heart." (4.) In *The Southern Presbyterian* of April 27, 1861, is an editorial on "Division of the Presbyterian Church," published almost *a full month* before the Assembly met. The editor says: "We have plainly and unequivocally report drawn up by the Hon. Stanley Matthews, of Cincinnati, and presented by him to the Assembly, from the Committee to whom the subject was referred, and was

expressed our conviction (in previous numbers of this paper), that a separate ecclesiastical organization of the Southern Presbyterian Church will be *desirable and necessary*." "As to the future relations between Northern and Southern Presbyterians, *ecclesiastically, we have no doubt of the issue*, and are very well content to let things take their course. We do not think it necessary or expedient to say or do any thing to hasten the *inevitable result*." "In the Assembly which will meet in Philadelphia on the 16th of next month, we suppose *there will be scarcely one commissioner from the Southern States.* If any such appear there, we are convinced *it will not be with the approbation of their constituents.*" Still earlier than this (April 6, 1861), in an article on "The next General Assembly," the same paper shows that the "SECESSION OF THE SOUTH" was "THE reason" urged by the leaders for a division of the Church, as follows: "Every thing we have seen and heard *against* a division of the Church, *in consequence of the secession of the South*, proceeds on the assumption that such division is desired and proposed on the ground of the abolition sentiments of Northern Presbyterians. We would again most earnestly protest against this. We do not know ANY ONE who desires a division of the Church ON THAT GROUND. The existence of a few out-and-out abolitionists in the Church at the North, and the radically unsound views of the majority of our brethren there on the slavery question, will be a reason to reconcile us to a separation from them; but it is a narrow and a shallow notion to suppose that is *the* reason (editor's italics) which will make such separation desirable and NECESSARY." Still earlier (March 30, 1861), the same paper says: "We do not know any one who favors a separate organization of the Church in the Confederate States, either on account of the act of the Assembly of 1818, or of any other action of the Presbyterian Church in the United States, or of the views of our Northern brethren in general on the slavery question. So far as we are aware, those who think such an organization will finally be best, and even necessary, form their judgment on OTHER REASONS *than these altogether*." We have seen what those "other reasons" are,—"the *secession* of the South,"—from the extracts given above from papers of a later date, where they *speak out* what in March they did not "think aloud" *quite* so plainly.

It is thus conclusively established that *the leaders*,—the men who had so much power over both Church and State,—had determined on *ecclesiastical* separation MONTHS BEFORE the Assembly met; and, also, WEEKS BEFORE the attack on Fort Sumter; and "THE REASON" for this was, "the secession of the South." These rulers in the *Church* thus made her *a tail* to the *State*, in her ecclesiastical *organization;* while, *personally*, they led both Church and State into "secession" at the start. They did not, at *that* period, deem the act of 1818, nor "the radically unsound views of the majority" of their brethren at the North "on the *slavery* question," as "THE reason" for division; for, the States having "seceded," every thing "on the *slavery* question" would be safe, of course. They therefore openly put the *division of the Church* on the ground of the *political secession* of the South. (5.) In view of the facts above given, the "Confederate General Assembly," by the pen of Dr. Thornwell, in their Address to the Christian world, justifying their separation from the Northern branch of the Church, "unanimously" perpetrate a serious libel upon adopted by the Assembly, at Newark, New Jersey, in May last.

It gives an historical sketch of the earlier deliverances of the Church on this subject, opening in these words:

In the opinion of the General Assembly, the solemn and momentous circumstances of our times, the state of our country, and the condition of our Church, demand a plain declaration of its sentiments upon the question of slavery, in view of its present aspects in this country. From the earliest period of our Church, the General Assembly delivered unequivocal testimonies upon this subject, which it will be profitable now to reaffirm.

As we have already given in this chapter a summary of these earlier testimonies, we omit from the report its historical sketch, and give in full the remaining portion, in which the doctrines of the Assembly, asserted at the present time are embodied. It is as follows:

Such were the early and unequivocal instructions of our Church. It is not necessary too minutely to inquire how faithful and obedient to these lessons and warnings those to whom they were addressed have been. It ought to be acknowledged that we have all much to confess and lament as to our short-comings in this respect. Whether a strict

the truth, when, referring to the action upon the Spring resolutions in the Assembly of May, 1861, they present that action as "the first thing" which led them seriously to contemplate separation. They say: "*The first thing* which roused our Presbyteries to look the question of separation seriously in the face, was the course of the Assembly in venturing to determine, as a court of Christ, which it did by necessary implication, the true interpretation of the Constitution of the United States as to the kind of Government it intended to form." Did not the "Presbyteries" of the South "look the question of separation seriously in the face," when they held special meetings for the purpose of revoking the commissions given to attend the Assembly, and when they *did* revoke them weeks before the Assembly met? The "Confederate General Assembly" *knew these things were so*, and knew, moreover, that the leaders had declared for "separation" even long before; and yet they "unanimously" try to deceive the world by declaring the contrary. This, we suppose, forms an element in the "manly *Christian* logic" of this Address of the "Confederate General Assembly," by reason of which its Louisville indorsers so warmly commend it to their readers, when they say with *equal* truth that it was "the fatal heresy of the late General Assembly (of 1861), in the unscriptural assumption of power in ecclesiastical courts over civic and political questions," which "caused the rending of the Church."

and careful application of this advice would have rescued the country from the evil of its condition, and the dangers which have since threatened it, is known to the Omniscient alone. Whilst we do not believe that the present judgments of our Heavenly Father and Almighty and Righteous Governor have been inflicted solely in punishment *for our continuance in* THIS SIN; yet it is our judgment that the recent events of our history, and the present condition of our Church and country, furnish manifest tokens that *the time has at length come, in the providence of God, when it is His will that every vestige of human slavery among us should be effaced, and that every Christian man should address himself with industry and earnestness to his appropriate part in the performance of this great duty.*

Whatever excuses for its postponement may heretofore have existed, no longer avail. When the country was at peace within itself, and the Church was unbroken, many consciences were perplexed, in the presence of this great evil, for the want of an adequate remedy. Slavery was so formidably intrenched behind the ramparts of personal interests and prejudices, that to attack it with a view to its speedy overthrow, appeared to be attacking the very existence of the social order itself, and was characterized as the inevitable introduction of an anarchy worse in its consequences than the evil for which it seemed to be the only cure. But the folly and weakness of men have been the illustrations of God's wisdom and power. Under the influence of the most incomprehensible infatuation of wickedness, those who were most deeply interested in the perpetuation of slavery *have taken away every motive for its further toleration.* The spirit of American slavery, not content with its defences to be found in the laws of the States, the provisions of the Federal Constitution, the prejudices in favor of existing institutions, and the fear of change, has taken arms against law, organized a bloody rebellion against the National Authority, made formidable war upon the Federal Union, and in order to found an empire upon the corner-stone of slavery, threatens not only our existence as a people, but the annihilation of the principles of free Christian Government; and thus has rendered the continuance of negro slavery incompatible with the preservation of our own liberty and independence.

In the struggle of the nation for existence against this powerful and wicked treason, the highest executive authorities have proclaimed the abolition of slavery within most of the rebel States, and decreed its extinction by military force. They have enlisted those formerly held as slaves to be soldiers in the national armies. They have taken measures to organize the labor of the freedmen, and instituted measures for their support and government in their new condition. It is the President's declared policy not to consent to the reorganization of civil government within the seceded States upon any other basis than that of emancipation. In the loyal States where slavery has not been abolished, measures of emancipation, in different stages of progress, have been set on foot, and are near their consummation; and propositions for an amendment to the Federal Constitution, prohibiting slavery in all the States and Territories, are now pending in the national Congress. So that, in our present situation, *the interests of peace and of social order are identified with the success of the cause of emancipation.* The difficulties which formerly seemed insurmountable, in the providence of God, appear now to be almost removed. The most formidable remaining obstacle, we think, will be found to be the unwillingness of the human heart to see and accept the truth against the prejudices of habit and of interest, and to act towards those who have heretofore been degraded as slaves, with the charity of Christian principle in the necessary efforts to improve and elevate them.

In view, therefore, of its former testimonies upon the subject, the General Assembly does hereby devoutly express its gratitude to Almighty God for having overruled the wickedness and calamities of the rebellion, so as to work out the deliverance of our country from the EVIL AND GUILT of slavery; its earnest desire for the extirpation of slavery, as the root of bitterness from which has sprung rebellion, war, and bloodshed, and the long list of horrors that follow in their train: its earnest trust that the thorough removal of this prolific source of evil and harm will be speedily followed by the blessings of our Heavenly Father, the return of peace, union, and fraternity, and abounding prosperity to the whole land; and recommend to all in our communion to labor honestly, earnestly, and unweariedly, in their respective spheres, for this glorious consummation, to which human justice, Christian love, national peace and prosperity, every earthly and every religious interest, combine to pledge them.*

* It must be confessed that there is point and force in the biting sarcasm which flowed from the pen of Dr. Thornwell, and was "unanimously" uttered by the "Confederate General Assembly" in their Address to the Christian world, when, after expressing satisfaction with the act of 1845, to which they refer in the first part of the following extract, they then speak in the latter part of the prevalent sentiment of the North and the actual condition of "the Northern section" of the Church:

FEATURES OF THIS REPORT.

We have already occupied so much space with the general subject of this chapter, that our observations upon this report *ought* to be brief. A few things, however, call for special notice.

1. It elicited an animated and somewhat protracted discussion, which was opened by Judge Matthews, and participated in by many members, among them some of the more distinguished in the Assembly, both in the ministry and eldership. After full consideration, it was adopted *with great unanimity;* some reports of the religious press said at the time, "unanimously," but others report "two or three faint noes" heard. These were supposed to be from some of the Border slave States.

2. The historical sketch given of previous deliverances, specifies those running from the earliest, 1787, down to that of 1818, and from the latter extended extracts are embodied; *but not the remotest allusion is made to the far-famed deliverance of* 1845! This is not at all remark-

"The Presbyterian Church in the United States has been enabled, by divine grace, to pursue for the most part an eminently conservative, because a thoroughly Scriptural, policy in relation to this delicate question. It has planted itself upon the word of God, and utterly refused to make slaveholding a term of communion. But though both sections are agreed as to this general principle, it is not to be disguised that the North cherishes a deep and settled antipathy to slavery itself, *while the South is equally zealous in its defence.* Recent events can have no other effect than to confirm the antipathy on the one hand, and strengthen the attachment on the other. The Northern section of the Church stands in the awkward predicament of maintaining in one breath that slavery is an evil which ought to be abolished, and of asserting in the next that it is not a sin to be visited by exclusion from the communion of the saints. *The consequence is, that it plays partly into the hands of abolitionists, and partly into the hands of slaveholders, and weakens its influence with both.* It occupies the position of a prevaricating witness, whom neither party will trust. It would be better, therefore, for the moral power of the Northern section of the Church, to get entirely quit of the subject." While we admit the pointedness of this sarcasm, we abjure the strange logic of one who prided himself on his logical power, that every "evil" which ought to be removed from among men, should necessarily be made a term of communion in the Church.

able, but it is very significant. Were there none so poor in the Assembly as to do that famous paper reverence? Its distinguished author was there. He of course took part in the discussion. He of course, as always heretofore, eulogized the work of his hands. He suggested some verbal modifications of the report, as did one or two others, and they were promptly and cheerfully accepted by the chairman of the committee; but nobody moved to insert a eulogy, or even an elegy, upon the deliverance of 1845, the paper with which *the whole South* had been "PERFECTLY CONTENTED FOR SIXTEEN YEARS!" This is indeed significant; it conveys an unmistakable lesson, and fully bears out the view we have already taken of this paper in previous pages.

3. This report takes a position upon slavery, so far as *terms* are concerned,—and we suppose these terms mean what they say,—which no other deliverance has ever taken. It speaks of "our continuance in THIS SIN," referring to the people at large. It also speaks of working out "the deliverance of our country from *the evil and* GUILT of slavery." It is true that the paper of 1818 says the severest things of the system that any one could desire; things which, from the language used, would seem to *imply* "evil," "guilt," and "sin." We do not see how that language can mean any thing else, and it was probably not intended to convey any other meaning by those who used it. But the paper of 1864 is the first instance of action by the General Assembly which has come squarely up to the mark and pronounced slavery, in terms, to be a "sin." This is, unquestionably, an advanced position. Words are things. And those who know the history of discussion on this subject, especially in the Church, know that this is a point where contending parties have erected their breastworks and "made a stand." The mass,

indeed, of those who have opposed slavery at the North, within the Churches,—and universally those who have claimed a monopoly of "conservative" sentiment and feeling,—have persistently maintained, that whatever else was true of slavery as an "evil," it was improper to call it a "sin." That is the term which has met with especial reprobation. Some would tolerate almost any other hard word of the English language but that. To mystify the uninitiated, and to instruct the learned more clearly, the Latin has been brought in to help our jejune tongue; and so, as we have all often heard, "Slavery is not a sin *per se*;" and "is not a *malum in se*." But the paper of 1864, using a Saxon term which is often upon the lips of men, calls it "this SIN."

As we are speaking of things simply from an historical stand-point, we are not called upon *here* either to condemn or to approve of this report, in its doctrines or terms, so far as to give our personal views of slavery. We shall do that in another chapter. We simply *now* note this as an *advanced* position, which no General Assembly has ever before taken. We presume the Assembly understood what they were about, and we presume they meant *just what they said.* It is in that light significant of the times in which we live, when men can speak what they believe to be the truth, without the main effort being to seek to conciliate somebody who might otherwise be mortally offended.

What the bearing of this feature of the report may be in the minds of the members of the Assembly, we of course do not know, any farther than may be gathered from the discussions, and not much light is there emitted upon the simple point in hand. Men differ about what slavery is, disagree in their definition of the system and of its nature, and probably members of the Assembly differ about the judgment pronounced upon this point, calling slavery a "sin." Some may understand merely the *system of slave laws* existing at the South; some may understand the *practice of slaveholding* under those laws, without which slavery is the merest abstraction; some may include both; and, according as each may understand the case, he may have voted in the Assembly, and may insist that his view is that which the body meant. This difference in men's reasons for a vote, and of the subject voted on, and as to what is the result of the decision, is not confined to slavery. It enters into all complex matters upon which men deliberate and act.

Nor do we know, beyond the possibility of mistake, what the committee or its distinguished chairman meant by this language; not because there is any obscurity in the terms employed, but because, in order to understand the exact meaning and *intent* of those who use them, we must know more fully the views of the system which, personally, they entertain. If we may judge, however, from the terms themselves, the *meaning* is clear and unmistakable. The *language* of the committee is certainly clear. When they speak of "the present judgments" of God as having been "inflicted" (though not "solely") "in punishment for our *continuance in this sin*," we cannot suppose for a moment they refer merely to the system of slave-laws at the South. There can be no actual sin without a sinner; nor can "punishment" be "inflicted" for "this sin" or any other, except upon the sinner. Even Christ was, legally, a sinner. Much less can a person or a people be punished for a "*continuance*" in sin, unless they are personally in the *practice* of sin. But what practice can be meant in this case? The upholding of slave-laws? This would be perfectly ridiculous, unless there were some *person* held in slavery under them, and some other person *holding* him there. This is the practice which we *suppose* the committee meant, or their chairman who drew the report; and the "continuance" of this practice, we *suppose*, is the "sin" meant, for whose "punishment" God's "present judgments" are being "inflicted."

There may be those at the South who are not personally in the practice of slavery, who yet connive at or approve of the slave-laws, and of the practice under them in which others are involved; and, so far forth, they are concerned in "this sin." There are also those at the North in the same category; not practising slavery, but conniving at the slave-laws and the practice of others under them. And as the report regards "the present judgments" as having come upon the whole people, as too manifestly is the case, the whole people are suffering this "punishment." The slavery of the South is in a sense a *national* thing, and involves, through its political and moral bearings, national responsibilities. For "our continuance in this sin," as a nation, we are as a nation punished. But what, as a nation, do we *continue* to approve, connive at, tolerate, or uphold, and for which we are punished? Can it be merely a system of laws, a bundle of rigorous legalities; or, is it not *these laws and the practice of the people who hold slaves under them?*

We of course readily admit the wide difference between *slave-laws* and *slaveholding*. We can imagine a set of legislators concocting a system of laws, without there being a slave or a slaveholder; a system under which they intend to introduce, at a future time, their chattels, when they can kidnap them. But in the *system itself*, without victims, however rigorous the laws, there would be no sin, although the legislators, from the mere *intention* of putting slavery in practice, might be at the time great sinners. We can understand, too, that in fact, there is, and always may have been, a great difference at the South among slaveholders; some approving the whole system, laws, practice, and all, and not wishing a change; others disapproving of certain features in slave-laws, and either acquiescing or striving to have them altered, but continuing the practice of slavery from choice; others condemning the laws and the practice but, seeing their way more or less hedged up toward emancipation, continuing still in the practice; though we think the number in this latter classification has for a long time been very small and growing beautifully less. These distinctions are palpable and real; and in judging of *individuals*, they cannot be properly left out of the account. So, also, we can imagine such a change to occur in the system at the South, as a possible thing, as would divest the laws of their odious features, and leave little or nothing else but the *relation* of master and slave, and the *practice* of slavery; though, unhappily, with all the ameliorating influences of Christianity (and we have the word of Dr. Stiles for it, that they are a people of purer and simpler Christianity than any other), the system of slave-laws has continued from generation to generation much the same.

But when we would speak of and characterize slavery as an INSTITUTION, as a thing standing out before all men, we must take it as *a whole* and take it *just as it is.* Nor is it material, practically, how it may be *verbally* defined; a point on which logomachy has run wild, and in which no two men have ever agreed. What the *system, as such*, is, can admit of no doubt. To speak of it properly, as an institution, all its elements must be embraced; the laws just as they are, and the practice just as it is, embracing the persons held and the persons holding them. And when the committee reported, and the Assembly enacted, that we were punished "for our continuance in *this sin*," we understand them to cover by these terms *all* that makes the institution *what it is.* If so, we regard it in this sense, and by these terms, as declaring what no General Assembly has ever before declared. In *no sense* has any previous Assembly ever declared slavery to be a "sin."*

4. It is the judgment of the Assembly that slavery is

* Some rather curious things were developed in the discussion upon this report in the Assembly. Dr. Rice is reported as saying: "He now expected to vote for the paper. *The war had not taught him any thing at all about slavery.* He had been accustomed to investigate the subject for a long time." "He *never* had believed that slavery *was of itself a sin.* He regarded it as an evil, and considered it a sin to undertake to perpetuate slavery." "*He had, since the war, learned nothing new.*" "It had been assumed that the act of 1845 was inconsistent with that of 1818. This he denied. It was not inconsistent with that act. He proceeded to explain the act of 1845, and showed that *it was less proslavery than that of* 1818. Why do not brethren read the whole document before they talk about it as a proslavery paper?"—*Philadelphia Presbyterian.* (1.) Although Dr. Rice may "never" have "believed that slavery *was of itself a sin,*" yet he voted for Judge Matthews's paper, which pronounces it "THIS SIN." Although the war may not have "taught him any thing *at all* about slavery," as his *speech* would indicate, yet his *vote* shows that he took with others an *advanced position* in a deliverance upon slavery. Some men advance without knowledge, and some without knowing it. Dr. Rice may have done both. (2.) Dr. Rice declares that the paper of 1845 is "*less proslavery* than that of 1818." If this statement should ever run the blockade with other contraband goods, we should be curious to know how it would be received in Dixie. What *will* "our Southern brethren" say, when they hear that it has been affirmed in the General Assembly, of the act of 1845, with which they had been "*perfectly* contented for sixteen years,"—and by the *author* of that act, who, they declare "has been distinguished as a defender of slavery and the South, and as an antagonist of the antislavery party,"—that the said act of 1845 is "LESS proslavery than that of 1818!" What *will* "our Southern brethren" say? If any of them have become, by the influence of the rebellion, addicted to what was currently reported in the early stage of it, of the late Major-General Bishop Polk, they may possibly do what "our army did in Flanders!" (3.) "He had, since the war, *learned nothing new,*" says Dr. Rice. Most men in this nation have no doubt learned a great many things "since the war" began. We hear this on every hand, from the President of the United States down. It is our humble opinion that the whole nation has learned much; has been led along in paths that they knew not of, in God's wonderful providence; and that the people will learn much more before "the war" is over. But Dr. Rice is perhaps the one exception, essential to prove the rule. If he has "learned nothing new" thus far, he probably will not hereafter. Some men are never willing to admit that they have any thing to learn, that they can be taught by anybody, or by any course of events. Is he one of them? Perhaps he is self-deceived on matters concerning "the war," as upon slavery, and takes a position here, too, in advance of the one he formerly was understood to hold, without being aware of it.

"the root of bitterness from which has sprung rebellion, war, and bloodshed, and the long list of horrors that follow in their train;" that hence, as it threatens our national existence, its continuance is "incompatible with the preservation of our liberty and independence;" and hence it urges all to efforts to remove it, regarding "the interests of *peace* and of social order identified with the success of emancipation."

5. It *virtually* approves of and indorses the measures of the Government, and the movements in certain Border States, looking to the entire removal of slavery from the land, in the exercise of both military and civil authority, and of the restoration of our national Union on the basis of universal freedom; regarding these things as calling for "gratitude to Almighty God."

TE DEUM LAUDAMUS.

We truly rejoice in this deliverance. We doubt not that Dr. Hodge in the *Repertory* is substantially correct in saying: "There cannot be a doubt that the sentiments of this paper are the sentiments of the Presbyterian Church in these United States." He of course means in the loyal States; and in this sense we say he is *substantially* correct: we wish we could say he is entirely so. But there are some Presbyterians in some of the Border States whose souls are filled with mourning and lamentation at this act of the Assembly; and there is one "religious" journal claiming to be the organ of the only *true* Presbyterians left in the whole land, whose wrath has taken new fire from the fuel here furnished.

We can, without qualification, adopt another statement of the *Repertory*, which says: "We think it may safely be assumed, that the report unanimously adopted by the Assembly, expresses the opinions and feelings of the vast majority of the people in the Northern, Western, and Middle States. In this view of the matter, we regard the adoption of such a paper a matter of great public importance. It is the revelation of a spirit of loyalty, and of devotion to the great cause for which the nation is now contending as for its life. In this view, it is matter for gratitude and encouragement."

It is of rather small consequence what that small fragment of the Church may think who groan over this deliverance. The mass of the loyal people, we verily believe, are convinced, after what slavery has attempted in this rebellion, that its death is just and its doom is near. We are, therefore, especially rejoiced, that the General Assembly of the Presbyterian Church, by an almost unanimous vote, has so explicitly put itself upon the record; has declared for universal emancipation, as essential to "peace," "social order," "liberty and independence;" and has pledged itself and the people to sustain the Government in its measures for the restoration of our National Unity.

TO GOD BE THE PRAISE!

CHAPTER XI.

KENTUCKY OPINIONS.—THE PAST AND THE PRESENT.

As no Border State has at any time exhibited, among the religious portion of its community, more decided convictions upon Slavery, *pro* and *con*, than Kentucky, we propose in this chapter to present some of the views expressed against the system, at different periods, by some of her eminent men and religious bodies.

That which claims the pre-eminence, on account of the sentiments announced, the source whence they emanate, and the time of their utterance, is an Address issued in the year 1835. It is from a Committee of the Synod of the Presbyterian Church in Kentucky, to the members of this Church throughout the State.

The authority under which it was issued is as follows, as found in the minutes of the Synod: "For the purpose of promoting harmony and concert of action on this important subject, the Synod do *Resolve*, That a Committee of ten be appointed, to consist of an equal number of ministers and elders, whose business it shall be to digest and prepare a plan for the moral and religious instruction of our slaves, and for their future emancipation, and to report such plan to the several Presbyteries within our bounds for their consideration and approval."

It is entitled: "An Address to the Presbyterians of Kentucky, proposing a Plan for the Instruction and Emancipation of their Slaves, by a Committee of the Synod of Kentucky."

The Committee were: "Messrs. John Brown, John

Green, Thomas P. Smith, J. R. Alexander, and Charles Cunningham, laymen; and Revs. Wm. L. Breckinridge, James K. Burch, Robert Stuart, Nathan H. Hall, and John C. Young, ministers."

Some of these persons yet survive. Dr. Young, whose name appears last on the list, was at that time President of Centre College, the post which Dr. William L. Breckinridge, the first on the list of ministers, now fills. This eloquent and pungent address was from the pen of Dr. Young, than whom no man ever stood higher in the esteem of the Presbyterian Church in Kentucky. Though long, we bespeak for it a careful perusal. If there is to be found in the English language a more decided condemnation of slavery as a system, we have not met with it. We have only to suggest to the reader that he constantly bear in mind that he is not reading a paper which emanated from Boston, and was designed for the latitude of New England, but rather an address written in Kentucky, and, under the authority of the Synod, made to the Presbyterians of the State. The chief portions of this Address are as follows:

DEAR BRETHREN—The will of Synod has made it our duty to lay before you "a plan for the moral and religious instruction," as well as for "the future emancipation," of the slaves under your care. We feel the responsibility and difficulty of the duty to which the Church has called us, yet the character of those whom we address strongly encourages us to hope that our labor will not be in vain. You profess to be governed by the principles and precepts of a holy religion; you recognize the fact that you have yourselves "been made free" by the blood of the Son of God, and you believe that you have been imbued with a portion of the same spirit which was in "Him who, though He was rich, yet for our sakes became poor." When we point out to such persons their duty, and call upon them to fulfil it, our appeal cannot be altogether fruitless. But we have a still stronger ground of encouragement in our firm conviction that the cause which we advocate is the cause of God, and that His assistance will make it finally prevail.

May He who "hears the cry of the poor and needy," and who has commanded to let the "oppressed go free," give to each one of us wisdom to know our duty and strength to fulfil it.

We earnestly entreat you, brethren, to receive our communication in the same spirit of kindness in which it is made, and permit neither prejudice nor interest to close your minds against the reception of truth, or steel your hearts against the convictions of conscience. Very soon it will be a matter of no moment whether we have had large or small possessions on the earth; but it will be of infinite importance whether or not we have conscientiously sought out the will of God and done it.

We all admit that the system of slavery which exists among us is not right. Why then do we assist in perpetuating it? Why do we make no serious efforts to terminate it? Is it not because our perception of its sinfulness is very feeble and indistinct, while our perception of the difficulties of instructing and emancipating our slaves is strong and clear? As long as we believe that slavery, as it exists among us, is a *light evil* in the sight of God, so long will we feel inclined to pronounce every plan that can be devised for its termination inexpedient or impracticable. Before then we unfold our plan, we wish to examine the system and try it by the principles which religion teaches. If it shall not be thus proved to be an abomination in the sight of a just and holy God, we shall not solicit your concurrence in any plan for its abolition. But if, when fairly examined, it shall be seen to be a thing which God abhors, we may surely expect that no trifling amount of trouble or loss will deter you from lending your efforts to its extermination.

Slavery is not the same all the world over. And to ascertain its character in any particular State or country, we must examine the constituents and effects of *the kind of slavery which there exists.* The system, as it exists among us and is constituted by our laws, consists of three distinct parts: *a deprivation of the right of property*, *a deprivation of personal liberty*, and *a deprivation of personal security.* In all its parts it is manifestly a violation of the laws of God, as revealed by the light of nature as well as by the light of revelation.

1. A part of our system of slavery consists in *depriving human beings of the right to acquire and hold property.* Does it need any proof to show that God has given to all human beings a right to the proceeds of their own labor? The heathen acknowledge it; every man feels it. The Bible is full of denunciations against those who withhold from others the fruits of their exertions. "Woe unto him that buildeth his house by unrigh-

teousness, and his chambers by wrong; that useth his neighbor's service without wages, and giveth him not for his work." Jer. xxii. 13. See also James v. 4; Lev. xix. 13; Deut. xxiv. 14, 15. Does an act which is wrong when done once and towards one individual, become right because it is practised daily and hourly and towards thousands? Does the Just and holy One frown the less upon injustice because it is systematically practised, and is sanctioned by the laws of the land? If the chicanery of law should enable us to escape the payment of our debts, or if a human legislature should discharge us from our obligations to our creditors, could we, without deep guilt, withhold from our neighbors that which is their due? No; we all recognize the principle that the laws of the God of nature can never be repealed by any legislature under heaven. These laws will endure when the statutes of earth shall have crumbled with the parchments on which they are enrolled; and by these laws we know that we must be judged in the day in which the destinies of our souls shall be determined.

2. *The deprivation of personal liberty* forms another part of our system of slavery. Not only has the slave no right to his wife and children, he has no right even to himself. His very body, his muscles, his bones, his flesh, are all the property of another. The movements of his limbs are regulated by the will of a master. He may be sold like a beast of the field; he may be transported in chains like a felon. Was the blood of our Revolution shed to establish a false principle, when it was poured out in defence of the assertion that "all men are created equal;" that "they are endowed by their Creator with certain inalienable rights; that among these are life, liberty, and the pursuit of happiness?" If it be a violation of the rights of nature to deprive men of their *political freedom*, the injustice is surely much more flagrant when we rob them of *personal liberty*. The condition of a *subject* is enviable compared with the condition of a *slave*. We are shocked at the despotism exercised over the Poles. But theirs is a political yoke, and is light compared with the heavy personal yoke that bows down the two millions of our colored countrymen. Does European injustice lose its foul character when practised with aggravations in America?

Still further, the deprivation of personal liberty is so complete, that it destroys the rights of conscience. Our system, as established by law, arms the master with power to prevent his slave even from worshipping God according to the dictates of his own conscience. The owner of human beings among us may legally restrain them from assembling to hear the instructions of divine truth, or even from ever uniting their hearts and voices in social prayer and praise to Him who created them. God alone is Lord over the conscience. Yet our system, defrauding alike our Creator and our slaves, confers upon men this prerogative of Deity. Argument is unnecesary to show the guilt and madness of such a system. And do we not participate in its criminality if we uphold it?

3. *The deprivation of personal security* is the remaining constituent of our system of slavery. The time was, in our own as well as in other countries, when even the life of the slave was absolutely in the hands of the master. It is not so now among us. The life of a bondman cannot be taken with impunity. But the law extends its protection no further. Cruelty may be carried to any extent, provided life be spared. Mangling, imprisonment, starvation, every species of torture may be inflicted upon him, and he has no redress. But not content with thus laying the body of the slave defenceless at the foot of the master, our system proceeds still further, and strips him in a great measure of all protection against the inhumanity of any *other* white man who may choose to maltreat him. The laws prohibit the evidence of a slave against a white man from being received in a court of justice. So that wantonness and cruelty may be exercised by any man with impunity upon these unfortunate people, provided none witness it but those of their own color. In describing such a condition, we may well adopt the language of sacred writ: "Judgment is turned away backward, and justice standeth afar off; for truth is fallen in the street, and equity cannot enter. And the Lord saw it, and it displeased Him that there was no judgment."

SUCH IS THE ESSENTIAL CHARACTER OF OUR SLAVERY. Without any crime on the part of its unfortunate subjects, they are deprived for life, and their posterity after them, of the right to property, of the right to liberty, and of the right to personal security. These odious features are not the excrescences upon the system, they are *the system itself;* they are its essential constituent parts. And can any man believe that such a thing as this is not sinful; that it is not hated by God, and ought not to be abhorred and abolished by man?

But there are certain EFFECTS, springing naturally and necessarily out of such a system, which must also be considered in forming a proper estimate of its character.

1. Its most striking effect is *to deprave and degrade its subjects, by removing from them the strongest natural checks to human corruption.* As there are certain laws impressed upon the elements, by which God works to preserve the beauty and order of the material creation, so these

are certain principles of human nature by which he works to save the moral world from ruin. These principles operate on every man in his natural condition of freedom—restraining his vicious propensities and regulating his deportment. The fires of innate depravity, which, if permitted to burst forth, would destroy the individual and desolate society, are thus measurably repressed, and the decencies and enjoyments of life are preserved. The wisdom and goodness of God are thus seen in implanting in man a sense of character, a desire for property, a love for distinction, a thirst for power, and a zeal for family advancement. All these feelings working in the minds of individuals, though not unmixed with evil, combine to promote their own happiness and the welfare of communities; and they are inferior, in the good which they produce, only to those high religious principles which constitute the image of God in the soul of man. The presence of these principles only can compensate for the absence of those natural feelings. Whenever, then, these natural feelings are crushed or eradicated in any human being, he is stripped of the nobler attributes of humanity, and is degraded into a creature of mere appetite and passion. His sensuality is the only cord by which you can draw him. His hopes and fears all concentrate upon the objects of his appetites. He sinks far down towards a level with the beast of the field, and can be moved to action only by such appeals as influence the lunatic and the brute. This is the condition to which slavery reduces the great mass of those who wear its brutalizing yoke. Its effects upon their souls are far worse than its effects upon their bodies. Character, property, distinction, power, and family respectability, are all withdrawn from the reach of the slave. No object is presented to excite and cultivate those higher feelings whose exercise would repress his passions and regulate his appetites. Thus slavery deranges and ruins the moral machinery of man; it cuts the sinews of the soul; it extracts from human nature the salt that purifies and preserves it, and leaves it a corrupting mass of appetite and passion.

2. *It dooms thousands of human beings to hopeless ignorance.* The acquisition of knowledge requires exertion; and the man who is to continue through life in bondage has no strong motive of interest to induce such exertion; for knowledge is not valuable to him, as to one who eats the fruits of his own labors. The acquisition of knowledge requires also facilities of books, teachers, and time, which can be only adequately furnished by masters: and those who desire to perpetuate slavery will never furnish these facilities. If slaves are educated, it must involve

some outlay on the part of the master. And what reliance for such a sacrifice can be placed on the generosity and virtue of one who looks on them as his property, and who has been trained to consider every dollar expended on them as lost, unless it contributes to increase their capacity for yielding him valuable service? He will have them taught to work, and will ordinarily feed and clothe them, so as to enable them to perform their work to advantage. But more than this it is inconsistent with our knowledge of human nature to expect that he will do for them. The present state of instruction among this race answers exactly to what we might thus naturally anticipate. Throughout our whole land, so far as we can learn, there is but one school in which, during the week, slaves can be taught. The light of three or four Sabbath-schools is seen glimmering through the darkness that covers the black population of a whole State. Here and there a family is found where humanity and religion impel the master, mistress, or children, to the laborious task of private instruction. Great honor is due to those engaged in this philanthropic and self-denying course, and their reward shall be received in the day when even a cup of cold water, given from Christian motives, shall secure a recompense. But, after all, what is the utmost amount of instruction given to slaves? Those who enjoy the most of it, are fed with but the crumbs of knowledge which fall from their master's table—they are clothed with the mere shreds and tatters of learning.

Nor is it to be expected that this state of things will become better, *unless it is determined that slavery shall cease.* The impression is almost universal that intellectual elevation unfits men for servitude, and renders it impossible to retain them in this condition. This impression is unquestionably correct. The weakness and ignorance of their victims is the only safe foundation on which injustice and oppression can rest. And the effort to keep in bondage men to whom knowledge has imparted power, would be like the insane attempt of the Persian tyrant to chain the waves of the sea, and whip its boisterous waters into submission. We may as soon expect to fetter the winds, seal up the clouds, or extinguish the fires of the volcano, as to prevent enlightened minds from recovering their natural condition of freedom. Hence, in some of our States laws have been enacted prohibiting, under severe penalties, the instruction of the blacks; and even where such laws do not exist, there are formidable numbers who oppose with deep hostility every effort to enlighten the mind of the negro. These men are determined that slavery shall be perpetuated, and they know that their universal education must be followed by their universal emancipation. They are then acting wisely, according to the wisdom of this world, when they deny education to slaves; they are adopting a measure necessary to secure their determined purpose. It is, however, policy akin to that which once induced the ruffian violators of female chastity to cut out the tongue and cut off the hands of their victim, to disable her from uttering or writing their names. She had to be maimed, or they would be brought to justice. It is such policy as the robber exhibits, who silences in death the voices that might accuse him, and buries in the grave the witnesses of his crimes. He is determined to pursue his occupation, and his safety in it requires that he should not indulge in the weakness of keeping a conscience. How horrible must be that system which, in the opinion of even its strongest advocates, demands, as the necessary condition of its existence, that knowledge should be shut out from the minds of those who live under it; that they should be reduced as nearly as possible to the level of brutes or living machines; that the powers of their souls should be crushed. Let each one of us ask, can such a system be aided or even tolerated without deep criminality?

3. *It deprives its subjects in a great measure of the privileges of the Gospel.* You may be startled at this statement, and feel disposed to exclaim, "Our slaves are always permitted and even encouraged to attend upon the ordinances of worship." But a candid and close examination will show the correctness of our charge. The privileges of the Gospel, as enjoyed by the white population in this land, consist in free access to the Scriptures, a regular gospel ministry, and domestic means of grace. Neither of these is, to any extent worth naming, enjoyed by slaves, as a moment's consideration will satisfactorily show. The law, as it is here, does not prevent *free access to the Scriptures;* but ignorance, the natural result of their condition, does. The Bible is before them, but it is to them a sealed book. "The light shineth in the darkness, but the darkness comprehendeth it not." Like the paralytic who lay for years by the pool of Bethesda, the waters of healing are near them, but no kind hand enables them to try their efficacy. Very few enjoy the advantages of a *regular gospel ministry.* They are, it is true, permitted generally, and often encouraged, to attend upon the ministrations specially designed for their masters. But the instructions communicated on such occasions are above the level of their capacities. They listen as to prophesyings in an unknown tongue. The preachers of their own color are still farther from ministering to their spiritual wants, as these impart

to them, not of their knowledge, but their ignorance; they heat their animal feelings, but do not kindle a flame of intelligent devotion. It has been proposed by some zealous and devoted friends of the colored race, to supply the deficiency of gospel ministrations among them by the employment of suitable missionaries, who may labor exclusively among them. We need not here speculate on the probable results of such a scheme, if carried into effect in a community where there is no intention to emancipate; for before there is found among us benevolence enough to adopt and execute it on a scale large enough to effect any highly valuable purpose, the community will be already ripe for measures of emancipation. Such a spirit of kindness towards this unfortunate race as this scheme presupposes, can never coexist with a determination to keep them in hopeless bondage. Further, there are no houses of worship exclusively devoted to the colored population. The galleries of our own churches, which are set apart to their use, would not hold the tenth part of their numbers; and even these few seats are in general thinly occupied So that, as a body, it is evident that our slaves do not enjoy the public ordinances of religion. *Domestic means of grace* are still more rare among them. Here and there a family is found whose servants are taught to bow with their masters around the fireside altar. But their peculiarly adverse circumstances, combined with the natural alienation of their hearts from God, render abortive the slight efforts of most masters to induce their attendance on the domestic services of religion. And if we visit the cottages of those slaves who live apart from their masters, where do we find them reading their Bibles and kneeling together before a throne of mercy? Family ordinances of religion are almost unknown among the blacks. We do not wish to exaggerate the description of this deplorable religious condition of our colored population. We know that instances of true piety are frequently found among them; but these instances we all know to be awfully disproportionate to their numbers, and to the extent of those means of grace which exist around them. When the missionaries of the cross enter a heathen land, their hope of fully Christianizing it rests upon the fact that they can array and bring to bear upon the minds of these children of ignorance and sin all those varied means which God has appointed for the reformation of man. But while the system of slavery continues among us, these means can never be efficiently and fully employed for the conversion of the degraded sons of Africa. Yet "God hath made them of one blood" with ourselves; hath provided for them the same redemption· hath in His providence cast souls upon our care, and hath clearly intimated to us the doom of him who "seeth his brother have need, and shutteth up his bowels of compassion from him." If by our example, our silence, or our sloth, we perpetuate a system which paralyzes our hands when we attempt to convey to them the bread of life, and which inevitably consigns the great mass of them to unending perdition, can we be guiltless in the sight of Him who hath made us stewards of His grace?

4. *This system licenses and produces great cruelty.* The law places the whip in the hands of the master, and its use, provided he avoid destroying life, is limited only by his own pleasure. Considering the absolute power with which our people are armed, it must be acknowledged that the treatment of their dependents is, in general, singularly humane. Many circumstances operate here to mitigate the rigors of perpetual servitude; and it is probably the fact that no body of slaves have been ever better fed, better clothed, and less abused, than the slaves of Kentucky. Still, they have no security for their comfort but the humanity and generosity of men who have been trained to regard them not as brethren, but as property. Humanity and generosity are at best poor guarantees for the protection of those who cannot assert their rights, and over whom law throws no protection. Our own condition we would feel to be wretched indeed, if no law secured us from the insults and maltreatment *even of our equals.* But superiority naturally begets contempt, and contempt generates maltreatment, for checking which we can rely not on virtue, but only on law. There are in our land hundreds of thousands clothed with arbitrary powers over those whom they are educated to regard as their property, as the instruments of their will, as creatures beneath their sympathy, devoid of all the feelings which dignify humanity, and but one remove above cattle. Is it not certain that many of these hundreds of thousands will inflict outrages on their despised dependents? There are now in our whole land two millions of human beings exposed, defenceless, to every insult and every injury, short of maiming or death, which their fellow-men may choose to inflict. They suffer all that can be inflicted by wanton caprice, by grasping avarice, by brutal lust, by malignant spite, and by insane anger. Their happiness is the sport of every whim and the prey of every passion that may occasionally or habitually infest the master's bosom. If we could calculate the amount of woe endured by ill-treated slaves, it would overwhelm every compassionate heart—it would move even the obdurate to sympathy. There is also a vast sum of suffering inflicted upon the slave by humane masters, as a punishment for that

idleness and misconduct which slavery naturally produces. The ordinary motives to exertion in men are withdrawn from the slave. Some unnatural stimulus must then be substituted, and the whip presents itself as the readiest and most efficient. But the application of the whip to produce industry, is like the application of the galvanic fluid to produce muscular exertion. The effect is powerful indeed, but momentary; and, if often applied, it is exhaustive and destructive to the system. It can never be used as a substitute for the healthful and agreeable nervous stimulus with which nature has supplied us. Equally vain is the attempt to supply by the whip the deficiency of natural motives to exertion; it produces misery and degradation. Yet, inadequate as is this substitute, it is the best that can be had; it must be used while the system lasts: the condition of the slave is unnatural, and his treatment must correspond to his condition. We are shocked to hear of epicures who cause the animals on which they feast to be whipped to death, that their flesh may be more delicate and delicious to the taste. We feel it to be disgusting and intolerable cruelty thus to inflict pain even upon a beast, merely to satisfy the cravings of luxury; and shall we excuse ourselves if a desire for ease or wealth leads us to sanction, sustain, and assist in perpetuating a system which, as long as it lasts, must lacerate the bodies and grind down the feelings of millions of rational and immortal beings?

Brutal stripes, and all the varied kinds of personal indignities, are not the only species of cruelty which slavery licenses. The law does not recognize the family relations of a slave, and extends to him no protection in the enjoyment of domestic endearments. The members of a slave family may be forcibly separated, so that they shall never more meet until the final judgment. And cupidity often induces the masters to practise what the law allows. Brothers and sisters, parents and children, husbands and wives, are torn asunder, and permitted to see each other no more. *These acts are daily occurring in the midst of us.* The shrieks and the agony often witnessed on such occasions proclaim with a trumpet-tongue the iniquity and cruelty of our system. The cry of these sufferers goes up to the ears of the Lord of Sabaoth. *There is not a neighborhood where these heart-rending scenes are not displayed.* There is not a village or road that does not behold the sad procession of manacled outcasts, whose chains and mournful countenances tell that they are exiled by force from all that their hearts held dear. Our Church, years ago, raised its voice of solemn warning against this flagrant violation of every principle of mercy, justice, and humanity. Yet we blush to announce to you and to the world that this warning has been often disregarded, even by those who hold to our communion. Cases have occurred in our own denomination where professors of the religion of mercy have torn the mother from her children, and sent her into a merciless and returnless exile. Yet acts of discipline have rarely followed such conduct. Far be it from us to ascribe to our people generally a participation in these deeds, or a sympathy with them; they abhor and loathe them. But while the system, of which these cruelties are the legitimate offspring, is tolerated among us, it is exceedingly difficult to inflict punishment upon their perpetrators. If we commence discipline for *any* acts which the laws of slavery sanction, where shall we stop? What principle is there which will justify us in cutting off a twig or branch of this poison-tree that will not, if carried fairly out, force us to proceed and hew down its trunk and dig up its roots? These cruelties are only the loathsome ulcers which show corruption in the blood and rottenness in the bones of this system. They may be bound up and mollified with ointment; they may be hidden from the sight; but they cannot be entirely removed until there is a thorough renovation within. Our Churches cannot be entirely pure, even from the grosser pollutions of slavery, until we are willing to pledge ourselves to the destruction of the whole system.

The voice of the civilized world has been lifted up in execration of the despot who recently dragged numbers of the unhappy Poles from their country, separating husbands and wives, parents and children. But they are his property by the same tenure by which we hold our slaves; and has he not a right, he may exclaim, to do as he pleases with his own? Nay, the security and peace of his dominions require this cruelty. He is not willing to relinquish *the property which he inherited;* and he may tell us, and tell us truly, that it cannot be retained in safety without the adoption of these horrid measures. Can we condemn his conduct, and yet justify our system of slavery? or can we condemn both, and yet be guiltless if we use no efficient exertions to terminate these cruelties among us?

5. *It produces general licentiousness among the slaves.* Marriage, as a *civil ordinance*, they cannot enjoy. Our laws do not recognize this relation as existing among them, and of course do not enforce by any sanction the observance of its duties. Indeed, until slavery "waxeth old and tendeth to decay," there cannot be any legal recognition of the marriage rite, or the enforcement of the consequent duties. For

all regulations on this subject would limit the master's absolute right of property in his slaves. In his disposal of them, he would no longer be at liberty to consult merely his own interest. He could no longer separate the wife and husband to suit the convenience or interest of the purchaser, no matter how advantageous might be the terms offered. And as the wife and husband do not always belong to the same owner, and are not often wanted by the same purchaser, their duties to each other would thus, if enforced by law, frequently conflict with the interests of the master. Hence all the marriage that could ever be allowed to them would be a mere contract, voidable at the master's pleasure. Their present quasi marriages are just such contracts, and are continually thus voided. They are in this way brought to consider the matrimonial engagement as a thing not binding, and they act accordingly. Many of them are united without even the sham and forceless ceremony which is sometimes used. They, to use their own phraseology, "take up with" each other, and live together as long as it suits their mutual convenience or inclination. This wretched system of concubinage inevitably produces revolting licentiousness. This feature in the slave character is so striking, as to induce in many minds the idea that the negro is naturally repugnant to the restraints of matrimony. From the ample and repeated testimonies, however, of such travellers as Park and Lander, who have visited this race in their native land, we learn that their character in this respect is in Africa the reverse of what it is here; that they regard the marriage rite with remarkable sacredness, and scrupulously fulfil its duties. We are then assured by the most unquestionable testimony that their licentiousness is the necessary result of our system, which, destroying the force of the marriage rite, and thus in a measure degrading all the connection between the sexes into mere concubinage, solicits wandering desire, and leads to extensive profligacy. Our familiarity with this consequence of slavery prevents us from regarding it with that horror which it would under other circumstances inspire. The sacredness of the marriage rite is the bulwark of morality, the corner-stone of domestic happiness. It is the foundation on which alone the whole fabric of an organized and virtuous community can be built. On it must rest all those family relations which bind together and cement society. Without it, we might herd together like brutes, but we could no longer live together as human beings. There would be no families, no strong ties of kindred, no domestic endearments softening the manners and curbing the passions. Selfish, sensual, and unrestrained, man would exercise his reason only to minister to the more grovelling propensities of his nature. Any set of men will approximate to this condition just in proportion to their approximation to the practical abolition of matrimonial restraints. And certainly never, in any civilized country, has respect for these restraints been more nearly obliterated than it has been among our blacks. Thus the working of our system of slavery diffuses a moral pestilence among its subjects, tending to wither and blight every thing that is naturally beautiful and good in the character of man. Can this system be tolerated without sin?

6. *This system demoralizes the whites as well as the blacks.* Masters are in a great degree irresponsible for the exercise of their power; and they generally feel that their object in possessing and exercising their dominion is their own utility, and not the good of those over whom they rule. Now, power can never be held or exercised without moral injury to its *possessor*, unless its exercise be subject to responsibility, or unless it be held *mainly* for the good of its *subjects, not of its possessor.* The lives of absolute monarchs furnish us with our most disgusting pictures of human depravity. Few, even of those who had been previously trained to self-control and virtue, have been able to withstand the corrupting influence of unrestrained power. And the effect is in some measure the same where despotic authority is possessed and exercised in a smaller sphere. No man, acquainted with the frailty of the human heart, would desire uncontrolled dominion over his fellow-men. We are sufficiently prone by nature to tyranny and a disregard of the rights and interests of others, without having these feelings developed, cultivated, and matured by a sense of irresponsibility, and by the habit of regarding ourselves as born to command, and others as born to obey. Where a consciousness of responsibility, equality, and dependence, does not check their growth, hard-heartedness, selfishness, and arrogance are in most men fearfully exhibited. And these odious traits of character must be peculiarly marked in those who have from childhood been trained in the school of despotism. The hand of one of our greatest statesmen has strikingly portrayed the demoralizing effects of this system on the minds and manners of the ruling class. "There must doubtless," says Mr. Jefferson, "be an unhappy influence on the manners of our people produced by the existence of slavery among us. The whole commerce between master and slave is a perpetual exercise of the most boisterous passions, the most unrelenting despotism on the one part, and degrading submission on the other. Our children see this, and learn to imitate it; for man is an imitative animal. This quality is the

germ of all education in him. From his cradle to his grave he is learning to do what he sees others do. If a parent could find no motive either in his philanthropy or his self-love for restraining the intemperance of passion towards his slave, it should always be a sufficient one that his child is present. But generally it is not sufficient. The parent storms, the child looks on, catches the lineaments of wrath, puts on the same airs in the circle of smaller slaves, gives a loose to the worst of passions; and, thus nursed, educated, and daily exercised in tyranny, cannot but be stamped by it with odious peculiarities. The man must be a prodigy who can retain his manners and morals undepraved by such circumstances."* Such, according to the testimony of one who had marked its operation with a philosopher's eye, is the character which slavery forms,—a character perfectly the reverse of that which the Gospel requires.

We forbear to picture before you the consequences of that indolence and aversion to all manual occupations which are necessarily engendered in youth surrounded by a servile class who are engaged in these pursuits. These consequences you have all seen and felt and deplored. Such are the evil effects to ourselves and our children of the system which we support. Thus we are made to eat of the bitter food which we prepare for others, and drink of the poisoned cup which our own hands mingled; the sword with which we unthinkingly destroy others is thus made to drink our own blood. These evils, if duly estimated, are alone sufficient to arm us with implacable hostility towards the system from which they spring. And, in view of these effects, we can almost adopt the opinion expressed a few years since on the scaffold, by one who was executed for the murder of a slave: "Slavery is a bad system; it is even *worse* for the master than it is for the slaves." It is a system which reminds us of the dark magic of ancient days, an art as fatal to those who exercised it as to those who were their victims.

7. *This system draws down upon us the vengeance of Heaven.* "God is just," and "He will render to every one according to his works." Oppression can never escape unpunished while He, who hath emphatically declared that he is the "Judge of the widow" and "the Father of the fatherless," is on the throne of the universe. "If thou forbear to deliver them that are drawn unto death, and those that are ready to be slain; if thou sayest, Behold, we knew it not; doth not He that pondereth the heart consider it? and He that keepeth thy soul, doth not

* Jefferson's Notes on Virginia, p. 319.

He know it? and shall He not render to every man according to his works?" Not a sparrow falls to the ground, we are told, without the notice of God; how much more doth He mark the abuse and oppression of a creature who bears His own peculiar image? "The very hairs of our head are all numbered;" much more are the groanings of the oppressed and the sighings of the prisoner recorded by Him who says that His name is "Gracious," and that His "ear is ever open to the cry of the poor and needy." The blood of Abel did not soak into the ground unheeded; it called down judgment upon the guilty man who had smitten his brother, and it drove him out a wanderer from the land of his birth, a fugitive from the presence of the Lord. But the sore cry of millions of the down-trodden has gone up to heaven from the midst of us; this cry is still swelling upward; and if there be righteousness on the throne of the universe, it must bring down vials of wrath upon the heads of all who are engaged in this guilty work. And when He cometh to execute vengeance, "who may abide the day of His coming?" Who can stand before His indignation? Who can stand up in the fierceness of His anger? We see the truth of what the prophet declares, that "the Lord is slow to anger;" but we are assured that it is equally true that He is "great in power, and will not at all acquit the wicked: the Lord hath His way in the whirlwind and in the storm, and the clouds are the dust of His feet."

Brethren, we profess to be Christians; we reverence the holy revelation which God has given; we look to its precepts for guidance, and to its denunciations for warnings. We know that the *principles* of the divine dealings are the same in every age, and that what God said to those of old, when we are in similar circumstances, He saith unto us. Listen, then, to one of the many intimations he has given us of the way in which He regards slavery, and the way in which He will punish it. "The people of the land have used oppression, and exercised robbery, and have vexed the poor and needy; yea, they have oppressed the stranger wrongfully. And I sought for a man among them, that should stand in the gap before me for the land, that I should not destroy it: but I found none. Therefore have I poured out mine indignation upon them; I have consumed them with the fire of my wrath: their own way have I recompensed upon their heads, saith the Lord God." Ezek. xxii. 29–31. Can we despise the instructions of the Almighty? Shall we shut our eyes and close our ears against the admonitions of the great Judge of the earth? Shall we not arise and "stand in the gap before Him for the land, that He may not destroy it?" Though our "nest may be built on high," and "our defence be the munitions of rocks," we cannot escape, if God rise up against us. He can blast our prosperity; He can drown us in blood; He can blot out our existence and our name from under heaven.

Let us remember too, that not only as a people, but as individuals, God will deal with us. The day is soon coming when every man's works which he hath wrought shall be tried as by fire, and we must then "eat of the fruits of our own ways."

We have now exhibited fairly, but briefly, the nature and effects of slavery. For the truth of our facts we refer to your own observations; for the correctness of our reasoning we appeal to your judgments and consciences.

* * * * * * * *

[After considering and answering various objections, the committee submit the following plan, and their closing appeal:]

The plan which we propose is, for the master to retain, during a limited period, and with a regard to the real welfare of the slave, that authority which he before held in perpetuity, and solely for his own interest. Let the full future liberty of the slave be secured against all contingencies by a recorded deed of emancipation, to take effect at a specified time. In the mean while, let the servant be treated with kindness; let all those things which degrade him be removed; let him enjoy means of instruction; let his moral and religious improvement be sought; let his prospects be presented before him, to stimulate him to acquire those habits of foresight, economy, industry, activity, skill, and integrity, which will fit him for using well the liberty he is soon to enjoy. That master is, in our opinion, doing most for the destruction of this system who thus sets in operation a machinery which, in a given and limited period, will not only unbind the body of the slave, but will, link by link, and in the only way in which it can be effected, twist off the fetters that now cramp his soul. If the master retains his authority over his servants only for a time, that he may enjoy ampler opportunities of employing means for their amendment and elevation; if he regards them as a trust committed to him by his Master and theirs, for their mutual benefit, and no longer as property, of which he has the uncontrolled disposal for his own selfish ends; if he acts and feels thus, he is not only free from guilt, but he is "bringing forth fruits meet for repentance," he is doing the work of righteousness and humanity.

* * * * * * * *

Brethren, there are three courses before you, one of which you must choose: either to emancipate immediately and without preparation, or to pursue some such plan of gradual emancipation as we propose, or to continue to lend your example and influence to perpetuate slavery. It is improbable that you will adopt the first course; if then you refuse to concur in the plan of gradual emancipation and act upon it, however you may lull conscience, you are lending your aid to perpetuate a demoralizing and cruel system, which it would be an insult to God to imagine that He does not abhor; a system which exhibits power without responsibility, toil without recompense, life without liberty, law without justice, wrongs without redress, infamy without crime, punishment without guilt, and families without marriage—a system which will not only make victims of the present unhappy generation, inflicting upon them the degradation, the contempt, the lassitude, and the anguish of hopeless oppression, but which even aims at transmitting this heritage of injury and woe to their children and their children's children, down to their latest posterity. Can any Christian contemplate without trembling his own agency in the perpetuation of such a system? And what will be the end of these scenes of misery and vice? Shall we wait until worldly politicians and legislators may rise up and bid them cease? We shall wait in vain. Already have we heard the sentiment proclaimed from high places and by the voice of authority, that a race of slaves is necessary to the existence of freedom. Is it from those who utter such sentiments that we expect deliverance to come? No; reformation must commence where we are divinely taught that "judgment must begin—*at the house of God.*" This work must be done; and Christians must begin it, and begin it soon, or wrath will come upon us. The groans of millions do not rise forever unheeded before the throne of the Almighty. The hour of doom must soon arrive, the storm must soon gather, the bolt of destruction must soon be hurled, and the guilty must soon be dashed in pieces. The voice of past history and the voice of inspiration both warn us that the catastrophe must come, unless averted by repentance. And let us remember that we are each of us individually responsible. We are individually assisting to pile up this mountain of guilt. And even if temporal judgments do not fall upon our day, we are not on that account the more safe from punishment. If we "know our Lord's will and do it not, we shall be beaten with many stripes." The sophistry and false reasoning by which we may delude our own souls, will not blind the eyes which "are as a flame of fire." A few years at most will place us where we would gladly give all the slaves of a universe to buy off the punishment that oppression brings down upon the soul. It may be difficult to do our duty, but it will be far more difficult to stand in the judgment without having done it.

Brethren, we have done. The hour is coming in which the slave and his master must stand together before the tribunal of God, a God who judges righteously. Are you prepared to place yourselves before Him who will decide upon your eternal destiny, and say that you have done justice to those whom you now hold in bondage? Are you prepared to say, "As I have done unto these, so let it be done unto me; as I have showed mercy, so let me receive mercy at the hands of my Judge." Anticipate, we beseech you, the feelings and decision of that great day which is fast hastening on; try yourselves now, as God will then try you. "What doth the Lord require of thee, but to do justly, to love mercy, and to walk humbly with your God?" Are you "doing justly" while you retain your fellow-men in hopeless boudage? Are you "loving mercy" while you are supporting a system that degrades and brutalizes beings whom God created in His own image? These are solemn questions. Let reason answer them, and let conscience decide your future course.

JOHN BROWN, *Chairman.*

JOHN C. YOUNG, *Secretary.*

The foregoing paper calls for no comment. It speaks for itself; it is from men of the highest character; and they describe the system of slavery as it existed *under their own observation.*

MOVEMENT FOR EMANCIPATION IN 1849.

The next step of public importance which we note, revealing the sentiments of the people of Kentucky, occurred in 1849. The Legislature submitted to the people the question of calling a Convention to revise the State Constitution, and the people decided affirmatively. The subject of slavery was a main topic of consideration in the canvass for the Convention. Many citizens, embracing many of the largest slaveholders, were in favor of providing in the new or revised Constitution for the removal of the system from the State. "For months previous to the election of members of the Convention to frame a new Constitution, the press teemed with arguments and appeals, public lecturers and orators travelled over the State to address the people, and county and State Conventions were held to embody and express the sentiments of the contending parties."*

A meeting was held in Lexington, on the 14th of April, 1849, which is thus spoken of:

The object of the meeting having been explained, in a few eloquent remarks by the Hon. Henry Clay and Rev. R. J. Breckinridge, on motion of the latter gentleman, the following resolutions were unanimously adopted:

1st. That this meeting, composed of citizens of the county of Fayette, met in pursuance of public notice, to consider the question of the perpetuation of slavery in this Commonwealth, considering that hereditary slavery, as it exists among us, (1) Is contrary to the natural rights of mankind; (2) Is opposed to the fundamental principles of free government; (3) Is inconsistent with a state of sound morality; (4) Is hostile to the prosperity of the Commonwealth; we are therefore of the opinion that it ought not to be made perpetual, &c.

The second resolution recommended the holding of a State Convention at Frankfort, on the 25th of April, to consider the subject of emancipation, and appointed thirty delegates. At this Convention, held on the day above named, "the Rev. Dr. R. J. Breckinridge submitted a document, which, after being amended with his concurrence, was adopted."

PRINCIPLES OF THE STATE CONVENTION.

We merely give the preamble, and the first and main point of the paper, as all that is essential to our purpose,

*The facts stated concerning this movement for Emancipation in Kentucky in 1849, we take mainly from an article in the *Biblical Repertory*, for October of that year, founded on an Address of Dr. R. J. Breckinridge, entitled "The Question of Negro Slavery, and the New Constitution of Kentucky." This Address is before us.

showing the judgment of the State Convention upon the character of the system which they sought to remove. This portion of the document is as follows:

> This Convention, composed of citizens of the Commonwealth of Kentucky, and representing the opinions and wishes of a large number of our fellow-citizens throughout the Commonwealth, met in the capitol on the 25th of April, 1849, to consider what course it becomes those who are opposed to the increase and to the perpetuity of slavery in this State to pursue in the approaching canvass for members of the Convention, called to amend the Constitution, adopts the propositions which follow, as expressing its judgment in the premises:
>
> 1. Believing that involuntary hereditary slavery, as it exists by law in this State, is injurious to the prosperity of the Commonwealth, inconsistent with the fundamental principles of free government, contrary to the natural rights of mankind, and injurious to a pure state of morals, we are of opinion that it ought not to be increased, and that it ought not to be perpetuated in this Commonwealth.

The other propositions of the paper, three in number, relate to matters of detail respecting the mode recommended to the Constitutional Convention for the ultimate and entire removal of slavery from the State. This paper is signed officially by "Henry Clay, of Bourbon, President," and by several Vice-Presidents and Secretaries.

EMANCIPATIONISTS DEFEATED.—CAUSES.

Dr. R. J. Breckinridge was an Emancipation candidate for the State Constitutional Convention, but was defeated; and it is said, that "not more than one or two emancipationists, if any, according to the public papers," were "elected." When, therefore, the Convention assembled, instead of providing for emancipation, they placed barriers in its way far greater than existed before; making a course of measures of some six or seven years duration necessary to reach the practical point in any system of emancipation, immediate or gradual, through constitutional and legislative forms. We have often heard it said in Kentucky, that while the largest slaveholders were in favor of emancipation at that time, the non-slaveholding vote of the State gave the Convention the proslavery character it possessed.*

The *Repertory* thus speaks of the failure of the emancipation cause, and of the agencies employed in its behalf:

It may be difficult for those out of the State to discern all the causes of this lamentable defeat. There are, however, some things connected with the subject patent to every observer. In the first place, the failure of the cause of emancipation is not to be referred to any want of ability on the part of its advocates. Those advocates comprise some of the most distinguished men not only of Kentucky, but of the Union; men who have no superiors in the power to control public sentiment. If the cause of freedom could have been carried, it must have been carried by such men. If any appeals could produce conviction, it would have been produced by the address mentioned at the head of this article. Self-interest, ignorance, and prejudice, are proof against any thing; but the human mind, when unbiassed, and sufficiently enlightened to comprehend their import, cannot resist such arguments, nor harden itself against such sentiments as are here presented. It must be conceded, then, that the cause of emancipation in Kentucky has failed for the present, in spite of the exertions of men of the highest order of talents of which the country can boast.

PRESBYTERIANS UNANIMOUSLY FOR EMANCIPATION.

Again, some seem disposed to refer this failure to the lukewarmness of the Churches in Kentucky. We are not prepared to speak on this subject for other Churches, but surely this reproach cannot fairly be brought against our own Church. *The Presbyterians have taken the lead in this struggle.* There is not a prominent man in the Synod of Kentucky, who has not been conspicuous for his zeal and efforts in behalf of emancipation. No names in connection with this subject are more

* The *Repertory* says on this point: "The impression seems very general that the emancipationists have been defeated by the slaveholders. This is a great mistake. A large and most influential class of the slaveholders are themselves emancipationists." "The fact, therefore, that the non-slaveholders in Kentucky have voted against emancipation, is not to be attributed to the influence of the slave-owners."

prominent than those of Drs. R. J. Breckinridge, John C. Young, William L. Breckinridge, *and of the Rev. Mr. Robinson, of Frankfort.* As far as we know, there is not a single Presbyterian minister whose name is found among *the advocates of slavery.*

We give these extracts because they state the case better than we can do, and because we wish the facts to go forth with greater weight than our individual authority could impart to them. They were written and published soon after the events occurred, and we are not aware that they have ever been called in question. The material facts which bear upon our immediate purpose are: that in 1849, "Presbyterians" took "the lead" in Kentucky for emancipation; that there was then "not a prominent man in the Synod" who was "not *conspicuous* for his *zeal* in behalf of emancipation;" that among the distinguished "names" than which none were "more prominent," is here given "the *Rev. Mr. Robinson*, of Frankfort;" and that there was, at that time, "not a single Presbyterian minister" in the Synod of Kentucky, "whose name was found among *the advocates of slavery.*"

DRS. HUMPHREY AND W. L. BRECKINRIDGE UPON EMANCIPATION IN 1849.

In the year 1850, Drs. William L. Breckinridge and E. P. Humphrey published a vindication of Dr. E. D. Mac Master from the aspersions cast upon him by Dr. N. L. Rice, in which they bear the following testimony to the position taken by Presbyterian ministers, elders, and Church-members, in Kentucky, for emancipation:

It is well known that during the past year a movement was made for emancipation,—that is, the ultimate extinction of slavery,—in the State of Kentucky. The first public meeting on this subject, of which we heard, was addressed by two Presbyterian ministers. The address to the friends of the cause throughout the State, calling a convention at the seat of Government, was drawn up by a Presbyterian minister.

When the Convention met, in April, 1849, there appeared, among its members, more than twenty Presbyterian ministers and ruling elders. * * * The Presbyterian ministers in Kentucky, so far as we know, almost without exception, *and the great body of the ruling elders and private members of the Churches, concurred in these views expressed by the Convention* [referring to the paper adopted as given above]. Nor have we heard of any expression of the public sentiment of the Church at large, censuring them in this behalf.*

According to this testimony, from two gentlemen who were at the time Pastors of Churches in the city of Louisville, the vast body of ministers, elders, and people of the Presbyterian Church in Kentucky, were, in 1849, in favor of the removal of slavery from the State.

POSITION OF DR. R. J. BRECKINRIDGE IN 1849.

The stand taken by Dr. R. J. Breckinridge is already shown by the resolutions he introduced, and which were

* The *direct* purpose of the article from which we here quote, was not to exhibit the sentiments of the writers or those of the people of Kentucky upon slavery. This is done very fully and satisfactorily, but it was only *incidental* to their main object. As said above, their direct aim was to vindicate a distinguished Theological Professor from the charge of being a disturber of the Church in propagating ultra-abolition doctrines, brought against him by Dr. Rice. They do this triumphantly, by showing: (1.) That Dr. MacMaster simply held the views formally set forth by the Church in which he was a minister; (2.) That these views were the same as Professors in other seminaries held; (3.) That they were the same as had been acknowledged by the ministers, elders, and people of Kentucky in 1849; (4.) That even Dr. Rice himself had professed to approve the action of Presbyterians in Kentucky in 1849; (5.) And that, so far from having been a disturber of the Church, the whole course of Dr. MacMaster showed, as illustrated by specific facts which they cite, that he had been specially prudent, and had said and done very little upon the subject of slavery; far less, indeed, in the line of writing and lecturing, than the man who had assailed him. Immediately following the quotation given above, Drs. Breckinridge and Humphrey say: "But what does Dr. Rice think of them [people of Kentucky] and their movement? They have said full as much as Dr. MacMaster has said against slavery, and they have done a vast deal more. If he must be disfranchised, proscribed, and hunted down, what is due to those whose little fingers are thicker than his loins? * * * This would seem to be sufficient to show that Dr. Rice's clamor against Dr. MacMaster is without the shadow of foundation. * * * We find in Dr. MacMaster's views on the subject, no objection to him as a friend, as a minister, or as a Professor."

adopted in the Fayette County meeting, and again by the paper adopted by the State Emancipation Convention which he presented. During the canvass for the State Constitutional Convention, Dr. Breckinridge issued an Address to the people, on "The Question of Negro Slavery and the New Constitution," from which we give a few sentences showing the character of the institution of slavery in his judgment, and the course he urged the people to take.

In the following paragraph he gives a graphic view of proslavery statements:

> The bulk, however, of the proslavery candidates for the convention and the bulk of that party, so far from agreeing that slavery is an evil —which it is the misfortune of the State to be obliged to tolerate—profess to consider it a great advantage and blessing, which it is our duty to foster, to enlarge, and to perpetuate. They desire to surround it with new constitutional guarantees, to make it more difficult to be abolished, in all time to come; and to secure the constitutional prohibition of manumissions within this State, and the constitutional guarantee of slave importations into it. The burden of their disquisitions is the divine origin of the right of property of man in man, the marked approval of slavery by Christ and His Apostles—the immense superiority of the people in slaveholding communities to all other people—the vast advantages of slavery, in a moral, social, and pecuniary point of view; the licentiousness, poverty, and degradation of the poor whites in all countries where there are no slaves; the turpitude, folly, and impracticability of all schemes of emancipation; the utter unfitness of negroes for any other condition than slavery; and, as the conclusion of the whole, the necessity for a larger surrender of power by the people in the new constitution in regard to slavery, in order that the institution may be placed on a footing at once more firm and more durable. I am aware that unless some collector of the essays, circulars, handbills, speeches, pamphlets, and newspaper articles to which our present discussions have given birth, shall transmit to posterity a fair sample of the political literature of our day, our children will hardly believe that such things were possible. In point of fact, the statements I have made come short of what I hear and read every day.

In the following paragraphs, Dr. Breckinridge shows the character and influence of the system of slavery, and appeals to the people in thrilling terms to take such a course as shall prevent its further increase and work its entire removal:

How clear is it, that Kentucky should place in a convention invested with such transcendent powers, none but pure, wise, enlightened, and trustful men; and that such men, when they are met, should act for Kentucky; for all Kentucky, and for her highest and largest good; and that Kentucky, therefore, is the great party in these affairs!

Now is it for the interest, the honor, the riches, the power, the glory, the peace, the advancement, the happiness, of this great Commonwealth, to exert her sovereign power in such a way, and to the intent, that involuntary, hereditary, domestic negro slavery shall be indefinitely increased and everlastingly established in her bosom? Men of Kentucky, ask yourselves that question; then lay your hands upon your hearts and answer it! Is it her bounden duty to increase and to perpetuate an institution which the whole civilized world except the fifteen slave States on this continent, and the Empire of Brazil, unites in condemning and denouncing? Is it her sacred duty to set at defiance the voice of the human race? Is it laid upon her by an irresistible obligation to do this in the face of a world struggling for freedom, and looking to this country for examples of liberty, justice, and right? * * * I shall not speak of the private condition of slaves, or their individual treatment. What now concerns us is the state of public law. The law, as to all other subjects, is often better on the statute-book than in practice; for the conduct of men is not always as good as their principles, or professions. On this subject, it is my opinion that the law is worse than the practice under it; and this is one of the anomalies of slavery, that *the evil element in it constantly gets the mastery.* Slavery, as it exists by law in this State, presents this aspect: 1st. The rights of property are absolutely and universally abolished, as to the slaves. 2d. The rights of person and character are unknown, as to them, except as the interest of the master and the public peace may demand the recognition. 3d. The institution of marriage, as between slaves, has no legal recognition, nor do marital rights exist as to them. 4th. The relation of parent and child, as between slaves, is not recognized by the law, except in determining questions of property. Now it is perfectly obvious that every one of these rights is inherent in human nature, and that their existence and their protection lie at the foundation of human society, which could not exist for a day, under any form, if these rights were universally abolished. Moreover, they are all of divine authority; and as the State itself—that is, human society—is ordained of God, we have one of God's institutions abolishing, as to immense numbers of His rational creatures, the very foundations on which He has erected that institution, and rendered possible the social state He ordained for those creatures. This is a condition of things for whose increase there can be no justification; and whose everlasting continuance can be defended only upon grounds which subvert the order of nature, the ordinations of heaven, and the foundations of the social state. * * * Our divine religion has been invoked against us. God, the creator of man, and his infinite benefactor, it is constantly alleged, is the great Author of the institution by which man has the most effectually defaced God's image in man. Jesus of Nazareth, the friend of sinners, meant, we are told, by His great law of love, that man should enslave his fellow-man; by His sublime revelation of the universal bond of human brotherhood, to teach us that we might afflict and crush all around us; by His royal law of doing to others as we wish them to do to us, to give us a rule by which to limit and restrict our bowels of compassion within rational bounds! These are great expositions; and the more to be cordially received, as they are uttered by those having no sort of interest or motive in perverting the word of God; and as they accord so precisely with the whole sentiments of God's people throughout all ages! Look around you, my countrymen. On which side of these questions is the great body of the disciples of Jesus Christ? On which side are to be found the most of those who seem to you to understand, to practise, and to love God's law? Why do you hear in popular addresses, and read in resolutions of popular assemblies, such denunciations of the Ministers of the Gospel, whose abuse is a staple theme, in a large portion of the slavery party? Ask your hearts, is not all this natural—is it not all just what might have been expected? Ask the fiercest of those who denounce us, whether, in their calm moments, they think Christian people and Christian ministers had better plead for or against the suffering and the oppressed—for or against the liberties of mankind? What is happening around us, has happened everywhere. What men have blushed to advocate upon their own responsibility, they have endeavored to justify in the name of the adorable God, and then traduced His servants for bearing testimony against them. But has that arrested the arm of the Lord? Follow His glorious word across the track of ages, and make with it the circuit of the world. Where was this institution of hereditary slavery ever abolished, where a divine revelation had not come? Where, on the other hand, has hereditary slavery held its ground unshaken, in the midst of the light of this Heaven-descended truth? Surely God's people know, if anybody knows, what is God's mind. Surely God's word, by means of His word, is a reliable exposition of what He designed that word to accomplish.

The record which is thus made by the Emancipation party in Kentucky, in 1849, is one, in our judgment, of which the persons concerned will never have cause to be ashamed. They took their noble stand in a great popular movement on the side of right; and though defeated, they were not dishonored. It is no doubt quite as clear now,—and perhaps far more palpable, as seen in the perils that are now upon the State and the Nation, growing out of slavery,—to all the surviving actors who favored emancipation in 1849, as well as to those who opposed them, that it would have been infinitely better for the State, had the people at large concurred in the system then sought to be inaugurated.

HON. GARRETT DAVIS ON SLAVERY IN 1849.

Mr. Davis, now in the United States Senate from Kentucky, was a member of the Constitutional Convention held in 1849. In a discussion on slavery in that body, he is reported as saying:

But it appears to me that any intelligent and carefully reflecting mind must come to the conclusion that slavery is to have but a transitory existence in Kentucky. The general sentiment of the world is against it, before which, in fifty years, it has receded vastly; and this sentiment is deeply and widely formed in our limits, and among our own people. * * * The history of slavery, as we have it, proves in all ages of the past that it *is progressing to its end.* That consummation is in the course of events, and when men throw themselves in the current of events to hasten, *or to retard,* they are but *straws.* Let all *straws* be kept out of that section of this *resistless* current which flows through Kentucky, *and let it roll on in its undisturbed power.*

We have said that those who took bold and decided ground for emancipation then, made up an enduring and honorable record. This is especially true of the Presbyterian clergy. Their posterity will not be ashamed of them.

A GLORIOUS RECORD TARNISHED.

But where do we find some of them now? On which side are they battling about slavery now,—not as the institution was then, reposing in peace, but—when it has risen up in its treasonable rage and is filling the land with carnage and wailing; when it is carrying fire and sword to the homes of Kentucky; and when all this is undertaken and prosecuted for the sole purpose of *perpetuating forever* the system which in 1849 the Presbyterians of Kentucky wished, unanimously, to remove from among them?

The "Rev. Mr. Robinson, of Frankfort," so "*conspicuous* for his zeal in behalf of emancipation" in 1849, is Dr. Stuart Robinson, of Toronto, Canada, now editor of *The True Presbyterian*, issued in Louisville, Kentucky. That paper, as we have proved in a previous chapter, is filled with treason against the Government, and is aiding the rebellion as far as it *dare go* in that direction. It of course advocates the system of slavery out of which the rebellion has arisen. Number after number of that paper has been *mainly* devoted to a vindication of slavery from the *extremest* proslavery position taken by the leaders of the rebellion in the South. In 1849, his "zeal" was "conspicuous" in maintaining the principles of the Emancipation State Convention of Kentucky, which declared slavery to be "contrary to the natural rights of mankind, and injurious to a pure state of morals." In 1862, '63, '64, when the nation is struggling for its life, against the foulest rebellion the earth ever saw,—a rebellion begun in the name of slavery, urged on for the sake of slavery, fighting for slavery, living for slavery, worshipping slavery, dooming a whole generation of its young men to a cruel death for slavery, and aiming to supplant universal liberty for slavery,—Dr. Robinson's "zeal" is made "conspicuous" in using all his power, through his paper, to convince the "Presbyterians" of Kentucky, hitherto opposed to slavery, that the system among them which they formerly denounced is "divine," an "ordinance of God," justified by law and by Gospel, the best condition for the negro race, in accordance with the law of nature, and all the other fine things which *Southern* rebels say of it; while, to dissent from this, to speak of slavery as did the Emancipation Convention of Kentucky in whose behalf his "zeal" was once "conspicuous," is "infidelity" in any man, and for the Church to do this is incurable "apostasy."

This is his former record; and this is his present one. We wish it could be said with truth that other Presbyterian ministers and members stand where they were *all* reported as standing fifteen years ago. But it is unquestionably true that *many* of them, judging from the editorials, correspondents, and support given to *The True Presbyterian*, have repudiated their former record, and now stand for the twin-powers, slavery and rebellion.

CHAPTER XII.

MODERN SOUTHERN VIEWS OF SLAVERY.

We have shown at some length, in previous chapters, the opinions entertained of slavery as an institution, both at the North and in the South, by the Church, by statesmen, and by the people, from before the establishment of the National Government down to a period within some thirty years; and they exhibit, with rare exceptions, a concurrent testimony against the system, on grounds both of principle and policy. Divines and statesmen, during the earlier period, as well in those States where it was established as elsewhere, regarded it as an evil to be tolerated rather than justified, and many of them hoped for its ultimate removal from the country, and aided schemes of emancipation with that end in view.

During the later period, a total revolution in opinion has obtained in the States in rebellion, embracing the Church and the world together, which has been for many years practically universal. It now approves what it once condemned, applauds what it once lamented, justifies what it once tolerated, blesses what it once denounced, and places under the divine sanction what it formerly consigned to God's withering curse.

As this change in Southern opinion is the fruitful germ which has brought forth this monstrous rebellion, we propose in this chapter to give some examples of the present *status* of this opinion, confining ourselves as before chiefly to the Church, as seen in the views of leading divines and ecclesiastical bodies. There is nothing in this aspect of the subject which requires that we should present this testimony in the chronological order of its utterance. It rather seems appropriate that we should exhibit some of the later expressions of opinion first, that we may see to what they have grown, and the baldness and boldness with which they are announced. We shall show, also, at the conclusion of this chapter, the development and progress of this modern opinion in the South in the order of time, and thus show how far the Church is responsible for leading and misleading the men of the world. Our chief object, however, is to set forth the sharp contrast between present and former opinions in the same section of country.

DEFENDED BY NORTHERN MEN.

We have entitled this chapter, "Modern *Southern* Views of Slavery," because the opinions here presented are mostly entertained in the South. But it will be seen, that among their stanchest advocates are found divines in the free and in the Border slave States. And what is a most significant fact in this connection is, that at no time since the existence of our Government have prominent Northern men been so bold in advocating and defending slavery,—many of them going to the extreme length of modern Southern opinion, and justifying it on every ground, human and divine,—as since the beginning of the rebellion caused by slavery, and during a short time previous, when the determination openly to resist the Government for the sake of slavery was in process of maturing. Volumes and pamphlets, of various ponderosity in size and argument, have been written by Bishop Hopkins, President Lord, Dr. Seabury, Professor Morse, and other men of equal and some of less distinction. Besides these, sermons have been issued, and portions of the periodical press have come to the rescue; while at least one professedly religious newspaper in Kentucky, conducted and supported by Presbyterians, is battling lustily and constantly as no religious journal within the State has ever been known to do before, going the full length of the most ultra Southern extremists in vindication of the system, and commending with special earnestness the works and writers to which we refer. There is a certain significance in these things which may be very puzzling to philosophers or very easy of solution to plain men.

POSITIONS TAKEN.

We state the positions which the modern defenders of slavery take, and give from their writings quotations which illustrate them, classifying both under two general heads: the sanction given to slavery by the *Law of Nature;* and the sanction claimed for it in the *Word of God.*

It must be borne in mind, as vital in the issue, that these positions, and the authorities and reasons for them, are presented by those who assert them not only to cover slavery in former times and in other nations, but are designed to exhibit the grounds on which *the present system of Negro Slavery in the South* is vindicated and sanctioned.

The views taken of the system by Southern extremists and their Northern "allies," though differing somewhat among their defenders, may be substantially reduced to the following form:

I. That slavery is in no sense the creature of local law, or indeed of any law of man, but is based upon the Law of Nature; that it is normally universal, found among all states of society and in every nation where it has not been positively prohibited, and has existed from the origin of the race to the present time; and that, therefore, "slavery is not municipal but natural," while "it is abolition which is municipal and local:" the grand conclusion from all which is, *that Negro Slavery as it exists in the United States is sustained by these sanctions.*

II. That slavery exists by the positive statutes of Divine Revelation; that it is sanctioned in the Decalogue, is an institution of the patriarchal age, has the approbation of the Mosaic code, was approved by all the prophets, and is interwoven with the whole history and ordinances of the Jewish Church; that it was sanctioned and regulated by Christ and the Apostles, and existed in the New Testament Church which they established; that it is placed by the Scriptures on the same footing with the civil, connubial, and parental relations, and is therefore "an ordinance of God" of the same character with them, in its rights, interests, duties, and permanency; that the system in the Southern States is the fulfilment of the prophetic curse upon Canaan the son of Ham; that it is essential to the intellectual and moral elevation of the negro race in the South; that it is the proper system for the evangelization of heathen; and that, as to the type of Southern negro slavery in particular, "it might have existed in Paradise and may continue through the Millennium:" the grand conclusion from all which is, *that Negro Slavery as it exists in the United States is sustained by these sanctions.*

AUTHORITIES FOR THESE POSITIONS.

We select a few passages out of enough to fill a volume, which it will be seen fully cover all the points in the foregoing paragraphs. We take them in such order, as far as convenience of extracting will admit, as will show their bearing upon each of the positions in the order in which they are announced.

I. *As related to Natural and Municipal Law.*

REV. JAMES H. THORNWELL, D. D., of Columbia, S. C.: "It has been contended that the right of property in slaves is the creature of positive statute, and, consequently, of force only within the limits of the jurisdiction of the law. * * * Slavery has never, in any country, so far as we know, arisen under the operation of statute law. It is not a municipal institution—it is not the arbitrary creature of the State, it has not sprung from the mere force of legislation. Law defines, modifies, and regulates it, as it does every other species of property, but law never created it. The law found it in existence, and, being in existence, the law subjects it to fixed rules. On the contrary, what is local and municipal, is the *abolition* of slavery. The States that are now non-slaveholding have been made so by positive statute. Slavery exists, of course, in every nation in which it is not prohibited. It arose in the progress of human events, from the operation of moral causes; it has been grounded by philosophers in moral maxims; it has always been held to be moral by the vast majority of the race. No age has been without it. From the first dawn of authentic history until the present period, it has come down to us through all the course of ages. We find it among nomadic tribes, barbarian hordes, and civilized States. Wherever communities have been organized, and any rights of property have been recognized at all, there slavery is seen. If, therefore, there be any property which can be said to be founded in the common consent of the human race, it is the property in slaves. If there be any property that can be called natural, in the sense that it spontaneously springs up in the history of the species, it is the property in slaves. If there be any property which is founded in principles of universal operation, it is the property in slaves. To say of an institution, whose history is thus the history of man, which has always and everywhere existed, that it is a local and municipal relation, is of 'all absurdities the motliest, the merest word that ever fooled the ear from out the schoolman's jargon.' Mankind may have been wrong—that is not the question. The point is, whether the law made slavery—whether it is the police regulation of limited localities, or whether it is a property founded in natural causes, and causes of universal operation. We say nothing as to the moral character of the causes. We insist only upon the fact that slavery is rooted in a common law, wider and more pervading than the common law of England—THE UNIVERSAL CUSTOM OF MANKIND." [The capitals are the author's.]—*Southern Presbyterian Review*, Jan., 1861.

ADDRESS OF THE "GENERAL ASSEMBLY of the Confederate States," penned by Dr. THORNWELL: "Whatever is universal is natural. We are willing that slavery should be tried by this standard. We are willing to abide by the testimony of the race, and if man as man has everywhere condemned it, if all human laws have prohibited it as crime, if it stands in the same category with malice, murder, and theft, then we are willing, in the name of humanity, to renounce it, and to renounce it forever. But what if the overwhelming majority of mankind have approved it; what if philosophers and statesmen have justified it, and the laws of all nations acknowledged it," &c.?—*Address, &c. "to all the Churches throughout the Earth,"* Dec., 1861.

An ANONYMOUS writer in the *Southern Presbyterian Review*, for April, 1861: "We shall endeavor to give a succinct description, rather than a formal definition, of the system as actually existing at the South. Slavery, then, is a constitution of the Law of Nature and of nations, by which, under certain providential conditions, one man has a right to incorporate into his family institution, and to hold under his rule, as the head of the house, a class of persons of a different, and, in all the attributes which fit men for self-government, an inferior race; and to exact from them, while in health and vigor, service and labor suited to their strength and capacity."

REV. SAMUEL SEABURY, D. D., of New York: "I call it American slavery. * * * It is this limited form of slavery which I propose to defend; not by an appeal to local or positive law, whether State or Federal, but by an appeal to the Law of Nature, or the principles of universal justice. * * * Where is the nation that has pronounced a state of servitude for life contrary to natural justice? What age, before our own, could point to moralists that proclaim it an offence against nature to hold slaves in the condition in which Providence has placed them?" *American Slavery Justified by the Law of Nature.* 1861.

THE TRUE PRESBYTERIAN, Louisville, Kentucky: "In every country and in every age slavery has existed, precisely as civil government and the family have existed. * * * The most polished and enlightened nations have recognized this relation. The Persians, the Greeks, the Romans, the Gauls, the Saxons, and the Normans, all held slaves, and they held them without any more doubt of their right to do so, than of their right to establish civil government, or to marry, or to rule their children. The greatest legislators and philosophers of antiquity, Solon and Lycurgus, Socrates, Plato, and Aristotle, all approved and regulated the institution. These master minds of the ancient world, reasoning upon the principles of human nature, discern this as one of the lawful relations of mankind."—*Review of Prof. Morse.*

Similar quotations relating to the first position might be given at much greater length, and from many other recent writers. We give a sample of the doctrine which covers the second position.

II. *As related to Divine Revelation.*

DR. THORNWELL: "That the relation betwixt the slave and his master is not inconsistent with the word of God, we have long since settled. Our consciences are not troubled, and have no reason to be troubled, on this score. We do not hold our slaves in bondage from remorseless considerations of interest. If I know the character of our people, I think I can safely say, that if they were persuaded of the essential immorality of slavery, they would not be backward in adopting measures for the ultimate abatement of the evil. *We cherish* the institution, not from avarice, but *from principle.*"—*Fast-Day Sermon, Columbia, S. C.*, Nov. 21, 1860.

Again: "Is it to be asked of us to renounce the doctrines which we believe have come down to us from the earliest ages, and have the sanction of the oracles of God? Must we give up what we conscientiously believe to be the truth? The thing is absurd."—*So. Pres. Review*, Jan., 1861.

ADDRESS OF THE "GENERAL ASSEMBLY of the Confederate States," penned by Dr. THORNWELL: "Slavery is no new thing. It has not only existed for ages in the world, but it has existed under every dispensation of the covenant of grace in the Church of God. Indeed, the first organization of the Church as a visible society, separate and distinct from the unbelieving world, was inaugurated in the family of a slaveholder. Among the very persons to whom the seal of circumcision was affixed, were the slaves of the father of the faithful—some born in his house, and others bought with his money. Slavery again, then, reappears under the law. God sanctions it in both tables of the Decalogue, and Moses treats it as an institution to be regulated, not abolished; legitimated, and not condemned. We come down to the age of the New Testament, and we find it again in the Churches founded by the Apostles under the plenary inspiration of the Holy Ghost. * * * Moses surely made it the subject of express and positive legislation, and the Apostles are equally explicit in inculcating the duties which sprung from both sides of the relation. * * * Moses and the Apostles alike sanctioned the relation of slavery. * * * We cannot prosecute the argument in detail, but we have said enough, we think, to vindicate the position of the Southern Church. We have assumed no new attitude. We stand exactly where the Church of God has always stood, from Abraham to Moses, from Moses to Christ, from Christ to the Reformers, and from the Reformers to ourselves. * * * The general operation of the system is kindly and benevolent; it is a real and effective discipline, and without it we are profoundly persuaded that the African race in the midst of us can never be elevated in the scale of being. As long as that race, in its comparative degradation, co-exists side by side with the white, bondage is its normal condition."—*Address, &c.*, Dec., 1861.

The Anonymous writer above quoted gives a specimen of the *position* taken and the *argument* for slavery propagandism into the Free States: "There is nothing in the nature of slavery to restrain its movements, any more than the possession of flocks and herds. So, when the patriarch Abraham emigrated to the new territory which God had given, he took with him not only his cattle but his servants, born in his house and bought with his money. If, therefore, there is nothing in the nature of slavery to restrain him, the Southern man demands: What sovereignty under heaven prevents him from emigrating, as Abraham did, with all his household and all his wealth, to the land which the Lord has given him, as tenant in common with his Northern and Western neighbors?"—*So. Pres. Review*, April, 1861.

Prof. Samuel F. B. Morse, of New York: "Man, from his very nature, dislikes restraints; he would at all hazards have his own way, and hence it is that no appeal takes a deeper hold of his passions and instincts than an appeal to his love of freedom. It was the original bait of the Tempter which lured man to his ruin. He did not comprehend that *slavery to God* was man's highest freedom. How shall such a nature, set on fire by a word that kindles at once all its fierceness, be curbed and repressed within the bounds of reason?"

The Professor answers his question by giving us his view of "the social system which *God has ordained.*" It has in it these four relations: the civil, or that between ruler and ruled; the connubial, or that between husband and wife; the parental, or that between parent and child; and the servile, or that between master and slave. He declares that all these are "ordained" and made equally authoritative by God, and the principles which govern them are alike found in the Scriptures. Again, after speaking of the antislavery views of some, as the "setting forth of a religious belief," he inquires: "And what is the opposite tenet, declaring *slavery to be an ordinance of God*, but the declaration of a *religious belief?*"

In commenting upon the views of Prof. DAVID CHRISTY, of Cincinnati,—who has collected the statistics showing the large numbers evangelized in Southern slavery, as compared with converts to Christianity on heathen ground, among many heathen nations, particularizing the poor success of missions in Liberia among the free blacks,—Prof. MORSE says: "These are stubborn facts, confirmed by careful, laborious, dispassionate research;" and then, from these facts, combating the position that slavery is incompatible with the principles of Christianity, says: "Experience shows that the converse of this dogma, as a general rule, is the truth. Christianity has been most successfully propagated among a barbarous race, where they have been enslaved to a Christian race."—*Argument on the Ethical position of Slavery in the Social System, &c.*

REV. STUART ROBINSON, D. D., Editor of the *True Presbyterian*, in an elaborate article, entitled, "Slavery recognized as a proper Social Order in the Church of God during every Era of Inspiration," introductory to his own doctrines, speaks of the opposite sentiments as "an *apostasy* from the truth of Christ," and as the "Iscariot treason of the artful demagogues who are manœuvring to force gradually upon the Churches and the conscientious people of the Border States, the antislavery heresies;" and of the persons who oppose them as those who "blaspheme God," and as "*apostates*, leading the Church to apostasy." The foregoing italics are those of the article. The positions then taken and the passages of Scripture quoted are those usually referred to concerning servitude in the time of Abraham and Moses: as that the Church was originally established by the covenant with Abraham, "a slaveholder," "the man called of God to be the father of the visible Church on earth;" that "a slaveholder and his slaves were expressly made the constituent members of the holy society;" that "no one who receives the Scriptures as of Divine authority, can deny that here is *the highest form of sanction of the principle of property in man*, at least under the patriarchal dispensation:" that the same system continued in the "Church Mosaic," where "slavery is again recognized as existing in the Church by command (the Decalogue), in reference to man-servants and maid-servants;" and that "both in the holy ordinance of the Passover, and in the holy law given to the Church, slavery is recognized and not excluded from the Church." Then, more especially of the system under the Mosaic code: "Such was the law of the Church, *as a Church.* Around this Church, as we have said, it was part of the mission of Moses to erect, as a protecting shell, a constitutional civil government, till, in fulness of time, the Church of one nation became the Church of all nations. Now, in that civil code, Divinely inspired, and under which Jehovah condescended to rule as political head of the nation, there could, of course, be no statutes in principle contrary to righteousness. Yet the civil code of Moses permitted and regulated slavery, *in the main recognizing the same principles of the modern slave codes of the Southern States.*" Having stated what "modern antislavery falsely represents to be the Mosaic slave code," he continues: "But nothing can be more explicit than the provisions of this code, for a system of hereditary and perpetual slavery, expressly distinguished again and again, from this temporary service as hirelings, or until the year of jubilee. Two statutes expressly allow slaves to be bought of surrounding heathen nations, and slaves to be made by capture in war from any heathen nations, except the seven nations of Canaan, who were to be utterly exterminated." It is then added, "that slavery entered into every department of the Hebrew social system by Divine sanction and example;" and, finally, the comforting conclusion is reached, that those who take the position against which the writer is mainly arguing, "must either trifle with the interpretation of Scripture or blaspheme the God of Israel."

Concerning slavery under the New Testament economy, Dr. Robinson thus discourseth: That "Jesus Christ, at His advent, found slavery existing, not only by the Mosaic law, but as part of every social structure in the civilized world;" that "He did not either expressly or impliedly exclude slavery from the Church;" and that "the propriety of slavery under the New Testament rests upon the sovereign will of Christ in not only allowing it in the patriarchal and Mosaic Churches, but in permitting it to continue in the New Testament Church, not repealing the law of usage existing, as we have seen, from the foundation of the visible Church. That this is the true view of the matter, will be more evident if we examine the practice and teaching of His Apostles, under the reorganized Church, after the outpouring of the Spirit. In every community out of which Christian Churches were gathered, slavery notoriously existed. Into the New Testament Churches, as into the Abrahamic and Mosaic, slaveholders and their slaves were admitted as constituent elements thereof. While care was taken to instruct the Churches that the ceremonial law of Moses had expired by limitation, not a word is said of a repeal of the *right of property in man.* * * * The duties of the relation of master and servant are discussed in common with the duties of parent and child, husband and wife." Commenting on Prof. Morse's work, referred to above, the *True Presbyterian* says: "Thus these four great relations of human life (the civil, matrimonial, parental, and servile) stand side by side, *equally approved of God, and equally rightful among men.* * * * The Saviour Himself, who corrected whatever else was wrong in man; apostles, saints, divines, martyrs, synods, councils, philosophers, statesmen, moralists; *all accepted slavery as being equally of God with civil government, marriage, or the parental relation.*"

Rev. Frederick A. Ross, D. D., of Huntsville, Alabama, says that "Slavery is of God;" of the relation of "master and slave," that "it is a relation belonging to the same category as those of husband and wife, parent and child;" and the work in which these doctrines are set forth at length and elaborated, is entitled, "*Slavery Ordained of God.*" Of himself, he says: "I am not a slaveholder. Nay, I have shown some self-denial in this matter. I emancipated slaves whose money value would now be $40,000." This was some years ago. He states the reason of referring to this: "I merely wish to show, that I have no selfish motive in giving *the true Southern defence of slavery.*" It is but justice to Dr. Ross to say, whether it reveals any inconsistency in his argument or not, that he is not a perpetualist. In addition to his own example to show this, he addresses "the Southern man of every grade" thus: "Let him know that slavery is to pass away in the fulness of Providence. Let the South believe this, and prepare to obey the hand that moves their destiny." Rather *prophetic* as well as didactic. Nor was Dr. Ross opposed to "the agitation," as many Southern men were, which he would perhaps say has brought on this "fulness" of time; but he rejoices in it, in this wise: "I believe He will bless the world in the working out of this slavery. *I rejoice then in the agitation* which has so resulted, and will so terminate, to reveal the Bible and bless mankind." As Dr. Ross's book was published in 1857, "the agitation" he "rejoiced" in is that which other Southern men lamented, and for which they threatened.

General Thomas R. R. Cobb, of Georgia: "One of the inmates of the ark became a 'servant of servants;' and in the opinion of many, the curse of Ham is now being executed upon his descendants, in the enslavement of the negro race."—*Historical Sketch of Slavery*, 1858.

Again, GENERAL COBB says: "They (Christ and the Apostles) simply treated slavery as they did all other civil government, as of God, so long as in His providence He permitted it to exist; and regulated, by precepts, the relation, as they did that of ruler and subject."—*Law of Negro Slavery*, 1858.

Again, GENERAL COBB says: "The test, then, is, does the institution of negro slavery tend to promote the physical, intellectual, and moral growth of the negro race?" He answers this question in the affirmative, and in another place, adds: "The inference would seem irresistible, that the most successful engine for the development of negro intellect is slavery."—*Law of Negro Slavery*, 1858.

REV. THOMAS SMYTH, D. D., of Charleston, S. C., says: "The war now carried on by the North is a war against slavery, and is, therefore, treasonable rebellion against the Constitution of the United States, and against the word, providence, and government of God. * * * Slavery, as a form of organized involuntary labor, has always and every where existed among the negro race. * * * What if God made slavery a part of man's and woman's original curse; what if God ordained, as a part of that penalty, that the earth should be brought into universal cultivation by a universally diffused race, through slavery in some form of involuntary servitude; what if God, by a positive, divine enactment, ordained that, through the history of the world, slavery should exist as a form of organized labor among certain races of men, and that lordship over such slaves should be a part of the perpetual blessing of the races of Shem and Japheth; what if God has actually embodied slavery in His moral law, and by there guarding, and protecting, and regulating it, has made it appertain to the present condition of humanity; what if He ordained and regulated it under the patriarchal, Mosaic, prophetical, and Christian dispensations; what if in the New Testament a curse is pronounced against fanatical opposition to slavery as antichristian, and a sentence of withdrawal from such as heretical, both in Church and State; what if, in these and other ways, God claims slavery, like other forms of government adapted to sinful human nature, as His own ordinance for good; what, then, must be thought of this war of the North against slavery, and this war of the South in its defence, as inwoven by Providence into the very texture of its body politic?"—*So. Pres. Review*, *April*, 1863.

Dr. Seabury, defending "American slavery as justified by the Law of Nature" (1861), thinks it might have existed, so far as the character of slavery is concerned, "in Paradise." He has a chapter on the "Theory of Slavery," in which he says: "But what (methinks I hear the reader exclaim), do you think there could have been bondage in Paradise? Pray, why not?"—"I see no reason, then, why the relation of master and servant should not have existed in a state of innocence, as well as that of husband and wife, parent and child."—"All this, I confess, proceeds on the assumption that slavery, or servitude for life, does no violence to Nature, but is good and agreeable to Nature."

The *True Presbyterian* warmly commends Dr. Seabury's book, in successive numbers of the paper, and says: "He argues that in this view of it, slavery being a condition so closely allied to that in which our wives, our sons, and our daughters are placed, by the laws of God and man, cannot be the degrading and hateful relation that modern abolitionists declare it to be. There is no debasement in it. *It might have existed in Paradise, and may continue through the Millennium.*" The "Millennium" phase is probably an advance movement on the part of the *True Presbyterian*, which Dr. Seabury may not yet have reached. At least, we have not yet discovered it in his book. But if slavery could have existed in "Paradise," we see no reason why it may not be continued in the "Millennium;" and we expect soon to see its modern defenders carrying it into Heaven, and perpetuating it forever. This we are prepared for by the following from the *True Presbyterian*, which shows how deeply and tenderly the system of Southern negro slavery has entwined itself among its Christian affections: "It is certainly remarkable that the Scriptures employ this very relation to express our subjection to Christ. Believers are constantly called the slaves of Christ: all bondage then is not disgraceful; here is an instance in which slavery is sweet and honorable. And if it be not degrading to our wives to obey their husbands, and to our children to obey their parents, we cannot see why it should degrade a slave to obey his master."—"*The slaves of Jesus Christ* love and revere their Divine Master, *and rejoice in their bondage;* and so may a slave love and revere his human master, and delight in his service."

We always supposed that the Apostle Paul understood the case, when he called a Christian, "the Lord's freeman" (1 Cor. vii. 22), but the Apostle who presides over the *True Presbyterian*, to instruct Kentucky Christians, is wiser than Paul; the Christian is, after all, but "the Lord's *slave*." Our Saviour said of His people: "Ye shall know the truth, and the truth shall make you free. If the Son therefore shall make you free, ye shall be free indeed." But this modern Apostle is wiser than Christ. All Christians are "the *slaves* of Jesus Christ;" and the negro slavery of the South is *the type* of the "bondage" in which they are to "rejoice" forevermore! But our object *here* is not to *argue* upon, but merely to *state*, the positions of the modern defenders of negro slavery. Every one of course knows that the original Greek word (*doulos*) is applied to the servant of Christ; but to argue from this, that every Christian is the *slave* of Christ, in the sense that the Southern negro is the slave of his master under Southern law, is about as good logic as *some* of these writers usually exhibit; and yet, this is the whole case, so far as the application of a common term to things totally distinct is concerned.

We have another witness to the Millennial phase of the case. REV. JOSEPH R. WILSON, D. D., of Augusta, Georgia, preached a discourse to his congregation in that city, Jan. 6, 1861, on the "Mutual Relation of Masters and Servants as taught in the Bible," the closing words of which are as follows: "And, oh, when that welcome day shall dawn, whose light will reveal *a world covered with righteousness*, not the least pleasing sight will be the institution of domestic slavery, freed from its stupid servility on the one side and its excesses of neglect or severity on the other, and appearing to all mankind as containing that scheme of politics and morals, which, by saving a lower race from the destruction of heathenism, has, under Divine management, contributed to refine, exalt, and enrich its superior race!"

REV. GEORGE D. ARMSTRONG, D. D., Norfolk, Virginia: "With civil government, marriage, the family, and slavery, they (the Apostles) dealt in the same way." "The Church must labor to make good masters and good slaves, just as she labors to make good husbands, good wives, good parents, good children, good rulers, good subjects." "The laws of our slaveholding States, at the present time, *ignore the marriage relation among slaves.* * * * The law in our slaveholding States, at the present day, gives to the master the right *to separate finally husband and wife among his slaves, and this at his pleasure and for his own profit.*"*—*Christian Doctrine of Slavery*, 1857.

* At this point, Dr. Armstrong introduces a long note from *Fletcher's Studies on Slavery*, which he regards as "the most elaborate work on slavery which has been published at the South." He quotes Fletcher as saying: "So far as our experience goes [Mr. Fletcher *possibly* means "observation" instead of "experience," and *possibly* not], masters universally manifest a desire to have their negroes marry, and to live with their wives and children *according to Christian rules.*" Now, if this

RIGHT REVEREND JOHN HENRY HOPKINS, D. D., Bishop of the Protestant Episcopal Church in Vermont: "The slavery of the negro race, *as maintained in the Southern States*, appears to me fully authorized, both in the Old and New Testaments, which, as the written Word of God, afford the only infallible standard of moral rights and obligations." Again, in another place: "The difference between the power of the Northern parent and the Southern slaveholder, is reduced to this, namely, that the master has a property in the labor of his slave for life, instead of having it only to the age of twenty-one."

The Bishop takes the positions and relies on the arguments so fully given in our quotations from others. He further says: "We have heard the boasted determination that the Union shall never be restored, until its provision for the protection of slavery is utterly abolished. And what is the result of all this philanthropy? The fearful judgment of God has descended to chastise these multiplied acts of rebellion against His divine Government." "If ever the Union of the States is re-established, it can only be, in my humble judgment, by a return to the old and Scriptural doctrine, once held alike by the whole Christian community, that slavery, in itself, involves no sin."—*View of Slavery, republished by the Author in* 1864.

ALBERT TAYLOR BLEDSOE, LL. D., Professor of Mathematics in the University of Virginia: "The institution of slavery, as it exists among us at the South, is founded in political justice, is in accordance with the will of God and the designs of His providence, and is conducive to the highest, purest, and best interests of mankind."—*Liberty and Slavery*, 1860.

REV. NEHEMIAH ADAMS, D. D., of Boston, among other apologetics

is so, one of two things must follow: either, Mr. Fletcher's knowledge of this "desire" is very limited; or, it is a mistake to suppose this "desire" is very prevalent, as his language would seem to imply. But granting that he is correct, the "desire" is wholly inoperative. This is shown in the simple fact that the laws which "ignore the marriage relation among slaves," remain the same on this point from generation to generation. Can any thing demonstrate the purely *venal* and *mercenary* spirit of that system of "Christian slavery" which Dr. Armstrong defends, more conclusively than this? Mr. Fletcher gives a good many *economical* and some *domestic* reasons why "masters" *should* "manifest" such "desire." But if it is "universal" among slaveholders, why don't these "masters" (for *they rule* in Southern politics) "manifest" that "desire" in their Legislatures, and have their laws changed? What but the *mercenary* spirit of the whole system prevents this "universal desire" from taking form *in law*, so that "final separation" could never occur? That any such "desire" exists "universally," will do to tell *to the marines*.

for the negro slavery of the South, says: "The Gospel is to slavery what the growing of clover is to sorrel. Religion in the masters destroys *every thing* in slavery which makes it obnoxious; and not only so, it converts the relation of the slave into an effectual means of happiness." If this is so, one would think there is very little "growing of *clover*" in the South. It is rather strange, when Dr. Adams was penning his apologies for slavery, that he did not think of a principle he elsewhere notices: "A Northerner at the South soon perceives, that, if he feels and shows in a proper manner a natural repugnance to slavery, *they respect him for it*, while they greatly *suspect and distrust* those from the North who seem in favor of the system."*

RESPONSIBILITY OF THE CHURCH FOR THE REVOLUTION IN SOUTHERN OPINION.

The reader may see, in what we have now given, that the present position of the Southern Church and of its Northern "allies," is a position of direct antagonism to that maintained by substantially the whole country, North and South, until within a period of some thirty years. The Southern section of the Union, for some years past, has with great unanimity maintained these extreme views.

It is now a very interesting inquiry, What portion of the community took the lead, and is therefore primarily responsible, for this ethical revolution? Under whose teachings, at first, was the general Southern mind brought to abjure its former sentiments, and adopt the "corner-stone" faith concerning slavery? Our own opinion is, that THE CHURCH, through its leading clergymen, in the pulpit and through the press, led the way, and that, for the most part, the politicians of the South were content to follow them. A mass of testimony exists on this point. We have space for a bare sample of it.

* When the Hon. Edward Everett made the first New England speech in Congress in defence of slavery, John Randolph exclaimed: "I envy neither the head nor the heart of any man from the North, who can defend slavery on principle."

EARLY POSITION OF REV. JAMES SMYLIE.

In proof of the point that the Church led the State, in the change of views on the merits of the system of slavery, may be cited an article from the *New Orleans True Witness*, a religious paper, edited by Rev. R. McInnis, a Presbyterian clergyman, a native Mississippian, who has the means of knowing whereof he affirms. It is under date of August 18, 1860. It may be added, also, that the Synod of Mississippi officially declare the same thing stated in this article, as to the leading responsibility for this change. The editor remarks as follows:

SMYLIE ON SLAVERY.—It is an interesting historical fact, that Rev. James Smylie, an Old School Presbyterian minister, *was the first person in our country who took boldly the position that slavery was not inconsistent with the teachings of the Bible.* He was one of the first Presbyterian ministers who came to the Southwest, and assisted in forming the Mississippi Presbytery, in 1816. The general view held at this time, and for many years after, South as well as North, was that slavery was an *evil.* The question had not been examined. All took it for granted that slavery was an evil, and inconsistent with the spirit and teachings of the word of God. Hence the sentiments expressed by our Church, in 1818—which, by the way, have been most shamefully garbled and misrepresented—*were at the time the sentiments of the whole country, and were regarded as a pretty strong Southern document; hence all the South voted for it.* In fact, so strong was the feeling for emancipation, that this act of 1818 discouraged it in our members, where the slaves were not prepared for it, while it condemned the "harsh censures and uncharitable reflection" of the more ultra men of the North. We have referred to this merely to call attention to the fact that *the opinion of the whole country was that slavery was an evil.* And we know of no man who took a different position, until Rev. James Smylie, in answer to a letter addressed to him as stated clerk of the above Presbytery, wrote a reply, in which he attempted to show that neither the Old nor the New Testament Scriptures declared slavery to be a sin, but both recognized it as an institution belonging to the great social system. This letter, which has long since been published, in a pamphlet of some eighty pages, small type, was not only the first, but it is, in our view, the ablest and most convincing Scriptural argument ever published on the subject. It shows research, ability, honesty, and is unanswerable. When the substance of this letter was delivered, in 1835 and '36, in the Churches of Mississippi, in the form of a sermon, the people generally, large slaveholders too, did not sympathize with him in his views. We recollect hearing him, on one occasion, for some three hours, and every person, without exception, thought him somewhat fanatical. *The idea that the Bible did sanction slavery was regarded as a new doctrine even in Mississippi.* Yet Rev. James Smylie—and a more honest man never lived—was honestly sincere in his convictions and his views, and he went ahead against the tide of public opinion. His Scriptural argument has never been answered, nor can it be. *This letter was the first thing that turned public attention in the South, and especially in the Southwest, to the investigation of the subject;* and every Scriptural argument we have seen is but a reproduction of this, while none is so clear, full, and unanswerable. It ought to be republished.

SOME TWO YEARS AFTER the publication of this letter, George McDuffie, a senator of South Carolina, announced similar views in Congress, and was regarded there as taking a strange and untenable position—one which met with little sympathy in that body. The fact is, the South had never examined the subject, and were finally driven to it by the intolerant fanaticism of ultra men at the North.

We mention the above facts, not for the purpose of provoking discussion, but merely to show the state of public opinion at the time on the subject of slavery; and to show that the South is indebted to a minister of our Church for the first clear and unanswerable argument against the generally admitted view that slavery was a *sin.*

PAPER OF THE SYNOD OF MISSISSIPPI.

It will be seen from the official document which follows, that Mr. Smylie began to make public his views somewhat earlier than the time mentioned by Mr. McInnis; at least, before he received the letter from the Presbytery of Chillicothe. The following is an extract from an obituary notice of Rev. James Smylie, of Mississippi, which was reported in the Synod of which he was a member, and by that body unanimously adopted:

Extract from the Minutes of the Synod of Mississippi, at a Meeting held in the City of Jackson, Miss., in December, 1853.

There is one production from his pen which produced a strong sensation in various parts of the United States. When the abolition excitement arose in the North, he resolved, as many others ought to have done, to give the Sacred Scriptures a thorough searching, to ascertain the doctrines and duties there inculcated in relation to slavery. He determined to investigate the subject in the most candid manner, and to receive whatever was taught with the most fearless and implicit faith. The result surprised himself. He found that the teachings of Scripture were *greatly at variance with the popular belief.* He wished to communicate his discoveries to others. He wrote a sermon on the subject and preached it at Port Gibson. *It gave great offence not only to the Church, but also to his brethren in the ministry, who seriously advised him to preach that sermon no more.* In the mean time, the Presbytery of Chillicothe (in Ohio) assumed the lofty position of instructors of their brethren of the South on the subject of slavery, exhorting them to abandon it as a heinous sin. They addressed a letter to the Presbytery of Mississippi on the subject. This letter was received by Mr. Smylie as stated Clerk. He wrote a reply, to be laid before the Presbytery for their adoption. He read this reply to one of his brethren before the meeting. As he had entered into the teachings of Scripture in relation to slavery, the reply was long; and many of his views differed from those of his brethren. On these two accounts he was told that his reply would not, in all probability, be adopted by the Presbytery. It was then agreed that the brother whom he had consulted should write another reply, in a different style and manner, and more concise, and that this should be offered if his was not adopted. The concise reply was adopted by the Presbytery, and the Chillicothe letter and the reply were published together in a religious newspaper at Cincinnati, and there was no further annoyance from the Presbytery of Chillicothe. *Mr. Smylie then determined that he would publish his views in a pamphlet form. Such was the variation of his sentiments from those of his brethren, that all whom he consulted, with but one or two exceptions, attempted to dissuade him from this step.* With that honest inflexibility of purpose and confidence in the correctness of his own conclusions which ever distinguished the man, he published his pamphlet. For a while he was covered with odium, and honored with a large amount of abuse from the abolitionists of the North, for teaching that the Bible did not forbid the holding of slaves, and that it was tolerated in the primitive Church. These doctrines are now received as true both North and South, and they constitute the basis of action of the most respectable religious bodies even in the North itself; so that Mr. Smylie has the high honor of giving the true exposition of the doctrines of the Bible in relation to slavery, in the commencement of the Abolition excitement, and of giving instruction to others far more learned and talented than himself.

JACKSON, MISS., *December 17th*, 1853. (Signed) J. H. VAN COURT, *Chairman.*

CONFIRMATORY TESTIMONY.

In Dr. Baird's "Southern Rights and Northern Duties," before referred to, we find incidental evidence confirmatory of the point that certain of the Southern clergy were earlier than Southern statesmen in announcing the new doctrines on slavery. John C. Calhoun has been deemed, along with Mr. McDuffie, named above, one of the earliest among Southern Statesmen to take extreme proslavery ground. But Dr. Baird places him in the rear of Mr. Smylie, in point of time. Speaking of the Anti-Slavery Society, he says: "This society was but three years old, when, in 1835, it acquired an illustrious ally in the business of slavery agitation in the person of Mr. Calhoun, who then, as he afterward avowed, began to act upon the policy which ruled his subsequent life."

Mr. Smylie began the work somewhat earlier. Nor is it supposed that he was impelled by any agitation at that time at the North. Even Dr. Baird says that "in 1835," "the antislavery party was an insignificant faction." And from that day forward it was but a small fraction of the people. We have heard Mr. Smylie, from his own lips, state what led him at first to examine the subject more fully, and finally to repudiate the views then universal at the South. We were a member of the Synod of Mississippi, and present, when the obituary concerning him was adopted; and from our personal knowledge, we know it was the common belief among all classes in the Church at the South, that he and other clergymen, chiefly in the Presbyterian Church, were the first to take open and broad ground on that platform which maintains the extreme proslavery views,—that Slavery is a divine system, an ordinance of God, on a par with the parental and matrimonial relations,—views which, at length, in the demands which were made in their name, plunged the country into treason, rebellion, and war.

It is, therefore, no slander upon the Southern Church and Southern Clergy to say that THEY LED THE WAY in the revolution in Southern opinion upon slavery. *They claim* to have done this; they deem it an honor; they glory in it; they will not divide the honor with politicians; but, as in regard to the rebellion, as we have shown elsewhere, they claim to have led both politicians and people. As a suitable reward for this noble work, they embalm the memory of those who took the lead in it, in solemn obituaries adopted in ecclesiastical bodies; and that these deeds may not perish from among men, they send these memorials for sacred deposit in the Archives of the Presbyterian Historical Society, that all men to the end of time may know wherefore they were thus highly honored!

CHAPTER XIII.

SLAVERY IN POLEMICS.—DIVINE REVELATION.

It seems almost to be a work of supererogation, at the present time, to argue for or against Slavery in the United States; to attempt to resolve questions with the pen which are in process of settlement by the sword, and which, before the ink we use is dry, may be determined forever. Our plan, however, would not be complete, unless we should give some attention to the reasonings by which the modern doctrines upon slavery are defended.

We shall not endeavor to emulate either the eloquence or the argument of those men of Kentucky, some of them of a former day, whose writings upon slavery we have already given; nor do we think the occasion calls for any thing to be said, or indeed that any thing can be said, against the special character and influence of the system, beyond what they have uttered. Our argument will bear chiefly upon points brought to view in the literature of the rebellion, and will aim to combat the positions taken by its instigators and abettors.

PRELIMINARY CONSIDERATIONS.

We have given, at great length, in the chapter immediately preceding, the doctrines announced by those who defend negro slavery as it exists in the South. It will be seen that the two propositions, numerically designated, which we have there laid down, are covered in every particular, and even more than covered, by the authorities we have cited. It will be seen, moreover, that every position taken by these authorities, is made to illustrate, apply to, and justify *the Southern system of negro slavery*. This is the specific and sole purpose for which their works are written and their reasonings elaborated.

We do not propose to exhaust the entire argument by which these extravagant positions may be met. That would require a volume instead of a chapter. So much has been written on this whole subject already, by able scholars, that it seems needless to waste many words upon it; and yet, it will scarcely do to say that at this time of day these extraordinary emanations are not worth noticing. From the sources indicated, and by the authority of great names, they are still spread before the religious public, with glowing commendation, while those who dissent from these high priests of the Southern Oracle are freely called by "religious" men "apostates," "infidels," "heretics," "French Jacobins," and the like. These authoritative responses have an influence upon many minds who draw their inspiration through the channels which convey them. They should be brought to the test of truth. We propose to notice only a few of the main points made, and to present our reasons for dissenting from them.

THE SCRIPTURES GROSSLY LIBELLED.

As incidental to the subsequent argument, we notice, in passing, the monstrous assumption of Dr. Robinson, editor of *The True Presbyterian*, that the servitude among the Jews, in the time of Abraham and Moses, is the essential type of negro slavery in the Southern States, as the systems are judged by their respective "codes," and by the facts. He asserts this in terms, several times over; and yet, no greater libel upon the truth was ever put into human language.

Let the reader first turn to the chapter where the paper

of the Committee of the Kentucky Synod sets forth the character of slavery in Kentucky, and notice the points made concerning the system, both as to the *law* and the *facts*, and remember that slavery in the Border States is always seen in its milder form as compared with the States farther South; and then let him note that it is the system as it prevails throughout the slave States, as seen under their "slave codes," which Dr. Robinson says is the counterpart of that which existed in the patriarchal and Mosaic ages, and which was sanctioned by the positive ordinances of God. Was ever a more palpable untruth uttered to deceive plain men? Whether this is so may be seen by comparison. Our own ears have been greeted with the satisfaction which certain people have expressed with their condition in holding this relation under the slave laws, from reading these very words in *The True Presbyterian*, and they have been led to believe that the venerated fathers of the Church who held a contrary opinion were ignorant of God's word; and we presume such unscrupulous dogmatism has beguiled and consoled many others in the same manner.

There is no call for mincing words in matters of such vital moment, where the interests of the State, the honor of the Church, the truth of the Scriptures, and the personal duty of men are all concerned; and hence we call such utterances by the only word which can properly characterize them. They are deliberate and positive libels upon the word and honor of God: and this we pledge ourselves to prove. The language in which they are uttered by Dr. Robinson is as follows:

"It will not do to attempt to parry the force of this *reductio ad absurdum*, by saying that slavery under Abraham was not THE SAME THING as by the SLAVE CODE OF THE SOUTH, for we shall see a little farther on, that the ancient slavery was, IN PRINCIPLE, JUST SUCH AS THAT

ENACTED BY THE SLAVE CODE OF THE SOUTH NOW." Of Abrahamic times, he says: "The language of that era was as THOROUGHLY PERMITTED BY THE INFLUENCE OF SLAVERY, as that of the Southern States now." Again: "The civil code of Moses permitted and regulated slavery, in the main recognizing THE SAME PRINCIPLES as the modern slave codes of the Southern States." Again: "The LAW OF SLAVERY in the Mosaic code, contemplates the slave as BOTH A PERSON AND A CHATTEL, JUST AS THE SOUTHERN SLAVE CODE DOES.

These declarations have one merit; they are direct, clear, and unmistakable. Their demerit is, their total want of truth.

POINTS OF DIFFERENCE BETWEEN THE JEWISH AND SOUTHERN SYSTEMS.

If any persons are so poorly acquainted with their Bibles and with the system of Southern slavery as to believe that the laws of the Jewish servitude and the "slave codes" of the Southern States are of "the same principles," we will point out to them a few characteristics of difference. We are not, at this point, to deal with the argument by which the writer attempts to prop up his assumption; we are only concerned with the assumption itself. It is a simple question of fact; a matter of truth or falsehood as to the agreement or disagreement of these systems. And it will be borne in mind, that, in order to sustain the position which Dr. Robinson takes, it is necessary to show, that in regard to each and every one of the essential characteristics of the Southern "slave codes," there is an exact and full correspondency in the laws of the Jewish system. If there is a failure to make out this complete correspondency in any one particular his assumption falls to the ground.

Among the radical principles in which the two systems differ are these.

1. By Southern law, slaves are "chattels personal." This is the legal definition in terms. The code of South

Carolina says: "Slaves shall be deemed chattels personal, in the hands of their owners and possessors, and their executors, administrators, and assigns, to all intents, constructions, and purposes, whatsoever."*

The Jewish system does not in this manner completely divest the bondman of his manhood. There is *no statute* in the Mosaic code so utterly dehumanizing as this, or which bears any correspondency with it. If so, let it be shown. We challenge its production.†

2. By Southern law, a slave can own no property; cannot control any of the avails of his own labor. This is expressly denied him. The civil code of Louisiana says: "A slave is one who is in the power of a master to whom he belongs. The master may sell him, dispose of his person, his industry, and his labor. He can do nothing, possess nothing, nor acquire any thing, but what must belong to his master."‡

In the Jewish system, *no statute* thus prevented those

* The most elaborate and authoritative work on slavery, recognized as setting forth *the law*, is that of General Thomas R. R. Cobb, of Georgia, published in 1858, entitled "The Law of Negro Slavery in the United States." In defining slavery, he says: "Slavery, in its more usual and limited signification, is applied to all involuntary servitude, which is not inflicted as a punishment for crime. * * * It has, at some time, been incorporated into the social system of every nation whose history has been deemed worthy of record. In the former condition the slave loses all personality: in the latter, while treated under the general class of *things*, he possesses various rights as a person, and is treated as such by the law." General Cobb was a lawyer of eminence, a brother of Howell Cobb; was an Elder in the Presbyterian Church, and a member of its General Assembly at New Orleans, in 1858; and was killed in battle at Fredericksburg, Va., in December, 1862.

† Dr. Mielziner, of Copenhagen, is spoken of as "the learned Jew," and as one of "the ablest writers upon the Hebrew economy;" Heinrich Ewald, of Göttingen, as "a great authority in Hebrew Antiquities;" Prof. Saalschütz, of Königsberg, as one "whose works on the Mosaic Polity are of the highest standing;" and Joseph Salvador, "the Rabbinical scholar of Paris;" all "men versed in the Hebrew language and in Jewish customs." These eminent Hebraists agree in this—that "the laws of Moses nowhere recognize *the right of property in man*, nor concede to the master an absolute proprietorship over the person of his servant."

‡ General Cobb says: "Of the other great absolute right of a freeman, viz., the right of private property, the slave is entirely deprived. His person and his time

in servitude from "acquiring" and "possessing" property. This alone settles the heaven-wide difference. But this is not all. There are statutes which inevitably imply that the Hebrew servant might and did acquire and hold property.

3. By Southern law, the slave is doomed to hopeless ignorance. It is a penal offence to teach him to read or write; even to teach him to read the word of God; much less is any legal injunction found for his religious training. The exceptional cases of actual instruction, unless it be oral, are in direct contravention of law.

No such *statutory prohibition* can be found regulating Jewish servitude. On the contrary, numerous *statutes enjoin* instruction in all religious duties, and open wide the door to all religious ordinances. It was a statutory offence against God and man for a Hebrew master to omit these things. Dr. Robinson himself gives the proof and illustration of this, in what he says of the regulations of the Jewish Church.

4. In many of the slave codes of the South,—perhaps in all,—colored persons, whether bond or free, are prohibited from merely assembling for the worship of God, even to receive oral religious instruction, or from meeting for any other purpose, without the presence of a specified number of white persons.*

There is *no such statute* as this regulating Jewish servitude.

5. By Southern law, *all* slaves are *vendible* "property."

being entirely the property of his master, whatever he may accumulate by his own labor, or is otherwise acquired by him, becomes immediately the property of his master."—*Law of Negro Slavery.*

* Under this feature of the slave code, General Cobb gives a judicial decision touching the authority of the "patrol" in times of danger from insubordination: "In South Carolina, it was held, that under the authority to disperse unlawful assemblages of negroes, the patrol had no right to interfere with an open assemblage for the purpose of religious worship, *where white persons were also assembled.*"—*Law of Negro Slavery.*

They are *sold*, by law, the same as mules, tobacco, and cotton. Without this feature of *vendibility* in the "slave codes,"—prevailing, so far as the law is concerned, *universally*, in the South,—the system would be comparatively worthless. Many families, and certain Border States, have found in this feature of the system one of the greatest sources of their wealth; and, for the sake of gain, masters sometimes *sell their own children*, begotten of slave mothers. *This is notorious.* This is also ACCORDING TO LAW; for, by the "codes," the child follows the condition of its mother,—*partus sequitur ventrem*,—and every one having *any* "black blood" belongs to the proscribed class. General Cobb, in his "Law of Negro Slavery," says: "The issue and descendants of slaves, in the maternal line, are slaves. The rule has been adopted *in all the States.*" This domestic traffic in slaves has been *the life, profit, and power of the system.* Without it, slavery in the extreme South, where it has been most profitable, and exerted its greatest power, at home and throughout the country, would shrivel and perish.

On the other hand, the Hebrew servitude was *wholly destitute*, both in *law* and *fact*, of this feature of *vendibility*, except in specified cases; as for crime, debt, and one other instance. The fact that these were *specified* cases, shows that the Jewish system knew nothing of that feature which is so prominently stamped upon the Southern system in practice, and which under *positive statute law* may be *universal.* This characteristic of the Southern "codes" is *nowhere found in the Mosaic law.* While Hebrews might "buy" of surrounding nations (in a sense which it is not, at this point, our purpose to consider), there is no evidence, either in *law* or *fact*, that any Jew ever *sold*, in the way it is commonly done in the South, and legally sanctioned as universal (except in the specified cases), *a single bondsman to any other Jew or to a heathen.* If this is denied, let the law and the case be shown. But yet, in order to make the Mosaic "code" *parallel* with the Southern, it must be shown that the *vendibility* of Jewish bondmen was, by the *statute, universal.* This is the *vital* point of correspondency to be shown; and this does not exist.

6. By Southern law, a slave cannot be a witness in any case against a white person. His master, or any other white person, may maltreat him in the extreme,—*may wilfully murder him,*—in the presence of fifty slaves who are as capable of testifying to the fact as any white person, and yet their testimony is worthless, *in law.**

Even Roman slavery, which many have regarded as the worst system that ever existed, was better than the Southern on this point. The Emperor Constantine not only allowed slaves to be witnesses, but gave those their freedom, by an edict, who testified against fraud, adultery, and certain other offences where freemen were involved.

* "Where a slave is killed, the presumption of law is the same as in other cases of homicide, that it was done maliciously. On account of the frequent and necessarily private relation of master and slave, remote most generally from the presence and view of any *white* person competent to be a *witness,* this presumption may and must often operate to the prejudice of the slayer, there being no means of proving the provocation given. Under this view, the Act of South Carolina provides, that where the homicide is committed, and no competent witness is present at the time to testify to the whole transaction, *the affidavit of the accused is admitted before the jury, explanatory and exculpatory of his conduct on the occasion.*"—"It would seem that from the very nature of slavery, and the necessarily degraded social position of the slave, many acts would extenuate the homicide of a slave, and reduce the offence to a lower grade, which would not constitute a legal provocation if done by a white person. Thus, in *The State* v. *Tackett,* it was held competent for one charged with the murder of a slave to give in evidence that the deceased was *turbulent, and insolent, and impudent to white persons.*"—"On account of the perfectly unprotected and helpless position of the slave, when his master is placed in opposition to him: not being allowed to accumulate property, with which to provide means for the prosecution of his rights; *his mouth being closed as a witness* in a court of justice; his hands being tied, even for his own defence, except in the extreme cases before alluded to; his time not being at his service, even for the purpose of procuring testimony," &c.—*Cobb's Law of Negro Slavery.*

No statutory prohibition of bondmen being witnesses can be found in the Mosaic code. Although there may be no statute authorizing testimony, as explicit as that of Constantine, yet the whole character of the Jewish system would naturally lead us to presume that those in servitude, otherwise competent, were allowed to testify against crime, whoever might be the offender. But the *absence* of any such positive, prohibitory statute, as is found in *all* the Southern "codes," marks the essential difference in the systems.

The foregoing, among many other differences in the two systems here compared, relate chiefly to the *individual.* There are strongly marked differences which relate to their *social* character.

7. By Southern law, *marriage* among slaves is a *nullity.* It has no legal recognition, existence, or protection. The master is authorized to separate, at pleasure and forever, those who *live together* under the name of husband and wife. This is often done in fact, for pecuniary gain and from other motives.*

On the other hand, the statutes of the Mosaic code regulating marriage are full and explicit, both positive and prohibitory, and these statutes were binding upon *all classes.* In the South, such unions as *are* formed among the slaves are often within the degrees of consanguinity and affinity forbidden by the Mosaic laws.

8. The whole family constitution *as God made it,* is utterly blotted out among slaves, by Southern law. The slave offspring of these teeming millions are the result of a systematic, perpetual, universal violation of the seventh

* "The inability of the slave to contract extends to the marriage contract, and hence there is no recognized marriage relation in law between slaves." "The contract of marriage not being recognized among slaves, of course none of its consequences follow from the contubernal state existing between them."—*Cobb's Law of Negro Slavery,*

command of the Decalogue; and this by the positive legislation of Christian States. These offspring may be torn from those who have borne them, and parents and children are often thus separated forever.*

Jewish servitude knew nothing of this wholesale and utter sweeping away of the most important institution God has given for the social, civil, and religious well-being of mankind. To charge this feature of the universal slave system of the South upon the Jewish system,—and, indeed, the same of every other point noticed,—and to say that *it is of God*, is to utter both falsehood and blasphemy.

The foregoing points show what Southern slavery is *as a system;* not the *evils incidental* to it, but what it is in its vital essence, and how it works, *by law;* evils which are inherent in it and inseparable from it, as both the General Assembly of 1818 and the Committee of the Synod of Kentucky affirm. The system, as such, could not exist a day without these radical legal features.

9. Our final point, therefore, in this comparison, is, that this system, by Southern law, is *made perpetual.* All slaves, legally considered, must look upon their posterity as doomed to it to the latest generation.

The Jewish system, to say the least of it, provided for the freedom of a portion of those in servitude at the year of Jubilee, and of another portion in the seventh year; while many able scholars (which we barely mention as a fact) contend that provision was made for the freedom of all who were held in servitude at the Jubilee.

On the other hand, many of the slave codes of the South

* "The marriage relation not being recognized among slaves, none of the relative rights and duties arising therefrom, belong strictly to the slave. * * * We may make the same assertion in reference to the relation of parent and child. In *some* of the States, both of these relations are *so far* recognized by the Legislature, as to provide by statute against their disruption in *public* sales."—*Cobb's Law of Negro Slavery,*

make it next to impossible for individual masters, when so disposed, to give freedom to their slaves ; while others prohibit emancipation altogether, making it a statutory offence.

There is thus a wide legal difference between the systems concerning *emancipation.*

PROFESSORIAL JUDGMENT OF THE CASE.

But we need go no further in this enumeration, though there are other points of marked contrast. THIS IS THE SYSTEM of the South which Dr. Robinson not only has the hardihood to *approve*, but which he has the unblushing effrontery to declare is of "THE SAME PRINCIPLES" as that which existed in the time of Abraham and Moses, *and which God incorporated into His Church!* For a more full delineation of it,—as a system *in practice*, inevitably resulting from such "codes,"—we again ask the reader to recur to the paper of the Committee of the Synod of Kentucky, and refresh his mind with what they set forth as the inherent essence of the system, AS SEEN IN REAL LIFE AMONG THEMSELVES, and then he will make some small approach towards understanding what *that specific thing is* which Dr. Robinson applauds and commends, and which he declares is taken into close fellowship by the Head of the Church!

If we were called upon to resolve the moral phenomenon presented in this case, we might, perhaps, adequately do it by citing what a distinguished Professor of Theology has written. The *Princeton Review*, for January, 1861, in an article on *The State of the Country*, says: "Most men, when they condemn slavery, have certain *slave laws* in their minds; laws which forbid the slaves to be instructed, which declare they cannot contract marriage, or which authorize the forcible separation of husbands and wives, parents and children. But Southern Christians condemn these laws as heartily as we do. INDEED NO MAN CAN BE A CHRISTIAN WHO DOES NOT CONDEMN THEM." Dr. Hodge here lays down the abstract principle. We shall not make the concrete application; but we abridge no man's liberty.

PROSLAVERY ARGUMENTS EXAMINED.

We come now to the arguments for slavery. We shall notice only some of the more prominent, and can give them but a comparatively brief examination. We shall take up those founded on Scripture first, and afterwards those drawn from the Law of Nature. The latter, indeed, will require no examination, provided negro slavery in the South can be sustained by the former; for if we have a "Thus saith the Lord" for it, in a written revelation, it is of little consequence to interrogate the less clear light of nature and reason.

What, then, do the Scriptures teach? At the outset, let the point which the advocates of the system must establish be distinctly kept in mind. THEY MUST SHOW THE DIRECT AUTHORITY OF SCRIPTURE FOR SOUTHERN NEGRO SLAVERY. They claim to be able to do this. They are confident they have done it. They deem those to be stupid who do not see it, and "infidel" who do not acknowledge it. We must then hold their arguments to this specific point.

So far as the present issue is concerned, it is wholly immaterial what the Scriptures of the Old and New Testaments may teach about the systems of their day, unless those teachings sanction negro slavery in the Southern States with the same kind and the same fulness of authority by which they sanction the Jewish and Roman systems of their own times, and concerning which it is conceded they directly speak. We may,—and of course we freely do,—admit *as true* every thing of *fact* and *principle* which is actually taught in the Scriptures concerning those systems; and yet, all which is thus true concerning them will go for absolutely nothing in the present argument, unless the *nexus* which it is claimed infallibly unites the modern system to the ancient, under the sanction of these divine teachings, is made as clear as the light.

Premising these plain points as fundamental, we take up several specific arguments separately. The order of examination, though not material, suggests, naturally, that which is first in importance.

THE ARGUMENT FROM THE DECALOGUE.

It is insisted by all Southern extremists that slavery is ordained in the Decalogue. Any references we here make to their language will be to the quotations given in a preceding chapter. Says Dr. Thornwell: "God sanctions it in both tables of the Decalogue." Dr. Robinson: "In two precepts of this law,—the fourth, concerning the Sabbath, and the tenth, concerning covetousness,—slavery is again recognized as existing in the Church by command, in reference to man-servants and maid-servants." Dr. Smyth: "God has actually embodied slavery in his moral law, and by there guarding, and protecting, and regulating it, has made it appertain to the present condition of humanity."

The Decalogue is permanent and universal in its authority. It is the law for man as man. If it "embodies" and "sanctions" the slavery for which Southern men contend, the argument is ended. The claim that it does, rests upon the meaning of two words. That meaning is assumed, in the quotations we have made, rather than established. It is, that the terms in the original, rendered "man-servant" and "maid-servant," in the fourth and tenth commandments, mean, necessarily, *slaves, in the sense of Southern slave law.* If the claim does not cover this, it is of no consequence in the present discussion. If it does cover and sustain it, we give up the point.

What then do these words mean? This is more or less a matter of opinion and exegesis, in which men differ. Much sholarship has been expended to ascertain the truth. We shall give eminent Jewish authorities, rather than our own opinion.

The Hebrew term rendered "man-servant," in the Decalogue, is *Ebed.* Remarking upon this word, Dr. Mielziner, before mentioned, the eminent Jewish scholar of Copenhagen, says, that it is "a name common to all who stood in a dependent or subordinate relation;" that it "has not the degrading meaning which we connect with the word 'slave' or 'bondman,' but often has the more mild signification, which we associate, in certain relations, with the term 'servant.'" Prof. Saalschütz, of Königsberg, says: that "the language of the Hebrews has *no word* for stigmatizing by a degrading appellation one class of those who owe service, and distinguishing them from the rest as 'slaves,' but *only one term for all* who are bound to render service to others. For males, this word is *Ebed*, servant, or *man-servant;* properly, *laborer;* for females, *Shifchah, Ama, maid-servant, maid.*"*

One of the most earnest advocates of a former day for the Scriptural authority for slavery in the South,—so far as deduced from the meaning of one of the words in question, as found in the Decalogue and elsewhere,—in noticing an objection to his view, says: "It is said, the Hebrew word *Ebed*, translated sometimes *servant*, some-

* Mielziner, *Die Verhaltnisse;* Saalschütz, *Das Mosaische Recht;* as cited by Dr. Thompson in his "*Christ. and Eman.*"

times *man-servant*, and sometimes *bond-servant*, does not mean a slave, but only a *worker*, one who is employed for a time, and even a relation of service of a highly honorable kind." He then makes this admission: "The word *Ebed* is translated as above, and *in itself properly signifies a worker, a laborer*, a person who does work of *any kind at all*, for another person."* This admission is all that is desired, and perfectly agrees with the eminent Jewish scholars referred to above.

If then the two words, found in the Decalogue, on which Southern men rest the whole argument for negro slavery, *from that source*, may have this wide latitude of meaning which the ablest scholars in Jewish learning give them, all the systems of slavery may perish throughout the earth, and no system ever again arise to curse the world, and yet this part of the Decalogue concerning "man-servants" and "maid-servants" would be just as applicable to society as ever. It would still be the law for mankind everywhere, and be appropriate wherever there were "laborers," or "workers," or "servants," who were yet in every sense *freemen*, and in no sense *slaves*.

An argument is pressed by some writers, drawn from the tenth commandment, which is not confined to the meaning of the words in question, but is deemed to be confirmatory of the essential meaning which it is claimed those words have. For example, it is said, that "man-servant" and "maid-servant" must indicate those who were held as "property," for *covetousness*, the sin here forbidden, always has reference to "property." The premises here are false. A person may "covet" that which is another's, whether it be his property or not. In point of fact this is often done. Many a person, in daily life, violates the tenth commandment, by coveting the

* "The Integrity of our National Union *vs.* Abolitionism," by Dr. Geo. Junkin.

"man-servant" or "maid-servant" who is but a *hired* laborer. More than this,—if the prohibition to "covet" a *servant*, in the tenth commandment, necessarily implies that the servant is "property," or a "slave" in the sense of Southern law, then the prohibition to "covet" a "wife," in the same commandment, implies that she also is a "slave" in the same sense. This is simply absurd. We readily grant that under the Jewish law, under the Roman law, under English law, and perhaps under law in every country in the world, the "wife" is, in a certain sense, the "property" of her husband. But who will pretend from this that there is a parallel in the condition of the "wife" under the Decalogue, and the condition of the "slave" under Southern law? And yet if the tenth commandment does not make the "wife" a "slave" in the sense of Southern law, no more does it make a "man-servant" or a "maid-servant" a "slave" in that sense. But if it does not make the "servant" a "slave" in that sense, then it makes him a "slave" in no sense applicable to the present case.

THE ABRAHAMIC AND MOSAIC SYSTEM.

Besides the Decalogue, there are two sources of authority for Southern slavery claimed from the Old Testament. One is, the system of servitude as regulated under Abraham; the other, as authorized by the code of Moses. For our purpose we may notice them together.

The specific point to be made out by our opponents is, that these regulations afford *precisely the same sanction* for Southern slavery that they do for the ancient system. We here pass by, entirely, the usual facts and reasonings urged to show that the Old Testament servitude was an essentially different system from that of Southern slavery, in all its elemental principles, designs, and actual working.

We have already stated certain points of difference. We pass by, also, the reasons for which many have supposed that system was established, or allowed and regulated. For the argument's sake, we here admit all that is claimed for the ancient system, as drawn from the two sources named.

What, then, was the fundamental authority for that system, both as to matter and form? It was sanctioned by the most direct and positive authority of God. The form of the sanction was through express revelation, embodying commands, covenants, and both positive and prohibitory statutes; by the several covenants made at different times with Abraham, and by the numerous statutes of the code of Moses. This, we presume, is the utmost which any one has ever claimed for the Jewish system, and this, for the sake of the argument, we at present concede.

Now, all we demand is this: Show us the same fulness of authority for Southern slavery, in matter and form, and we instantly yield the ground. Give us positive Divine sanction, through express revelation; give us the commands, covenants, statutes, and ordinances,—or even *one* of any of all these,—which as specifically designate negro slavery in the South as do those of the Old Testament unquestionably designate the ancient system,—that is, let these commands designate the race of Southern masters with the same definiteness that Jewish masters were designated, and point out the particular people who may and those who may not be enslaved, as is done in the Jewish code—do all this, and we will say no more. But until this is done, the indispensable *nexus* is wanting. Until this is done, it is just as reasonable to send us to the statutes of the Tycoon as to the statutes of Moses for *authority* for Southern slavery.

We have never been able to see,—and we sincerely desire some one to explain,—how it is that the Southern system is *necessarily hitched on* to the Mosaic, so that the ancient inevitably draws the modern along by its authority. This is a thing which is *assumed.* We insist that it shall be *proved.* The only semblance of a connection between the two which Dr. Robinson in his long argument attempts to make out, expressly in order to show that the Southern system is authorized by the ancient, is, that in their "principles," tried by their respective "codes," the two systems are "the same." That he deems this the vital and turning point in the case, is seen in the fact that he presses this declaration at four different stages of his argument, in nearly the same words, all of which we have given. But we have already shown that this assumed sameness is utterly groundless.

AUTHORITY IN CONTRAST.

But suppose, for the sake of the argument, that we admit this assumed identity in "principles,"—admit that these "codes" are, in every characteristic, precisely the same; that the Southern is an exact copy, word for word, of the Mosaic,—still, no shadow of sanction for the Southern system can result from such identity. It is an identity in AUTHORITY which must be established; but *that* does not result from an identity in "principles." If we look at the real sanction for the two systems,—admitting, for the moment, that they are alike in "principles,"—we shall see the world-wide difference between them in this vital matter of authority.

For the Jewish, there is this authority: GOD ALMIGHTY did, by express revelation, *Himself* ordain a code for the benefit of *a specific people*, Jewish masters, "chosen" by

Himself; and HE did also, by express revelation, designate the people who should *serve them* under that code.

For the Southern, there is this authority: SOUTHERN LEGISLATORS do, without revelation, *themselves* ordain this code, four thousand years afterwards, for the benefit of *another specific people*, Southern masters, "chosen" by *themselves;* and THEY do also, without revelation, designate the people who shall *serve them* under that code.

Now, can Southern masters, by virtue of this identity in the "principles" of the respective codes, claim divine sanction for slavery? This assumed identity is nothing to the purpose. It is, as before stated, an identity in AUTHORITY which must be established,—which shall embrace it in form and substance, as *directly from God*,—or Southern slavery can receive no support from the Jewish system. Such identity of authority, no man can show; nor any other kind of authority by which the Southern system can be sheltered under the Jewish. DIRECT REVELATION is what is demanded to meet the case.

If this total want of Divine sanction for Southern slavery, —in the matter and form stated,—be not conclusive against its being authorized by the ordinances regulating Mosaic servitude, then this result follows of logical necessity: that any system of slavery which men may choose to inaugurate,—at any time, in any place, among any people as masters, over any people as slaves, by any means, in any manner, from any motive,—may immediately claim, on precisely the same grounds, when once fully established among a people, the same Divine authority, and must at once be acknowledged as coming under this broad shield of the Divine protection; and he who does not admit all this of any system "got up to order," is, in the language of Southern extremists, an "infidel," an "apostate," and "blasphemes the God of Israel!" This is the inevitable logical result of the position taken and the argument presented.

We deem the foregoing considerations conclusive against the assumption that Southern negro slavery is of necessity sheltered under the ordinances, covenants, statutes, and commands, of the Old Testament system of servitude, and may therefore challenge for itself Divine sanction on such grounds. Make the "principles" of the ancient system to embrace just what you please,—covering every fact which the Scriptures declare,—and yet, if these covenants and statutes do not, *upon the very face of them*, show the Divine and direct *designation* of negro slavery in the South, as clearly as they designate the Jewish system, they no more authorize Southern slavery than they authorize the system of the Algerine corsairs.

THE NEW TESTAMENT ARGUMENT.

The argument for Southern slavery drawn from the New Testament, rests upon a different basis from that drawn from the Old. It is not claimed that ordinances and covenants of precisely the same character as those regulating Jewish servitude, are found for the system of Greek and Roman slavery of the time of Christ and the Apostles. It is insisted, however, that they recognized it as existing, in the State and in the Church, in their day; that they gave no command for its removal from either, but gave directions for the duties of masters and servants; and that it is placed in the same category with the matrimonial and parental relations, and is, therefore, like them, an "ordinance of God," of permanent and equal authority: from all which is drawn the broad conclusion that the negro slavery of the South is a lawful system, and is on like grounds an "ordinance of God." These points, it will be seen, are covered by the quotations previously given.

As in the argument on the other branches of the subject, so here, we shall pass by many points which are often effectively made in opposition to some of the positions taken and the conclusions reached in favor of slavery.

SLAVERY HANGING BY A WORD.

All who have paid any attention to discussions of the subject, know that much has been written upon the meaning of a single Greek word. *Doulos*, in New Testament discussions, has figured as largely as *Ebed*, in the Old.

Dr. Robinson inquires, in the article to which we have before referred, "What can be more absurd, than the dogma of white-cravatted infidelity, that 'servant' (*doulos*), in Scripture, means a hireling, or apprentice, not a slave?" This is his entire *argument* upon the point, in an elaborate paper in which he says: "We have aimed to present at one view an outline of the whole argument against the anti-slavery dogmas, as gathered from the inspired teaching of the Church in all these eras," embracing both the Old and New Testament dispensations.

We would remind Dr. Robinson that his distinguished friend, Dr. Thornwell, always wore a "white cravat." He should therefore regard that part of his argument as disposed of. So far as there is any point in his inquiry about the meaning of the word in question, we propose to meet it with something better than a sneer; something, too, that will probably have more weight with him than any thing we could say.

PROF. LEWIS ON DOULOS.

Prof. Tayler Lewis, occupying the chair of Greek in Union College, is an eminent scholar; and from a commendatory notice of an article of his which has appeared in *The True Presbyterian*, we presume its editor may be in a state of mind to heed what he says about *doulos.* He says of the Professor: "It may be a weakness of ours, but we confess to a particular sympathy with, and pleasure in, the curious, semi-platonic and scholarly, but earnest and soul-reaching method in which Prof. Tayler Lewis *always writes of the Scriptures, and their interpretation.*"

Upon this, we are certainly justified in commending Prof. Lewis's "interpretation," which is "always" so valuable, to Dr. Robinson. We do not remember the color of Prof. Lewis's cravat, but we heard an apdress from him in New York some years since, and he then had on a blue coat with gilt buttons. He thus discourseth:

Much learning has been exhibited in respect to the word *douloi.* There is no doubt that it *may* denote the servile condition. It is equally clear that it is a term of government, and may signify a *subject* from the highest to the lowest rank. It may imply both ideas. But there *is* a word in the Greek language that has the one, the lowest one, *exclusively and forever.* It is always *servile.* It is ever used to denote slaves as *property,* and in a property sense. As thus employed, it is exceedingly common in the classical Greek—*always* used, we may say, when the *servile* notion is to be expressed *simple and unmixed.* It must have been very familiar throughout Asia Minor, and wherever Paul found the reality or the semblance to the relation. It is the word *andra podon.* It is of the neuter form, to express vileness, to denote that that to which it is applied is regarded as a *thing* or chattel, without will, or a true acknowledged personality. When slaves are statistically enumerated as property, they are called *andra poda,* just as cattle or flocks are called by similar neuters, *to kteno, ktenea, ktemata, probata.* It is an interesting query: Why is this servile word, so common in Athenian Greek, *never found in the New Testament?* It is because there is *no idea acknowledged there which it could properly express.*

We now give Dr. Robinson all the benefit he can derive from *doulos,* with all the aid he can get from the entire coterie of those who claim that the word necessarily means a "slave;" and we leave it wholly to him to choose the color of their cravats. We trust that Prof. Lewis's "scholarly" performance may prove "soul-reaching" to the whole of them.

PROF. LEWIS ON SLAVE-TRADERS.

There is an exegesis from Prof. Lewis, following the above extract, which is further serviceable here. It knocks certain declaimers for Southern slavery, and those who denounce *man-stealing*, completely "off their pins," and turns the argument against them with a force which should make them wince. The Professor says:

> There is one word used in the New Testament, a derivative of this word (1 Tim. i. 10), but in such a way that it will do the man who is hunting Scriptural pleas for slavery no good. It is *andra podistes*, rendered *man-stealer*, but clearly wrong. The form of the ending shows that it does not denote an occasional act, an occasional theft, but a business, an occupation *Andra podistes* is not a *man-thief*, but a MAN-TRADER, a SLAVE-TRADER, or a SLAVE-DEALER; one whose business is to sell an *andra podon:* just as *kermatistes* (John ii. 14) does not mean *money-stealer*, but *money-seller*, *broker*, "money-changer." So in the Memorabilia, Socrates metaphorically calls the Sophists who took pay for their lectures, *andra podistes*, men who sold themselves for *servile hire*. Look at the association in which this term is found (1 Tim. i. 10), and then judge whether the idea of that thing in which the *andra podistes* dealt, or the idea of *human property*, could ever have been applied by the Apostle to a *man*, much less to a *Christian brother*. What an ungodly crew!—"the unholy and profane, murderers, fornicators, SLAVE-TRADERS, liars, perjurers, and all else that is opposed to pure doctrine."

Who does not remember to have heard this passage often quoted from Timothy to show direct condemnation by Paul of the practice charged upon certain men for enticing away slaves from the South, calling them "men-stealers!" We are not defending theft; nor do we refer to this passage to justify the practice charged. "Let every tub stand on its own bottom." We refer to it to show that it has nothing to do with condemning that practice. But it has much to do with another thing. It condemns *men-traders*. It is a bolt wielded by the Apostle Paul, under the guide of inspiration, which crushes at one blow *the whole domestic slave-trade, and all concerned in it*,—to say nothing of the foreign slave-trade,—on the ground claimed by all the advocates of Southern slavery, that these teachings of the Apostle bear as directly on that system as they did upon the Greek and Roman slavery of his time; a domestic slave-trade which is the very *life and power of the whole system*, and out of which certain of the Border States have coined millions of wealth. This is another "scholarly" performance, which we hope also may prove "soul-reaching" to all who may need the benefit of it.

We now leave Dr. Robinson in company with his *doulos*, and we place alongside of him the *andra podon*, the *andra podistes*, and the Apostle Paul; the latter a "noble old Roman citizen." We do not know the color of Paul's cravat, nor the color of that of any of these Greek gentlemen; so we cannot tell whether their company will be agreeable or otherwise.

We cannot close this part of the subject without giving another extract from Prof. Lewis. He is speaking of the use proslavery men make of some of Paul's teachings; and the sarcasm will apply to all, but especially to Professors Morse and Christy, *The True Presbyterian*, and all others who with them (and we do not know of any exceptions) deem slavery an essential antecedent to the most successful evangelization of a "barbarous" race:

> And now, to take these *holy things*, and make from them an argument in favor of slavery as it exists in the United States, of cotton growing slavery, our trafficking, mercenary, *property-claiming* slavery, that will sell a man, his children, and his children's children, for its own worldly gain, and then content itself with the poor, conscience-soothing plea, that perhaps he may, somehow, *get Christianized in the process!* It is rank sacrilege.

SLAVERY AMONG THE RELATIONS.

The position in which slavery is mentioned by the Apostles, among certain recognized and permanent relations in society, is deemed by many the most formidable argument in its favor. It is presented by all the advocates of the Southern system, and is regarded as conclusive and overwhelming. It is substantially this: that slavery, in the New Testament, is placed on an equality, as to authority and permanency, with the civil, matrimonial, and parental relations, as, with them, "an ordinance of God." This claim, taken in connection with the conceded fact that injunctions are given to both masters and servants, as well as to the persons filling the other relations, is deemed as presenting a valid and unanswerable sanction for Southern slavery. It is the argument from the greater to the less; from the acknowledged authority of three relations,—the civil, matrimonial, and parental,—to the authority of a fourth, the *servile*. As they are classed together, and the duties of each are specified, their authority is equal, and the relation in each case permanent. That is the argument.

Says Dr. Ross: "Slavery is of God," and "Slavery is ordained of God;" as between master and servant, "it is a relation belonging to the same category as those of husband and wife, parent and child." Says Dr. Thornwell: "The Apostles are explicit in inculcating the duties which sprung from both sides of the relation." Speaking at length of the four relations, Prof. Morse calls them, "the social system which God has ordained." Dr. Robinson: "The duties of the relation of master and servant are discussed in common with the duties of parent and child, husband and wife." The *True Presbyterian:* "The Saviour Himself accepted slavery as being equally of God with civil government, marriage, and the parental relation." And so say they all.

THE REDUCTIO AD ABSURDUM.

The exalted position here given to slavery involves these logical absurdities: (1.) It makes slavery an essential and universal element of society. (2.) It makes emancipation a sin.

These are inevitable deductions from the doctrine maintained. We no longer wonder, therefore, that men who hold the doctrine can write books, like Mr. Fitzhugh, of Virginia, on "The Failure of Free Society," nor that among certain Southern men, as Drs. Palmer, Thornwell, and Armstrong, there should have been such lamentations of mourning and sorrow over the condition of things in the Free States, concerning which, however, they know so little. We are no longer surprised that they should wish to make slavery universal. We no longer wonder that this stupendous rebellion is prosecuted in the interest of this doctrine; for the institution it defends is one of the very pillars of the whole social fabric, of the family, of the State, and of the Church. Let us glance at these two points.

SLAVERY UNIVERSALLY ESSENTIAL.

1. The doctrine propounded upon these relations makes slavery an essential and universal element of society. How can it be otherwise, if it is in all respects equal to the matrimonial, parental, and civil relations? Writers generally have considered three of these relations as "ordained of God," viz., the civil, or that of ruler and ruled; the connubial, or that of husband and wife; the parental, or that of parent and child; that these three belong to society universally, as God designed it, and are essential

to the *existence*, as well as to the well-being, of mankind in a social state; and that these three are all which God has directly "ordained" for that end. But our modern philosophers make a fourth, the *servile*, which they place in "the same category." We do not see, therefore, on this basis, why slavery is not essential to the very existence of society, in the form in which God has authorized and organized the social state.

Can society be maintained without civil government?—or without marriage?—or without the parental relation? No Christian will pretend it. Nor, upon this theory, can it be maintained without slavery. Strike down *any one* of the other relations, and society perishes. Blot out civil government, and anarchy reigns and society is in ruins. Destroy marriage, and the race becomes extinct, or universal concubinage must perpetuate it; and in either case, destruction to the parental relation is the result. So, also, upon this theory, society can no more be perpetuated without slavery than without these other relations, for it is equally with them an "ordinance of God," and in "the same category." This is the inevitable logical result from the premises; and it demonstrates the perfect absurdity of giving *slavery* that position among the authoritative and permanent relations of society.

But is it said, that all that is meant is, that slavery is merely a universally *admissible* relation? Then we ask, in reply: Is civil government merely an admissible institution, that may be continued or dispensed with at pleasure? Is marriage, as an institution or relation, merely admissible; and may it be set aside altogether for the institution of "free love?" May the parental relation be supplanted by any substitute which would result from overthrowing the matrimonial? Not one of these three institutions, involving these relations, is *merely admissible* in the

Divine organization of society. *It cannot be organized and perpetuated, as God designed it, without them.* They are each and all *enjoined as essential* to its existence and perpetuity. Then, of logical necessity, on the ground now claimed, *slavery* is also *enjoined*, as a universal, permanent, and essential element, in the Divine organization and continuance of society. This conclusion is unavoidable; or, the premise that slavery is an "ordinance of God," in "the same category" with these other relations, is altogether untenable.

EMANCIPATION A SIN.

2. So, also, of logical necessity, this doctrine makes emancipation a sin. One of the things which is always insisted upon by proslavery writers is, that the New Testament is *utterly silent about emancipation.* Well, let it be granted; and then what follows? If slavery is an "ordinance of God" in the sense that marriage is, what right have we, by emancipation, to destroy the relation essential to it, in any case, without express revealed authority from God? To do so is sin. Can we set aside marriage, in any case, by sundering the relation of husband and wife, except upon the ground for which the Scriptures expressly provide, without heinous sin? Can we sever the parental relation without sin? Can we overturn lawful civil government without sin? Are not all these essential to society, and "ordained of God?" No more can we, upon the doctrine claimed, set aside slavery without sin; neither, on the one hand, by proclamation, or law, or military power, or by any other wholesale measures; nor, on the other, in any individual case. To do this in any way or to any extent, without an explicit "Thus saith the Lord," from His word, either expressly permissive or directory, is to sin against

God with a high hand, if slavery is His "ordinance;" and this is, also, to overthrow one of the pillars of society.

INVASION OF GOD'S PREROGATIVE.

The case of Dr. Ross is most remarkable for a Christian minister. He writes a book, entitled, "Slavery Ordained of God." In the book he tells us that "Slavery is of God;" and the relation essential to it he puts into "the same category as those of husband and wife, parent and child." What next? He tells us that he has been a slaveholder, but is not one now. He has "emancipated his slaves," and the act cost him "some self-denial." He does not boast of the act, but evidently regards it as redounding to his credit.

This case presents a singular mixture of morals and logic, and we presume Dr. Ross does not stand alone. It is a sound principle, on every ground, that the only authority which can warrant a person in setting aside a just law or ordinance, is the authority that established it; and not only so, but the manner in which it may be set aside must be as clearly set forth as are the provisions of the ordinance itself. This principle may be applied to the matter in hand. Dr. Ross and his co-laborers claim slavery to be a Divine "ordinance;" that this is a doctrine of written revelation; and they are out of patience with those who dissent. They do not pretend that they have any revelation for emancipation. On the contrary, it is one of their cardinal doctrines in defence of the system, that the word of God is utterly silent on the subject of emancipation. And yet Dr. Ross coolly tells us that he has "emancipated his slaves," or, in other words, that he has deliberately abolished an "ordinance of God;" one which is in "the same category" with marriage and the parental relation, and which, therefore, is essential to human welfare; that he did it with "some self-denial," but nevertheless he did it, and thinks it well, and wishes others to think so. We should suppose that such an unwarranted invasion of the Divine prerogative ought to have cost him "some self-denial," and not a little. Would he thus repudiate his wife, and banish his children? Why not, with equal authority?

THE RELATIONS IN DIALOGUE.

But we are not done with the absurdities of this doctrine. We have noticed two, which are absurdities in logic. There is another, partly logical and wholly practical.

It is a little remarkable that this equality of authority for these several relations is urged to sanction the system of negro slavery in the South,—and is deemed an argument of such force as to put to silence all opposition,—when, notoriously, the matrimonial and parental relations, as an "ordinance of God," on which the servile relation is made to rest for its sanction, are, among the slaves, *utterly ignored in law, and have no existence in fact.* It is most amazing,—it puts all logic to the blush, and presumes upon ignorance of what is universally known, or supposes a stultification of conscience, touching the sacredness and authority of ordinances on which the whole social fabric rests, that would be criminal,—to see men seriously urge the lawfulness of a given relation, on the ground of the lawfulness of two other given relations, where the latter are confessedly binding upon all who enter into the family state, when these two are utterly repudiated, in law and in fact, among the entire people on the one side for whom the lawfulness of the first is claimed.

Good morning, Mr. Smith. Do you live in South Carolina?

Yes.

Do you deem negro slavery a divine institution?

Certainly.

On what ground?

The relation between master and slave is upon the same ground as the matrimonial and parental relations. They are all alike "ordinances of God."

Do these other two relations exist among your own slaves, Mr. Smith, as "an ordinance of God?"

They live together, and have children.

Are they lawfully married?

Our "slave code" does not recognize marriage among slaves, so that we can exactly call it "an ordinance of God;" for, it must be confessed, it allows us to sell and separate any that live together, and their children; and in fact that is often done, and done against the consent of the parties.

Does it not look a little queer, then, Mr. Smith, that you should urge a divine sanction for slavery on such a ground as that?

Our ablest divines have presented that argument often; it appears sound.

Their reasoning is bad enough, at best; but it would not be quite so strikingly objectionable, practically, if the other two relations were hedged about by your laws as slavery is. Your "slave code" is burdened with laws about one of these relations, securing all the interests of slavery; but the other two are ignored in law, among the slaves. Is not that a singular argument for the one, which is based upon the other two, where the two have no existence?

Oh! but our laws secure the rights of husbands and

wives, parents and children, as truly as they do those of masters and slaves.

How is that, Mr. Smith? Did you not say that the laws make no provision for marriage among slaves, and that they gave you authority to break up and separate families at pleasure, and that this was often done?

Yes; but it was of the laws about these two relations among the whites that was meant.

Ah! you mean, then, that two of these relations were "ordained" for the white race only, and that the other was "ordained" for the negro. Is that it, Mr. Smith?

Well—it is about that—practically.

Then the argument of your divines to show God's sanction for slavery, drawn from the social relations, is this: that because he has "ordained" marriage and the parental relation for the whites, he has *therefore* "ordained" slavery for the blacks. Is that it?

Well,—they are more skilled in these things; you must consult them.

Good morning, Mr. Smith.

Such is about the point and pith of the argument for negro slavery in the South, drawn from the matrimonial and parental relations, for the sanction of the system as an "ordinance of God." Two of the relations are made for the master only; the other for the slave.

A SOUTHERN FAMILY ESTABLISHED.

Let us bring the argument for negro slavery based upon these several relations, as each an "ordinance of God," to a practical test in another way. Leaving abstractions, let us take a real case. We shall assume that the *civil* relation of ruler and ruled, with regard to the case now to be considered, exists properly, and we shall notice only the other three relations.

Here is a family of four persons. It consists of John Smith and Mary, his wife, John Smith, Jr., their son, all white persons; and Peter, a negro slave, held as a "chattel" under the "code" of South Carolina, in the name of the elder Smith. It is claimed that these three relations, in this concrete case, have equally the sanction of Scripture, and that each is an "ordinance of God." How does this appear? Each of these relations had a beginning, as to that particular family and these particular persons. How could they, of right, be formed, so as to make each one, when formed, an "ordinance of God?"

There is no difficulty in regard to the first two. When John Smith wanted a wife, whom had he a right to marry? Any woman in the wide world, not within the prohibited degrees of consanguinity or affinity, who was willing to marry him. The marriage of John and Mary was based upon mutual consent. The relation of husband and wife was thus properly formed between them, and the demands of the law of God were fully met, and thus the first "ordinance" is established in this family under the divine sanction. John Smith, Jr., is the offspring of these parents, begotten and born in lawful wedlock. The second or parental relation is thus formed in this family, according to the "ordinance of God," and is therefore brought fully under the divine sanction.

We have now only to provide for Peter, and to see if we can exalt his relation into an "ordinance." How shall it be done? There appear to be some practical difficulties in the way of bringing him under God's "ordinance," as a slave to John Smith, though he is John's slave under South Carolina law.

Whatever is done for Peter's relief, must be done in accordance with the Scriptures, for it is an "ordinance of God" that is to be established.

DIVINE ORDINANCES PLAIN.

All God's ordinances are explicit. If they involve the instituting of a *relation*, they show how it is to be formed, and what is essential to it. Is it a union with the Church? The Scriptures show in what this consists, the terms of communion, the requisite qualifications, and how membership is to be formed. Is it severance from the Church? They point out the offences which justify it, the officers who are to judge, and the several successive steps to be taken. Is it of baptism, or of the Lord's supper? They are full upon every point touching persons and things. Is it of marriage? They declare who may and who may not join to constitute this relation, and point out the sin of violating the law. Is it of divorce? They define what may and what may not sever the relation of husband and wife.

And so on through every ordinance; every thing essential to the case is made clear. And, be it observed, it is not merely *the duties* of these several relations which the Scriptures make plain. It is the *relations themselves* upon which they give light; the *persons* who may enter into them, and all the *requisites for their formation.*

THE SERVILE RELATION AS AN "ORDINANCE."

Now, how are we TO FORM *this relation* between master and slave, so that it may be an "ordinance of God," with the same undoubted certainty as to the *persons* who may be *masters* and the *persons* who may be *slaves*, and all other things essential to it, as in the case of every other conceded "ordinance of God?" Do the Scriptures give us any light whatever on these points? How can we, at the start, put Peter into the family of John Smith, of South Carolina, so that the relation which Peter will then sustain to John as his slave, will be in the same sense an "ordinance of God" that the marriage tie by which John and Mary are husband and wife, is an "ordinance of God?" *What is there in Scripture*, as regards this "ordinance," *to show that Peter might not just as well have been the master, and John the slave?* We put aside mere abstractions at present, and we wish the doctrine applied to this concrete case. If it cannot explain the relation existing between John and Peter, and how it was *originally formed* as an "ordinance of God," the doctrine cannot apply to any case. It must first *establish* the relation between John, the master, and Peter, the slave, and then vindicate it as God's ordinance. What is the process for doing this, pointed out in Scripture?

We have no difficulty in putting Peter into the family of John Smith as his slave, under *the statute law* by which he is held. We can kidnap him from Africa, by Col. Lamar and the slave ship *Wanderer;* or we can transmit him by inheritance from the honorable family of Smith, in the line of John's ancestors; or we can buy him of Wade Hampton with John's money; or we can give John a "clean bill of sale" from a friend as a gift, with "one dollar" as a consideration. We can exhaust all the possible modes by which he could have been made and held a slave, and brought into this relation to John Smith, any one of which would stand the test of South Carolina law; and yet, we fail to find any one of them, or all of them together, anywhere *set forth* as the modes by which this relation may be *constituted*, so as, without question, to make it an "ordinance of God," as the matrimonial and parental relations are acknowledged to be; while, *how* to exalt Peter into "an ordinance" in a *Scriptural manner* is the vital question at issue.

Now, can it be possible, that a relation where such momentous interests are involved, can be elevated to the dignity of a divine "ordinance," founded on revelation, and put on a par with the matrimonial and parental relations,—a relation, as in negro slavery in the South, involving life, liberty, the grossest ignorance, ignoring marriage, breaking up families,—and yet, the Scriptures be *utterly silent* on the manner of its *formation*, and the persons who may enter it, on the one side and the other, while they are so full on these points touching every other relation where an "ordinance of God" is concerned? *Credat Judæus Apella.*

THE ONLY LOOPHOLE, AND THAT CLOSED.

There is but one possible resort by which any advocate of this doctrine can attempt to relieve the case of Peter; and that we have already met, and it will avail him nothing. *The New Testament can throw no light upon it.*

The only thing left is to go back to the time of Abraham and Moses, to the Jewish law, which would allow Peter to be "bought with (John's) money," as "bondmen" were then bought of the "heathen." But that resort presents sundry difficulties which we have already noticed.

As we are now confined to a specific case, we say as before, that until you show as unequivocal commands as Abraham and Moses had, commands as directly addressed to the present race of masters as those ancient commands were addressed to the Jews as a distinct people, you can gain nothing by that resort; and if John Smith claims that he has a right to Peter, under those ancient commands, he must show, that he, John Smith, infallibly belongs to the present class to whom like commands are addressed, or that a similar command has been addressed to him in person. All this must be as certain *antecedently* as the claim which any Jew could make, and *then* John

Smith can proceed, but not before, to possess himself of Peter.

If these positions are not tenable, then we say as before, that any person or any number of persons, without *any authority whatever* from God, may at any time, and in any country, get up a system of slavery "to order," and immediately place it under the ancient Jewish law, with the same good reason that the Southern system can be placed there.

We here drop the discussion upon the Scriptural claim of Southern slavery to a recognition by both the Old and New Testament. There are other arguments which are often advanced for the claim which it is unnecessary to notice. If those which we have considered cannot be maintained, the claim must fall. On which side lies the truth, we leave the reader to judge.

CHAPTER XIV.

SLAVERY IN POLEMICS.—LAW OF NATURE.

It is of comparatively little consequence to Christian men, what the "Law of Nature" may teach about slavery. When we have a written Revelation from God, and are told that slavery is "sanctioned," "ordained," "established," "regulated," and "sanctified," by express "commands," "covenants," "statutes," and "ordinances" of His word, we are satisfied with simply examining this Revelation. If the negro slavery of the South can be justified by the Scriptures, and in all the modes claimed, that is quite enough; the Law of Nature cannot add any thing to this testimony. So, on the other hand, after being so confidently referred to the Scriptures for full proof for negro slavery, if we find the evidence fail, we need not be sent to Nature to have the case mended. That cannot supply our need, while we have Revelation as "an infallible rule of faith and practice."

But we are not afraid of Nature, her Law, or her teachings. In examining the subject, however, so as to derive any practical benefit, and especially so as to settle the question before us, we are met at the outset with difficulties.

DISAGREEMENT ON WHAT IS THE LAW OF NATURE.

Men are not agreed upon the meaning of the phrase, "Law of Nature;" upon what Nature herself is, as a moral teacher; upon the extent, character, and authority of her teachings; whether she is an independent and authoritative teacher, or to be limited by Revelation; or how her teachings are to be interpreted, and by whom. These and a thousand other things come up for settlement before we can make even a beginning in our investigations. We are then completely at sea touching this whole matter; and it is the merest folly for those who have a perfect guide in a written Revelation, in all questions of morals, to leave that to follow an *ignis-fatuus.*

Dr. Seabury, in defending slavery as resting on the "Law of Nature," defines the phrase as follows: "By the Law of Nature, according to the best usage among the ancients, and universally among the moderns, is meant, as we have said, that rule of fitness which the Deity has established for the government of men, considered as reasonable creatures, and intended for mutual society." Upon this definition, three things may be observed. (1.) Here is an admission that this law is not understood alike; for he speaks of the "*best* usage among the ancients." They then differed among themselves, as all men know. (2.) Men also now differ as to which was the "best usage" among differing opinions in former times. Dr. Seabury is a case in point. As we shall see hereafter, he dissents from the opinion of one of the highest authorities "among the ancients." (3.) Nor is this law understood alike, "universally among the moderns;" for nothing is more certain than that men now, as they have always done, on ten thousand questions,—and this very question of slavery, in all its bearings, is a striking example of the fact,—widely differ as to what "that rule of fitness" is, of which he speaks. Modern apologists for negro slavery, —and he among them,—deem the system of the South pre-eminent in its "fitness" for both master and slave; the very best condition of things, "intended for mutual society," as taught by both Nature and Revelation.

Others totally dissent from these opinions. It is simply the determination to push this doctrine and illustrate this "fitness" by extending negro slavery far and wide, which is now deluging this nation in blood. The upshot of the whole matter, therefore, is, that it is ludicrously absurd,—not to say criminal,—to pretend that all men now agree upon the "Law of Nature," as Dr. Seabury here defines it.

The Law of Nature,—so far as there is any such thing, whether we understand it or not,—is the Law of God. He speaks through both Nature and Revelation. His utterances from them are harmonious. They are but different volumes to unfold His will. Where men have not Revelation, Nature is their guide. But what is the guide in such a case? We refer only to human opinions as we find them; what answer do they give? Is this guide the knowledge of God's will which men may gather from His works of creation and providence?—or, within a narrower view, from the condition of human society?—or, in a still narrower, from the voice of the individual soul, the reason, the conscience?—or, from the general judgment or consent of mankind?—or, is it from all these combined?—or, is it from something different from them all? Here, again, the philosophers of the world are disagreed, and he who attempts to follow them will find himself befogged and in despair.

DISAGREEMENT IN APPLYING THE LAW OF NATURE.

To show the bearing of all this upon the case in hand, we need only observe that some writers declare, with an assurance which awes timidity into submission, that the Law of Nature justifies slavery; that it is founded in it and approved by it; and that hence all nations have recognized slavery as proper on such grounds. But other writers as directly declare that the Law of Nature condemns slavery; that wherever slavery has existed, though it may have prevailed ever so widely, it has always been in violation of this law, and an infringement upon the inherent rights of man. And thus the ablest men are in conflict on that which is vital to the whole question. They disagree upon matters of fact and of principle; upon what the law itself is; whether it approves or condemns; and differ upon its application.

When Christian men cannot agree about the meaning of a written Revelation concerning slavery, it is worse than idle to make an appeal to the Law of Nature, where the matters presented for its justification are vastly more indeterminate and inconclusive.

MORAL PHASES INVOLVED IN THE APPLICATION.

It will often appear, both in the investigation of this branch of the subject and that concerning slavery being authorized by the Scriptures, that men's views as to matters of fact, principle, interpretation, and application, covering all that bears upon the justification of slavery, are more or less shaped and modified by the circumstances of their education, and also to a degree, no doubt imperceptibly to themselves, by their interests. It is an undoubted fact, that with the rarest exceptions, the men who have justified and defended slavery as a divine institution, as an "ordinance of God," have been those who were in some way interested in the system, directly or indirectly; sometimes through a pecuniary interest, and sometimes through their social or other relationships.

It is no impeachment of human nature, except as fallen and blind, and no unjust invasion of any proper principle within the province of morals, to say that arguments in favor of human bondage,—and especially that system of *chattelism* which so *dehumanizes* both the master and the slave as to make a man formed "in the image of God," the marketable, vendible commodity of another man, as a horse and an ox,—when universally presented by those who are interested in the system, should be scrutinized with some degree of suspicion. If any persons to whom this may apply do not feel themselves complimented, the fault is not ours; it is the fault of the case. Whatever else may be said of the Law of Nature, this is a true principle, as gathered from the universal observations of mankind,—meaning now, under this view of the law, simply the universal state of the human race, as *fallen* beings,—that all men are more or less swayed in their judgments, reasonings, and feelings, *by their interests*, and often and to a degree without being aware of it. This is as truly settled in the convictions of mankind as any other fact or principle.

We see no reason why the principle should not be applied to judgments, reasonings, feelings, in favor of slavery; but, on the other hand, every reason why it should be so applied. If the justice and force of the application in any manner depend upon the *degree* of interest in the subject, then we have only to look at what men are now doing in this terrible rebellion, undertaken and prosecuted for the sake of slavery, to see how closely their opinions, urged in favor of the system, should be scanned.

ILLUSTRATIVE CONTRADICTIONS.

Let us, now, in order to come directly to the matter in hand, first give an example or two to show the contradiction of writers upon the point whether slavery is justified or condemned by the Law of Nature.

Dr. Seabury writes a book, published since the rebellion began, entitled, "American Slavery distinguished from the Slavery of English Theorists, and Justified by the Law of

Nature." He says, it is "necessary to bring the question of slavery to the test of the Law of Nature." And further: "Is not the institution agreeable to the Law of Nature, as well as the law of the land, and to the Scriptures? This is the question which I propose to examine." He then proceeds:

Where is the nation that has pronounced a state of servitude for life contrary to natural justice? What age, before our own, could point to moralists that proclaim it an offence against nature to hold slaves in the condition in which Providence has placed them. * * * If slavery has, in fact, existed among most nations; if no nation has proclaimed it a violation of natural justice; and if the most eminent men of all times, legislators, sages, and moralists, have confessed a state of servitude for life, no matter what name they have given it, to be consistent with justice, then we have, to this extent, the consent of mankind in its favor; and from this consent we are entitled to infer, not indeed its expediency in every country and every state of society, but its agreement with, or non-repugnance to, the Law of Nature.

And he proceeds to defend "American Slavery" on the ground that it is in "agreement with" this law.

SLAVERY AGAINST NATURE.—CODE OF JUSTINIAN.

Over against this broad claim, we put the declarations of the Justinian Code, which will be admitted to be conclusive upon the point in hand. We need scarcely say, that philosophers, statesmen, moralists, accord to it the highest authority. From the *Institutes of Justinian*, we take the following:

Concerning the rights of persons, Title 3.—The first division of persons in regard to their rights is this: that all men are either freemen or slaves. *Freedom* (from which men are called free) is the *natural* power which one has of doing what he pleases, unless prevented by force, or by law. *Slavery* is when one person is subjected to the dominion of another by authority of the law of nations, CONTRARY TO NATURAL LAW. Slaves are so denominated, because our commanders were accustomed to sell, and thus to preserve instead of slaying them.*

So, also, in the *Pandects* or *Digests*, Lib. 50, Tit. 17, Sec. 32, the same doctrine is laid down, that slavery is contrary to the Law of Nature:

> In regard to the Civil Law, slaves are not reckoned as persons; but it is *not so according to Natural Law*, for according to that law, ALL MEN ARE EQUAL.†

It seems that the doctrine upon human rights laid down in the Declaration of Independence as among "self-evident" truths,—"that all men are created equal," taken in the true sense there intended,—was older than the days of Thomas Jefferson. It appears, too, that slavery is contrary to the Law of Nature,—"contra naturam," *against nature*,—instead of being in "agreement with" it, as Dr. Seabury asserts, provided we take as our guide authorities which are regarded as among the highest in the world. But the advocates of "American Slavery" cannot be turned aside by such slight obstacles as the Institutes of Justinian, even when their appeal is made to a principle which such an authority, if any, is deemed competent to settle.

THE JUSTINIAN CODE OVERTHROWN.

Dr. Seabury is of course aware that the Justinian Code contradicts his position, and he labors to avoid its force. He concedes that it is "a great authority on a subject of

* "*De Jure personarum*, *Tit.* 3.—Summa itaque divisio de jure personarum hæc est: quod omnes homines, aut liberi sunt, aut servi. Et libertas quidem (ex qua etiam liberi vocantur) est naturalis facultas ejus, quod cuique facere libet, nisi quid vi aut jure prohibetur. Servitus autem est constitutio juris gentium, qua quis dominio alieno contra naturam subjicitur. Servi autem ex eo appellati sunt, quod imperatores captivas vendere, ac per hoc servare, nec occidere solent."

† "Quod attinet ad jus civile, servi pro nullis habentur; non tamen et jure naturali, quia quod ad jus naturali attinet omnes homines æquales sunt."

this sort;" speaks of it as "a code which it took centuries to mature," and in reference to the Law of Nature, says that this code "is one of the ablest developments of its principles ever made by unassisted reason;" and admits that it "declares slavery to be an abnormal state of society, upheld by force, and in violation of justice." How, then, does he reconcile the Justinian Code with his own position? Or, rather, how does he seek to invalidate its authority?—for that is really what he undertakes to do, after giving it such high praise. The task is most easily accomplished, and the resort is eminently worthy of a philosopher. He thinks it "just possible" that we "impute to the code a flagrant inconsistency."

He first brings against this code, hoary with that wisdom "which it took centuries to mature," the charge that its definition of the Law of Nature is "different from that in which the phrase is commonly taken;" that is, "different" from his own definition. This ought not to disturb our equanimity. We should freely allow any man to prefer his own wisdom if he likes, even though it should clash with that which it took "centuries to mature." We have seen, however, that his own definition has elements palpably irreconcilable with notorious facts. But that is a small matter. It is, so far, mere criticism, and that is within the capacity of any one, even upon the Justinian Code. The great philosophical feat is yet to come.

He gives the observations of the Code upon the Law of Nature, as embracing and illustrated by the law of procreation, which appertains to "all animals, whether they are produced on the earth, in the air, or in the waters;" and which says that "the rest of the animal creation" as well as man, have a "knowledge of this law by which they are actuated;" and then the learned commentator upon Justinian proceeds to say:

Now by the Law of Nature, in this large sense of the phrase, man is as free as the beasts of the field; and to say that slavery is against Nature, or the Law of Nature, in this sense, is merely to say that no precedent or analogy could then be drawn in favor of slavery from the brute creation. I say, could *then* be drawn in favor of slavery; for the ancients were undoubtedly ignorant of the astonishing facts which modern naturalists have brought to light in respect to a certain species of ants; and which, if then known, would have restrained them from saying that slavery was contrary to Nature, even in Ulpian's sense of the word. But they were ignorant of these curious facts, and they pronounced slavery contrary to Nature, on the supposition that no precedent or analogy in its favor could be drawn from the brute creation.

SLAVERY FROM AN ANT-HILL.

What, now, are these "curious facts" about "a certain species of ants," which are to demonstrate, in spite of the Justinian Code, that "American Slavery is justified by the Law of Nature?" The good Doctor does not leave us in distress long. Like a skilful physician he comes to our relief; and here is the unfailing specific:

Among facts, all of which are wonderful, not the least remarkable and instructive is, the mutual good-will and affection which prevail between *the negro ants and their masters;* and that, too, maugre the fact that the relation had its origin in hostility and violence.

There it is!—"American Slavery" resting on an *ant-hill!* Not so bad, either; for "the logic of events" helps that of Dr. Seabury, in revealing that its foundations, just now, are a little porous.

Who shall dispute hereafter that this is an age of progress? The great Southern statesman, Mr. Stephens, builds a new empire on a foundation whose "corner-stone" is slavery; and he boasts that no nation was ever so built before. At this bold announcement the world stood aghast. And now, this great New York Doctor tells us what this "corner-stone" rests upon—an ANT-HILL. And the *True Presbyterian* commends to the good people of Kentucky, in several successive issues of the paper, the Doctor's book as being very able, and as putting the defence of slavery "on grounds distinct from any yet presented" in their columns. We see wherein the distinction lies. We have failed to discover, however, that the paper has exhibited the *Ant-hill* doctrine. As this is one of the most "distinct grounds" on which the Doctor "justifies slavery," we recommend its insertion.

ANT-SLAVERY.—STRIKING ANALOGIES.

This feature of the defence of the negro slavery of the South is altogether so rich and instructive, that we must give a further extract from Dr. Seabury upon *Ant*-slavery. He quotes joyously from a work on Natural History, thus, where the author is speaking of the habits of certain species of ants:

> It is both warlike and powerful, and, unlike the rest of the tribe, its habits are far from being industrious. Enough has been said to show that the proceedings of some insects so nearly resemble human actions, as to excite our greatest wonder: but the habits of the legionary ant are still more surprising than the proceeding of the chiefs which we have just described. It is actually found to be a *slave-dealer*, attacking the nests of other species, stealing their young, rearing them, and thus, by shifting all the domestic duties of their republic on strangers, escaping from labor themselves. This curious fact, first discovered by Huber, has been confirmed by Latreille, and is admitted by all naturalists The slave is distinguished from its master by being of a *dark ash-color*, so as to be entitled to the name of *Negro*—an epithet now appropriated to the *Formica fusca*, or ash-colored ants. *Their masters are light in color* The *negro* is an industrious, peaceable, stingless insect; the *legionary*, a courageous, armed, and lazy one.

Here is a pretty striking analogy, it must be admitted between the "habits" of *one* of the two classes of ants, and certain Southern masters—"far from being industrious;" "slave-dealers;" "escaping from labor themselves;" "warlike, courageous, armed, and lazy." Pretty good.

SLAVE-TRADE JUSTIFIED.

It will be seen, also, that not only is "American *slavery*" here "justified," but all its concomitants are sanctioned in the same manner. Both the foreign and domestic slave-trade is carried on by these ants. The master tribe are represented as "attacking the nests of other species, stealing their young, rearing them," and thus having "servants" of their own. This is precisely the way slavery began in our country—"stealing" men, women, and children, from Africa. We presume, therefore, that Dr. Seabury and his warm admirer and patron, the *True Presbyterian*, go in for reopening the African slave-trade,—which, also, the leading rebels of the South were in favor of,—justifying it upon the "Law of Nature;" that is, the proceedings about an *Ant-hill.* We shall not lack for a definition of that controverted phrase hereafter.

But there is more in an Ant-hill than at first appears—when stirred up a little; and especially in this one. How does Dr. Seabury know, that which he so confidently assumes, that the Justinian Code can be so easily overthrown by a tribe of ants? How does he *know* that "the ancients were undoubtedly ignorant" of ant-wars and ant-slavery? Does he presume they never saw an Ant-hill? They knew a great deal more than has come down to us in books. His reasoning, even should we allow it any value, is wholly built on his own ignorance rather than upon theirs. He argues from a negative premise. If he is so confident they did not know these things, let him show the evidence of it. If he is so sure of their ignorance, let him relieve his own. This is certainly incumbent on him, when he is arguing for the perpetual bondage of human millions from the quarrels of an Ant-hill. But it is of very small moment whether "the ancients" were "ignorant" in this matter or not. The Justinian Code is likely to survive this assault.

CANNIBALISM JUSTIFIED ON SIMILAR GROUND.

This hill is as pregnant of conclusions as of ants. If the "habits" of the lower species of animals are to be a guide to man in his moral relations, they may justify many other things besides negro slavery. If the Law of Nature, on this ground, sanctions slavery, it also sanctions *cannibalism*. Did the good Doctor never hear of animals devouring each other? Fishes live upon fishes; insects upon insects; and the various tribes of carnivorous animals live upon each other. May mankind then eat one another? If it be said that no animal ever devours one of precisely the same species, we should demand proof, as upon the proposition that "the ancients" never saw an Ant-hill. As it is a negative proposition, it would require a larger amount of evidence than the Doctor may be able to give. But we waive that. Even though it were true, that the carnivorous animals eat other species only than their own, —of the contrary of which we have had ocular demonstration,—we could get along with that difficulty very easily. The Anglo-Saxon need only eat the negro. Some wise men make them of a different race entirely; others say that they are at least of a different species of the *genus homo*. The case then is clear. Cannibalism is established upon the Law of Nature.

ITS PRACTICAL ADVANTAGES.

Besides this solid foundation for cannibalism, it has its practical illustrations and its advantages in certain cases.

The examples become less numerous as Christianity advances, but that is no matter; the Gospel of the Law of Nature is older than the Christian era. We can follow the New Zealanders and the Feejees, and can instruct modern missionaries to re-establish their ancient and well-observed customs.

And then, this might be a serviceable argument among the rebels. It is said they are scarce of food. If the Doctor's book is among them, as is most likely, we think they will see that upon his premises they might serve up their fat negroes as meat for their armies. If "necessity is the mother of invention," they may do it without his aid. And it may be well, too, as a measure of safety; for if they do not eat their negroes, the negroes will be very apt to devour them; and, in either case, we do not see but the Law of Nature would be equally well and profitably illustrated.

But seriously,—and in fact we have been serious all along,—is it not a sorry sight, to behold a grave divine of the metropolitan city of New York, at this time of day, dealing out such stuff to a sensible people, for the "justification of American Slavery by the Law of Nature;" helping thus, by the silliest of all imaginings, to prop up a tottering system of human bondage that has plunged his country into a bloody war which is slaying by myriads both bondmen and freemen! And is the sight any less humiliating, to see a Presbyterian newspaper, claiming to be "religious," attempting, week after week, to enlighten the benighted people of Kentucky, in the year of grace 1864, by commending such a work to them in the highest terms of approval? If any thing can exceed the infatuation of rebel politicians and their coadjutors in the South, in attempting to overthrow their Government by armed rebellion, it is the infatuation of rebel sympathizers, exhibited in such feats of literary accomplishment as the one here noticed, and many more like it.*

DR. THORNWELL'S ARGUMENT FROM NATURE.

A similar view may be taken of the argument of Dr. Thornwell, about slavery being justified by nature, as found in the "Confederate General Assembly's" Address to the Christian world, and in the *Southern Presbyterian Review*, extracts from both of which we have given.

In the former, he says: "Whatever is universal, is natural. We are willing that slavery should be tried by this standard." Let us then apply the test. Sin is "universal" among men. Is it, therefore, "natural;" that is, right, justifiable?

But here is more logic of the same sort. Dr. Thornwell proceeds: "We are willing to abide by the testimony of the race, and if man, as man, has everywhere condemned it; if all human laws have prohibited it as crime; if it stands in the same category with malice, murder, and theft, then we are willing, in the name of humanity, to renounce it, and to renounce it forever."

Here is a carefully framed sophism which spoils the whole argument. It takes a good logician to be a good sophist, and Dr. Thornwell was the former when he chose

* General Cobb declares, that "even learned judges in slaveholding States, adopting the language of Lord Mansfield, in Somerset's case, have announced, in judicial decisions, that 'slavery is *contrary to the law of nature*.'" He refers to such decisions as found in the reports of Southern courts. He remarks upon the point, as follows: "The course of reasoning, by which this conclusion is attained, is very much this: That in a state of nature all men are free. That one man is at birth entitled by nature to no higher rights and privileges than another, nor does nature specify any particular time or circumstances under which the one shall begin to rule and the other to obey. Hence, by the law of nature, no man is the slave of another, and hence all slavery is contrary to the law of nature. While "learned judges in *slaveholding* States" thus *judicially* announced, years ago, this doctrine, "learned" divines in *non*-slaveholding States, in a time of rebellion and war in behalf of slavery, are trying to prop it up by every possible means; by nature, revelation, and all other "aid and comfort' they can give to rebels in arms!

to be. His reasoning here is based upon an assumption, and one which is notoriously contrary to fact. Have men universally reprobated the crimes which he specifies? Have "all human laws prohibited" each one in the catalogue? Did the laws of Sparta, for example, prohibit and punish "theft," or rather its detection? Were not many things sanctioned there by law, even under the teaching of their great lawgiver, Lycurgus, which are now reprobated?—when, "to teach the youth of Lacedæmon cunning, vigilance, and activity, they were encouraged to practise theft in certain cases; but if detected, they were flogged, or obliged to go without food, or compelled to dance round an altar, singing songs in ridicule of themselves."

Have "all human laws prohibited" all other crimes which are now upon the statute-books of enlightened States? Nobody will pretend this. What then does the argument amount to, based upon universal condemnation of specified crimes, when no such condemnation exists? Suppose then slavery has not been universally condemned among nations; neither has "theft;" nor has "murder," in all the degrees and phases of that crime in which it is now condemned by Christian States. This argument, then, amounts to just nothing at all. It is a skilfully framed sophism, and nothing more; and Dr. Thornwell was always skilful.*

* If there is any thing of special value in the legislation of ancient Pagan nations as an example for a Christian people, take the following, as one among a thousand cases, from one of the greatest lawgivers of antiquity. It was one of the "peculiar institutions" of Sparta: "A singular custom was the flogging of boys (*diamastigosis*), on the annual festival of Diana Orthia, for the purpose of inuring them to bear pain with firmness. The priestess stood by with a small, light, wooden image of Diana, and if she observed that any boy was spared, she called out that the image of the goddess was so heavy that she could not support it, and the blows were then redoubled. The men who were present exhorted their sons to fortitude; while the boys endeavored to surpass each other in firmness. Whoever uttered the least cry during the scourging, which was so severe as sometimes to prove fatal, was consid-

PAGAN AN EXAMPLE FOR CHRISTIAN STATES.

But wiaving all this, and admitting the assumption to be true,—of, even admitting the implied affirmative assumption, that slavery has been universally *approved* among nations; admitting, as the *True Presbyterian* says, that "the Persians, the Greeks, the Romans, the Gauls, the Saxons, the Normans, all held slaves,"—is not this a most humiliating exhibition for Christian men to make?—to appeal to the Pagan States of antiquity for an example to guide Christian States and Christian men, at this time of day, in their highest moral duties towards their fellow-men?

Has the Gospel produced so little effect in our day, and in our country, that its TEACHERS must go back two thousand years to Paganism for a guide in ethics where the most important interests of humanity are involved?—that they must seek shelter from the scorn of men, for *slavery*, in those Pagan States which have long since been *purged of slavery*, and this too by the influence of that very Christianity which they preach and profess to exemplify as a light and a guide for all mankind? Oh, shame, where is thy blush!

There is another aspect of the case presented by Dr. Thornwell which deserves notice. Leaving the negative, he turns to the positive view of the subject, and immediately following what we have given above, triumphantly adds: "But what if the overwhelming majority of mankind have *approved* it; what if philosophers and statesmen have justified it, and the laws of all nations acknowledged it," etc.? We have already met this in part, but it claims a word or two more.

ered as disgraced, while he who bore it without shrinking was crowned, and received the praises of the whole city."

SLAVERY SUBMITTED TO A POPULAR VOTE.

How easily he here slides from what just before was assumed to be the "universal," to what he is now content with calling a "majority!" Suppose we admit that "the overwhelming majority of mankind have approved" of slavery, does that settle any thing about the *right* of the case? Are mankind always right in their judgments? "What if philosophers and statesmen have justified it;" what then? Are they infallible? Is not the whole race in sin,—as this distinguished theologian held,—with judgment, heart, conscience, biased to evil? And do we not all recognize the fact that men may and do change their opinions; that the world may improve in its moral judgments, and that it is doing so daily upon a thousand questions hoary with age?

But is this representation true in point of fact? Can any one for a moment suppose that "the overwhelming majority of mankind approved" of slavery, at the time the Justinian Code was promulgated?—a code containing the "matured wisdom of centuries?"—a code which pronounced slavery to be "against nature"—*contra naturam?* This claimed approval of a former day is untrue in point of fact; and if it were true, it would establish nothing to the purpose upon the question of *moral right.*

But if this question is to be settled by the voice of a popular "majority,"—rather a singular tribunal for Dr. Thornwell to erect to decide a *moral* question, and still more singular for the "Confederate General Assembly of the Presbyterian Church" to propose for the determination of *any* question, while they have joined their fellow-citizens in rebellion against the constitutionally expressed will of the whole American people,—but if this is the tribunal, the voice of the "majority," suppose we take a vote *to-day;* what would be the decision upon slavery? Suppose we submit it, at the present moment, to a vote of the whole civilized world? Would the advocates of negro slavery be willing to abide the result? For our part, we certainly would. If, then, it is to be determined by a popular "majority," we propose it to all civilized and Christian States and Christian people, *Anno Domini* 1864.

THE INEVITABLE CONCLUSION.

We can not pursue the subject further, of the relation of slavery to the Law of Nature. One of the very highest authorities on this point, the Code of Justinian, settles the question satisfactorily. We do not think such philosophers as Dr. Seabury, nor even such logicians as Dr. Thornwell, writing an Address for the "General Assembly of the Confederate States," will overthrow the position of that code, that slavery is "contra naturam," without more successful efforts than they have yet made. The Law of Nature does not sustain the system; but its greatest expounder positively condemns it.

Nor are the arguments any more conclusive which attempt to sanction the negro slavery of the South by an appeal to the word of God. That system is wholly destitute of the positive "commands" and "ordinances" by which the Old Testament system of Jewish servitude was regulated; and when the attempt is made to justify it by the "matrimonial and parental relations" in connection with which it is mentioned in the New Testament, the effort is involved in inextricable absurdities.

AMERICAN SLAVERY FOUNDED ON HUMAN LAW.

But passing both these, we maintain that the only foundation on which American negro slavery rests, with any show of *legal right* in the institution which is even plausible, is that of *human law*. Dr. Thornwell elaborately argues against this, in quotations before given. He says: "It has been contended that the right of property in slaves is the creature of positive statute, and, consequently, of force only within the jurisdiction of the law." Against this position he arrays himself. His proofs, however, are mere *dicta*, and his reasonings fallacious. That we may be seen to do his argument justice, we refer the reader to a previous page where it is given at length. We can here only notice it briefly. He says in opposition to the doctrine which he recites above, the italics being his own:

> Slavery has never, in any country, so far as we know, arisen under the operation of statute law. * * * Law defines, modifies, and regulates it, as it does every other species of property, but *law* never *created* it. * * * The point is, whether the *law* made slavery—whether it is the police regulation of limited localities, or whether it is a property founded in natural causes, and causes of universal operation.

CONFLICTING AUTHORITIES.—LAW VERSUS DIVINITY.

Dr. Baird, in his "Southern Rights and Northern Duties," takes *both* sides of this question. This will allow him to defend whichever side may be attacked. Speaking of one of the planks in the Chicago platform of 1860, he avers that slavery is the creature of positive law, as follows:

> Nay, further, this declaration pronounces unconstitutional *the laws by which slavery acquired* EXISTENCE *in eight of the Southern States*—all those which have passed through a territorial condition.—p. 9.

He then takes the other side, denying that slavery is the creature of positive law, as follows:

> So far is it from being true, as commonly assumed, that slavery was *originated* and now *exists in the States by virtue of special local statute*,

such statute is probably nowhere to be found in the laws of any people except Israel. Certainly there never was a law passed in any State of the Union, whether prior to or since the Revolution, establishing slavery.*—p. 18.

When Doctors of Divinity disagree upon law, as Drs. Thornwell and Baird here do, and the latter with himself, it is well to see what certain Doctors of Law say upon the point. We will detain the reader with but two examples out of many.

Daniel Webster is conceded to have been among the ablest, if not decidedly the ablest, constitutional lawyer of the country, well called the "Defender of the Constitution." He dissents from both the points made by both these Divinity Doctors, regarding the constitutional right to slavery in the Territories, and the existence of slavery by positive law. In his speech in the United States Senate, in 1848, on the "exclusion of slavery from the Territories," alluding to the Southern States, he says:

They have a system of *local legislation on which slavery rests;* while everybody agrees that it is *against natural law,* or at least against the common understanding which prevails among men as to what is natural law. * * * I do not intend to deny the *validity* of that local law, where it is established; but I say it is, after all, *local law.*

Chief-Justice Shaw, of Massachusetts, gives his opinion in a judicial decision, as follows:

Slavery being odious, and *against natural right,* cannot exist except by the force of *positive law.* * * * *Each State* may, for its own convenience, declare that slaves shall be deemed property, and the laws of personal chattels shall be deemed to apply to them; as, for instance, that they may be bought and sold, delivered, attached, and levied upon; that trespass will lie for an injury done to them, or trover for converting

* Dr. Baird is "certainly" mistaken. In the State of Georgia, at least, slavery originated in the very way he denies,—through "a law passed" "*establishing slavery.*" Gen. Cobb says: "With the exception of Georgia, where it was at first prohibited, no law is found on our statute books authorizing its introduction."—*Law of Negro Slavery.*

them. * * * If a note of hand made in New Orleans were sued on here, and the defence should be made that it was a bad consideration, or without consideration, because given for the price of a *slave sold*, it may well be admitted that such a defence could not prevail; because the contract was a legal one by *the law of the place where it was made.*

Thus Law *versus* Divinity, stands under the authority of great names on both sides.

ORIGIN OF NEGRO SLAVERY IN THE UNITED STATES.

Whatever may have been true of other systems,—as, in ancient times, originating in some countries prior to legal recognition,—that of negro slavery in this country, both as a system and as involving property in slaves, did arise and has continued "under the operation of statute law." The origin of slavery in some other countries is so remote that it can be traced only to the mists of the fabulous ages, and then it is very convenient to assert that it rests on the Law of Nature, "is a property founded in natural causes," or general custom, or rests on some other vague foundation; but its origin in this country is too recent and too well known to admit of doubt; and it will be borne in mind that Dr. Thornwell's abstract reasonings are made to bear upon and justify, and are by him directly applied to, the system of the South. *The legal status of that system is coincident with its origin in this country.*

ITS HISTORY TRACED.—AFRICAN SLAVE-TRADE.

Let us look at the historical facts of the case. Negro slavery began in this country in 1620. Negroes were brought from Africa into Virginia, and there sold as slaves. That was the first positive connection of the system with what is now the United States. Negroes were afterwards brought, at different times, during many years, and disposed of in the same way. Every portion of the country that finally possessed them, obtained them in this manner, or by purchasing in this country those originally brought from Africa, or their descendants. These were the germs of the *system*, and of all *rights* embraced in it, so far as it had a foothold in the United States; and every slave that has since been held here has been held by a tenure which had such an origin.

Now, out of what did the system, thus begun, arise, and on what does it still legally rest? The system arose, in this country, "under the operation of" the African slave-trade; and that trade, in every country which carried it on and encouraged it, beginning centuries before the introduction of slaves into Virginia, was legalized by "statute law."

It arose from the highest civil authority known, being legalized by Ferdinand of Spain, in 1501; by Charles V., in 1516; Queen Elizabeth sanctioned it 1567; James I. in 1618. The Dutch vessel which brought the first cargo of twenty negroes into James River, in 1620, was engaged in the trade under charter.

The system which thus *began* "under the operation of statute law," *continued to increase* in the same manner. Charles I. granted a charter to a company to carry on the slave-trade in 1631; and Charles II. in 1662, at the head of which was the Duke of York, the King's brother. The Royal African Company was chartered in 1672, embracing among its members the King, the Duke of York, and other noblemen. In 1688, Parliament abolished all exclusive charters; and in 1698 the slave-trade was thrown open to all persons, and negroes were exported duty free.

While the laws of England secured a monopoly to British subjects in bringing slaves to British Colonies, French and Portuguese Companies, under authority granted by Spain, brought them to the Spanish Colonies. Philip V of Spain, and Queen Anne of England, formed a treaty to promote the trade in 1713. In the reign of George II., 1750, it was declared by Parliament that "the slave-trade is very advantageous to Great Britain;" and as late as 1788, Parliament passed acts regulating the trade. The French Government encouraged the trade in 1784, by paying a bounty to vessels engaged therein.

Besides all these foreign charters, the Colonies of Great Britain in this country passed acts regulating the trade, and directly engaged in it under the legal authority of the mother country.

FOUNDED IN HUMAN LAW, OR WITHOUT LEGALITY.

And thus it is as certain as any historical facts can make any thing certain, that the *system* of negro slavery in the United States *did arise* "under the operation of statute law," and did continue to *expand* and *progress* under the highest and most "positive statutes" of all the civilized nations of the world. And it is further true, *that no negro was ever held in this country, as a slave, "as property," whose status as a slave, and as "property," did not arise, either in his own person or through his ancestors, in just that manner.* And it is further true, that all the statutes which have ever been passed in this country concerning slavery, in any of the States, have tacitly assumed as legal and authoritative all the charters under which Africans were brought to this country; and all the legal basis for the *system*, as it has ever since existed in this country, and all the legal basis of *property right* in the slave under the system, rests ultimately, so far as law in this country is concerned, on the presumed legality of that authority under which the African slave-trade was carried on; or, it *originated* in the local and positive laws of the respective States.

POSITIVE LAW.—INEVITABLE CRIME.

If any persons choose to go beyond the slave-trade, and push the subject on into darkness, to endeavor to find a foundation in "natural causes," or something else, for the system in this country, the case will not be benefited. We say nothing now of the *moral* right of the slave-trade, which has since been pronounced "piracy" by the laws of enlightened nations, and which of course, if so now, was always so, in a moral point of view,—but if it was once *legal*, as in a technical sense it was, then it covered the whole process of what was necessarily embraced in the trade: the obtaining of the negroes in Africa, whether by purchase, or by kidnapping them; the bringing of them to this country; and the sale of them to the subjects of Great Britain in the Colonies.

Now, if those who wish to escape the position, that the system arose "under the operation of positive statute," choose to go into Africa, on what basis will they there place it? "It is a property founded in natural causes, and causes of universal operation," says Dr. Thornwell. What are those causes, in this case? *Captures in war* were the most common. We have, then, visions of the most revolting wars among barbarous tribes; wars expressly undertaken to provide victims to sell to the slave-trader; villages sacked and burned, and large districts of country laid waste; the basest treachery, fraud, and brutality practised, and every spectacle at which humanity shudders. All this, so well known to the world, is then the alternative furnished, by the facts of the case, which must inevitably be accepted as the only basis upon which negro slavery in this country can rest, either as a system, or as embodying a property right in the slave, the moment the theory is abandoned that both had their origin in "positive law." If the advocates of the system prefer the alternative, they are quite welcome to the superior satisfaction it must afford them.

POSITIVE LAW THEORY SUSTAINED BY THE HIGHEST SOUTHERN AUTHORITY.

General Thomas R. R. Cobb, of Georgia, whom we have before several times quoted, fully sustains the *legal basis* which we have laid down both for the system and the property right, referring it to the "purchase" made in Africa, which, as we have said, was covered by the legalized traffic which always originated either in such "purchase," or in kidnapping; and General Cobb distinctly repudiates the latter process as furnishing any "legal claim" whatever, leaving those who reject the theory of "positive law" nothing to stand on. He says:

> We have seen in a preliminary sketch the history of the introduction of negro slavery into the United States. The origin of the system is found, therefore, *in purchase*, of persons already in a state of slavery in their own land. The *law* does not go back of that fact, to inquire into the foundation of that slavery there, but, recognizing the rights of the master there to sell, sustains the title of the purchaser from him. It was alleged, and, doubtless, was true, that the slave-traders sometimes stimulated or were engaged in kidnapping free negroes on the coast of Africa, who were afterwards sold as slaves. *Such a foundation could not sustain a legal claim to the bondage of the victim.*

This work of General Cobb,—"Law of Negro Slavery,"—is of the highest legal authority in the South. He cites, in connection with the foregoing extract, several judicial decisions of Southern courts sustaining the positions taken. As "kidnapping" in Africa was held to invalidate the "legal claim," one of these decisions lays down the principle by which the courts are governed, that "the presumption is in favor of the slavery there."

THE IMPREGNABLE CONCLUSION.

The *status* of negro slavery in the United States, rests, therefore, by the highest legal authorities *of the South*, upon a different basis from that to which Dr. Thornwell and others assign it. It is unquestionably true, in point of fact, that vast multitudes who have been held in slavery in the United States, ever since the origin of the system, have been held upon a "foundation" which, if traced back, "could not sustain a legal claim to the bondage of the victim." Their slavery was founded in "kidnapping." It was, therefore, by these high Southern authorities, from first to last, illegal. The "presumption" by which the courts are governed, and which in such case would, of course, be in favor of the "legal claim," was no doubt a principle absolutely necessary to save the claim in multitudes of cases; and as the interest of every master would be in favor of the "presumption," the claim would always be safe.

General Cobb well says: "The law does not go back of that fact;" that is, of the "purchase of persons already in a state of slavery in their own land." It is perhaps well, *morally* considered, that it does not, for, as before stated, there is nothing "back of that fact" but force, fraud, treachery, crime of every sort, in the perpetration of which the victims have been brought into slavery and their bondage perpetuated; and the same crimes have entered into the traffic by which some other systems have been established. And yet, *legally* considered, there was no necessary reason for stopping even there. If any persons, therefore, choose to "go back of that fact" where Southern courts are content to stop, and should "inquire into the foundation of that slavery" in Africa, they would still be obliged to "fetch up" on a basis of "positive law."

The African systems prevailing have the public consent of the chiefs and of the tribes; the usages by which slavery is regulated among them are settled; the modes of reducing one another to slavery, as for example by captures in war, are recognized; "the right of the master there to sell" is an acknowledged right; and these, and all other essential regulations of those systems, dating back as far as any certain knowledge of those people extends, are, among those tribes, of the *nature* of "positive law." The Southern courts do not decline to "inquire into the foundation of that slavery" because there was any difficulty in finding a legal basis for it, but because they must have some place to begin, and they might as well begin with the "purchase" founded on "recognizing the rights of the master there to sell" as anywhere else; and yet, that "right to sell" must, of course, rest on the right of possession, which, if inquired into, would inevitably involve the *legal* status of "the foundation of that slavery." If that "foundation had not thus been tacitly assumed to be legal, "the rights of the master there to sell" could not have been legal, nor "the title of the purchaser from him;" and, in that case, as in "kidnapping," no "legal claim to the bondage of the victim" could be sustained. But the African slavery was *assumed to be legal*, as the right to "sell" and to "purchase" under it was deemed legal. The basis, therefore, of even the African systems, is, so far as we can trace it, a basis of "positive law."

The same principle of recognizing those only as *legally* held in bondage in this country, who were *legally* held in slavery in Africa, which General Cobb declares to be the rule in Southern courts, was early acted upon in Massachusetts. General Cobb says: "The Puritans insisted that the traffic should be confined to those who were captives in war and *slaves in Africa*. Hence, when, in 1644 or

1645, a Boston ship returned with two negroes captured by the crew, in a pretended quarrel with the natives, the General Court ordered them to be restored to their native land." This shows that all parties, at that early day, deemed negro slavery in this country as having no other proper origin than a legal one.

THE CONSOLING ALTERNATIVE.

If any persons choose to go still further, and search for "natural causes and causes of universal operation," under which they *imagine* those African systems may have come into being prior to their having any legal status,—of which they *know* absolutely nothing with certainty,—they will, in all probability, find, as before stated, only fraud and force, and all the cruelties and crimes which the facts which *are* positively known suggest.

If this affords any better foundation for satisfaction to the Christian conscience, we do not know that it would be wise to disturb it. It may be convenient to attempt to push the system, to avoid a legal origin, on into African darkness, but we do not think it is sensible.

But, be all this as it may be, there is nothing clearer under the light of the heavens, than the contrary of Dr. Thornwell's assertions. "Slavery," in *this* country, *did* arise, and is continued, "under the operation of *positive law*." Such is the testimony of history, of Southern law, and of Southern judicial decisions: connecting its *legal status here* with its *legal status in Africa*.

As we stated in the beginning of the discussion upon the "Polemics" of Slavery, our space by no means allows us to present an *exhaustive* consideration of the subject. Nor is this necessary. We have noticed a few points which are radical, and which are always relied upon as the main positions from which the system is defended. If these are untenable, all the rest is mere skirmishing.

We freely confess that we take very little interest, at present, in any discussion with the pen upon the right or wrong of slavery; and perhaps the reader will take far less. We shall not blame him if he does. A discussion concerning it is going on in the country, of infinitely deeper moment to every American citizen. As its friends have appealed to the sword in its defence, let its merits be decided with that weapon; and may God sustain the right!

CHAPTER XV.

REVIEW AND CONCLUSION.

WE bring this work to a close in the present chapter. Several subjects on which we had proposed to dwell, and some chapters fully written, are entirely omitted, to avoid swelling the volume to a larger size.

The general subject which has enlisted our pen is one that must deeply interest every American citizen, as indeed it has awakened the interest and stimulated the inquiries of the whole civilized world.

THE EXTERNAL SITUATION.

It is safe to say that no contest of arms in modern or ancient times has embraced elements of wider range, in their bearing upon the general welfare of mankind, than the great American struggle now progressing. At the outset, it so seriously disturbed the industrial concerns of the two largest nations of Western Europe, to name no more, threatening thousands of operatives with starvation and endangering the public tranquillity, that it was feared they would, in self-defence, become parties to the quarrel, and thus enlarge the theatre of war. And during every stage of the strife thus far, an uneasy feeling about "foreign intervention" has more or less constantly haunted the minds of the people.

This was counted on by the leaders of the rebellion as an absolute necessity, involving, as they supposed, the daily bread of millions, and the regular flow of business in all the channels of trade. Without this hope, it is highly improbable that they would have ventured on a bloody revolution. But they believed they were masters of the situation; that they had but to speak, and the world would obey. Hence, they defiantly proclaimed: "It is a remarkable fact, that during these thirty years of unceasing warfare against slavery, and while a lying spirit has inflamed the world against us, that world has grown more and more dependent upon it for sustenance and wealth." "Strike now a blow at this system of labor, and the world itself totters at the stroke." It is not wonderful, under this hallucination, that in their schemes of treason they should have attempted to justify themselves on the ground that they were discharging a "duty" in this regard which they owed "to the civilized world."

That the industry of the nations has suffered, and that their internal quiet and peace with us have been imperilled, is unquestionable; but that the world's industry, its trade, its tranquillity, were absolutely tied to the stake which they held, the event has disproved. It is nevertheless true that this belief, begetting the confidence that foreign intervention were a necessity, nerved them to strike the first blow; and it is also just as true, that the foreign aid which they have actually received, by land and sea, during every hour of the war, has enabled them to strike every subsequent blow with more effect, and that without such aid the rebellion would long since undoubtedly have been crushed.

RESPONSIBILITY OF FOREIGN POWERS.

This feature of the case shows the magnitude and bearings of the contest, not only by revealing what has been put at hazard, touching the actual necessities of toiling millions, but it draws into a deeper channel the great question of international comity. That the United States, in contest with a rebellion against its lawful authority, provoked by no governmental aggression, as the greatest statesman of the South declared,—a rebellion begun and prosecuted solely for independence in the interests of negro slavery,—should have encountered, under the name of "neutrality," the early, consistent, determined opposition of the great powers of Western Europe, in aiding the rebellion in ships, munitions of war, and in every other way which was possible or safe, presents a view which gives no satisfaction to those who prefer peace to war, and international friendship to enmity.

But the facts cannot be set aside by any sentimental philosophizing. They are written in deeds of blood. They mark every battle-field where lie bleaching the bones of the slain. They are imprinted on every rebel breastwork mounted with English cannon. They are seen in every rebel platoon armed with English rifles. They are found on the deck of every piratical cruiser, built in English ports, carrying English guns, supplied with English powder, and manned by English seamen. The tale which these outfits of a "neutral" power tell, is read in the death-cries of our fathers, husbands, sons, and brothers, and is heard in the midnight wail of the homeless widow and the orphan. It is read in the perils which still hang over our national destiny, and in the alternate hope and fear which thrill the hearts of millions, lest, after all the sacrifices made for our national honor and safety, for human freedom at home and for down-trodden man abroad, our national disintegration should fall a prey to foreign jealousy of our rivalship and greatness, through a perfidy as venal as the hypocrisy of the powers which exhibit it is transparent.

THE COMING RECKONING.

It is not in human nature to pass over these things without a settlement. It may come soon, or it may be deferred. That the day of reckoning will come, we have no more doubt than that there is a God in the heavens. The deeds which demand it are imprinted on the memory of this generation indelibly. The impression will be transmitted to the generations to come. In God's own time and manner, whether soon or hereafter, the debt will be paid with compound interest. We but speak, as we verily believe, the common mind and common heart of this nation.

For the depredations upon American commerce committed by English piratical cruisers, we doubt not a demand will be made by our Government. That a record of every case is scrupulously made, we do know. Whether the demand for compensation will be complied with, we do not know. Whether refusal will be made a *casus belli*, is of no material concern. Full compensation for actual losses at sea would be but as a grain of sand in the scale of accumulated obligations. There are debts incurred which can never be paid in pounds, shillings, and pence. There are duties to be discharged which can be met only by an exhibition of the national power of the United States towards those who have forever blackened their honor in endeavoring to work our ruin; who have, with a meanness and a littleness which no words can adequately express, seized upon the hour of our domestic calamity to cripple the rivalry of our power by division, to humble our honor in the dust, that they might lord it over us, as they have always lorded it over the smaller States of Europe. In no other way can this balance be adjusted.

RETRIBUTIVE JUSTICE.

But this is "vengeance," cry the timid and the meek. It is *justice*, we reply; and a justice which will meet the approval of Heaven. It will conserve the ultimate interests of humanity, and preserve the peace of the world. A nation, to make itself respected, must exact that which is just, and inflexibly hold to the right and the true. If it permit wrong after wrong to be heaped up mountain high, with no effort at redress, it sinks into contempt, becomes the prey of every power, and can never count securely on peace; while, on the other hand, such a course hazards the peace of the world.

The principle of *justice* is the highest recognized by writers on international law as proper between nations. This they must exemplify in practice. It is on this ground alone that we insist that the United States owes a debt to herself and to humanity, respecting the great powers of Western Europe, which she must eventually discharge. That it is a debt of the clearest *justice*, we shall not waste words to argue with any one who chooses to dispute it. That it will be cancelled, we have no manner of doubt.

ESSENTIAL DISCRIMINATIONS.

That we have warm friends in both England and France we all know. We honor Victor Hugo, and others of the French Academy. Looking to England, we praise God for her John Bright and her Richard Cobden in her Parliament; for her Professor Newman and Goldwin Smith, among scholars; for her *Star* and her *News* of the London press; and for hosts of others. But her Government, her aristocracy, and hordes of her merchant princes, have been our sworn enemies, to the full extent that their selfish interests and their sordid fears would permit. With the government and the aristocracy, the interest is concentrated in their power; with the trading classes, in the pocket.

As for their opposition to slavery, so demonstrative in days that are past, it was strong, and their weapons were always burnished and ready, so long as slave products were filling their coffers with gold. But when a rebellion arose to make slavery more secure than ever, to expand its area and perpetuate its power, with honorable exceptions they wheeled promptly about in support of the war waged in its interest, and against the Government seeking its overthrow, because their profits from the institution were diminished.

POCKET PHILANTHROPY.

We shall never be at a loss hereafter for an exact standard by which to measure British philanthropy, in a cause where the interests of down-trodden millions are concerned. Its criterion is the pocket. They are for their freedom and elevation, so long as their actual bondage helps the pocket. They are for their slavery and degradation, if their freedom or their efforts to obtain it endanger the fulness of the pocket.

We would not revile our British brethren; we have friends among them, and relatives. But the great Napoleon once said, that they were but a nation of shopkeepers.

While we thus speak, we shall ever honor those, in Parliament and out of it, who have raised their voices for freedom and humanity, and for our right to manage our internal affairs in quelling a foul rebellion without their interference; resisting on the one hand class interests and governmental power at work to reach their sinister ends, and on the other that narrow spirit which measures every thing by the value of a farthing. For them we have an abiding affection.

OUR CAUSE MISREPRESENTED.

The class for whom we have the deepest contempt, among foreign nations, embraces those who are looked up to as guides of public opinion. The impression they have most studiously sought to make is, that ours is a mere contest for power, for territorial aggrandizement. This they reiterate in Parliament, upon the hustings, through the press. They say it so often, so boldly, and in such places, that it is not wonderful that many among the people who take their cue from them believe it.

But this is not only the basest of falsehoods, but, the worst of all is, *they know* it to be so; and this is true when applied to Lords Palmerston and John Russell in Parliament, and to the columns of the *London Times*. We presume that neither of these high dignitaries, nor the great Thunderer, will care for our individual opinion; nor we for theirs. The only importance the case has in our eyes, is, that they delight in stabbing our national life through their personal and official villany.

FOREIGN ENMITY PERSISTENT.

Let it not be said that we are stirring up bad blood. That element has already been infused into our international relations by the course of the powers of which we speak. We take the case simply as they present it. In a great contest for existence, we treat those abroad as those at home; as friends or as foes.

If it be said, that these foreign powers are more friendly now than formerly, we answer that we see no proof of it. If it be said that there is less danger of intervention now than formerly, or no danger at all, we admit it. But it is because they see it to be useless, or that in intermeddling there may be danger. Those who have been our enemies abroad are so still. Give them an opportunity, and they would show it. Let our national capital be taken, or any extraordinary disaster to our arms occur, and all the aristocracies of Europe would shout for joy, and the echoes would be heard over the earth. Let Jefferson Davis and his Slave Confederacy be recognized by us, and their exultations would rend the very heavens.

While the great antagonistic elements of American and European civilization exist before the eyes of the world's millions, it is perfectly idle to say that the ruling powers of Europe have any other wish than our national dismemberment and total overthrow. If we are pointed to the large numbers of the middle classes, we find this to be true: the more influential among them, as a whole, would be for or against us, as their own commercial profits would be enhanced by the one course or the other; while those honorable exceptions who sympathize with our Government against rebellion, are but the exceptions, and are well-nigh powerless against those who sway the destinies of European politics.

THE POPULAR MASSES WITH US.

Turning away from the rulers to the teeming millions, and though we do not find them arrayed in court dresses and rolling by in aristocratic pomp, the view is refreshing. They have a true sympathy with popular liberty, a heart detesting oppression and a hand raised to strike it down, whether the sceptre of power be the mace of the nobleman or the whip of the slave-driver. They watch our contest with an intensity of interest surpassed only by our loyal citizens.

They have confidence in our triumph. This is seen in

their actions. At no period in our history has immigration from Europe been so rapid as during the war. This is not by reason of the large bounties paid to soldiers. This may influence some. But the mass come with their families, and to better their condition. Our taxes do not deter them. The fear of national ruin does not deter them. They believe we shall triumph. They see in that triumph the inauguration of popular liberty on a grander scale than is promised in any other land of the broad earth. They come to enjoy it, and to secure a heritage for their children. As friends of liberty and of the oppressed everywhere, we welcome them from every nation under the wide heavens.

Another token of sympathy from the heart of *the people* of Europe, is seen in their Addresses to the People of the United States, encouraging them in the contest with slavery and rebellion. Many of these have been received since the war has been progressing; several coming from the people of the British Isles, and others from Continental countries.

One of the latest, just heralded to the world as we write, is from the people of Geneva, one of the earliest and firmest homes of popular liberty in Europe. It is thrilling to the heart of every true American, and must nerve the arm of the soldier in battle, to hear the echoes of these eloquent voices from among the hills of Switzerland. They close their Address, made to the "People of the American Union," in the words: "Hail, Liberty! Hail, Republic of the United States!"

We rejoice in the response which has been made to this Address by the Secretary of State. Mr. Seward says: "Your Address adds strength to the already strong claim which binds the first Federal Republic of America to the oldest and foremost Federal Republic of Europe. The people of Switzerland may rest assured, whoever else may fail, that it will not be the people of the United States which will betray the republican system to foreign enemies, *or surrender it to domestic faction.*"

God grant that this pledge of the Secretary of State, made on behalf of the Government and People of the United States, may be kept inviolate!

THE INTERNAL SITUATION.

We have looked at the aspect of things from without; at the adverse influences operating against us in foreign nations; and at the favorable influence we are exerting upon the masses of the people, and the interest the *real people* of Europe take in our struggle.

We turn our view within, and look at some things at home. This has, indeed, been the theme of our entire writing. We do not desire to repeat or to recapitulate what we have said, but we will notice a few points of the general subject, suggested by what has already gone before.

We take it for granted that no subject has ever so interested the American people, since they have been a people, as that which now rocks this nation on its deepest foundations. We can conceive of no subject, next to one's personal salvation, which can take so deep a hold upon the mind and heart of an American citizen, as that which involves the great issues bound up in our present contest.

WHAT THE CONTEST EXHIBITS.

What is at stake?—what is involved?—what has called mighty armies into the field?—for what are we pouring out our best blood, and covering all the plains of the South with the mangled limbs of the slain?—and for what are we encumbering ourselves and our children with a debt under which generations will groan?

To hear some people talk, and to read what some people write, it would seem that we are merely engaged in a partisan contest, a political scramble. They therefore bid the combatants desist, rush into each other's arms, and fall upon each other's necks in loving embrace. We should rejoice at the spectacle.

We envy not the head or the heart of that man who cannot take a higher view of the "situation" than this; who cannot see in the elements of the strife that which is infinitely above any partisan or sordid interest; but who, from his stand-point, is ever prating of "peace," and gloating over the horrors of the war. Peace is a lovely and heaven-descended messenger, and war is a grim-visaged visitant of woes. No one in this fair land will welcome the coming of the one and the eternal departure of the other with more hearty rejoicing than shall we. But we are free to say, that we have no wish for this happy result, until peace can be so determined as shall give us a *security* for peace. We have no wish to fight these battles over a few years hence, and *continually.*

This contest exhibits, on the one side, a rebellion in arms against lawful Government, gotten up by disappointed demagogues, to make their rule more secure over the victims of their cruel bondage, four millions of negro slaves, and to extend the system indefinitely, and to continue it perpetually; originating in the false hue and cry, that the Government was to be administered against their vested rights.

On the other side, the Government, in the exercise of its constitutional rights, and in the discharge of its God-given duty, sustained by the people, is engaged in putting down this rebellion by Heaven's ordained means, the sword; and as the rebellion sprung out of the interest of the leaders in negro slavery, and has its chief support in that system, the Government is determined, as a necessary means to its own salvation, to destroy slavery, and let the oppressed go free.

This is the contest, and this is the whole of it. It is then a contest for national life, by a lawful Government, against a foul rebellion, seeking its overthrow. This is the simple and sole issue: a lawful Government contending against a wicked rebellion.

FRIENDS AND FOES.

In such an issue, it is impossible that there should be but two parties; just as the House of Representatives unanimously resolved—"patriots and traitors."

The question is so simple, it cannot be otherwise. It is incapable of division. It is maintaining our National Unity, or allowing it to be destroyed; triumphing over the rebels, or allowing them to triumph over us. On this issue, one or the other must conquer. The contrary is a simple impossibility; even a compromise cannot prevent it. If we maintain the Union intact, we conquer them. If it is dissolved, they conquer us, for it is for our nationality we are contending. If we maintain the Union, even with a compromise on slavery, or on any other question, still we conquer; for the maintenance of our nationality is *the vital* question. So that, in any view, as they are contending to dismember the Union, and we to preserve it, one party or the other must triumph, and that involves the conquering of the other party. No other result is physically possible.

It is on this simple issue that we say, that every man is either a friend or a foe of the Government; helping to maintain our nationality, or aiding to overthrow it. Indifference, or neutrality, in this case, we deem not to exist in any man's bosom, in point of *fact*. We do not believe any American citizen is or can be neutral. But if it be possibly so in any case, his position is a *criminal* one, before God and man; and for such a man, if he *has* a soul, we feel infinitely less respect than for many who are in open arms against the Government.

We will not argue here the right of the case. We only say, that those who are living under the protection of the Government,—in the loyal States, where its flag still waves,—and are aiding rebels in arms, or even tacitly sympathizing with them, are in a position, and doing a work, or entertaining a sentiment, which is offensive to God, and will eventually cover them with odium.

SUBORDINATE QUESTIONS.

There are many questions on which loyal men may honestly differ: as upon the necessity of destroying slavery, in order to save the Government; or, if it is to be removed, the proper manner of its termination; or, whether it shall be destroyed in the rebel regions only; and upon arbitrary arrests, habeas corpus, and other important questions.

We regard these, of necessity, each and all, independent of and subordinate to the *vital* issue of our nationality; and we regard *that* as vital, simply on the ground that right, truth, honor, justice, law, order, and every other principle involving good government, demand that it should be maintained; and because, unless it is maintained, we shall have eternal war instead of any enduring peace.

This being our judgment, as we are now at war, we say, let the war be prosecuted until rebellion is crushed, and peace can be maintained on firm foundations. Other questions, even slavery, we deem subordinate; for, as we have tried to show in a previous chapter, we think it has the poorest possible chance for life, in any issue of the war;

and yet, we greatly prefer to see no vestige of it survive the rebellion.

ADMINISTRATION AND GOVERNMENT.

We take the same view, substantially, concerning the present Administration, or any other that may be for the time in power. Men and policies are subordinate, and as far as possible should be so treated, or left out of the account altogether. The NATION, the GOVERNMENT, the UNION; these are the vital matters.

We think some persons make a serious mistake in failing utterly to sustain the *Government*, because they are not friendly to the *Administration;* having personal objections, or dissenting from some points of its policy. Some truly loyal people are found in this category; many who are at heart disloyal, present such objections as a cloak for their treason.

Any Administration actually in office, embodies for the time the authority, the power, and the dignity of the Government, and as such justly demands all the obedience and honor due to the highest civil authority. Nor can we, *practically*, distinguish between them. We can, indeed, readily understand the difference between the Government and any particular Administration in power; for the Government is permanent, while Administrations and their policies are evanescent and conflicting. But the difference is wholly abstract or theoretical. Government, independent of an Administration, is an inoperative lifeless body; while an Admin'stration is essential to give it soul, activity, life, power. No Government, whatever its form, acts, or can act, but by and through an Administration. Laws are not self-executing. Constitutions have no inherent vitality. Constitutions and laws are made by the people, and for the people; but they must be executed by the people's servants; through a personal administration, and that of fallible men.

As it is impossible to have an operative Government but through an Administration, so it is impossible to support a Government, but by supporting its Administration. If men dissent from certain measures of the policy of an Administration, they must still support it, if they support the Government.

TRUE PRINCIPLE OF SUPPORT.—OBJECTIONS.

In a great contest for national life, the truly loyal will make as few objections, and give as generous support to those in power, who are endeavoring to save the nation and crush rebellion, as is compatible with their conscientious convictions of duty. No other principle can be adopted as a rule of action, consistent either with personal honor or national safety.

But it is lamentably true, that many who claim to be opposed to the rebellion, and in favor of putting it down, *entirely withhold* their support from the Government in its efforts to crush it, because they dissent from some measures adopted for that end. And it is further lamentably true, that when these objections are summed up, those who hold the aggregate amount constitute a large body of citizens. Some dissent, because the Government does not go far enough and fast enough; others, for precisely the opposite reasons; some, because the Government has meddled at all with slavery; others, because it did not make war upon it from the first, or sweep it at once away by proclamation; some, because it has suspended the privilege of the writ of habeas corpus; others, because it has committed errors in arresting disloyal citizens; and on a hundred other points which naturally arise out of such a contest among such a people, many are found to dissent, and as far as possible *wholly withhold* their support; who, at the same time and in the same breath, *claim* that they are loyal, and who would resent it as an insult should any suspicion of disloyalty be cast upon them.

There is another phase of the case which is even worse. Some are not content in withholding support, but take pains to throw every obstacle in their power in the way of the Government, being careful not to overstep the line of personal safety. We need not specify the numerous ways by which this is done, by public men and private. The facts are simply notorious. Others are content with speaking against the Government, where no other motive is apparent than the pleasure afforded in abusing those in power, or for personal relief.

The obvious objection to this whole course, and to any and every part of it, in those who *claim to be loyal*, must commend itself to every person of discernment. It tends to hamper the Government, and give the most substantial "aid and comfort" to the rebellion. It will be truly wonderful, with such dead weights upon it, if the Government shall succeed at all in putting down the rebellion. It is wonderful that it can have any success, with *such* friends, either in its civil or military policy. And yet, these very "friends" are complaining that it does not succeed.

No person will understand us as in the least invading the inherent right of every American citizen freely to canvass any measures of Government, and to approve or to condemn, according to his best judgment, when it is done in a proper manner. As we have said before, men are nothing, administrations are nothing, policies and measures are nothing, in a great contest with treason, except as they bear upon the great issue, *national salvation.* The point we urge is, that the *Administration*, in power for the time, *must* be supported, or the *Government cannot* be;

and in a time of civil war, the *truly loyal* will give that generous support which patriotism demands, the *withholding* of which is a sin against God, and a crime against humanity.

OPPOSING THE ADMINISTRATION.—CHANGE DEMANDED.

There is still another phase of "loyalty," so called, which deserves a passing notice. So intense is the feeling of some who claim to be loyal, that they proclaim that they will not give one iota of influence to sustain the Government, to aid the war, or to crush the rebellion,—all which they profess to wish to see accomplished,—until we can have a change of administration. They deem its measures so impolitic or wicked, its aims so selfish, and its conduct so corrupt, that until there is a change they cannot conscientiously aid the Government in any possible way; in recruiting its armies, or sustaining those now in the field, or in any other measure tending directly to crush the rebellion.

To mere partisans, who wish to get into power or to be carried upon the back of some one who does, we have nothing to say. To reason with partisan prejudice and passion is seldom profitable. For another class, who claim to be loyal, and whose position is that above designated, we have a word.

There are two ways of disposing of corrupt officials, both of which are provided for by law. One is by impeachment; the other by dismissal at the end of their term of office, that is, by electing some one else. In regard to the Administration at Washington, as Congress will not meet till after the Presidential election, the latter is relied upon to work the change essential to bring to the support of the Government those who cannot support it until a change occurs.

Leaving politicians to discuss probabilities, let us look at what all must admit may possibly occur on the first Tuesday in November next.

LOYALTY PRACTICALLY TESTED.

Mr. Lincoln has been nominated for re-election. General Frémont is also a candidate for the Presidency. A candidate is to be nominated at Chicago by the Democratic party. Perhaps others may be put in nomination.

It will be admitted that Mr. Lincoln may possibly be re-elected. Suppose he should be, what will those do who claim to be loyal,—some of whom believe that they personally embody an unusual amount of that sentiment,—but who declare that they cannot and will not support the Government, or help to crush the rebellion, while Mr. Lincoln is in power? Will they add four years more of total inaction, or opposition and vituperation, to the time already expended in that way, if the contest with treason should continue so long, while other citizens are using all their influence, even pouring out their blood, to sustain the Government against its enemies? Will they do that, and still claim to be *loyal?*—still claim a larger amount of patriotism than their fellow-citizens?

But this is a many-sided question. There are other possibilities. The election of General Frémont, we may assume, is secured. A certain class of those who suspend support of the Government upon a change in the administration will then of course become very zealous in its support. But suppose the friends of Mr. Lincoln should then say they would withhold all support while General Frémont was in power; would their loyalty suffer no detriment?

Or if the Chicago nominee should be elected, and on coming into power should announce such a policy upon the *manner* of dealing with the rebellion as would not satisfy the friends of the present Administration, but yet was determined on maintaining the Union intact, would it be the part of good citizenship to withhold support from the Government, or malign it, or throw obstacles in its way, because every measure of the new Administration could not be approved?

But if the policy of the *present* Administration, as to the *manner* of dealing with the rebellion,—objected to from opposite grounds, and for conflicting reasons, by different and disagreeing classes,—can justify a total withholding of support, the same dissent from some measure of policy in any *future* Administration may justify like inaction or opposition. We are then brought back to the principle already announced,—and there is no other safe ground to occupy,—*the duty of every citizen to sustain the Government, by sustaining the Administration for the time being in power, by whatever party elected, in crushing rebellion and preserving our nationality, even though some measures of its policy for these ends may not be approved.* Any other principle than this has in it the germ of anarchy and ruin. If we may withhold support from the Government until all men are agreed in every measure of its policy, we must wait till doomsday—and still wait.

LOYALTY ABOVE PARTISANSHIP.—VIOLENCE.

Let no one imagine that we view things from a partisan stand-point. Far different from that is our feeling; far different has been our action; far different will both be in the future. We have given, as we have had ability, our influence to sustain the Government in overthrowing rebellion. As we have done it under this Administration, so shall we, and so should we have done, under any other. Whoever may be elected in

November next to administer the Government shall have our unfailing support. We know of no other stand in Christian honesty to take. So it would have been in the past. Had Jefferson Davis, who was sought to be put in nomination at Charleston, been elected President of the United States in 1860, he would have been our President, and we should have given his administration that support always demanded as a Christian duty.

It is believed by some,—indeed, we have heard it said by those whose opportunities are good for gaining information, beyond what appears in the papers, about secret organizations against the Government,—that in case Mr. Lincoln should be re-elected, his administration would not be tolerated, and that he would be assassinated.

That there are men base enough for this is of course true. That there are secret organizations for this purpose may be also true. That there are men, all through the loyal States, ready for *any thing* which will destroy the Government and give triumph to the rebellion, is beyond doubt true. But we have not lost faith in the loyalty of the people at large. Desperadoes, in a time of revolution, are ready for any thing. But we do not believe that *partisanship* has so corrupted the masses of the people who are for sustaining the Government and putting down the rebellion, that they would for a moment countenance a *revolution* against any Administration which the people, should constitutionally put in power. If Mr. Lincoln is re-elected, it will be hailed with joy by his friends, and be quietly submitted to by his foes. If any other candidate is elected, the same result, *vice versâ*, will be seen. Politicians may gnash their teeth, on one side or the other, as the issue shall be determined, and desperadoes, whether within or without the Golden Circle, may organize, and arm, and bluster; but THE PEOPLE have too much at stake to inaugurate or support a *revolution*, whoever may attempt to lead it, against any Administration constitutionally elected. Their experience with the rebellion now on their hands, convinces them that one thing of this very sort is enough at a time.

GOD REIGNS—OUR TRUST.

We have said we have not lost confidence in the people. Much less have we lost faith in God. That He presides over the destinies of this nation we know from His word, for He presides over all. And though His word does not reveal the path opened for us in the future, His providence, as we have attempted to show elsewhere, is shaping events, as we believe, through our eventual purification, for a more glorious career for this people. We may yet have to pass through a fiercer furnace than that now glowing. If so, it will be just. We eminently deserve it.

But whatever is in store for us, whether greater trials or speedy deliverance, and by whatever means, we know that all events are in His hand, and that He will do His pleasure. He works through all policies, all men, all events, and reaches His ends infallibly and gloriously.

THE PATRIOT'S REWARD.

The national contest in which we are engaged, places a stamp upon men and things which time can never efface. Those who are sustaining the Government, *the truly loyal*, will have their names and their deeds transmitted to posterity with honor. They will go down to coming generations in a grander halo of glory than that which encircles the memory of the patriots of the Revolutionary Era; for, if successful, the good which will be vouchsafed to the nation in its salvation from anarchy, and in the triumph of freedom, will far eclipse that which was secured by its birth and independence. If they fail, their reward in the esteem of the wise and the good will be none the less, for success is not the criterion of merit; and it will still be true, that they battled for right, for law, for order, for freedom, for humanity, against treason and rebellion opposing good government, and forging stronger fetters to body and soul for millions in human form.

But they cannot fail. God is in the contest, and His strong arm will give them the victory. All who share in the conflict will share in the reward which a grateful people will bestow upon them. As we have been accustomed to venerate the names of those who signed the Declaration of Independence, and on every anniversary of our nation's birth to honor the surviving representatives of the Revolutionary army, so it will be in the days to come concerning the present war. The men who have led our armies to battle, and the soldier who has stood in the ranks, will alike be honored for acts of greater prowess, for sacrifices in a greater cause, and for securing results of far higher interest to the nation and to mankind.

The noble and the brave who have fallen will be honored. Their deeds of valor will be rehearsed by their comrades; they will be cherished in the family circle made desolate by their untimely death; their example will be transmitted as worthy of imitation; every village churchyard, every city cemetery, and the burial places in every rural neighborhood, will exhibit mausoleums of enduring marble, on which their names and their battles shall be inscribed, before which the stranger will pause in mute admiration, and upon which devoted affection will hang garlands of unfading laurel. But the most enduring monument to their patriotism will be erected in the hearts of their countrymen. From the highest commander who has fallen, to the private, each will be held in grateful and affectionate remembrance. Each succeeding generation will embalm their memory, and time will waft its fragrance until time shall be no more!

THE TRAITOR'S DOOM.

The patriot's reward has its counterpart in the traitor's doom. There are chapters in the history of this contest of loyalty and treason among the darkest in the annals of the human race. If we had an enemy on earth, we could wish for him no sorer punishment than that which is in store in the righteous judgment of posterity for all those who have plotted, instigated, aided, abetted, or in any way, at the South or in the North, helped on this godless and heaven-defying rebellion.

Of the two classes,—those at the South who have openly aided and fought for it, and those in the loyal States who have secretly or openly aided it while enjoying the protection of the Government,—the latter are infinitely more abhorred, both on earth and in heaven. Posterity will accord with this judgment, now universally entertained among the loyal. Every dictate of human reason and every principle of religion declares it.

"The memory of the wicked shall rot," is a saying of Holy Writ. This may prove true of the "wicked" in this rebellion. The Scripture does not state when the process shall begin or when the work shall be finished. We trust the period in this case will be distant. Valuable purposes to this nation and to mankind will be served by holding their "memory" up to the gaze of men.

We wish our children and our children's children to know when, how, for what, and by whom, this rebellion was begun and prosecuted. We wish them to know, from the words of the rebels themselves, that it was begun with no sufficient reason, that it was to overthrow lawful authority, that it was to extend and perpetuate human bondage. We wish them to know the agency of the Church in this work, the zeal of the ministers of religion, and the organic indorsement of ecclesiastical bodies. We wish them to know the truth, and the whole truth, that they may understand the awful guilt of men, and watch more narrowly the interests which God has consigned to their faithful keeping.

Future Bancrofts and Prescotts will write the elaborate histories of the rebellion; and we hope some Peter Parley will tell its simple tale in the pages which will be read in every school-house and rehearsed at every fireside.

Let its story thus go abroad over the wide earth and among all people, until the sun shall no more rise upon a master nor set upon a slave; let it go down through all the generations of men to the end of time; and then, LET THE MEMORY OF THE WICKED ROT!

THE END.

www.ingramcontent.com/pod-product-compliance
Lightning Source LLC
LaVergne TN
LVHW021230110826
845150LV00002B/289

* 9 7 8 1 4 2 5 5 6 2 7 9 3 *